W9-AFE-066

WITHDRAWN

Music, Politics, and Violence

EDITED BY SUSAN FAST
AND KIP PEGLEY

Music, Politics,
and Violence

WESLEYAN UNIVERSITY PRESS

Middletown, Connecticut

Wesleyan University Press
Middletown CT 06459
www.wesleyan.edu/wespress
© 2012 Wesleyan University Press
All rights reserved
Manufactured in the United States of America
Typeset in Galliard by Integrated Publishing Solutions

Wesleyan University Press is a member of the Green Press Initiative.
The paper used in this book meets their minimum requirement for recycled paper.

Library of Congress Cataloging-in-Publication Data

Music, politics, and violence / edited by Susan Fast and Kip Pegley.
p.   cm.
Includes bibliographical references and index.
ISBN 978-0-8195-7337-7 (cloth: alk. paper)—ISBN 978-0-8195-7338-4
(pbk.: alk. paper)—ISBN 978-0-8195-7339-1 (ebook)
1. Music and violence. 2. Music and war. I. Fast, Susan. II. Pegley, Kip.
ML3916.M878   2012
306.4′842—dc23   2012020964

5 4 3 2 1

Contents

Acknowledgments

This book represents the culmination of a long journey. After watching the first mass-mediated post-9/11 benefit concert unfold its narrative of American jingoism, delivered through a normative representational politics newly emboldened by the crisis, we thought it urgent to write about these events. We published two essays together and then began thinking about a larger project. Some of the post-9/11 critical literature turned us toward a consideration of violence and a desire to bring together scholars whose work engaged with the subject of music and violence, particularly as it played out within the context of the nation-state, either as an instrument of governmentality, or as a foil to it. We would like to thank the authors who have contributed to this volume: for their intellectually rich and important work and for their patience as the book went through numerous revisions; contributing to an edited collection can seem like an endless process, and their generosity and cheerfulness throughout made our experience so much easier and pleasurable.

The McMaster University Arts Research Board provided funding to hire a research assistant as this project was drawing to a close. This assistant was Laura Wiebe, whose editing, fact-checking, and work on permissions in the penultimate version of the manuscript was simply extraordinary, as her work always is. We also thank Katherine Mazurok, our research assistant at Queen's University, whose keen editorial eye during the last edit of the manuscript was invaluable. We would also like to acknowledge Suzanne Crosta, Dean, Faculty of Humanities; Mo Elbestawi, V.P. Research, McMaster University; and the Social Science and Humanities Research Council of Canada and the Queen's University Office of Research Services for providing financial support as the book went into production.

We owe a debt of gratitude to the series editors at Wesleyan University Press, Annie Randall and Harry Berger, for supporting this project and for their many helpful comments that improved the manuscript. We would also like to acknowledge the anonymous reviewers of the manuscript whose comments helped strengthen the arguments we make in our introduction, as well as those in a number of the essays. Thanks also to the team at Wesleyan: Parker Smathers, Susanna Taminem, and Leslie Starr.

We thank the IASPM Canada 2010 program committee for inviting us to present portions of the introduction in a plenary session and Martin Daughtry for serving as respondent to our presentation at that conference. It was the perspicuity of his comments that prompted us to invite him to write them up as a postscript to the book, and we thank him for taking the time and energy to shape those comments into a thoughtful conclusion to the volume.

In 2010, as we were working on a crucial draft of this book, Kip was suddenly diagnosed with cancer. She would like to thank her family, friends, and colleagues who gave her such tremendous support as she went through treatment, and to the staff at the Princess Margaret Hospital, Toronto, for their exceptional care. A special thanks to Julie L'Heureux, Susan Fast, and Barbara Clarke for their love and bravery, and to her family, Mom, Dad, Fred, Patricia, and Ellen, for standing next to her every step of the way. Thank you, Susan, for our long conversations about culture and about life over many years, and for sharing your intense love for music as well as your infectious curiosity for what it all means. Finally, Kip would like to thank Catherine Kellogg for her intellectual generosity as we wrote the introduction. More importantly, thank you, Catherine, for giving so wholeheartedly when the news of illness came, for setting everything else aside and supporting me physically, psychically, and emotionally so beautifully as I went through treatment and recovery. There are no words.

Susan would like to thank Catherine Graham, Liss Platt, and Stan Hawkins for their willingness to listen to ideas, often not quite fully formed; her thanks to these colleagues — also friends — and her sister, Louise Punnett, for their constant support. Thanks to Kip for pursuing this project through all the many twists and turns of work and life, even her difficult illness; for her intellectual openness; and for sharing an unbridled passion for music and how it works to produce culture. She would like to dedicate her work on this project to her mother, Frieda, and late father, Abe, who came together amid the violence of war — World War II. Their experiences in that conflict shaped their lives and those of their children in many ways, one of them being her intellectual interest in the subject of this book.

Introduction

≽➤❈

SUSAN FAST AND KIP PEGLEY

Although it is now commonplace to observe that we can destroy ourselves and the planet in ways unimaginable to those living even two generations ago, the sheer fact of this capacity has given rise to an unprecedented interest — from sociologists, philosophers, lawyers, political scientists and psychologists — in the meaning and workings of violence. Given that, as Martin Cloonan and Bruce Johnson observe, there is often a "tacit assumption that . . . music is inevitably personally and socially therapeutic,"[1] it might at first blush seem odd that those who study music have also recently become interested in the subject of violence.[2] But music, as much as any other cultural object, is implicated in such phenomena as the power, reach, and seeming unassailability of global capital, the unleashing of new technologies of destruction, human aggression, the proliferation of laws of war, genocide, nation building, concepts of otherness, and discourses of "tolerance." Just as poetry or photography can "frame" acts of violence, or be framed so as to interpret those acts in particular ways, as Judith Butler has argued,[3] so too can music.

Despite music's richness as a medium for understanding violence or conflict, the scholarly fields of musicology and ethnomusicology, until quite recently, have paid relatively little attention to either concept.[4] There are notable exceptions, of course, dating to the end of the twentieth century, when conflict-centered ethnomusicological, musicological, and popular music texts began to emerge; in the aftermath of 9/11, this area of research quickly swelled. Noteworthy books targeting a particular people, musical genre, conflict, or means for conflict resolution included Pettan's *Music, Politics, and War: Views from Croatia* (1998); Sweeney's *Singing Our Way to Victory: French Cultural Politics and Music During the Great War* (2001); Wolfe and Akenson's *Country Music Goes to War* (2005); Daughtry and Ritter's *Music in the Post-9/11 World* (2007); McDowell's *Poetry and Violence: The Ballad Tra-dition of Mexico's Costa Chica* (2008); Urbain's *Music and Conflict Transfor-mation* (2008); Cooper's *The Musical Traditions of Northern Ireland and Its Diaspora* (2009); and Pieslak's *Sound Targets* (2009). Enough research has been conducted that there are also articles that survey the fields of music and war, and music and peace studies, wherein authors provide an overview of the existing literature and suggestions for theoretical models.[5]

Of particular relevance to the present volume is the recent work of John Morgan O'Connell and Salwa El-Shawan Castelo-Branco, whose collection *Music and Conflict* (2010) brings together established ethnomusicologists to explore conflict and possibilities for conflict resolution in a cross-cultural perspective. In his introduction to the volume, O'Connell explores how conflict may be defined and utilized within ethnomusicological analyses, but, as he explains, the complexity of the term makes this a challenging task:

> Conflict can be viewed negatively, as the logical outcome of economic inequal-ity and social disparity leading inevitably to violent rupture where the status of a dominant elite is called into question. Conflict can also be viewed positively when economic difference promotes social mobility. . . . [C]onflict by defini-tion implies the possibility of conflict resolution, an equivocal position that calls into question its fixity as a concept.[6]

He also rightly argues that by exploring conflict cross-culturally, we come to understand it as a relative concept that is intrinsically dependent upon the context within which it is situated.[7] For instance, conflict could be identified as such for strategic purposes rendering it plausible that what might be considered as conflict within one cultural setting might be over-looked within another. It is for this reason that musicological *and* ethno-musicological studies are needed to more fully understand the multifaceted ways in which conflict is expressed and interpreted cross-culturally. What-ever the context, O'Connell sees music in a "paradoxical" position: either it is used to escalate conflict or it is used to promote conflict resolution.[8] In other words, conflict is the condition that engages both rational and non-rational domains, often resulting in violent outbursts, but always leaving open the possibility for eventual peace.[9]

While in some respects our work builds upon the ethnomusicological and musicological scholarship described above, our choice of the term *vio-lence* in this volume, over the more commonly used *conflict*, is a deliberate departure from existing literature. Moreover, while there are many gram-mars of violence, the specific tradition of thinking violence to which we hope to contribute is concerned with its theorization within a political context, as that which occurs between, among, and within nations in their various states of ascendency and decline, a tradition that can be traced back through such texts as Walter Benjamin's "Critique of Violence"; Franz Fanon's "Concerning Violence"; Hannah Arendt's *On Violence*; and more recently, those debates and conversations that follow on from these. They include Giorgio Agamben's permanent "state of emergency/exception," Jacques Derrida's "new violence," Wendy Brown's examination of tolerance, Judith Butler's work on borders, nations and their relation to the state, and the linked question of those lives deemed illegal and/or ungrievable; and Slavoj Žižek's concepts of "objective" and "subjective" violence.[10] Inasmuch as the system of national states works to cut or divide up the world — through borders, passports, citizenship papers, counting and managing its populations through the science of the state itself (statistics) — it is a system that is defined by both violence and sovereign power. The essays in this book investigate the uses of music within and between national borders, mostly as a means through which divisions are strengthened and deepened; hence these uses of music contribute to the very idea of the nation-state as a violent entity and are directly concerned with ideas about violence emerging in the critical literature.

Our aim in this introduction is to situate music and the ways in which it gets taken up in the essays that follow within some of the recent critical discourse on violence, a discourse that has often addressed arts such as film, poetry, photography, and fiction, but which has either examined music quite uncritically or neglected it altogether. There are three critical trajectories explored in this introduction that are relevant to the essays presented here: the first is Slavoj Žižek's categorization of violence and his discussion of how best to speak/write/reflect on it. We then explore notions of belonging and/or "otherness" within and across nation-states, including the concept of multiculturalism. These ideas are central to Judith Butler and Gayatri Spivak's discussion of the nation, Wendy Brown's examination of "tolerance," and the "crisis of sovereignty" as articulated by Jacques Derrida. Finally, we explore memorials and postmemorials; to this end we consider Judith Butler's analysis of media frames, which, as she argues, can sway the onlooker to believe that some lives are worth more than others. Butler's work is then placed in dialogue with Sharon Rosenberg's analysis of public memorials — events that frame public memory and, as such, hold the power to commit injustices and violences to those already dead.

The nine essays that follow mirror this movement: from the conceptualization of music that participates directly in the production of objective and subjective violence, through its use in rituals of reconciliation and rebuilding, and finally as a means through which to memorialize and remember violent pasts.

Slavoj Žižek has been a remarkably influential thinker in the past decade, yet his work has seldom been taken up in studies on music. In his book *Violence: Six Sideways Reflections*, Žižek categorizes violence in a way that has been central in our decision to frame this project in those terms. His is largely an investigation into the conditions of possibility *for* violence and so he makes a distinction between what he terms "subjective" and "objective" violence.[11] As he explains, if subjective violence is empirical, visible, and quantifiable (war, genocide, terrorism), its condition of possibility is objective violence, the "non-violent zero level,"[12] which includes the systemization or "objectification" of exploitation and oppression that appears to be the *way things have to be*. This objective violence is the violence that holds the "'normal,' peaceful state of things"[13] intact, the "neutral" backdrop against which subjective violence explodes. There are two kinds of objective violence. The first is "symbolic": the violence (racism, gender discrimination, etc.) that is embodied in hegemonic forms of discourse, particularly language. But its scope extends beyond these particular instances: language as a whole does violence through its very organization. "[T]here is something violent in the very symbolization of a thing," Žižek suggests, "which equals its mortification."[14] When one communicates, then, it is impossible to escape some level of symbolic violence (even the words we use to characterize Žižek's ideas commit a symbolic violence to his text as we privilege one particular interpretation of his ideas over other possible readings). Acknowledging that symbolic violence is inherent to every utterance, however, should not discourage us from following its traces to see when and how, through repetition, it generates power that can then be utilized against agents, particularly in the form of subjective force.

"Systemic" violence, meanwhile, is "the often catastrophic consequences of the smooth functioning of our economic and political systems."[15] Specifically, this is the violence of capitalism, the violence inherent in the process that Marx called the "objective condition"[16] of exploitation: appropriating wealth and distributing it to the affluent at the expense of the vast majority of the world's people who live in poverty. Žižek instructs us to "resist the fascination of subjective violence," to turn our attention away from obvious eruptions of violence in order to notice how "objective violence" makes those local explosions of violence possible, and indeed, inevitable.[17]

One of the threads that Žižek follows, and which is relevant to our discussion here, is his argument that in order to justify the unfair economic order and feel that we are still "acting" against global imbalances, we now stand behind the figure of what he calls the "liberal communist," philan-

thropists like Bill Gates and George Soros, who initially might have to op-
press third-world lives but then give back and redistribute wealth in significant, generous, forms. Žižek argues that while celebrating the aid individuals
like Gates and Soros provide we usually overlook their own co-responsibility
in creating the oppressive conditions under which so many live. "Charity,"
in his words, "is the humanitarian mask hiding the face of economic oppression."[18] He rejects the idea that in the face of "urgent" humanitarian
crises (often, in his estimation, "fake" and played up by the media), there
should necessarily be action: his answer to the question, "Do you mean we
should do *nothing*" is, in fact, "YES, precisely that!"[19] Instead of acting, he
argues, we should sit back and reflect, heed Lenin's advice to "'learn, learn,
and learn' what causes violence."[20]

As Paul Taylor argues, the media's heightened attention on celebrity culture over the past several decades provides a powerful example of how our
focus has been directed away from asking the important questions:

> The manner in which the relatively new celebrity cultural frame of reference
> has become the *lingua franca* for the discussion of a disproportionate number
> of traditionally political and economic issues within the media demonstrates a
> blend of symbolic and objective violence. Symbolic violence is manifested in
> the excessive concentration upon celebrity figures to the exclusion of more
> politically important issues, and as this form of symbolic violence becomes the
> predominant background value of the media, it enables objective violence to
> continue largely unchecked and unquestioned.[21]

Since "charity rock" has become a significant presence in contemporary
culture, beginning with George Harrison's *Concert for Bangladesh* and increasing exponentially in the aftermath of 9/11, this is one instance where
music can help us think through, and bring out the complexities inherent
in the issues around objective violence that Žižek raises. Although the staging of a mass-mediated benefit concert in response to humanitarian disaster
began with *Live Aid* in 1985, it has been in the wake of 9/11 that this form of
response to catastrophic events has become commonplace. As one CBC
News reporter noted prior to the 2010 Haitian earthquake benefit concerts,
"By now, it's almost standard procedure: a major natural disaster is often
followed by a star-studded made-for-TV benefit concert."[22] We have simply
come to expect a celebrity-drenched musical response to mass human suffering.

In many instances, benefit concerts perpetuate a second layer of symbolic
violence through the choice of performers (largely white and male) and the
preeminence of rock music over other genres, reinforcing the hegemonic
order where rock is taken seriously, pop and other genres not as much. In

fact, benefit concerts provide a good example of how the concept of liberal tolerance operates. In the wake of significant criticism that, especially, black artists had been seriously underrepresented at *Live Aid*, the organizers of subsequent benefit concerts made space for "minorities," but in a manner, as Wendy Brown expresses it, that "manages" the threat of difference. Women, black and other performers who fall outside the white and male rock tradition are invited into the performance but are rarely, if ever, given the same amount of time, or the prime spots (beginning or ending the concert, for example), or their otherness is immediately neutralized through following their performance with someone who reinforces the normative. As Brown argues, this is what the troublesome idea of liberal tolerance looks like: "[w]hat is tolerated remains distinct even as it is incorporated. Since the object of tolerance does not dissolve into or become one with the host, its threatening and heterogeneous aspect remains alive inside the tolerating body."[23] This idea allows performers and genres that fall outside of the dominant culture of popular music to participate, but ensures, by limiting where and how they appear in the concert, that they do not usurp power.[24]

The critique has run deeper than this, however. For example, the mixing of musical performances that create a festive atmosphere with such serious issues as poverty or the fallout of natural disasters can confuse the purpose of the event and tend to highlight, in an obscene way, the privilege of the performers and audience members in contrast to the devastation of those for whom money and/or awareness is being raised. They can perpetuate objective violence by not asking people to question or challenge reasons for inequity but instead encouraging them to feel like they are acting generously. This can be understood as part of the larger set of difficulties with recent trends in development awareness and fundraising. According to John Cameron and Anna Haanstra, "sexy" world development is a recent phenomenon: it was only a few decades ago that development portrayed the image of the helpless "other" from the global south — a representation sometimes referred to as the "pornography of poverty" — designed to provoke viewers' sympathy and guilt. Instead of feeling guilty about their affluence, individuals in the global north now can both feel that they are making lives better in lands far away while simultaneously celebrating consumption.[25] April Biccum argues further that we should consider not only how development articulates these unequal relationships but also how it serves individual national narratives. For instance, she points out that within the particular context of Britain, African development has, since 1997, become embedded within its national narrative "with the global citizen as both raison d'être and mode of delivery,"[26] and that the government has been "marketing" development through a series of subject-producing exercises that bear the mark of empire.[27] Indeed, in the case of benefit concerts, discourses of power certainly operate on the level of nation, since many of them, perhaps especially those that occurred in the wake of 9/11, perpetuate entrenched narratives of national identity (Canada as a nation of benevolent peacekeepers; the United States as the land of freedom, for example).

But this analysis, as Žižek's, shuts the door on the possibility that benefit concerts (or "charity" in general) may also do some good. While it is probably true that sitting back and doing nothing may hasten the demise of capitalism (an idealistic Marxist vision and one probably offered by Žižek as nothing more than a provocation), this seems like a luxurious solution proposed by those who live in comfort, and is, ultimately, also a kind of violence. While benefit concerts may be problematic in a number of ways, they do bring the world's attention to various issues, in some cases causing governments to act (as with *Live 8,* the series of concerts organized around the G8 summit in 2005, twenty years after *Live Aid*, with a purpose not of raising money but awareness around the issue of poverty, and pressuring Western leaders to pledge more aid to Africa, which they did do). And while some at the concerts may care only about the music, not the issues, others may become newly conscious of issues about which they would otherwise remain blissfully ignorant. In other words, these events *are* a means through which to reflect on what causes violence. While some artists may be more interested in appearing at a benefit concert to promote their career than to participate in an act of charity, they are still using their celebrity power to focus attention on a particular issue. As for other artists who take up the causes seriously, their power to move the hearts and minds of their fans should not be underestimated, nor should they categorically be viewed as naïve about the depth and complexity of the issues, including those outlined above: it is an elitist idea that popular culture cannot offer a means through which to engage in serious reflection. The question remains: would we rather simply have our music celebrities be celebrities and not use the considerable power of music to make us think about the world? In short, do benefit concerts serve to both perpetuate and eradicate objective violence simultaneously?

>≫⸻

Žižek also argues that in writing about violence, direct and factual accounts serve to perpetuate it. "The only appropriate approach to my subject," he writes in *Violence,* "seems to be one which permits variations on violence kept at a distance out of respect towards its victims."[28] In this context, Žižek evokes Adorno's famous dictum: "It is barbaric to write poetry after Auschwitz,"[29] modifying it as follows:

> Adorno's famous saying, it seems, needs correction: it is not poetry that is impossible after Auschwitz, but rather *prose*. Realistic prose fails, where the poetic evocation of the unbearable atmosphere of a camp succeeds. That is to say, when Adorno declared poetry impossible (or rather barbaric) after Auschwitz, this impossibility is an enabling impossibility: poetry is always, by definition, 'about' something that cannot be addressed directly, only alluded to. One shouldn't be afraid to take this a step further and refer to the old saying that music comes in when words fail.[30]

We understand Žižek to suggest that, especially in the case of violence, speaking beyond or in place of language is a useful characteristic of music, but we also know the dangers of thinking about music in this way. This notion of music as somehow "naturalized" means that it is figured as lying outside of the social, that the individual can interpret musical sounds broadly with respect to their own experience, with little recourse to a larger social context, or at the very least, that music is considered too abstract to signify the social very particularly. But these ideas about music are themselves situated in a very particular time and place.

The famous line to which Žižek refers can be traced back to the nineteenth century when artists spoke loftily of music's transcendent power. Heinrich Heine, for instance stated famously that "when words leave off, music begins."[31] But Heine is not alone, and many such references exist, from Beethoven: "Music is a higher revelation than all wisdom and philosophy"[32] to Victor Hugo: "music expresses that which cannot be said and on which it is impossible to be silent."[33] This sentiment lingered within various traditions in the twentieth century, echoed in the words of Aldous Huxley, who stated that "After silence, that which comes nearest to expressing the inexpressible is music."[34] This notion of how music functions and produces its effects is tied to nineteenth-century romanticism and has continued to hold sway in some circles to the present day. It is one of the reasons that music can be so easily dismissed in discussions about pressing social matters such as violence. But one only need look outside of the white, Western high-art tradition to understand the social constructedness of this idea of music. For instance, African-American jazz saxophonist and composer Charlie Parker said: "Music is your own experience, your own thoughts, your wisdom. If you don't live it, it won't come out of your horn."[35] Similarly, jazz saxophonist John Coltrane: "My music is the spiritual expression of what I am — My faith, my knowledge, my being. . . . When you begin to see the possibilities of music, you desire to do something really good for people."[36] Linking their musical practice with their everyday life experience, and connecting it deeply to the social, the human, is dramatically different from the conception of music that Žižek and the romantics before him construct. In short, Žižek's idea that music can be used to "keep violence at a distance" is itself caught up in a particular social tradition of thinking about how music works.[37]

In Žižek's formulation we are left with the notion that music, like poetry, cannot address something directly, that it is "evocative," but not "realistic," that it can only "allude" to something; that it is not only a different medium from prose, but one that somehow works beyond language or in place of it. Or even before it. For an example of the latter, Žižek points to the first movement of Arnold Schoenberg's *Five Pieces for Orchestra* (1909), the title of which is "Premonitions." Žižek argues: "There may well be some common truth in the wisdom that, in a kind of historical premonition, the music of Schoenberg articulated the anxieties and nightmares of Auschwitz before the event took place."[38] Žižek goes on to say that in this movement, "Schoenberg 'extracted' the inner form of totalitarian terror," that he "evoked the way this terror affects subjectivity."[39]

Since Žižek says nothing more about how he thinks Schoenberg "extracted the inner form of totalitarian terror" in this piece, we can only speculate: is it the lack of a tonal center, of the ability to connect to, hang on to, or anticipate what might come next? The seeming disconnectedness of the musical gestures? The pictorial qualities (the idea of fleeing or being chased that we might get through the string ostinato)? The cacophony and bombast of the incredibly loud climax? The collapse of this climax into a pathetic, whimpering (non) conclusion? Is it because Schoenberg has done away with musical sounds that traditionally signify beauty and calmness? If so, then for Žižek, "the inner form of totalitarian terror" is created by not knowing what comes next, a lack of predictability, the lack of a center and this, of course, is a response that is deeply situated within Western culture, where a lifetime of listening to tonal music constructs that system as normative. It is important to note that Schoenberg in fact reluctantly provided titles for each of the five pieces at the request of his publisher and only included them in later editions of the work. Without Schoenberg's titles all of these musical gestures could be read differently. The title frames the piece of music for us in a particular way, although the word "premonitions" could allude to a lot of things other than the terror of war. The particular association of the work with war developed through a further discourse about the piece, primarily based on the date of composition — 1909; many commentators believed that Schoenberg's piece foreshadowed the horrors of the First World War. Žižek is, then, perpetuating an entrenched discourse about this piece, accepting it without interrogating its socially situated premises.

But perhaps Žižek would still hold on to his interpretation even without all the extra-musical framing, since he understands atonality as producing chaos, something Schoenberg and his fellows in the Second Viennese School would have no doubt found amusing. Žižek cites Alain Badiou, who uses the term "atonality" to refer to worlds "which lack the intervention of a Master-Signifier to impose meaningful order onto the confused multiplicity of realty." The idea is pressed further to suggest that postmodernity tries to dispense with the ordering Master-Signifier and is atonal in its drive for socio-sexual equality where binarisms are eliminated. As he argues: "Badiou's excellent example of such an 'atonal' world is the politically correct vision of sexuality as promoted by gender studies with its obsessive rejection of binary logic: this world is a nuanced world of multiple sexual practices which tolerates no decision, no instance of the Two [*sic*], no evaluation . . ."[40] Postmodernism's sexual equality with no Master-Signifier and no binarisms is clearly a bit nightmarish for Žižek. But Schoenberg, who developed "total chromaticism," identified it in 1926 as "the emancipation of the dissonance,"[41] in other words, equality of all notes of the scale, the doing away with hierarchy: pitch freedom. No longer need we be led by the nose through relative keys, leading tones, and secondary dominants: we are released from the sonic expectations that conditioned Western listeners for centuries. Atonality for Schoenberg does not necessarily conjure "totalitarian terror" as it does for Žižek; in fact, for Schoenberg, it is its own freedom from terror. Using the term "atonality" without fully unpacking it misrepresents the intentions behind an important musical tradition, and Žižek's thoughts on *Five Pieces for Orchestra* renders for the reader a potentially misleading, terror-filled listening guide.

Žižek also uses music to "evoke," we presume something about violence, in another way. He gives each chapter in his book two titles: a musical tempo and/or articulation marking and a conventional title. There is no explanation of the musical titles, so we assume that he includes them as a way of demonstrating his idea that music (here not even music itself, but written allusions to music) evokes, but does not pin down meanings. But in fact these tempi roughly correspond with those indicated in the score of Beethoven's String Quartet No. 14 in C# Minor, Opus 131.[42] Perhaps Žižek wants to invoke the general pathos of this quartet, or perhaps he knew that Beethoven dedicated the quartet to Baron Joseph von Stutterheim as a way of showing gratitude to the Baron for taking his nephew into the army after a failed suicide attempt, a fact that links the piece directly with two kinds of subjective violence.[43] We're probably not supposed to get too analytical about these titles, but Žižek falls prey to a kind of symbolic violence in his choice here, what he himself calls "the relations of social domination reproduced in our habitual speech forms . . ."[44] For those in the know, his choice frames the arguments of his book in the context of perhaps the most dominant composer in the dominant tradition of Western (high) art music, a music that, until quite recently in the West, has been considered the proverbial gold standard by which other musics of the world have regularly been deemed "primitive." The choice of the C# minor quartet is particularly interesting in this respect, since it signals, along with the composer's other late quartets, the genre of classical music through which nineteenth- and twentieth-century composers expressed some of their most complex and intricate ideas — this is not the classics "lite," but rather the kind of music consumed by the elite of classical music listeners. It is "difficult" music, not intended for the uninitiated, hence the choice positions Žižek's arguments within a particular class hierarchy. Further, Beethoven has been at the center of narratives of German nationalism since his death, some of these narratives, such as his embrace by Hitler as an example of a "good" composer who possessed the "German heroic spirit," highly fraught. And if we want to push the questionable cultural associations of Beethoven's music further, we might also bring into this discussion the — albeit controversial — comments on Beethoven by Susan McClary, not about this particular piece, but about one of the most revered of Beethoven's works, the ninth symphony. McClary called the point of recapitulation in the first movement of that piece "one of the most horrifyingly violent episodes in the history of music," because of the way in which cadential arrival for the first theme (the protagonist) is kept at bay until it "finally erupts. . . . It is the consequent juxtaposition of desire and unspeakable violence in this moment that creates its unparalleled fusion of murderous rage and yet a kind of pleasure in its fulfillment of formal demands."[45] Indeed, there is an element of aggression in other of Beethoven's works as well: the insistence of the final cadence of the fifth symphony, for example, or, for that matter, the unending repetition of the sharp, angular, *loud* main motive of the finale of the C# minor quartet.

But what should readers unfamiliar with these connections do with the information Žižek provides? Is he suggesting that they engage these ideas about violence in chapter 1, for example, slowly, but not too slowly, and very expressively? Is it the pathos of the fugue that opens the C# minor quartet that he intends to evoke? Why in chapter 2 is the instruction to move from a moderately fast tempo back to "adagio" (slowly). If these tempo markings are not intended as a means through which to engage the ideas (which, in our attempted analysis here seems quite ridiculous), then might they be commenting on the nature of the ideas themselves? It is difficult to know. Most importantly, despite what he may think, his choices situate his engagement with music in a particular set of social circumstances: they are from the tradition of classical Western music, are only found in musical scores, and they are in Italian. To which reader is he speaking by using them, and whom does he alienate?

What we have tried to challenge here are the ways in which Žižek attempts to naturalize music, allowing it to function as a sort of transcendent language that may allude to the social (the terror of the camps), but diminishes or voids its political import and its particular social-situatedness. While the ways in which he categorizes violence are a useful means through which we can understand it as a pervasive and systemic presence, we cannot use music to keep our reflections on violence at some respectful distance. Indeed, we must uncover *precisely* how music does its cultural work, which is what the essays in this volume seek to do.

Violence, Belonging, and Singing

In the last book he wrote before his death, Jacques Derrida said, "Consider the context we've inherited from the end of the Cold War: a so-called globalization or *mondialisation* that is more inegalitarian and violent than ever." Globalization — or what he insists on leaving untranslated as *mondialisation* or "world-wide-ization" — has not resulted in the cosmopolitan "perpetual peace" envisioned by Kant in the eighteenth century, but rather, has produced a world with decreasing democratic or political accountability. The eclipse of the sovereignty of the national state gives rise to a kind of "war by other means," whereby the supreme value of accumulating capital is increasingly unfettered by the trappings of democracy and its inefficiencies.[46]

Derrida writes in this context that "a new violence is being prepared and, in truth, has been unleashed for some time now, in a way that is more visibly suicidal or autoimmune than ever."[47] By the "new violence" Derrida is referring to the fact that world wars no longer happen exclusively in a theatre battleground, where paid members of one nation-state's military force are pitted against others. Chemical or nuclear weapons, biological terrorism, viruses in computer systems, are unleashed against civilians and combatants alike. At the same time, what is more "visibly suicidal or auto-immune" is captured by such features of modern political reality as "proroguing," that is, shutting down Parliament, as happened in Canada in 2009, some argued as a means to squelch debate on a key topic of government accountability in the Afghanistan war, or giving the executive branch of government in the

United States extraordinary powers after 9/11, gestures that attack democracy and the rule of law, purportedly, *in order to save them*. Given the increasingly fragile distinction between states, it becomes more and more difficult to tell the difference between friend and enemy: one's state includes more and more of "them" and so one must murder more and more of "them" in order to immunize oneself. The others are *inside*, and so it becomes necessary to kill more and more of oneself.[48] Thus, with the crisis of sovereignty, we are witnessing not only the end of the juridical form of warfare, which is to say, the end of wars fought between sovereign nation-states, we now see such wars as the "war on terror," whose target is potentially everywhere, or the "war on drugs," whose target is a poor, largely black American underclass, or Arizona's "immigration war," reflected in a 2010 law that allows police to stop, question, and demand documentation from anyone suspected of being in the state illegally.[49]

The threat from within is taken up in Judith Butler and Gayatri Spivak's 2007 collaborative book entitled *Who Sings the Nation-State?* Through a brief consideration of this text, we hope to uncover how music is introduced as a mode of critique and a strategy for understanding how the nation can be disarticulated and, simultaneously, how it can serve as a means through which notions of otherness are engaged. We also hope to demonstrate how a more thorough consideration of the musical text might have further complicated — and enriched — their analysis.

The title for the book was inspired by illegal resident protests that took place in Los Angeles in 2006. These protests were launched after President George W. Bush responded to the news of a new Spanish-language recording of the "Star Spangled Banner" — called "nuestro hymno" or "our anthem" — by stating that the anthem ought to be sung in English. Protesters took to the streets singing the American anthem in Spanish, and Butler and Spivak center their discussion on the use of language in this rendition of the anthem. In particular, they ask who this "we" might be, to whom the anthem, and hence the nation, belongs when it is sung in a language other than English. The authors saw these protests as an example of "the moment when a national majority seeks to define the nation on its own terms and even sets up or polices norms of exclusion deciding who may exercise freedom, since that exercise depends upon certain acts of language."[50] (This analysis is interesting to consider in the context of the Canadian national anthem, which is regularly sung in two different languages.) Butler reads their public rendition as an act of performative speech that "is the very freedom of expression for which it calls or, rather, it is the very call of freedom."[51] Rather than heed Bush's opinion — and, by extension, that of the hegemonic majority — the protestors' subversive performance insists that the "we" to whom the anthem and nation belong be extended beyond the English-speaking population.

Butler and Spivak acknowledge that singing the "Star Spangled Banner" in Spanish "does not make the anthem any less sing-able," hinting at the centrality of melody to the definition of the anthem. But they do not take this analysis any further. They also say that "singing is a plural act — an articulation of plurality,"[52] but even if they mean this to refer only to group singing of the anthem (as opposed to singing in general, which they don't make clear), it isn't really the case. Group singing in unison — the way the national anthem is usually sung — serves to homogenize and unify a population; indeed, that is the purpose of an anthem. It is plural insofar as the group constitutes a "we," but this "we" is articulated as having a single identity through melody. Butler asks if singing the national anthem in Spanish "is . . . still an anthem to the nation," and whether such a performance "can . . . actually help undo nationalism."[53] To these questions she says she does not have an answer. Would taking the intactness of the melody into account make these questions more answerable, or answerable in a different way?

While the discussion surrounding a translation's transformative power to prompt political change is insightful here, we can't help but wonder what we could learn about intentionality and what is politically permissible if we set the lyrics to the national anthem aside and consider only the music. What does it mean that the protesters translate the words but sing the melody largely intact? Does the translation necessitate a change in melodic shape, or possibly the addition or deletion of notes? And if the melody is altered, when and how can it be altered and still maintain its identity and "integrity" as the anthem? At what point would changes in the melody be deemed disrespectful, an act of rebelliousness, or even violence toward the idea of the nation, or a way of reclaiming the nation from hegemonic control?

We have a perfect example to consider, of course, in Jimi Hendrix's famous — and controversial — rendition of the American national anthem at Woodstock. In *Who Sings the Nation-State?* Butler calls for a reconsideration of what she calls a "sensate democracy" within which would be explored "the relationship between song and what is called the 'public.'"[54] Although Hendrix's performance is probably quite familiar, it is worth reflecting on just what he accomplished in terms of Butler's notion of "rethinking certain ideas of sensate democracy, of aesthetic articulation within the political sphere."[55] In that performance, Hendrix played a blues/rock-inspired version of the anthem on electric guitar, his characteristic use of extreme distortion and feedback wreaking timbral havoc on the melody. By virtue of his use of this instrument and timbre alone, the anthem became generically framed in a way it never had been before. The distorted electric guitar sets up a generic frame for Hendrix's performance through which we must understand it, that is, as an expression of rock music. As Eric Clarke observes: "In simple terms, national anthems (like flags and coats of arms), as the emblems of nationhood, stand for the cultural status quo, and are expected to remain unchanging and inviolate, while the rock music of this period is predominantly countercultural and is associated with the constant change that is the consequence of a fundamentally performance-based (as opposed to text-based) and improvisatory musical tradition."[56] That means an alignment with rock's rebelliousness, with its challenge to certain forms of hegemony (perhaps long gone now, but certainly still operative at the end of the 1960s), thereby arguably reclaiming the nation, through this generic frame, for youth culture and, by virtue of its connection with the blues, potentially also for African Americans. This frame stands prior to a more detailed analysis of the performance. Hendrix interpolates new musical material, thereby altering the melody and in fact creating a commentary that calls into question the values of the nation: right after playing the melody that accompanies the lines of lyric "And the rocket's red glare, the bombs bursting in air" he makes a long digression from the melody that is undoubtedly intended to mimic bombs bursting. While in traditional performances this lyric is understood as celebrating America's power, here Hendrix's musical interpolation calls such a celebration into question through articulating the chaos and violence of armed conflict — the repeated launchings of bombs, the moment of impact, what sound like the wails of the injured — and, with the addition of a repeated tritone that sounds like an ambulance siren, the human injury and loss that is a consequence of war, specifically, in 1969, the time of this performance, the war in Vietnam. Later in the piece, Hendrix interpolates a version of "Taps," a melody normally played at the funeral of a soldier which also points to the human cost of war.

Not surprisingly, this rendition provoked significant opposition, particularly within the southern United States (Hendrix had included this piece in his concerts for a year and continued to include it in his set list until his death in 1970). Was it patriotic? Or was it meant to express dissatisfaction with present-day America? For over forty years now, Hendrix's precise intentions have prompted debate. Pop critic Al Aronowitz of the *New York Post*, for instance, heard it as an oppositional gesture: "You finally heard what that song was about, that you can love your country, but hate the government."[57] Similarly, Charles Cross claims that the piece "became part of the sixties Zeitgeist, captured forever on film as an antiestablishment rallying cry."[58] Indeed, Hendrix himself stated that his rendition of the anthem was a form of critique:

> When it was written then, it was played in what they call a very, very beautiful state, nice and inspiring, your heart throbs, and you say, 'Great! I'm American!' But nowadays when we play it we don't play it to take away all this greatness that America's supposed to have. We play it the way the air is in America today. The air is slightly static, isn't it? You know what I mean?[59]

Yet Hendrix also muddied the interpretive waters by telling talk-show host Dick Cavett on September 9, 1969, less than a month after his performance, that he didn't understand the controversy and thought his rendition was "beautiful." As he simply stated, "I'm American, so I played it." If Hendrix meant this work to be an overt political manifesto, he failed to mention this to reporters, his friends, or even his band mates.[60] Regardless of his intentions, however, it is entirely possible to *hear* this rendition, to quote Cross, as informed by a Zeitgeist and part of a larger critique of American involvement in the Vietnam War, and perhaps on the American glorification of war in the anthem more generally. As such, it is also a similar, if not *more* powerful, intervention into who might belong in the nation than changing what language the anthem is sung in.

The Hendrix example is only one of many that could be offered as a way into the use of music as a means through which to articulate notions of otherness and belonging in the context of the nation-state. As far back as documentation exists, music has been used as a means through which discourses of belonging — to regions, nations, ethnicities, classes — have been articulated, largely through the use of musical instruments and/or structuring systems that make one people's music sound distinctive from another's.[61] Music is a "universal" language only insofar as every known culture has it; other claims to its universality (or "timelessness") are in fact veiled expressions of hegemony. A classic example of this is the way in which ideas of universalism have been pitted against the "rise" of regional or national musics in the Western European art music tradition. There are numerous points in the history of this tradition during which these tensions have played out, but the emergence of national styles in response to musical universalism arises with particular force in the nineteenth century, which, as Richard Taruskin notes, "saw the rise of nationalism to supremacy among ideologies."[62] This coincided with the rise of European nation-states and included the promotion of composers who would help define the nation through sound. In particular, these composers, among them Smetana, Chopin, Sibelius, and the "Russian Five," drew on "folk" music styles to accomplish this task, following, of course, Herder's theory that what made communities different from one another, what, in fact, expressed a particular community's "essential" and "authentic" character, was their language, customs, and arts.[63]

The systematic scholarly study of Western art music also began in the nineteenth-century university, and it too was linked with the project of nation building. While the history of the development of the modern university lies outside the scope of the present writing, it bears noting that the model presently used worldwide was conceived by German philosopher Wilhelm von Humboldt, who, in 1810, established the first modern university, the University of Berlin (now Humboldt University). As Bill Readings has observed, this modern university not only served as a platform for nineteenth-century scholarly pursuits, but also functioned as the glue for developing the German nation-state.[64] No longer responsible for inculcating reason alone, modern universities like this one came to include the study, preservation, and indeed production of culture *for* the nation-state. Thus, the development of the modern state was intimately tied to the study, taxonomization, historicization, and preservation of music as the cultural artifact of a sovereign "people" (*volk*) united into a commonwealth. Musicology, defined from its early stages largely by German scholars, became a discipline that put the Austro-German tradition of music at its center.

The importance of music (and its study) to the development of German nationalism in the nineteenth and twentieth centuries should not be understated. As Philip V. Bohlman writes:

> In the language of German nationalism, music occupies a symbolic position of exceptional importance. In the service of history and of the nation, music has the power to become German and to express the essence, to muster and constitute all that lies at the center. The Germanness of music is not simply a matter of sloganism. It shapes literary and scholarly languages; at certain moments including those of the most aggressive German nationalism.[65]

Indeed, as Pamela M. Potter has argued, the scholarly study of German music resulted in German musicologists using their research for extensive state-strengthening purposes after World War I. With substantial support from the government and the SS, their pro-state agenda exceeded that of all other university scholars as they publicized and forwarded German musical legacies. According to Potter, their efforts in turn not only served to support the Nazis' rise to power, but survived to subsequently provide a revisionist version of early music history.[66] Moreover, musical nationalism during World War II was substantiated as truth by so-called "scientific" experiments, which perpetuated the most ugly of racisms, among them *Blut und Boden* ("blood and soil").[67] As such, German music was linked with a biological race that risked contamination from without, necessitating an eradication of that potential threat.[68] This is, of course, an extreme case of symbolic violence, and while we highlight the German example here, it is crucial to reiterate the tremendous extent to which music and music history have been powerful tools in the production and maintenance of hegemonic power worldwide. The German context is exceptional, but it is one of many examples of musical nationalism that has crossed continents and defined national borders — and, by extension, who belongs inside or outside a border — for time immemorial.

Music as Healing: Memorials and Postmemorials

Once we acknowledge that music can be used as a tool of subjective and objective violence, as well as a means to address "the other" both outside and increasingly inside "our" borders, we are compelled to consider how music might also be used as a means of healing and reconciliation. How can an art form — any art form — assist in understanding violent events and help us to heal from their trauma?

One medium that has been carefully considered with respect to its effectiveness to communicate, motivate, and change individuals over the past decade has been the visual image, including the photograph. Given the recent dominance of visual media that have saturated us with images, the scholarly attention to the power of the photograph is not surprising.[69] Since 9/11 — including the wars in Iraq and Afghanistan — we have been bombarded by an overwhelming number of violent images, much of it through news coverage of the wars, and it has become easy to forget that until World War II, violent images like these were relatively rare.[70] How this wash of images actually affects viewers, however, is still of considerable debate. On the one hand, this deluge of visual information has resulted in what some political scientists and media studies scholars have coined the "CNN effect": contemporary media have become so powerful, they argue, that they not only alter public opinion, but have begun to alter state foreign policy.[71] On the other hand, as David Campbell points out, viewers have also been described as suffering from "compassion fatigue" from having viewed too many such images, so many in fact that they have dulled audiences' senses and rendered them politically immobile.[72]

In her 2003 book *Regarding the Pain of Others*, Susan Sontag distilled these arguments and provided a thoughtful perspective on the role of contemporary photography in representing violence. In this work, Sontag importantly complicates our understanding of the photograph, arguing that it is not the deluge of images that dulls our feelings toward violence, but rather, viewer passivity.[73] Sontag argues further in *Regarding the Pain of Others* — as she did in her landmark 1977 text *On Photography* — against unquestioned assumptions about the photograph's intrinsic power. Importantly, Sontag believes that because a photograph cannot produce ethical pathos in a viewer, it does not have the capacity to change a viewer's mind about something like war. Unlike prose, which, she posits, is subject to interpretation and has the ability — even if only momentarily — to move the reader toward change, photography gives the viewer only a partial "imprint," not a full explanation of its content. As Butler summarizes it, "For Sontag there is something of a persistent split between being affected and being able to think and understand, a split represented in the differing effects of photography and prose."[74] Instead, the photograph's power hinges upon how well it fits into the viewer's "relevant political consciousness."[75] Ultimately, according to Sontag, what photographs lack that is necessary to produce meaning and understanding of an event is a *narrative*.

It is interesting to consider Sontag's arguments alongside Žižek's position, i.e., that "[r]ealistic prose fails, where the poetic evocation of the unbearable atmosphere of a camp succeeds."[76] While Žižek and Sontag appear to hold opposing views on the issue, they both understand prose, with its capacity for narrative, as fundamentally distinct from other artistic forms such as poetry or photography, which they view as "evocative." In her discussion of Sontag, Judith Butler questions her insistence on the power of narrative over photography to change minds, arguing that a photograph is "not merely a visual image awaiting interpretation; it is itself actively interpreting, sometimes forcibly so."[77]

The argument that lack of narrative is photography's shortcoming, thus limiting its effects, in Sontag's words, to "some kind of sentimentalism,"[78] has serious ramifications for the study of music — if we include it alongside poetry and photography as other to prose/narrative — and might seem to derail the arguments we have been trying to put forward about it in this essay. Can non-texted, non-programmatic music be persuasive? Can it move us to action? Can it change our minds? Since the 1970s, a deep pool of influential musicologists, music theorists, and music critics — Edward T. Cone, Joseph Kerman, Peter Kivy, Lawrence Kramer, Fred Maus, Susan McClary, Jean-Jacques Nattiez, and Anthony Newcomb, among many others — have explored the question of music's narrative potential. While their particular methodologies differ across subdisciplines, many of these scholars have been interested in whether music can be said to engage a plot, or be said to have narrative agents.[79] In a more recent consideration of the topic, Jerrold Levinson argues that a narrative comprises three parts: first, it must represent something outside of itself, second, it must represent states of affairs or events, and finally, it must represent temporality or causality between those states of affairs or events.[80] While the first two conditions are difficult to ascertain within a piece of instrumental music, the third condition, Levinson contends, would require music to have significant referential power that lies beyond its capacity. Accordingly, he posits that music is not capable of narration, but instead, it can convey "non-narrative representation."[81] To this extent, he argues, music can only really *suggest* gestures and actions, but falls short of fully *representing* them.[82] Fred Maus agrees, and has suggested that rather than think of music as narrative, we should value it as a "kind of drama that lacks determinate character."[83] Music is best understood then as having expressive actions and personae that appear before us as opposed to a narrative form whereby those actions are recounted to us by a narrative agent.[84]

If music lacks the narrative capacity we attribute to prose, then what is the possibility for music to move and change us, to help us understand incomprehensible violence and help us cope with our individual or collective trauma from war? According to Cathy Caruth, an individual experiences trauma for two reasons: either they cannot integrate a memory into their own experience, or they cannot communicate their painful knowledge to others.[85] Many forms of art, including prose and dramatic plays are able to communicate on our behalf, to convey that which we are unable to ourselves. Music, however, does not have the narrative capability of communicating in this same way. Instead, music can help us achieve a heightened emotional response to an event or topic, as Sontag argued on behalf of photographs, which too have the potential to evoke sentiment. But beyond this, as we have argued through our examples given above, the forms, instruments, and individual gestures used in music are socially coded: they tell stories because of the ways in which they have been used repeatedly in particular sociocultural contexts. While instrumental music, like photographs, might not always tell a linear, or teleological story, as Maus suggests, we do understand its formal and gestural signs as socially meaningful and able to reify what we believe or, perhaps, even change it.

So, for example, we might be able to make a case that Hendrix's performance of the "Star Spangled Banner" changed listener's minds to consider differently the glorification of violence in the lyrics of that song. And there are certainly other situations within which music *can* shape the listener's response to conflict so as to provoke a change of mind. In her 2009 book *Frames of War: When Is Life Grievable?* Judith Butler articulates the contexts within which listeners/viewers might engage with non-narrative art (although she does not take up music) in a way that would move them beyond the sentimental. According to Butler, it is crucial that we not only examine the content of the media, but also the frame within which an art form is presented. "In my view," Butler notes, "interpretation is not to be conceived restrictively in terms of a subjective act. Rather, *interpretation takes place by virtue of the structuring constraints of genre and form on the communicability of affect — and so sometimes takes place against one's will or, indeed, in spite of oneself.*"[86] Butler's analysis of recent war coverage in the popular media is handled through a series of case studies — poetry written by Guantánamo inmates, the media and "embedded reporting" in the Iraq war, and the photographs from Abu Ghraib, among others — through which we are able to glean how various frames are used to communicate information around these texts and encourage us to respond in particular ways. It becomes clear through her analysis that how these texts are framed by the American government is crucial in limiting the power of sympathetic affect for the "enemy" and securing public support for the war here at home.

By analyzing these texts, Butler tries to show how frames can be used to depict lives differently, some as already lost, already beyond hope, while "we" are presented as stable, righteous, and not so precarious. "[T]he frames that, in effect, decide which lives will be recognizable as lives and which will not, must circulate in order to establish their hegemony," she argues.[87] An important reason that their lives are read as ungrievable is because they are subjected to force, yet unprotected by legal or even civil rights. Law is operative but without meaning to those who are subject to it and through this lens we are disconnected from the victims, and able to disengage from their plight. Instead of accepting the frames through which we see — or, perhaps more accurately, don't see — their lives, Butler argues instead for the importance of frames that communicate their precariousness. If we can comprehend their instability and insecurity and recognize their lives as fragile and in need of protection, then we can challenge the power exerted against them, often unfairly and illegally, by our own governments. This is not an effort to relate to or understand their identity but rather their vulnerability, which ultimately connects us all, if to greater and lesser degrees.

We would like to take up Butler's argument through the examination of one critical frame often used to make sense of violence through music: the memorial. A memorial is an object or event that serves as a tribute to a person or event; closely related is the postmemorial, differentiated from the memorial because it is at least one generation removed from the event. To many minds, memorials and postmemorials may present as little more than benevolent and loving tributes. Following Butler, however, we argue that these also serve as political memory-framing devices, shaped by decisions about how and where the event is organized, who and how many are invited to participate, how it is described in the media and other public documents, and what sort of memorial is planned (a monument, a concert, a service, a day of remembrance, etc.). The relationship between the music and the frame (the memorial), then, is dialectical: memorials are framing devices that help "encode" music cross-culturally, that is, they infuse particular pieces with meaning so that this music, through its repetition at such events, may be deemed "appropriate" for future social grieving (Barber's *Adagio for Strings* is often performed at contemporary memorials, thus rendering this music sad, mournful and emotionally powerful within Western societies). But each subsequent memorial, each new "frame" is different, and the music chosen (or omitted) for each unique memorial in turn informs the way we remember the particular memorialized event. In other words, the music and frame must work seamlessly together to create a shared meaning, otherwise the frame is exposed and called into question. How then does the frame (including the music within that frame) tell us about what should be remembered? What must we also forget in order to remember an event in a particular way?

To shed light on the contemporary problematic of memorialization under consideration here, we would like to focus momentarily on one horrifically violent day in Canadian history. On December 6, 1989, a twenty-five-year-old white male named Marc Lepine entered the École Polytechnique, an engineering school affiliated with the University of Montréal. Armed with a legally obtained semi-automatic rifle and a knife, Lepine walked into a fourth-year mechanical engineering class of sixty, and asked the male students and two male professors to leave. He then shot six women while screaming they were a "bunch of feminists," after which he walked down hallways and into other classrooms killing eight more women before turning the gun on himself. This event, the deadliest single-day shooting in Canadian history,[88] has since been known as the "Montréal Massacre."

Many memorializations were held immediately following the 1989 event, as well as at the ten- and twenty-year anniversaries of the killings. But as Sharon Rosenberg asks,[89] what *exactly* was remembered at these memorials? While immediately following the event, numerous writings spoke to its singularity (killings at the hands of a "madman"), feminists soon urged Canadians not to see this act in isolation, but as part of a broader problem of violence against women in Canada, and, by 1991, the Canadian government passed a new gun control law and announced December 6 as a National Day of Remembrance.[90] The discursive practice of remembering what happened on December 6, then, shifted the meaning of the event from a singular atrocity to an "emblematic" day with the hope it would help us change a larger social problem. In effect, these fourteen became symbolically configured, their stories standing in for all Canadian women whose unnecessary deaths at the hands of their perpetrators remain untold. Those who had been silenced now had a powerful (emblematic) narrative that received nationwide attention. As Rosenberg points out, however, symbolization of this sort requires some distance, be that emotional, relational, or geographic;[91] as a result, remembering the women's identities as individuals became secondary and even contradictory to this strategy of remembrance. Moreover, becoming an event that came to represent violence against women more broadly required a partial erasure of the difficult political fact that these women were murdered because they were labeled as feminists.[92] To be effective emblematically, an important reason behind these killings — that Lepine was a raging antifeminist — must be erased from public memory.

The politics surrounding the memorialization of December 6 are cited at some length here to illustrate how memorials — intentionally or not — help us as a public remember, but only partially. It is possible to take this argument one step further, as Pierre Nora has done, to suggest that memorials might even serve as a means to help us forget. Monuments, or physical memorials, Nora argues, risk relieving communities of their own memory work: "The less memory is experienced from the inside the more it exists through scaffolding and outward signs."[93] Could it be the case, then, James Young asks, that the inverse is true, and that the more memory takes externalized forms the more it does our memory work for us, thus allowing us to forget more easily?[94] In other words, could the desire to memorialize events originate from the opposite desire to forget them?

The use of instrumental music within the context of the memorial is a clear instance of how its entrenched sociocultural codes can be deployed to help frame the narrative of the event, even if the music alone might not be considered "narrative" in a traditional sense. For one brief example, it is useful to consider how both instrumental and texted music was used as part of a memorial to perhaps the most traumatic event Americans have experienced in modern-day wartime: the attacks of September 11, 2001, or 9/11. On October 28, 2001, almost seven weeks after the events, a memorial service was held at the World Trade Center in New York City, the site where the majority of the lives were lost. While this was one of many tributes, benefits, and memorials held in the fall of 2001 across the United States and beyond its borders, this one was singular and worthy of our attention here because (1) of its location (it was held at the World Trade Center which was still quietly smoldering); (2) this was the first time that the thousands of family members of those lost were formally invited to the site; (3) those in attendance included high-ranking political and religious figures; and (4) it was mass-disseminated to home audiences through CNN. Although the fifty-five-minute service could have taken many forms, it was kept relatively simple. As anchor Aaron Brown stated during CNN's live broadcast, "This is not a day for speeches. It is a day for music and a day for prayer." Brown thus acknowledges music as part of the process of private contemplation enacted publically, of music's ability to help us reflect and *feel*, while at the same time linking it to the process of healing, of which prayer is also a part. The ceremony opened with Officer Daniel Rodriquez of the New York City Police Department singing "The Star Spangled Banner," followed by an opening prayer by Cardinal Egan, the Archbishop of New York. The first musical performance of the day was by a classical music celebrity, Italian tenor Andrea Bocelli performing Schubert's "Ave Maria" (circa 1825), accompanied by the Orchestra of St. Luke's. After Bocelli, New York Police Department chaplain and Muslim leader Iman Izak-El Mueed Pesha spoke a prayer, followed by Russian violinist Ilya Gringolts, who performed a Yiddish traditional song entitled "Raisins and Almonds." Rabbi Joseph Potasnick, also a chaplain to the New York City Fire Department, then offered his prayer. Renée Fleming followed with the Christian hymn "Amazing Grace," followed by the first "pop" song of the service: Andrew Lloyd Webber accompanied Irish vocalist Shonagh Daly in a rendition of his song "Let Us Love in Peace" from his 2000 musical *The Beautiful Game*. Reverend Franklin Graham (Billy Graham's son) read the Lord's Prayer and a benediction, followed by American composer Samuel Barber's 1936 *Adagio for Strings* (performed by St. Luke's Orchestra). Fleming then returned to close the memorial with her version of "God Bless America," followed by a closing benediction by Cardinal Egan.

How might this musical set list contribute to an overarching national narrative that day? Officer Rodriquez, who sang the opening anthem, was dressed in his uniform; significantly, he is not a celebrity or a professional musician, but "one of the people," and also represents the first responders to the attack, around which a discourse of heroism linked to national identity and pride was created immediately after the attacks. That Rodriquez sang in uniform also served to provide structure and instill confidence: New York City may still be burning, but those who protect the city have returned to work and will continue to fulfill their duties. The concert *proper* started, however, with European-born performer Andrea Bocelli, who represented support for America from beyond its borders; with the selection of "Ave Maria," a piece of music from the Western classical and sacred (Christian) tradition, his performance also communicated a gravity, seriousness, and sense of (Western) cultural history. If we were to take into account Celine Dion's now-famous quote — "if God would have a singing voice, He would sound a lot like Andrea Bocelli"[95] — then there might be further reason for Bocelli to begin the memorial.

After Bocelli's performance, the Muslim and Jewish religious representatives spoke and Ilya Gringolts performed his solo violin piece. This constellation of individuals was likely the least familiar to the Christian mainstream audience and undoubtedly were grouped together to form a segment: they followed the "star" power of Bocelli and, importantly, appeared not at the beginning nor at the end of the memorial, but embedded "safely" within the mid-section as a kind of "contained inclusivity," echoing again Wendy Brown's ideas of the safe inclusion of "others." The event then made an important shift: the music turned back to the English language and to another star as American Renée Fleming sang perhaps the most well-known piece of the day, "Amazing Grace." Given that it is a staple at American public events, its Christian roots have been conflated with American national identity. British-born Andrew Lloyd Webber's song followed, which once again gave America foreign support not through cultural weightiness but rather this time through the lightness and hope of pop music. St. Luke's Orchestra then performed Barber's *Adagio for Strings*, one of the most haunting and often played instrumental works following traumatic events, and then Fleming, who has been called "America's Beautiful Voice,"[96] concluded the musical portion of the event.

The memorial's musical selections, then, could be read as contributing to a frame that encouraged a preferred reading. The event featured three non-American performers, each of whom served a different purpose: Bocelli opened with weighty seriousness and a sense of old-world history, while Webber contributed a "pop" lightness (a role not shared by any of the American performers). Gringolt, meanwhile, was nested between the Muslim and Jewish speakers and contributed to an ideal of American inclusivity (although it is important to point out that he appeared in a secondary role within the artist lineup). A hegemonic version of America came clearly into focus as the hour progressed: the music (as well as the speakers) represented the country's Christian background ("Amazing Grace"), moved to *Adagio for Strings* (a new-world, more modern classical work than Schubert's "Ave Maria"), and concluded with "America's Beautiful Voice" inviting God to bless the nation. These musical selections, then, "progressed" from England to contemporary America, and intimated that the position formerly held by the United Kingdom — imperial dominance — now belongs to the United States, thus justifying the United States' upcoming military efforts.[97] By the end of the ceremony the American audience was assured through the musical selections and performance order that its self-perception as an open, inviting people was still intact, and that it could be both grounded and uplifted through its international relationships, but that ultimately, God and America stood alone, resolute, powerful and justified.

But what and whom are forgotten or marginalized musically in this program? How does the music reinforce what is important to remember? How will the music, along with the speakers, performance order, and the like, communicate what will be important to recall at the twenty-fifth or fiftieth or one-hundredth anniversary of the event? How this event is remembered in the years or decades that follow and how music contributes to that collective memory will no doubt be informed by current political ideologies. Regardless of how the event is memorialized, we might want to consider a few critical questions: How does music contribute to the shifting social discourses of a traumatic memory? How can music help erase some memories and replace them with others? Can music hold both emblematic remembrance (necessary in large-scale horrors like the Holocaust or the millions of dead or dying as a result of HIV/AIDS) *and* hold us accountable to the ruptures that precipitated these conditions? Because music can be so emotionally moving and because it can bring us back to an idea, event, or person so powerfully, is it possible that we willingly hand over to a work the responsibility of remembering for us? Can music be a means by which we face the specificity of a tragedy while also broadening the horizon to consider the context leading up to the event? What would it mean to have music at a memorial that forces us to layer the complexities of uncomfortable remembering? (Could we imagine Afghan classical or folk music being played at a future post 9/11 memorial?) Could we bear to hear what it says about our past, about what has changed and about what has remained the same, and about our hope for a nonviolent future?

The essays that follow center on issues relating to music and violence, issues that cross political boundaries, time periods and media. It is impossible for nine essays to constitute a geographically comprehensive volume; instead, they were chosen because they provide sound and engaging case studies of musical practices ranging from well-known and large-scale events to regionally specific and still-emerging histories. The chapter order follows the three broad themes we have explored in this introduction: those that appear early in the volume explore how music participates in both objective and subjective violence (Attfield, Baker, Baade, and Deaville); the authors featured in the second section (McDonald, Vicente, and Miller) explore violence and reconciliation, while those who appear at the end of the volume (Ritter and Wlodarski) address healing, post-memorials and memory. In the Afterword, J. Martin Daughtry invites us to consider violence with regard to an unlikely perpetrator (the voice), and provides a reflection on how each of the chapters engage with objective, subjective, and/or violent memory.

Throughout this volume we seek to reveal how music and violence are closely — and often uncomfortably — entwined. While it may be already apparent to readers how music can either challenge or support subjective violence, the authors demonstrate in their work how music is also a particularly rich medium for perpetuating symbolic violence, which, in turn, often becomes part of a much larger systemic oppression. In organizing the essays, it became clear that many of them address music's relationship to symbolic and subjective violence concurrently. This is not entirely surprising — as the saying goes, "violence begets violence." Accordingly, the contributions could have been ordered in a number of different ways and the reader may discover numerous points of connection other than those drawn forward here. What unites all of this work, however, is the position that music is never neutral, and that we cannot turn a blind eye to how it is used for violent purposes in the realm of the political. Further, if we contend that the opposite of violence is neither peace nor nonviolence but rather *empowerment*,[98] we afford space to think about music intellectually as an *active* agent rather than as a passive art. Music, in this sense does not "keep violence at a distance"; it either contributes to it or challenges it directly, and, sometimes, both. We hope that as readers engage with the essays that follow, they do so with the knowledge that music does not come in just "when words fail." Instead, music must be understood as both critical and central in creating a fully realized "sensate democracy," a project to which we hope this volume contributes.

Notes

1. Bruce Johnson and Martin Cloonan, *Dark Side of the Tune: Popular Music and Violence* (London: Ashgate, 2009), 1.

2. See, for example, Johnson and Cloonan, *Dark Side of the Tune*, although they define and take up "violence" in music in ways distinctly different from how we approach the subject in this book; see our discussion below.

3. Judith Butler, *Frames of War: When Is Life Grievable?* (London: Verso, 2009).

4. Samuel Araújo and Members of the Grupo Musicultura, "Conflict and Violence as Theoretical Tools in Present-Day Ethnomusicology: Notes on a Dialogic Ethnography of Sound Practices in Rio de Janeiro," *Ethnomusicology* 50, no. 2 (Spring/Summer 2006): 289. See also John Morgan O'Connell, "Introduction: An Ethnomusicological Approach to Music and Conflict," in *Music and Conflict*, eds. John Morgan O'Connell and Salwa El-Shawan Castelo-Branco (Urbana: University of Illinois Press, 2010), 8.

5. See Samuel Araújo, "Conflict and Violence as Conceptual Tools in Present-Day Ethnomusicology: Notes on a Dialogic Ethnography of Sound Practices in Rio de Janeiro," *Ethnomusicology* 50, no. 2 (Spring/Summer 2006): 287–313; Margaret Kartomi, "Towards a Methodology of War and Peace Studies in Ethnomusicology; The Case of Aceh, 1976–2009," *Ethnomusicology* 54, no. 3 (Fall 2010): 452–83; Svandibor Pettan, "Music in War, Music for Peace: Experiences in Applied Ethnomusicology," in *Music in Conflict*, 177–92; John Morgan O'Connell, "Music in War, Music for Peace: A Review Article," *Ethnomusicology* 55, no. 1 (Winter 2011): 112–27.

6. O'Connell, "Introduction: An Ethnomusicological Approach to Music and Conflict," 2–3.

7. O'Connell, "Introduction: An Ethnomusicological Approach to Music and Conflict," 3.

8. O'Connell, "Introduction: An Ethnomusicological Approach to Music and Conflict," 12.

9. O'Connell, "Introduction: An Ethnomusicological Approach to Music and Conflict," 3.

10. See Walter Benjamin, *Reflections: Essays, Aphorisms, Autobiographical Writing*, trans. Edmund Jephcott, ed. Peter Demetz (New York: Schocken Books, 1978); Frantz Fanon, *The Wretched of the Earth*, trans. Constance Farrington (New York: Grove Press, 1963); Hannah Arendt, *On Violence* (New York: Harcourt, Brace & World, 1970); Giorgio Agamben, *State of Exception*, trans. Kevin Attell (Chicago: University of Chicago Press, 2005); Jacques Derrida, *Rogues: Two Essays on Reason*, trans. Pascale-Anne Brault and Michael Naas (Stanford, CA: Stanford University Press, 2005), and "The 'World' of the Enlightenment to Come (Exception, Calculation, Sovereignty)," trans. Pascale-Anne Brault and Michael Naas, *Research in Phenomenology* 33 (2003): 9–52; Wendy Brown, *Regulating Aversion: Tolerance in the Age of Identity and Empire* (Princeton, NJ: Princeton University Press, 2006); Butler, *Frames of War*; Judith Butler and Gayatri Chakravorty Spivak, *Who Sings the Nation-State? Language, Politics, Belonging* (London: Seagull Books, 2007); and Slavoj Žižek, *Violence: Six Sideways Reflections* (New York: Picador, 2008).

11. While we recognize Žižek's definitions of "subjective" and "objective" violence (the latter of which includes "systemic" and "symbolic" violence) as particular, he was not the first to theorize the various modes of violence. Pierre Bourdieu previously articulated symbolic violence — the form through which communication, including music, is exerted — as "the violence which is exercised upon a social agent with his or her complicity." Pierre Bourdieu and Loïc J. D. Wacquant, *An Invitation to Reflexive Sociology* (Chicago: The University of Chicago Press, 1992), 167. Bourdieu himself acknowledged that one of the pitfalls of his definition is that the agents could be interpreted as willing participants in this

violence (167). Žižek does not discuss the role of the social agent against whom symbolic violence is exerted, but rather describes the violence as coming from above, that is, the "imposition of a certain universe of meaning" (2). We have chosen to work with Žižek's definition because we too are most interested in how symbolic power is generated from positions of hegemonic power regardless of agent complicity.

12. Žižek, *Violence: Six Sideways Reflections*, 2.

13. Žižek, *Violence: Six Sideways Reflections*, 2.

14. Žižek, *Violence: Six Sideways Reflections*, 61.

15. Žižek, *Violence: Six Sideways Reflections*, 2.

16. Karl Marx, *Capital: A Critique of Political Economy: Volume III, Part II, The Process of Capitalist Production as a Whole*, ed. Friedrich Engels (New York: Cosimo Books, 2007), 744.

17. Žižek, *Violence: Six Sideways Reflections*, 11.

18. Žižek, *Violence: Six Sideways Reflections*, 22.

19. Žižek, *Violence: Six Sideways Reflections*, 7.

20. Žižek, *Violence: Six Sideways Reflections*, 8.

21. Paul Taylor, *Žižek and the Media* (Cambridge: Polity Press, 2010), 146.

22. Greig Dymond, "Benefit Concerts: An Abbreviated History," www.cbc .ca/news/arts/things-that-go-pop-blog/2010/01/benefit-concerts-an-abbreviated -history.html (accessed November 14, 2010).

23. Brown, *Regulating Aversion*, 28.

24. For critical reflections on the cultural politics of benefit concerts see Susan Fast and Kip Pegley, "*America: A Tribute to Heroes*: Music, Mourning, and the Unified American Community," in *Music in the Post-9/11 World*, eds. J. Martin Daughtry and Jonathan Ritter (New York: Routledge, 2007) 27–42 and "Music and Canadian Nationhood Post 9/11: An Analysis of *Music Without Borders: Live*," *Journal of Popular Music Studies* 18, no. 1 (2006): 18–39, as well as Reebee Garofalo, *Rockin' the Boat: Mass Music and Mass Movements* (Cambridge, MA: South End Press, 1992).

25. John Cameron and Anna Haanstra, "Development Made Sexy: How It Happened and What It Means," *Third World Quarterly* 29, no. 8 (2008): 1476.

26. April Biccum, "Marketing Development: Live 8 and the Production of the Global Citizen," *Development and Change* 38, no. 6 (2007): 1124.

27. Biccum, "Marketing Development," 1112.

28. Žižek, *Violence: Six Sideways Reflections*, 4.

29. Theodor W. Adorno, *Prisms* (Cambridge, MA: MIT Press, 1983), 34.

30. Žižek, *Violence: Six Sideways Reflections*, 4–5.

31. As quoted in Laurence J. Peter, *Peter's Quotations: Ideas for Our Time* (New York: Morrow, 1977), 343.

32. Marion M. Scott, *Beethoven* (London: JM Dent, 1974), 125.

33. Available online at: http://thinkexist.com (accessed November 25, 2011).

34. SheetMusicFox.com, "Free Music Quotes by Famous Musicians," www
.sheetmusicfox.com/quotes.html (accessed January 3, 2010).

35. Available online at: http://thinkexist.com (accessed November 25, 2011).

36. http://beatsnrants.tumblr.com/post/763171592/quote-john-coltrane
(accessed on November 25, 2011).

37. For foundational scholarly work that began to challenge romantic notions
of music as imprecisely evocative see, for example, Susan McClary, *Feminine
Endings: Music, Gender and Sexuality* (Minneapolis: University of Minnesota
Press, 1991); Ruth Solie, *Musicology and Difference: Gender and Sexuality in Music
Scholarship* (Berkeley: University of California Press, 1995); and Katherine
Bergeron and Philip V. Bohlman (eds.), *Disciplining Music: Musicology and
its Canons* (Chicago: University of Chicago Press, 1992).

38. Žižek, *Violence: Six Sideways Reflections*, 5.

39. Žižek, *Violence: Six Sideways Reflections*, 6.

40. Žižek, *Violence: Six Sideways Reflections*, 35.

41. Arnold Schoenberg, *Style and Idea*, ed. Leonard Stein, trans. Leo Black
(London: Faber and Faber, 1975), 261.

42. Michael Steinberg, "The Late Quartets," in *The Beethoven Quartet Companion*, eds. Robert Winter and Robert Martin (Los Angeles: University of California
Press, 1994), 245.

43. Michael Steinberg, "The Late Quartets," 245.

44. Žižek, *Violence: Six Sideways Reflections*, 1–2.

45. McClary, *Feminine Endings*, 128. In an earlier version of this essay ("Getting
Down off the Beanstalk: The Presence of a Woman's Voice in Janika Vandervelde's
Genesis II," which appeared (unpaged) in the February 1987 *Minnesota Composer's
Forum Newsletter*), McClary likened this moment in the piece to "the throttling
murderous rage of a rapist incapable of attaining release." She was, predictably,
widely castigated for daring to speak in such a way about a cultural icon.

46. Derrida, *Rogues*, 155–56.

47. Derrida, *Rogues*, 156.

48. Derrida, *Rogues*, 105–6.

49. For more information on the conflict in Arizona, see Terry Greene Sterling,
Illegal: Life and Death in Arizona's Immigration War Zone (Guilford, CT: Lyons
Press, 2010).

50. Butler and Spivak, *Who Sings the Nation-State?* 59–60.

51. Butler and Spivak, *Who Sings the Nation-State?* 48.

52. Butler and Spivak, *Who Sings the Nation-State?* 59.

53. Butler and Spivak, *Who Sings the Nation-State?* 69.

54. Butler and Spivak, *Who Sings the Nation-State?* 63.

55. Butler and Spivak, *Who Sings the Nation-State?* 62–63. For a musical analysis of this piece that corresponds to ours, but which offers much more detail about the use of distortion and feedback see Eric F. Clarke, "Jimi Hendrix's 'Star Spangled Banner,'" in *Ways of Listening: An Ecological Approach to the Perception of Musical Meaning* (New York: Oxford University Press, 2005), 48–61.

56. Clarke, "Jimi Hendrix's Star Spangled Banner," 54.

57. As cited in Charles Cross, *Room Full of Mirrors: A Biography of Jimi Hendrix* (New York: Hyperion, 2005), 271.

58. Cross, *Room Full of Mirrors*, 272.

59. As cited in Rob Kirkpatrick, *1969: The Year Everything Changed* (New York: Skyhorse Publishing, 2009), 190.

60. Cross, *Room Full of Mirrors*, 271.

61. A number of early ethnomusicological writings addressed the question of how humans engage with musical sounds, which, in part, serves to form a sense of community and differentiates them from other groups. See, for instance, Alan Merriam, *The Anthropology of Music* (Evanston, IL: Northwestern University Press, 1964), John Blacking, *How Musical Is Man?* (Seattle: University of Washington Press, 1973), and Anthony Seeger, *Why Suyá Sing* (Cambridge: Cambridge University Press, 1987), 137. Studies that address questions of music and nationalism are too numerous to mention here. For an excellent overview of the subject in Western art music, including an extensive bibliography, see Richard Taruskin, "Nationalism," in *Grove Music Online, Oxford Music Online*, www.oxfordmusic online.com (accessed November 11, 2010). See also Georgina Born and David Hesmondhalgh (eds.), *Western Music and Its Others: Difference, Representation, and Appropriation in Music* (Berkeley: University of California Press, 2000), and Ronald Michael Radano, *Music and the Racial Imagination* (Chicago: University of Chicago Press, 2000). Of particular note for the present writing is Philip V. Bohlman, *Music, Nationalism and the Making of the New Europe*, 2nd ed. (New York: Routledge, 2011). In this text, Bohlman provides an excellent overview of the history and issues at the intersection of music and European nationalism from the Middle Ages to the present day.

62. Taruskin, "Nationalism."

63. Johann Gottfried von Herder, *Abhandlung über den Ursprung der Sprache* (1772, English translation 1827), cited in Taruskin, "Nationalism."

64. Bill Readings, *The University in Ruins* (Cambridge, MA: Harvard University Press, 1996), 61.

65. Bohlman, *Music*, 134.

66. Pamela M. Potter, *Most German of the Arts: Musicology and Society from the Weimar Republic to the End of Hitler's Reich* (New Haven, CT: Yale University Press, 1998), 260.

67. Bohlman, *Music*, 50.

68. For more information, see Uli Linke, *Blood and Nation: The European Aesthetics of* Race (Philadelphia: University of Pennsylvania Press, 1999), as cited in Bohlman, *Music*, 50.

69. Susan Sontag's 1977 text *On Photography* (London: Allen Lane, 1978) remains a seminal text on photographic representations of violence, although since 9/11, a series of further writings on photography and representation have appeared. For more on this topic see Sontag's 2003 text *Regarding the Pain of Others* (New York: Farrar, Straus and Giroux, 2003), and Stuart Allan and Barbie Zelizer's *Reporting War: Journalism in Wartime* (London: Routledge, 2004).

70. David Campbell, "Representing Contemporary War," *Ethics & International Affairs* 17, no. 2 (Fall 2003): 102.

71. See Sontag, *Regarding the Pain of Others*, 104.

72. Campbell, "Representing Contemporary War," 99.

73. Sontag, *Regarding the Pain of Others*, 102.

74. Butler, *Frames of War*, 70.

75. Sontag, *On Photography*, 19.

76. Žižek, *Violence: Six Sideways Reflections*, 4–5.

77. Butler, *Frames of War*, 71.

78. Sontag, *On Photography*, 24.

79. See, for instance, Edward T. Cone, *The Composer's Voice* (Berkeley: University of California Press, 1974); Peter Kivy, "Music as Narration," *Sound and Semblance: Reflections on Musical Representation* (Princeton, NJ: Princeton University Press, 1984), 159–96; Lawrence Kramer: "Musical Narratology: A Theoretical Outline," *Indiana Theory Review* 12 (1991): 141–62, repr. in *Classical Music and Postmodern Knowledge* (Berkeley: University of California Press, 1995); Jean-Jacques Nattiez, "Can One Speak of Narrativity in Music?' *Journal of the Royal Music Association* 15, no. 2 (1990): 240–57; Fred E. Maus, "Music as Drama," *Music Theory Spectrum* 10 (1988): 56–73; Fred E. Maus, "Narrative, Drama, and Emotion in Instrumental Music," *Journal of Aesthetics and Art Criticism* 55, no. 3 (1997): 293–303; Anthony Newcomb, "Schumann and Late Eighteenth-Century Narrative Strategies," *19th-Century Music* 11 (1987–88), 164–74.

80. Jerrold Levinson, "Music as Narrative and Music as Drama," *Mind and Language* 19, no. 4 (2004): 429.

81. Levinson, "Music as Narrative and Music as Drama," 429.

82. Levinson, "Music as Narrative and Music as Drama," 431.

83. Maus, "Music as Drama," 128.

84. Levinson, "Music as Narrative and Music as Drama," 434.

85. Cathy Caruth and Thomas Keenan, "'The Aids Crisis Is Not Over': A Conversation with Gregg Bordowitz, Douglas Crimp, and Laura Pinsky," in

Trauma: Explorations in Memory, ed. Cathy Caruth (Baltimore: Johns Hopkins University Press, 1995), 256.

86. Butler, *Frames of War*, 67 (emphasis added).

87. Butler, *Frames of War*, 12.

88. Charles Grandmont, "Massacre of 14 Women Haunts Montréal Ten Years Later." *National Post*, December 5, 1999, www.canada.com (accessed May 23, 2010).

89. Sharon Rosenberg, "Neither Forgotten, Nor Fully Remembered: Tracing an Ambivalent Public Memory on the Tenth Anniversary of the Montreal Massacre," *Feminist Theory* 4, no. 1 (April 2003): 8.

90. Rosenberg, "Neither Forgotten, Nor Fully Remembered," 13.

91. Rosenberg, "Neither Forgotten, Nor Fully Remembered," 20.

92. Rosenberg, "Neither Forgotten, Nor Fully Remembered," 18.

93. Pierre Nora, "Between Memory and History: Les lieux de mémoire," trans. Marc Roudebush, *Representations* 26 (1989): 13, as cited in James Young, *The Texture of Memory: Holocaust Memorials and Meaning* (New Haven, CT: Yale University Press, 1994), 5.

94. Young, *The Texture of Memory*, 5.

95. www.andreabocelli.com/site.html#/en/biography (accessed November 17, 2010).

96. www.renee-fleming.com (accessed November 14, 2010).

97. Thanks to Harry Berger for bringing this point to our attention.

98. See Global Oneness Project, www.globalonenessproject.org/opposite -violence-isnt-non-violence (accessed November 25, 2010).

PART I

❦

Objective
and
Subjective
Violences

❦

The chapters in Part I ask how, in the context of war, music becomes a means through which violence is perpetuated off the battlefield, how it is used as a mechanism to extend and deepen the physical wounds suffered in war by further delineating categories of difference and separation — what we explored in the introduction through Žižek's category of "objective violence." In chapter 1, Nicholas Attfield explores how those writing for the journal *Neue Zeitschrift für Musik* during World War I strove "for a full national politicization of the country's musical life," resurrecting all manner of patriotic song and engaging in debate about the national identity of prominent composers — who could be claimed as German and who could not (unsurprisingly, Beethoven plays a major role in this discourse). The object of this violence, as he points out, is changeable, from musics outside German borders (and by extension, the cultural creators of that music) to, by the 1920s, musics made by "unpure" Germans from within those same borders. That this violence was written into a canonical text like the NZM is crucial: racism perpetuated through well-known sources that lacked ideological pressure from a specific governing authority made its content seem more autonomous, more authorial, even "truthful." The objective violence unearthed in this first chapter, then, is the symbolic form: the written language communicates about music in ways that violently separates German from non-German, insider from outsider, purity from contagion.

While Attfield's essay focuses on the written word, Catherine Baker's is directly concerned with how music itself perpetuates symbolic violence. In chapter 2, Baker carefully documents the story of folk-pop singer Neda Ukraden, a popular Yugoslavian singer during the 1970s and 1980s. During the historical reconstruction of the country in the early 1990s, however, her career took a turn as the newly independent Croatian government sought to erase its Yugoslavian past, tighten ethnic identity, and nationalize its culture. Ukraden, who left for Belgrade (Serbia) after the outbreak of war in 1992, was stripped of her Croatian identity and presented emphatically as Serb. Her music, in turn, was deemed undesirable for broadcast in Croatia, even though the songs were often written by Croatian songwriters. Resurrecting Ukraden's music — previously loved by many Croatians — would require a performance of the "correct" ethnicity; accordingly, Croatians re-recorded her music and brought back her songs into "Croatian show business" (even though these performers too had to secure their safety by distancing themselves politically from Ukraden). Music, then, was used in the service of symbolic violence: songs were revised to make artists disappear and erase a history the new government best saw as forgotten. This revisionist cultural history, like that articulated in Attfield's previous chapter, is testimony to the power of language (words *and* music) to symbolically rewrite the past, sever relations, and direct future nationalist agendas.

In chapter 3 Christina Baade analyses three performances of the popular WWII song "Lili Marlene" and explores how it reflected (and constructed) nationhood, gender, and desire by *both* German and Allied troops. In particular, she demonstrates how multiple versions of the song were carefully constructed not only to bridge the distance between the troops and their loved ones at home, but also to represent the nationally foreign performers as dangerous temptresses. While the troops sang along with longing and desire, they were unaware of how calculated the production of these records was, how both the BBC and German radio stations manipulated the song, sometimes by promoting a version, sometimes by frustrating its airplay, or even by opting instead for new renditions that served clear, ideologically motivated, nationalistic goals. Like Baker's analysis of how music was revised in the 1990s to enforce a stable, and ethnically unambiguous Croatian identity, Baade's work here uncovers how one song — which could have expanded our understanding of those with whom we were engaged in conflict — instead was revised to limit our capacity for empathy and connection in a gesture of symbolic (auricular) violence.

In chapter 4, James Deaville shifts the era and media focus to explore the use of diegetic and non-diegetic sound in American news broadcasts of two wars. Whereas music "humanized" early televised reports from "the first television war" (Vietnam), Deaville shows that by the 1990s the incorporation and organization of sounds and visuals resulted in nothing short of "infotainment." Indeed, by the start of the Persian Gulf War (1991), CNN tapped music's power as "the ultimate hidden persuader,"[1] taking the leap of integrating all its production elements — including live reporting, music, graphics, and the like — to effectively communicate a preferred (pro-Bush) position on the war, convincing viewers that the United States was not only justified in its actions, but would also be victorious. This new level of visual and sonic integration resulted in a spectacle already familiar to viewers from video games and filmic texts, saturated with the images and sounds of subjective violence. As Paul Taylor argues, music here is part of "the media [that] systematically uses symbolic violence to focus on subjective violence in order to avoid confronting the extent to which our society is based upon a corresponding amount of systemic objective violence."[2] Music, in other words, accompanies shocking images in a symbolic media storm that excludes any sort of comprehensive analysis of the (systemic) reasons leading up to this war. Not only does music not promote understanding, one could argue that it participates in symbolic *mis*understanding.

Notes

1. Nicholas Cook, *Music: A Very Short Introduction*, 2nd ed. (Oxford: Oxford University Press, 2000), 122.
2. Paul Taylor, *Žižek and the Media* (Cambridge: Polity Press, 2010), 147.

CHAPTER ONE

"A Healing Draft for a Sick People"

War in the Pages of the
Neue Zeitschrift für Musik, 1914–1918

NICHOLAS ATTFIELD

I tell you, fate sends war: the value of this cruel medicine is so seldom under-stood, because the doctors of men could never be so bold as to prescribe it readily as a healing draft for a sick people. . . . War is a nation-creator: as it shakes the borders of countries, it binds countryman to countryman ever tighter, gives to the ignorant a sense of the splendor of the Fatherland, warms the withered soul with love's light.[1]

These words, the work of the nineteenth-century German historian Hein-rich von Treitschke, might reasonably alarm the modern reader. After a cen-tury of apocalyptic conflicts, not to mention the desperate pleas for peace that they have brought in tow, the notion of war as something salutary — as healer, creator, or binder — rings with an alien tone. Even if we can imag-ine, in the abstract at least, a "just" war, a conflict for some semblance of greater good, many of us would countenance this only as a last resort. In the twenty-first century, war and "love's light" are quite divorced, if not dia-metrically opposed.

It will come as no surprise that I quote Treitschke's statement from a source that appeared in September 1914, at the onset of the first mass con-flict of the past century — the "Great" War that it seemed unlikely would ever be superseded. It may be more surprising to learn that I quote it not from Treitschke's original,[2] nor from a bragging political manifesto, nor from some Clausewitzian general's treatise on war, but from the pages of a music journal.[3]

The *Neue Zeitschrift für Musik* is among the world's longest-running dedicated music journals, and is certainly one of its best known. This notoriety stems in part from the famous story of the journal's beginnings: in 1834, Robert Schumann and his band of like-minded crusaders had sought through its publication to "erect a barrier against convention," that is, against what they saw as the artistic philistinisms of their time. Thus a markedly idealistic venture, the *Neue Zeitschrift*'s first issues (appearing twice weekly from April 3, 1834) had aimed to create a professionalized critical front far beyond the narrow bounds of contemporary journals: a union of theoretical inquiry with "belletristic pieces," and critiques of new works with comprehensive chronicles of European concert life — all the while standing apart from the guiding hand of any particular music publisher or contemporary authority.

Schumann was similarly uncompromising in outlining the journal's stance toward music history. As he wrote in his first solo editorial of 1835, the "recent past," characterized only by an empty mechanical virtuosity, would have to be rejected as an "inartistic period," whereas the "creations of the [more distant] past" would be drawn upon in order to "prepare and facilitate the advent of a fresh, poetic future." Through the invocation of Bach, Mozart, and the other German masters, then, and through wide-reaching critical engagement with the most promising musical phenomena of the present, the future could be grasped whole-handedly. In all, the *Neue Zeitschrift* had started out from a potently liberal-modernist position resonant with the Leipzig milieu in which it had been conceived.[4]

Indeed, as the journal's reputation and readership expanded in the latter half of the nineteenth-century, this commitment to a "progressive" ("fortschrittlich") orientation became something of a mantra, variously interpreted, for subsequent editors.[5] Franz Brendel, the music critic and historian who acquired the journal's editorial rights from Schumann in 1844, certainly hid behind it when he chose to publish Richard Wagner's notorious essay "Das Judentum in der Musik" ("Judaism in Music") in 1850. If the journal were to remain "free-thinking" in the exalted German sense — as Brendel's editorial and Wagner's pseudonym *Freigedank* suggested — then these kinds of points of view would have to be honored.[6]

Sharply drawn as its debates were, though, the journal's nineteenth-century identity was played out on what might fairly be called the socio-aesthetic battlefields of its heartland. Overt eulogies to war, or clamor for its good effects in the manner of Treitschke, are not a key part of its nineteenth-century program. In spite of various displays of military prowess — 1864, 1866, 1870–71 — music and armed conflict were kept at a distance. Moreover, in the years directly before the Great War, this division still pertained in the pages of the *Neue Zeitschrift*. Now under the leadership of Friedrich Brandes, the director of music at the University of Leipzig,[7] it continued to offer, apparently quite unaffected by events on the European political stage, broad swathes of news items and reviews of concerts and other musical events from around Germany and Austria, as well as from other important centers — Rome, London, and Paris.

But as the tone of many of these reports testifies, the journal's careful balance had gradually tipped toward study of the revered past, largely at the expense of Schumann's and Brendel's visions of the future. In other words, the *Neue Zeitschrift* had become something of a conservatively colored and historically oriented *Traditionsblatt* (roughly translated, a "journal in support of tradition"). Leading articles in 1912 and 1913 addressed, to take a brief sample, the latest research on Johann Adolf Hasse, Bruckner's First Symphony, Wagner's relationship with his mother, and the vexing question of Bayreuth's rights with regard to performances of *Parsifal*.[8] Felix Draeseke's oratorio trilogy *Christus*, the work of an acidly antimodernist composer,[9] also met with a warm reception on the journal's opening pages, and experiments with quarter-tones were raised as a possibility only to be roundly dismissed.[10] Meanwhile, advertisements for Wagner editions, the suites and symphonies of now rather obscure composers (August Scharrer? M. J. Erb?), and tastefully bound volumes of the *Neue Zeitschrift* itself tempted the reader's reflections away to more venerable historical realms.

If there is the occasional glimmer of a laissez-faire attitude toward new aesthetics and new compositional means, then singled out for criticism still is their nurturing society. F. A. Geissler's leading article of October 10, 1912, may permit a certain liberty on the part of modern composers ("Who knows where all these different [creative] efforts will lead? May in future music never lose its desire to be the sounding expression of the *Zeitgeist*"),[11] yet it also brutalizes the force — and for that matter the *Zeitgeist* — that drove them:

> And who would dare dispute that the spirit of capitalism, which many people in all seriousness prize as a splendid achievement of modern times, has also taken control of music? It is not only that every composer grasps and clamors for his gold, dreaming of monstrous royalties and limitless profit, but that, through the cults of virtuosity and personality, our musical life has declined so far into capitalism that "big names" arise whose highest hope is an American tour — not for the sake of fame, but for dollars. . . . [T]hese are the first in the dance before the golden calf.[12]

Given this context, the impetus behind the printing of Treitschke's statement only two years later is easily identified: its call for war appears as a cry

for the thresholding of the present, a measure needed to halt the degenera-
tion of musical life and purge Germany of its manifold cultural sicknesses —
of which Geissler's rampant capitalism, materialism, and superficiality were
only a few.[13] Indeed, this was a project that, in broad outline, could be
traced back to Schumann and his original conception.

Yet at the same time, the appearance of such an overtly saber-rattling
statement heralded a will to a distinctly twentieth-century nationalist-
conservative advance into the political fray. Now a widely respected and
disseminated publication, read by musical professionals as well as intrigued
amateurs in the home, the *Neue Zeitschrift* could play a significant role in
shaping what music — German music — ought to be. And since, from time
immemorial, music had stood at the heart of German cultural identity, this
shaping process necessarily engaged with questions of national identity, an
old problem given new life by the presence of enemy forces massing around
the country. It is these facets of the *Neue Zeitschrift*'s participation in the
war — their inception, the debates they encompassed, the crises of confidence they concealed, and, crucially, the trajectory they followed as the conflict progressed — that are the subject of the present essay. We begin with
the phenomenon that, as Treitschke's statement sat in the journal's presses,
was already spreading all over the country.

The "spirit of 1914" raged throughout the country in that year's summer
months. With the Austrian ultimatum to Serbia on 23 July and news of the
mobilization of Russian troops a week later, crowds of urban Germans
flooded to their local newsstands, the better to express en masse a newfound patriotic fervor. At fever pitch, songs were sung, bands played, flags
were waved, and student-led processions wound through town centers.
Imperial Germany, it was widely believed and reported, had been the victim of an attack by its bellicose neighbors. It had been forced to defend
itself. And, as many of those thronging in the town centers urged, so it
would: with superior government, an ardent press, vocal support from significant cultural figures,[14] a military that was the envy of Europe and the
world, and the glory of swift and crushing victories in the unifying wars of
living memory, nothing other than ultimate triumph was to be expected.
This war, so it was repeatedly said and written, would be the start of another new era of national unity and patriotism, bringing clear-air transcendence of petty loyalties of class or religious confession. *Gesellschaft* — mere
society — would mature into *Gemeinschaft* — community. Why would many
of those Germans in their crowds have any fear of defeat or humiliation?

Why would they, for that matter, have any concern that the conflict would last beyond Christmas?[15]

Those behind the *Neue Zeitschrift* evidently felt no different. On August 20, 1914, a week before the resounding German triumph at the battle of Tannenberg, the leading music article of that week's issue is squeezed into a feuilleton-like fringe. In its place comes a declaration from editor and publisher that, while ultimately rather trivial in content, marks the adoption of a defiant tone in what were now clearly felt to be extraordinary circumstances. "To our readers," it begins in overly massive font, "in spite of the conditions of war that have reigned throughout Europe in the past months . . . we shall permit the limitation of our journal only insofar as we shall, for the time being . . . publish a double edition every fourteen days."[16]

This announcement serves, more significantly, as a visual cue for the metamorphosis of the journal's usual fare. From this issue onward, alongside the traditional scholarly contributions on Beethoven, Brahms, and the like, tumbles out a multitude of strongly patriotic articles. Here and subsequently, reproductions of statesmen's speeches and historians' dicta litter the journal's pages: quotations from Tacitus's *Germania* ("they stir no foreign people to war and terrorize none with plunder and pillage; it is precisely this that serves as the highest proof of their splendour and their power")[17] and the venerable historian Karl Lamprecht ("it is as though the nation, and every individual German, had become bestowed with high courage and free thought")[18] shore up the reader's national feeling, if, that is, the lines from Frederick the Great's "Ode an die Deutschen" and Bismarck had not been sufficient for the task.[19] The texts of all manner of songs and poems, too, reprinted from other sources in regular profusion, stress German qualities in adversity and profess everlasting devotion to the fatherland. In one case, a "Deutsches Kampflied" ("German battle-song") is put forward as a replacement for the national song "Wacht am Rhein" — for, owing to German territorial advances in the West, the river in question no longer formed the country's border, but had become an almost entirely German fixture.[20]

The provision of musical texts, once an occasional feature, also became commonplace. From late 1914, many issues include a patriotic song or march as supplement, often newly composed and always transcribed for piano, so that they might all the more easily be played and sung as *Hausmusik* in the parlor — a simple unifying gesture for the family, a show of support for the country's troops, and a connection, however fleeting, between home front and battlefront. A devotional text by Otto R. Hübner serves as a good example. Set by Karl Thiessen, it traces the outline of a Haydn-like imperial hymn "with patriotic enthusiasm." "For German," its first strophe closes, "means eternally loyal."[21]

Heil dir, mein Vaterland—musical supplement to the December 31, 1914, edition of the *Neue Zeitschrift für Musik*.

But most interesting of all are the articles that question whether or not German cultural and musical spheres ought to be influenced by what were still perceived as events "external" to it. At first glance, this may seem like something of a *post facto*, and rather futile, debate: whether the journal's administration liked it or not, its correspondents' columns frequently complained of privations caused by the war.[22] Yet at stake were less these inevitabilities and more the issue of whether, and if so to what extent, German music should accommodate the aims of the country's war effort — how, in other words, political ideology might guide its musical counterpart. The consensus seems to have been, indeed, that the latter should keep closely in step with the former: in the journal's very first wartime issue, for example, we find a short report entitled "Feinde hinaus!" ("Out with the enemy!") that details the decision of the *Allgemeine deutsche Musikerverband* to bar all members from enemy countries.[23] One issue later, the possibilities of placing foreign musicians operative in Germany under house arrest come under discussion.[24]

Other correspondents wanted to reclaim German composers and works for the nation's honor. In December 1914, Max Unger angrily, perhaps nervously, refutes a Parisian claim that Beethoven had in fact been a Belgian — first with the elucidation of his family tree, and second with reports of his indignation toward the French, and particularly Napoleon.[25] Another short demands that Beethoven's Ninth Symphony remain unperformed during the conflict, as Schiller's thoughts of a "brotherhood of man" in the finale "must seem all the more alienating" in view of current events. "Our kisses for this vile world and its armies can only be bombs and grenades now," it continues, while "Be embraced, ye millions!" ["Seid umschlungen, Millionen!"] would "hopefully take on quite another meaning for the mishmash of enemy troops" — when, of course, the German army surrounded them on the battlefield.[26]

Still others wanted to explore these ideas even further, to develop their observations of such practices into lengthy polemics. Wilhelm Tappert's article "Our Musical Programs and Germany's Enemies — a Provocation" from September 1914 drives for a full national politicization of the country's musical life. For all too long, writes Tappert, Germany's concert halls had been invaded by foreign music and musicians — a situation made all the more shameful by the German people's ready acceptance of it, and resulting neglect of their musicians ("How often have we overlooked the plain simplicity [*schlichte Einfachheit*] of native music in favor of Latin rubbish and Muscovite jingle-jangle!").[27] The balance ought to tip the other way round; far beyond a position of mere narrow-minded chauvinism (this latter an invention, Tappert reminds us, of the French), this redress would display the "rightful feelings of a people, that, in this time of holy earnest, would turn to shame if a program of our artists gave room to foreign composers at the expense of native ones."[28] Harking back to Max Unger's rejection of Beethoven-as-Belgian, Tappert closes with the gruesome claim that that composer "would sooner have had both hands hacked off than play in front of a Frenchie [*Franzmann*]," and a familiar quotation ("Ehrt eure deutschen

Meister") from *Meistersinger*. The imagined naif whose question opens the article — "What has the war to do with our music programs?" — would, at this ending, have been left in little doubt.[29]

So a repel-all-borders approach, in tune with the official political rhetoric of the day, became entirely commonplace in the pages of the journal, its definition of Germanness based on apparently straightforward categories of nationality and national boundaries. But at the same time a group of much thornier questions had also been raised: what were the *inward* characteristics and qualities of the German? What was the uniquely German condition? How were Germans superior — in culture, in mind — to those that faced them across the front lines? And by the same token, what exactly was Germanness in music? Everywhere the simple question resounded: *was ist deutsch?*

This was, of course, nothing new. Crises of German identity, fuelled by the marked political, confessional, and territorial differences of German-speaking peoples, had pervaded its literature since at least the Enlightenment.[30] Indeed, Friedrich Nietzsche, one of the problem's most recent and eloquent interlocutors, had made the ambivalence, and the asking of the very question, part of the identity itself: in 1886, finding the Germans to be a "'people in the middle' [*Volk der Mitte*] in every sense," he distinguished them as "more unfathomable, . . . more full of contradiction, . . . more appalling to themselves" than other groups — an undefinable collective among whom it is "characteristic" that "the question 'What is German?' never dies out."[31]

Shortly before Nietzsche, Richard Wagner had explored similar ground in a famous essay titled with the key question "Was ist deutsch?" and it was from this musically inflected version of the identity question that most of the *Neue Zeitschrift*'s commentators took their cue. In September 1914, the appearance in the journal of a well-known excerpt from Wagner's essay — aligning the birth of the modern German spirit with the emergence of Bach, and stressing the propensity of the German artist never to strive for advantage, fame, and recognition[32] — sparked an eruption of responses to the same questions. These are, inevitably, sharper, more militaristic, and more jingoistic in tone than much that had appeared in the previous hundred years; equally inevitably, they are written with a vagueness that clings to articles of faith and pseudo-science rather than rigorous analysis of the complex issues at hand.

Otto R. Hübner — he of the supplement *Heil dir, mein Vaterland* — writes in mid-1915 of a German race marked by specific character traits "that have just as naturally sprung forth from our German soil and climate as have its unique animals and plants."[33] This race, Hübner claims, had long been inwardly marked by their "bravery, love of the truth, and loyalty," their "great vigour and vitality" — qualities proven on the battlefield that, in the artistic sphere, translated into a perpetual battle against the "fashionable artist and the prevailing fads of the day."[34]

As for music, if Slavic examples propounded a certain "soft sentimentality," a "surrendering femininity," then their German counterparts displayed a "sober masculine inwardness [*Innerlichkeit*]." These were characteristics on which German composers of the future should build as they fashioned "entertainment, joyfulness, cultivation, education, enthusiasm, and emotion."[35] The "trash art [*Afterkunst*]" that harried so much of the present would have to be replaced by music that fulfilled "the exalted task of every true art" — to lift mankind "above the mundane and to ennoble his inner life."[36]

In a similar vein, Otto Viktor Maeckel gives voice to his disdain for many musical paths recently followed, and makes use of these to define what German music was not (and, by implication, what it was or ought to be). He recommends an "energetic dispatch of the French Impressionists, Expressionists, and Modernists [*Neutöner*]," who, like a disease, had "infected" the younger generation of German composers.[37] Wholly French national, this "Unmusik" and its "narcotic effect" were a bad habit that would have to be abandoned if the headlong German rush toward "musical decadence [*musikalische Dekadenz*]" was to be halted.[38] More stridently yet, Adolf Prümers, writing of what he calls the "delousing [*Entlausung*]" of German music, concentrates the themes of Hübner's and Maeckel's polemics into a single outburst:

> The German masters from Bach to Wagner have taught us what Germanness is: *German art is massive, outstanding ability*, no infirm touch, no mathematical calculating of dissonance, of quartertones or wholetones! German art brims over with strength! German art has nothing to do with sickly whining between the steps of scales, the picking to pieces of the flower of tonality, the crumbling of the granite of harmony — the immature, unfinished, or unclear![39]

But wherever their focus lay, and whichever issue they wanted to resolve, these articles from the war's first eighteen months present a firm consensus on one matter. Hübner dreams of a reform of German music that the war could only facilitate, for it had "re-awakened a strong feeling for life in so many people" who had "flung away so much rubbish with their inner strength."[40] Tappert, enchanted by the "clash of sabres and the crack of the flintlock in high descant" against the "splendid rumbling bass of our cannons' thunder," eagerly awaits the final victory of this "powerful medicine [*Gewaltkur*]."[41] Prümers, again the histrionic, proclaims that the war had already "smashed this worthless work of men, this tower of Babel, to pieces with mighty fists." "Truly," he adds, "it was high time that it came for *this* art! High time that it completely annihilated it!"[42] In the final analysis, little matter the state of German culture, the progress of its disease. The war had come, and it was a force for good.

Die Ihr Blut und Leib und Leben
Für uns habt dahingegeben,
Tote Brüder, nun ruht aus.
Keiner Schmerzenswehen Schrecken
Kann aus diesem Schlaf Euch wecken.
Ruhet aus! Ihr seid zu Haus!

Überstanden ist die Hölle
Der Granaten und Schrapnelle.
Nun schützt Mutter Erde Euch!
Durst und Hunger, Frost und Fieber,
Sturm und Regen sind vorüber,
Mutterschoss ist warm und weich.

Blood, body, and life
You have given for us
Dead brothers, be at peace.
No throes of terrible pain
Can wake you from this sleep.
Be at peace! You are at home!

Overcome is this hell
Of shrapnel and shell.
Mother Earth keep you now!
Thirst and hunger, frost and fever,
Storm and shower are all past,
Mother's womb is warm and soft.

These two stanzas form the first half of a poem reproduced in the *Neue Zeitschrift* on February 4, 1915. No author is acknowledged. A simple title alone — "Epitaph, 1914 at Bixschoote" — indicates that these words had been inspired by a series of battles around the West Flanders town of Bixschoote (today Bikschote) in November 1914. An attempted German advance had there been driven back by stolid British and French resistance.[43]

These stanzas are perhaps the first hint in the journal's pages that the spirit of 1914 was vulnerable. Their brief evocation of appalling pain, of the terror of modern warfare's weaponry, and the distress of a soldier's daily life, provide a first inkling of the horror of this conflict, in tentative contradiction of the rhetoric of the previous August. Though the poem's two concluding stanzas hurriedly reassert that rhetoric (stressing devotion to "the greatest thing we know: the German people and the Fatherland"),[44] their bombast has inevitably, if still only timidly, been gainsaid.

By 1916, indeed, these kinds of negative responses were becoming ever more commonplace. Germany and its allies were now fully engaged on two fronts, outnumbered and underequipped, and fated to a conflict that had lasted far longer than most strategists had forecast. Particularly in the West, long campaigns with very little territorial advance and uncountable casualties began to generate a real sense of despair at the battlefront; simultaneously at home, the "total" mobilization of manpower and resources in response to this crisis resulted in severe privations in many areas of daily life. In theory, the German public were protected from the battlefronts' bad tidings by media censorship, but loopholes existed of necessity: families had to be informed of the deaths of loved ones, and local casualty statistics — however judiciously presented — could be stitched together to give an impression of the picture at large.

The horrible means of many of these deaths, moreover, as the epitaph from Bixschoote hints, were becoming widely known. For, as many Germans were now shocked to realize, this was no war of sabers, flintlocks, and cannon (as we saw Wilhelm Tappert fantasize). It was no romantic adventure into a foreign land — in one month, out the next with glorious spoils of war and tales to tell, and the honor of having served one's country. Rather, it had become an incessant slaughter, with the honest German rifleman one of many millions of lambs, no match whatsoever for the new mechanized warfare of the twentieth century. An entire generation was being hewn down by merciless machine-gun fire, splinters of grenade, disease, or simply hunger — and, in what was now a war of attrition, there was little sign of this carnage relenting.[45]

We, of course, are far more accustomed to such accounts of the Great War; but then we have the benefit of iconic texts that reported and stylized these experiences. Several examples are worth briefly quoting. Erich Maria Remarque's *Im Westen nichts Neues* (*All Quiet on the Western Front*), first published in 1929, fictionalizes some reminiscences from the author's short period of active service in the West in mid-1917. An early passage captures this change in the conception of war, the stunned realization of a young soldier rejecting the values of his elders in the midst of the horror of battle:

For us youngsters of eighteen, they were supposed to have been our mediators and guides to the world of maturity, the world of work, of duty, of culture, of progress — to the future. We often made fun of them and played jokes on them, but fundamentally we believed in them. The idea of authority, whose bearer they were, was associated in our minds with a superior insight and a more humane wisdom. But the first death that we saw shattered this belief. We had to recognize that our generation was more honest than theirs; they surpassed us only in words and in cleverness. The first bombardment showed us our mistake, and under it the world as they had taught it to us broke in pieces.[46]

The tortured conciseness of a list from the book's end is no less striking:

Shells, gas clouds, and flotillas of tanks — crushing, corroding, death.
Dysentery, influenza, typhoid — choking, burning, death.
Trenches, hospitals, mass graves — there are no other possibilities.[47]

Ernst Jünger's *In Stahlgewittern* (lit. "In Storms of Steel"), first published in 1920, is the work of a man similarly experienced at the front, and is yet more graphic:

A strange feeling of unreality oppressed me as I stared at a figure streaming with blood, whose leg hung loose from his body at an odd angle, and who unceasingly gave a hoarse cry for help, as though eager death had him already by the throat. . . . Just what was that? The war had shown its claws and torn off its friendly mask.[48]

An epiphany it truly was; and, in defiance of the censors, it also made its way into the pages of the *Neue Zeitschrift für Musik* — those previously a vessel for the spirit of 1914. True, this was no overnight change, and alongside the journal's commonplace historical inquiry some of the old jingoism remained: an ardent demand for a new national song to replace the *Kaiserlied* "Heil dir im Siegerkranz" — which was tainted by having the same tune as "God save the King" — appeared in early 1917, as did, once again, the irritable refutation of Beethoven's Belgianness.[49]

But two remarkable leading articles stand out from this period, and are well worth quoting at length and reading in the presence of the reminiscences of Jünger and Remarque. The first, "Die Überlebenden" ("The survivors") is by the same Adolf Prümers who had written in 1915 of the necessity of German musical life's "delousing," of "annihilation" as the deserved fate of modern music. As his essay of March 1916 opens, the ineffable forces of war and fate have anthropomorphized into a stalking, Jünger-like figure of death, no longer a healer or conqueror, but a "choker [*Würger*]":

Death is enjoying a good harvest; he has become simply insatiable! When will this choker's grip finally relent? Seas of blood have filled about him: the most beautiful specimens of youth, the most priceless fruit of mature age have fallen; many a proud tree has lost his crowning glory and been uprooted![50]

The survivors, writes Prümers, must turn their flagging wills to iron; the longer they stared at this "inheritance of war," the more lucid their senses would become, the more grasping their hands, the more willing the spirits that would drive them to work. For the music of the dead — these "last fervent cries of farewell to life and art" — would have to be completed and performed in its creators' honor. Through these tasks, the survivors would act as "priests" to the works of the fallen, led by holy thoughts of their comrades and ever watched by the critical eye of the "wilder Knochenmann" — Schubert's skeletal figure of death.[51]

Developing further the natural metaphors with which he began, Prümers heaps his despair on the near disappearance of an entire generation of the young. The thousands of "buds and blooms" that had lived in the "paradise of music," he says, had been obliterated by the war. He is adamant that they should not be treated as mere statistics, but as "individual personalities":

We will not say: a thousand dead; we will not measure the mountains of corpses by the cubic meter; we will ask: what did this person or that person mean to us? What did that person's individuality or personality mean to us?[52]

At home, too, Prümers sees that many creative artists had been sapped of their energies; with nerves shattered, their inner desire to create had been "temporarily extinguished."[53] Though here and there a "lonely sound" could be heard, Prümers is doubtful that time would bring these sounds together into euphony. Better, then, that German music try to return to the glory of a former age, "to grasp heartily the act of creation as in earlier days of peaceful, industrious labour."[54]

So just as war had become an all-annihilating death, just as time was now the only possible healer, so Prümers's other categories had been turned on their heads. War's creative spark is made a consuming flame; the hoped-for German hegemony becomes a wistful look to the past; respect for one's elders is colored by a fragment of the generational fury of Jünger and Remarque. And just as those 1920s accounts would focus autobiographically on the experiences of a lone soldier, so Prümers switches round his lens from the collective to the individual: What did that person mean to us? Most of all, the strident German patriotism of the previous years is largely absent: though "German publishers and concert halls" are briefly called upon to honor those who "died for German ideals," the blatant rabble rousing, the apportioning of war guilt and slandering of enemy nations have evaporated entirely.[55]

The second leading article of note is far less oriented toward a desperate future. Rather, it deals with the simple expediencies of musical life in the present. Written by Hans Schorn and published in July 1917, its curt title is "Klaviere und Klavierwerke für Einarmige" — "Pianos and piano works for people with one arm." Here the realities of war lead Schorn to a discussion of a collection of difficulties that, then as now,[56] would rarely cross the minds of most musical professionals: many soldiers, once "passionate pianists," were returning from the front with damaged or absent arms. In initial review, Schorn praises an article from the *Frankfurter Zeitung* that had provided a detailed overview of works for the left hand alone, whether exercises or arrangements of two-hand pieces, for the benefit of players and their teachers alike.[57]

Yet what concerns Schorn is that the needs of those pianists with only a *right* hand were not comparably met. For reasons that remain obscure, the majority of soldiers disabled by arm injuries were returning from war service with a damaged left arm. They could find few pleasing works to assuage their previously budding musicality: as Schorn notes, there was a dearth of original music for the right hand alone — the instrument's bass, with its resonant harmonic possibilities, being a more effective register for a solo piece or part than the treble, and many pedagogical works having focused on the usually weaker left hand. Left-hand studies rearranged, as the *Frankfurter Zeitung* had prescribed, were liable to lose their character entirely. Schorn thus suggests a number of more imaginative solutions, among them the arrangement of orchestral works for three hands (though here he fears an emphasis on a "rather embarrassing impression of the makeshift [*Notbehelf*]") or the manufacture of an organ-like keyboard for the feet, the usual pedal being placed above "at the service of the remaining arm-stump or artificial limb."[58]

In any case, again there is little stress placed on patriotism or the superiority of German culture. Here is tragic expediency and necessity only. And, in circumstances like these, in which the "understandable desires of thousands" for some scrap of musical solace needed addressing, Schorn even demands that "aesthetic considerations" would have to step back. Finally, in the grim face of war, the once higher mission of German art — the uncompromising idealism at its core — necessarily made its retreat.

The war's last sixteen months brought a more distant retreat in the pages of the *Neue Zeitschrift* — largely into historical and abstract philosophical matters, with now only the occasional glimmer of the spirit of its early years. A more relaxed attitude toward the art and artists of enemy countries becomes evident, with the printing of a lengthy apologia for Gounod on what would have been his one-hundredth birthday,[59] and the serialized translation of Romain Rolland's *Beethoven* (1903) — a presentation of no little irony, indeed, since Rolland had argued for Beethoven's non-German roots.[60] Finally, buried beneath an investigation into the life of Johann Gallus Mederitsch — the young Grillparzer's piano teacher, no less — the Armistice passes silently.[61]

But some things also rang curiously familiar. In November 1917, Rudolf Felber's leading article — on the need to rediscover and nurture a "Will to art" — complained bitterly of how the war years had further "intensified and coarsened" the "trivializing tendencies" evident in peacetime.[62] Specifically, "popular melody [*der Gassenhauer*]" had been raised to a principle in the new wave of operetta, becoming an "insidious and deadly disease" slowly infecting native music. In a direct echo of Geissler's words some five years earlier, Felber remarks that the modern composer's practice had become little more than a "dance before the golden calf."[63]

If earlier fears for the health of German culture had been momentarily repressed under the weight of deathly despair, then, they had not been destroyed. Never forgotten, they waxed gradually in strength from the war's end, metamorphosing all the while into something the more bitter. Fuelled by the newly radicalized political right's catchwords — *Novemberverbrecher*, *Dolchstoss* — and adopting its hateful stance toward all that was "foreign," these new forms of *Geist* fashioned an image of Germany as betrayed from the inside ("stabbed in the back"), her righteous war effort sabotaged by those who sought political revolution and the reins of power.

The *Neue Zeitschrift*, for its part, lost its qualifier from the beginning of March 1920, becoming simply the *Zeitschrift für Musik* — a change that passes without comment, but to which it is tempting to ascribe a deliberate turning away from all that was expressly "new" in art, and an anxious entrenchment in "eternal" values demonstrated by the music and aesthetics of the past. Indeed, as the decade drew on, the somewhat fanciful subtitle of "Unabhängiges Organ für Musiker und Musikfreunde" ("Independent Organ for Musicians and Music-Lovers") that the journal had displayed during the war years — and which resonated with Schumann's original conception — was gradually honed to a nationalistic razor's edge: from the "Kampfblatt für deutsche Musik and Musikpflege" (loosely, "Campaign Journal in Support of German Music") in 1923, it became two years later the "Monatsschrift für eine geistige Erneuerung der deutschen Musik" — a "Monthly Journal for a Spiritual Revival of German Music."

From 1921, these developments were guided by the hand of a new editor, Alfred Heuss (1877–1934), a music critic of considerable eminence and reputation.[64] Under his watchful eye and poison pen, German musical life was made subject for almost a decade to the unbending rejection of much that Heuss held to be the threatening "new." If it pressed at the boundaries of sexual decency, it was labeled "perverse";[65] if it allowed popular styles to infiltrate those more venerated, it was derided as "wanton" and "frivolous;"[66] if it appointed controversial avant-gardists into its coveted positions, it "struck a blow against German music,"[67] became accused of collusion with "Jews and Bolshevists" — the inchoate group that, for Heuss and his collaborators, conspired against and threatened direly the musical, cultural, and spiritual future.

For Heuss, as for others beyond number, it was high time for that purge of German culture that the Great War had failed to bring. But this time, with Germany's enemies identified within as much as without, no cataclysmic conflict was called for outright. Rather, a mass movement — grouping aesthetics and culture together with politics as worldview — would promise the desired effect, citing the stifling categories of biology and background to force identity on some, and to exclude others by violence. Heuss, for his part, put himself forward as one musical spokesperson for Alfred Rosenberg's "Kampfbund für deutsche Kultur" ("Campaign League for German Culture"), the thinly veiled Nazi organization dedicated to the indoctrinating of the so-called "apolitical" but culture-loving German middle classes into the ranks of the party faithful. And so, when supporters of the National Socialists disrupted the premiere of Kurt Weill's *Aufstieg und Fall der Stadt Mahagonny* in Leipzig in March 1930, he was on hand to capitalize on the furor and to foretell for the readers of the *Zeitschrift*, in terrible terms, the next step taken:

> And on 9 March, a great breach has been smashed into the sturdy wall [of the new art], smashed by the theatre-going public that broke through its imposed chains on the spot, and now aims its devastating criticism not only at the work itself, but at the theatrical authorities and the big-city press. . . . We shall state on this occasion once again that far more important than modern music is the *worldview* that stands behind it, and without which it is done for from the inside out. We should occupy ourselves with this above all. . . . The date of 9 March has opened the eyes of many, many people, and shown them, we hope, how strong the few — as they are for the time being, at least — can be, so that they might, in short, bravely intercede not only for art but for mankind itself. The thousands will become hundreds of thousands; the hundreds of thousands will become millions — if only those who can raise their voices will recognize the obvious duty that is theirs.[68]

Notes

1. "Ich sage, das Schicksal sendet den Krieg: denn darum eben wird der Wert dieses grausamen Heilmittels so selten verstanden, weil sich kein Arzt unter den Menschen erdreisten darf, den Krieg wie einen heilenden Trank einem kranken Volke auf Tag und Stunde zu verordnen. . . . Der Krieg ist ein Völkerbildner, er bringt nicht bloss die Grenzen der Länder ins Wanken, er kettet auch den Landsmann fester an den Landsmann, gibt dem Gedankenlosen eine Ahnung von der Herrlichkeit des Vaterlandes, erwärmt das vertrocknete Gemüt mit einem Strahle der Liebe." All translations are my own unless otherwise stated.

2. See Heinrich von Treitschke, *Historische und Politische Aufsätze* 4th ed. (Leipzig: S. Hirzel, 1870), 787.

3. In section "Noten am Rande," no author given, *Neue Zeitschrift für Musik* (henceforth *NZfM*) 81 (1914): 490.

4. I have summarized the history in this paragraph and the one preceding from John Daverio, Robert Schumann: Herald of a "New Poetic Age" (New York, 1997), 105–30. The quotation from Schumann, given here in Daverio's translation, is found originally in NZfM 2 (1835): 2.

5. See, for example, the summary of *NZfM*'s editorial forewords in the late nineteenth century in Rika Shishido, *Die Neue Musik-Zeitung (1880–1928): Geschichte, Inhalt, Bedeutung* (Göttingen: Hainholz, 2004), 160–62.

6. On Brendel and Wagner's essay, see Jens Malte Fischer, *Richard Wagner's "Das Judentum in der Musik"* (Frankfurt-am-Main: Insel, 2000), 18–21.

7. Brandes (1864–1940) had studied under Hermann Kretzschmar in the 1880s in Leipzig, and had become known as a composer and conductor of men's choruses, as well as a music and literary critic. He took up the university job in Leipzig in 1908 — after Max Reger left it vacant — and became editor of the *NZfM* in mid-1910. See Max Unger, "Friedrich Brandes. Zu seinem 50. Geburtstag am 18. November." *NZfM* 81 (1914): 548, and *Riemann Musik-Lexikon*, 12th ed., s.v. "Brandes, Friedrich."

8. *NZfM* 79 (1912): 1–3 (Georg Kaiser, "Neues von Johann Adolf Hasse"), 69–71 and 81–83 (August Stradal, "Anton Bruckners erste Sinfonie in c-moll"), 173ff. (*Parsifal*: a debate sparked, incidentally, by Arnold Schönberg's article "*Parsifal* und Urheberrecht"). Also Adolph Kohut, "Wagner und seine Mutter," *NZfM* 80 (1913): 377–80.

9. H. W. Draber, "'Christus' von Felix Draeseke," *NZfM* 79 (1912): 113–14. Aside from his compositions, Draeseke was known for his conservative *Kampfschrift* "Die Konfusion in der Musik" (1906).

10. Max Unger, "Das Vierteltonsystem und die moderne Musik," *NZfM* 79 (1912): 161–63.

11. F. A. Geissler, "Moderne Musik und moderne Kultur," *NZfM* 79 (1912): 567.

12. "Und dass auch der Geist der Kapitalismus, den manche Leute allen Ernstes als eine hervorragende Errungenschaft der modernen Zeit preisen, in der Musik zur Herrschaft gelangt ist, wer wollte das bestreiten? Am Golde hängt, nach Golde drängt nicht nur jeder Tonsetzer, der von ungeheuren Honoraren und unermesslichen Tantièmen träumt, sondern durch das Virtuosentum und die Steigerung des Personenkultus ist unsere Musikausübung insoweit dem Kapitalismus verfallen, als die 'grossen Namen' in Frage kommen, deren Höchstes eine amerikanische Tournee ist und zwar nicht des Ruhmes, sondern der Dollars wegen . . . die sonst die ersten beim Tanze um das goldene Kalb sind." Geissler, "Moderne Musik," 566.

13. New and experimental music was certainly another — as implied, for example, by Unger, "Das Vierteltonsystem," 161–63. I am not convinced that Jewish influence on music was yet widely classed as another "sickness": while anti-Semitism was unquestionably a powerful force of the period, and though we might certainly arrive at a suspicion of a muted version of it from Geissler's "golden calf" remark, I do not see it as an overt or governing principle in the journal at large — this would be to apply a post-1918 judgment retrospectively. On the contrary, several later essays offer a rebuttal of anti-Semitic views: see Adolf Prümers, "Das deutsche Musikleben und seine 'Entlausung,'" *NZfM* 82 (1915): 276, and Paul Dietzsch, "Heine und Chopin," *NZfM* 84 (1917): 123.

14. I think here of Thomas Mann and the literary scholar Friedrich Gundolf, some of whose opinions on the war are presented in Peter Gay, *Weimar Culture: The Outsider as Insider* (New York: Harper & Row, 1970), 11–12.

15. See Roger Chickering, *Imperial Germany and the Great War, 1914–1918*, 2nd ed. (Cambridge: Cambridge University Press, 2004), 13–23; and Jeffrey Verhey, *The Spirit of 1914: Militarism, Myth and Mobilization in Germany* (Cambridge: Cambridge University Press, 2000). As both these authors point out, the belief that all Germans felt enthusiasm for war is a social myth created and exploited by conservative politicians after the event. Local, and particularly rural, studies of response to the war also show considerably less spirited reaction.

16. Friedrich Brandes, "An unsere Leser," *NZfM* 81 (1914): 469.

17. In section "Noten am Rande," no editor given, *NZfM* 81 (1914): 490.

18. Karl Lamprecht, "Geistige Mobilmachung," *NZfM* 81 (1914): 481.

19. In section "Noten am Rande," no editor given, *NZfM* 81 (1914): 491.

20. The "Kampflied," by Ferdinand Avenarius, was borrowed from the pages of another conservative periodical, the *Kunstwart*. See *NZfM* 81 (1914): 482.

21. Supplement to *NZfM* 81/52 (31 December 1914).

22. See, as just one example, the "Noten am Rande" article entitled "Hilfsvereinigung für notleidende Künstler Gross-Berlins" in *NZfM* 81 (1914): 482. No author given.

23. In section "Noten am Rande," no author given, *NZfM* 81 (1914): 473.

24. In section "Noten am Rande," no author given, *NZfM* 81 (1914): 482.

25. Max Unger, "Beethoven 'der Belgier,'" *NZfM* 81 (1914): 557–59.

26. In section "Noten am Rande," no author given, *NZfM* 82 (1915): 301–2.

27. Wilhelm Tappert, "Unsere Musikprogramme und Deutschlands Feinde. Eine Anregung," *NZfM* 81 (1914): 487.

28. Tappert, "Unsere Musikprogramme," 487.

29. Tappert, "Unsere Musikprogramme," 487–88. It is worth adding that responses to Tappert's article arrived at what, under the circumstances, were more moderate positions. Bruno Schrader criticizes patriots who would exclude all but German music, but believes in a removal of all non-German performers; a "Direktor Pochhammer" from Aachen writes that Germans should adopt the higher moral ground and prevent the "true artwork" from entering into the "conflict of nations." See Bruno Schrader, "Berliner Brief," *NZfM* 81 (1914): 511–12, and Pochhammer, "Soll die Kunst in den Streit der Völker hineingezogen werden?" *NZfM* 81 (1914): 549–50.

30. This is a massive topic, broached only in miniature here. A starting point for further discussion, with particular emphasis on music, is Bernd Sponheuer's essay "Reconstructing Ideal Types of the 'German' in Music," in *Music and German National Identity*, ed. Celia Applegate and Pamela Potter (Chicago: University of Chicago Press, 2002), 36–58.

31. Friedrich Nietzsche, *Jenseits von Gut und Böse: Vorspiel einer Philosophie der Zukunft* (1886; reprint, Stuttgart: Reclam, 1988), 163.

32. Richard Wagner, "Der deutsche Geist. Aus Wagners Schrift 'Was ist deutsch?'" *NZfM* 81 (1914): 485. The original was published in the *Bayreuther Blätter* in February 1878.

33. Otto R. Hübner, "Zukünftige Musik," *NZfM* 82 (1915): 193.

34. Hübner, "Zukünftige," 193.

35. Hübner, "Zukünftige," 194.

36. Hübner, "Zukünftige," 195. As *der After* translates literally as "anus," my rendering of *Afterkunst* as "trash art" is a considerable euphemism.

37. Otto Viktor Maeckel, "Musik und Künstler des feindlichen Auslandes," *NZfM* 81 (1914): 533.

38. Maeckel, "Musik," 534.

39. "Was deutsch ist, haben uns die deutschen Meister von Bach bis Wagner gelehrt: *Deutsche Kunst ist grosses, überragendes Können,* kein unsicheres Tasten, kein mathematisches Berechnen der Dissonanzen, der Vierteltöne, der Ganztonleiter! Deutsche Kunst strotzt von Kraft! Das süssliche Gewinsel zwischen den Stufen der Tonleitern, das Zerzupfen der Tonblüten, das Zerbröckeln der Akkordgranite, das Unreife, Unfertige, Unklare hat mit deutscher Kunst nichts zu tun!" Prümers, "Das deutsche Musikleben," 276. His emphasis.

40. Hübner, "Zukünftige," 195.

41. Wilhelm Tappert, "Feinde ringsum! Krieg gegen die deutsche Musikwissenschaft," *NZfM* 81 (1914): 518.

42. Prümers, "Das deutsche Musikleben," 276. His emphasis.

43. See, for example, the report "Allies Gaining Ground" in the *Times* (London), November 9, 1914, 8. No author given.

44. No author given, "Grabschrift 1914 bei Bixschoote," *NZfM* 82 (1915): 37.

45. This paragraph and the previous one use information from Chickering, *Imperial Germany*, 65–129.

46. Erich Maria Remarque, *All Quiet on the Western Front*, trans. A. W. Wheen (London: Putnam, 1929), 19–20. Translation modified.

47. Remarque, *All Quiet*, 306–7. Translation modified.

48. Ernst Jünger, *The Storm of Steel: From the Diary of a German Storm-Troop Officer on the Western Front*, no translator given (New York: Howard Fertig, 1975), 3. Translation expanded and modified.

49. In section "Noten am Rande," *NZfM* 84 (1917): 171 and 274–76. No authors given.

50. "Der Tod hält reiche Ernte; schier unersättlich ist er geworden! Wann endlich wird dem Würger die Hand erlahmen? Meere voll Blut sind ihm geflossen; es sank der Jugend schönste Zier, es brach des reiferen Alters kostbare Frucht, manch stolzer Baum verlor seine Krone und entwurzelte!" Adolf Prümers, "Die Überlebenden," *NZfM* 83 (1916): 89.

51. Prümers, "Die Überlebenden," 89.

52. "Wir sagen nicht: tausend Tote; wir messen die Berge von Leichen nicht nach Kubikmetern; wir müssen fragen: was war uns Dieser und Jener? Was war uns der Einzelne, der Persönliche?" Prümers, "Die Überlebenden," 89.

53. Prümers, "Die Überlebenden," 89.

54. Prümers, "Die Überlebenden," 89.

55. Prümers, "Die Überlebenden," 89.

56. I except with this generalization the recent collected volume edited by Neil Lerner and Joseph N. Straus, entitled *Sounding Off: Theorizing Disability in Music* (New York: Routledge, 2006).

57. Hans Schorn, "Klaviere und Klavierwerke für Einarmige," *NZfM* 84 (1917): 229. It is perhaps worth adding that many of the most famous works for piano left-hand — the concertos, for example, of Ravel, Korngold, and Janáček — were commissioned by pianists who had lost their right arms during the Great War, but were not composed until the 1920s.

58. Schorn, "Klaviere und Klavierwerke für Einarmige," 230.

59. Bertha Witt, "Charles Francois Gounod. Zum 100. Geburtstag, 17. Juni 1918," *NZfM* 85 (1918): 129–30.

60. Compare, for example, Romain Rolland, "Beethoven," *NZfM* 84 (1917): 253 with Rolland, *La vie de Beethoven*, 28th ed. [of *Beethoven*] (Paris: Hachette, 1953), 4.

61. Alexander Fareanu, "Johann Gallus Mederitsch," *NZfM* 85 (1918): 293.

62. Rudolf Felber, "Der Wille zur Kunst," *NZfM* 84 (1917): 341.

63. Rudolf Felber, "Der Wille zur Kunst," 341–44.

64. See Oliver Hilmes, *Der Streit ums "Deutsche": Alfred Heuss und die Zeitschrift für Musik* (Hamburg: von Bockel, 2003).

65. Alfred Heuss, "Über Franz Schrekers Oper 'Der Schatzgräber,'" *ZfM* 88 (1921): 567–70.

66. Alfred Heuss, "Der Foxtrott im Konzertsaal," *ZfM* 90 (1923): 54–55.

67. Alfred Heuss, "Arnold Schönberg — Preussischer Kompositionslehrer," *ZfM* 92 (1925): 583–85.

68. "Und in diese festgefügte Mauer ist nun am 9. März eine starke Bresche geschlagen worden, geschlagen von einem Theaterpublikum, das kurzer Hand die ihm auferlegten Fesseln brach und nun seinerseits nicht nur an dem Stück selbst, sondern auch an den Theaterbehörden und einer grossstädtischen Presse vernichtende Kritik übte. . . . Wir sagen denn auch dieses Mal einzig noch, dass weit wichtiger als die ohnedies innerlich erledigte moderne Musik die *Weltanschauung* ist, die hinter ihr steht. Mit ihr vor allem gilt es sich zu beschäftigen. . . . Der 9. März hat vielen, sehr vielen die Augen geöffnet und ihnen hoffentlich gezeigt, wie stark zunächst verhältnismässig wenige sein können, so sie, kurz gesagt, für die Würde keineswegs der Kunst allein, sondern des Menschen überhaupt, mutig eintreten. Aus den Tausenden werden Hunderttausende, aus diesen Millionen werden, wenn zunächst die, die ihre Stimme erheben können, ihrer selbstverständlichen Pflicht sich bewusst sind." Alfred Heuss, "Wird es endlich dämmern? Zur Mahagonny-Theaterschlacht am 9. März im Neuen Theater zu Leipzig," *ZfM* 97 (1930): 395. Emphasis in original.

CHAPTER TWO

The Afterlife of Neda Ukraden

Negotiating Space and Memory through Popular Music after the Fall of Yugoslavia, 1990–2008

≫≋

CATHERINE BAKER

An essay by Dubravka Ugrešić tells the story of the singer "Neda U.," who "came from Sarajevo, and her songwriter, N., [who] came from Zagreb." Neda "became . . . a Serb" during the war in Croatia when the Yugoslav National Army (JNA) and Croatian Serb rebels opposed Croatia's secession from Yugoslavia. Neda's music was no longer played once war broke out, but a young Croatian singer re-recorded her hits "to make N.'s music Croatian again."[1] The singer, Neda Ukraden, had performed some of the 1980s' most famous Yugoslav pop songs. The songwriter, Đorđe Novković, had composed extensively for Ukraden and many other singers based inside and outside Croatia. Novković would be integrated into the restructuring of Croatian culture, entertainment, and media initiated by Croatia's nationalist government during and after the fall of Yugoslavia. Ukraden, who moved from Sarajevo to Belgrade when war broke out in Bosnia-Herzegovina in April 1992, would not.

This chapter uses the course of Ukraden's career during and after the disintegration of Yugoslavia to illustrate how musical biographies become subject to recontextualization and reworking in conditions of ethno-political conflict where nationalists perceive ambiguous figures as threats. Former Yugoslavia had been a federal state containing many options for ethnic identification and allowing for persons, texts, and symbolic cultural markers to be identified in multiple ways. Yugoslav policy did not aim to erase ethnic identifications completely but rather to force them into the background and foreground a consciousness of "brotherhood and unity," within a con-

text of official fear of overt nationalism as a denial of Yugoslavia's legitimacy.[2] Between 1990 and 1992, political competition for resources after the
collapse of state socialism fractured this Yugoslav state into nation-states
based on a different single dominant ethnic identity in each entity. To make
the existence of each new nation-state meaningful, multiple identities had
to be erased in a violent process this author has described elsewhere as a
"war on ambiguity."[3]

It is well-known that the goals of nationalist leaders in what proclaimed
themselves the successor states of Yugoslavia were achieved through wars
that, in Croatia and Bosnia-Herzegovina, used the strategy of ethnic cleansing to kill hundreds of thousands of civilians and displace yet more people
from their homes in order to create ethnically homogenous, nonambigu-
ous territories. These acts were paralleled by nonphysical interventions
against markers of Yugoslavia (ethnic ambiguity and socialist iconography)
in many other fields of life; indeed, in Slovenia, which underwent only ten
days of war while separating from Yugoslavia, this symbolic violence was
the primary form of discursively establishing the nation-state. The many
attempts to accommodate the ethnically complex figure of Neda Ukraden
within one or another national narrative, either as a member or more often
as an excluded Other, took place in this context and can be best understood
by turning to a subfield of nationalism studies that focuses on the ideological work of nationalism in the everyday. Michael Billig's *Banal Nationalism*
identified the daily reproduction of the nation in "the embodied habits of
social life," such as handling currency, as creating reminders of nationhood
that were so familiar they operated on an unconscious level.[4] This perspective has since been applied specifically to popular culture by Tim Edensor.[5]
The nationalizing regimes of Croatia and other new nation-states with a
similar logic were striving for this very outcome: to create so coherent and
strong a national identity among members of the majority nation that it
might go unmarked. Contradictory sources of ambiguity, such as a musician who could equally well belong to several nation-states at once, had
either to be incorporated or excluded.

The power of nationalism to destabilize national and international politics received more attention in the 1990s than at any time since the end
and aftermath of World War I, when the uncertainty over which nationalist
claims to the territory of former multinational states would be recognized
had similarly been internationalized as a political problem. Responding to
events in former Yugoslavia, a major theme of many 1990s works on nationalism (such as Michael Ignatieff's *Blood and Belonging: Journeys into the
New Nationalism*) was how its ethnic dimensions could legitimize and motivate violence.[6] The constructivist turn in studies of nationalism since the

mid-1990s, building on though often disagreeing with Benedict Anderson's influential *Imagined Communities* (1983), was in turn a response to discussions of nationalism that took the existence and importance of ethnic identity as a given. Critical nationalism studies, problematizing the construction and legitimization of nations and their constituent elements (ethnic groups, languages, and so on), find their apogee in the work of Rogers Brubaker, who believes that scholars' tools should be the processes of identification and categorization not the concepts of identities or groups.[7] Brubaker goes on to argue that nationalism in 1990s Eastern Europe was not a "return" of identity after socialism but a set of practices that newly constituted persons and places as national.[8] The post-Yugoslav "afterlife" of Neda Ukraden, a person whose mobility between future nation-states had previously been unremarkable, demonstrates these practices at work.

Historical Background

The first Yugoslav state, a centralized kingdom ruled by the Karađorđević dynasty from Serbia, was established in 1918 after World War I and collapsed during World War II in 1941 after army officers rejected a pact with the Axis. Axis powers (Germany, Italy, Hungary, Bulgaria) directly occupied parts of Yugoslav territory and installed puppet governments in the Croatian and Serbian capitals, Zagreb and Belgrade. Yugoslavia experienced not only the global conflict but also a brutal civil war between Serbian royalists ("Četniks"), the "Ustaše" forces of the so-called Independent State of Croatia (NDH) and a Partisan army organized by the Yugoslav Communist Party and led by the charismatic Marshal Josip Broz Tito. The Partisans finished the war as the only Communist party to have liberated their country without help from the Red Army.

The second Yugoslav state, officially the Socialist Federal Republic of Yugoslavia, was progressively decentralized so that the branches of the Party in the six republics (Bosnia-Herzegovina, Croatia, Macedonia, Montenegro, Serbia, and Slovenia) acquired more and more responsibility. In 1974, the last of federal Yugoslavia's four constitutions created two devolved "autonomous provinces" in the largest republic, Serbia: Vojvodina in the north and Kosovo in the south. A group of Serbian political scientists labeled the idea a deliberate ploy to weaken Serbia's influence in the federation and called for constitutional revisions.[9] In the 1980s, after Tito had died and a severe economic crisis shattered the myth that the Yugoslav style of socialism provided for its people better than any other system, authors and intellectuals in Serbia expanded the constitutional critique by writing on topics that had not previously been open to the public: the massacres committed by Partisans during World War II and the Communist prison camp on the island of Goli Otok, where alleged Stalinist sympathizers had been sent after the Tito–Stalin split in 1948.

The political tensions that led to the disintegration of the second Yugoslavia arose from a clash between the centralizing ambitions of the new Serbian party leaders and aspirations in Slovenia for the northernmost, richest republic to have more freedom of action within the federal system. The decision of the Serbian party president, Slobodan Milošević, to revoke the devolution of Kosovo and Vojvodina in 1989 (giving Serbia control of three out of eight votes on the rotating presidency that had replaced Tito), shocked his counterparts in Slovenia and then Croatia into gradually considering more drastic measures. Were Slovenia to secede altogether (as every republic — ostensibly — had the right to do), Croatia would be perpetually outvoted on the federal presidency by Milošević's bloc of votes, which now included the three Serbian representatives plus Montenegro. Yugoslavia's last prime minister, Ante Marković, launched a last-ditch attempt to keep the federation together by introducing a package of economic reforms, having the presidency meet in various republics and setting up a pan-Yugoslav television channel to supplement the radio and television stations controlled by each republic, which were becoming de facto national broadcasters. He proverbially did too little, too late.

The election of Franjo Tuđman, the leader of the nationalist HDZ, as Croatian president in May 1990 led to a clash between the Croatian government and the leaders of the Serb minority in Croatia. They, backed up by the media Milošević controlled in Belgrade, claimed fears that the genocide of the Second World War — when the Ustaše had massacred Serbs, Jews, other minorities, and political opponents — would be repeated if they lost Belgrade's protection. When Slovenia and Croatia both declared independence in June 1991, the Yugoslav National Army (JNA) moved in to stop the secessions. The fighting lasted only ten days in Slovenia but many months in Croatia, as the JNA linked up with the Croatian Serb militias. The "Homeland War," as it was known in Croatia,[10] saw one-third of Croatian territory occupied by the Croatian Serb authorities. Ethnic cleansing — committing massacres in order to induce the population of a wider area to flee — took place on both sides of the lines as the belligerents aimed to establish ethnically homogenous territories under their control.

Under President Franjo Tuđman, whose Croatian Democratic Union (HDZ) party governed Croatia from May 1990 until January 2000, political speech-making, print/electronic media, academic debates, educational practices, and reconfigured public space all contributed to a new conceptual matrix requiring people to identify primarily as Croats.[11] Individuals' contributions to Croatia (and political loyalty to presidential discourse) decided their (non)integration into the new cultural space and public life. However, the idealized image of an ethnically homogeneous national community did not account for many personal/professional lives that routinely involved crossing Yugoslavia's internal borders. This discrepancy between "social and political spaces"[12] threatened to undermine Croatian (and Serbian) nationalist elites' rhetoric of homogeneity. Indeed, certain authors argue that wartime Croatian/Serbian leaders used media to depict ethnicity as the basis of identity and break down the practices and memories of cross-border interaction.[13] A representational "media war" thus accompanied and facilitated the violent "ethnic war."[14]

Acceptance by, and into, the 1990s Croatian media depended on individuals publicly presenting their present and past careers to fit a new public ideology dictating that: the most important level of identity was national; Tuđman's ruling party existed to establish and defend the Croatian state as the state of all Croats; the previous (Yugoslav) regime had repressed the Croatian will to independence (e.g., by suppressing Croatian culture); and acting against the "state-building" flow of Croatian history excluded one from the nation proper. Although individuals continuously revise their own biographical narratives anyway,[15] 1990s Croatian public life went further: public figures deliberately revised their relationship to space and memory to emphasize their contribution to political/cultural "state-building." The resultant ethnic biographies selectively reinterpreted individuals' origins/ achievements according to contemporary political needs. Stef Jansen found that Croatian villagers too withheld "evidence of previous social complexity"; he speculated that this evidence needed repressing because it threatened the state's cherished Croatian/Serbian binary.[16] Celebrities' public presentation contributed to a climate where the same discourses became necessary in everyday life.

In January 1992, a ceasefire in Croatia allowed the Serbian and Croatian governments to turn their attentions to Bosnia-Herzegovina (BiH), where they both had territorial ambitions. The choice to leave the federation or become exposed to threats from other republics now fell on BiH, but by the time a referendum on independence was held in March 1992, Serb and Croat nationalists had already set up entities on the republic's territory. A month after the declaration of independence was realized, the JNA turned most of its equipment and staff in BiH over to the Army of Republika Srpska (VRS) under the command of Ratko Mladić. While the VRS — joined by volunteer paramilitary units (including so-called "weekend warriors" from Serbia who went on short excursions to fight in BiH) was attacking non-Serb villages in eastern and northwestern BiH, the Croat Defense Council (HVO) was waging its own campaign in Herzegovina and eastern Bosnia. The Sarajevo government organized the Army of Bosnia-Herzegovina (ABiH), which was originally intended as a multiethnic defense force but took on an increasingly Bosniak character as the war went on.

The Dayton Peace Agreement that ended the Bosnian war in December 1995 provided for two ethnically defined entities (the Muslim–Croat Federation and Republika Srpska) as well as wide-ranging powers for the international agencies in BiH to establish and intervene in the state's political process. Although intended to lay the groundwork for liberal democracy in BiH, it created a system where citizens only belonged to a political community through their membership of one of the country's three "constituent" ethnic groups — Bosniaks, Croats, or Serbs.[17] As such, it perpetuated the wartime ethnopolitics, which had sought to assign every individual to an ethnic group and erase heterogeneity. The repercussions of the war on ambiguity in former Yugoslavia outlasted the armed conflicts.

Yugoslav Popular Music in the 1980s: Genre and Ambiguity

Neda Ukraden was born to Serb parents in Imotski, in Croatia's Dalmatian hinterland (Dalmatinska zagora). They soon moved to Bosnia, where she was educated. In the 1970s she began singing with the group Kamen na kamen and producer Nikola Borota Radovan, and belonged to the genre of Yugoslav "newly composed folk music" (NCFM),[18] which was converging with "light-entertainment" pop ("zabavna" music).[19] Ukraden, like several singers, blurred the NCFM/"zabavna" boundaries (as, most famously, did the emblematic 1980s star Lepa Brena).[20] After signing for the Zagreb-based label Jugoton in the early 1980s she sang many songs by Croatian pop composers, particularly Rajko Dujmić then Đorđe Novković.[21] Their arrangements used typical 1980s pop techniques and set folk rhythms on synthesizers; their introductions usually included semi-folk techniques like multivocal singing or synthesized folk panpipes (frule).

The well-known Belgrade-based pop/folk lyricist Marina Tucaković often worked for both Brena and Ukraden. Tucaković used different variants of the "Serbo-Croatian" language for different clients: Brena sang in "ekavica," the lexis and constructions generally recognized as "Serbian." Tucaković's lyrics for Ukraden and other Croatian clients used "ijekavica," the variant spoken in Croatia and most of Bosnia.[22] This difference perhaps reflected the fact that Brena belonged to Belgrade's recording/promotional network and Ukraden (like Tucaković's Croatian clients) belonged to Zagreb's; since Ukraden came from Sarajevo, she would also speak ijekavica herself. As Yugoslavia disintegrated, linguistic markers became clues to ethnicity:

speaking/writing/singing in ekavica immediately coded one as Serb, while using ijekavica in Croatia affirmed Croatianness.[23] The exclusion of ekavica from the Croatian state media and popular culture was perhaps the most enduring constriction of cultural space along national lines — yet even when Ukraden the performer became personally unsuitable, her songs' content could still be considered suitably Croatian. The unacceptability of standard Serbian/Bosnian NCFM in Croatia (given the Serbian-ness, eastern-ness and Balkan-ness of its ingredients) did not extend to the folk-pop crossover developed by some Croatian composers, which had originated in Jugoton's cross-border collaborations. As federal Yugoslav politics and media disintegrated, these once-routine activities became increasingly difficult.

As the economy, politics, and the media in Croatia became more and more detached from the rest of Yugoslavia in the months before the republic declared independence, show business followed. The Zagreb studio of the national Yugoslav broadcaster was reconstituted as Croatian Radio and Television (HRT) and dropped as much material as possible from other studios — most of all from TV Belgrade, which had upset Croatian television workers even before HDZ's election victory with its pro-Milošević, anti-opposition, anti-Croatian spin on the news and its preference for the Cyrillic script, in which the Serbian language was written (Croatian used Latin script). HRT's withdrawal from Yugoslav broadcasting prevented unwelcome counternarratives about the Croat–Serb relationship intruding into national cultural space, representing a symbolic limiting of national boundaries but also a very real limiting of access to alternative information sources.

The Croatian entertainment industry, meanwhile, became increasingly closed to Serbian music, especially after an incident on May 2, 1991, when a Serb militia murdered twelve Croatian police officers in the village of Borovo Selo. Few details of the exclusion of Serbian performers were made public, although one weekly's television supplement indicated in May 1991 that many Serbian/Bosnian singers had stopped being broadcast on Croatian TV.[24] Croatia's cultural separation from Yugoslavia and Serbia was untidier than it appeared in the state tabloid, *Večernji list*. In this newspaper, deliberate Croatian action against Serbian products was minimized, any Serbian action vice versa was detailed as anti-Croatian aggression, and Croatian independence was presented as the last-resort option — much as Tuđman commented when Croatia seceded.[25] *VL*'s silence on the withdrawal of Serbian music contributed to a much broader ideological picture, which contrasted Croatian innocence against Serbian aggression. Thus, anything Croatia did could and would be considered self-defense.[26]

Renegotiating the Past: The Management of Ethnic Biography

The years 1990 and 1991 also saw a renegotiation of the relationship between Croatia's past and present, which normalized the current state-sanctioned historical narrative and minimized the previous, socialist state's historical narrative.[27] Socialist street names were replaced with names expressing the nationalist narrative of continuous Croatian statehood and great historical rulers.[28] Even show business reporting reoriented itself toward Croatia rather than Yugoslavia. In early 1990 *Večernji list* used "domestic show business" to mean all-Yugoslav show business;[29] without explanation, "the domestic" gradually came to mean only musicians still based in Croatia. Continuing to work in Croatia helped demonstrate commitment to the national cause, but public figures were also tacitly obliged to demonstrate their loyalty to Croatia, their contribution to "state-building" activities (often through fundraising "humanitarian" concerts for the army/refugees), and their record of never having obstructed Croatia's political or cultural independence. Croatian Serbs also had to distance themselves from the Serb rebellion (by stating that they and other Serbs were in no danger in Croatia) and correct the Croatian Serb failure to acknowledge the Croatian state; silence was not good enough: writers, journalists and sports officials all asked this of Serbs.[30] In this ethnicized atmosphere, performing the necessary "hrvatstvo" ("Croatness") required a primarily ethnic slant on one's personal biography.

Yet Tuđman's conception of ethno-national identity was also political: challenging the nation-state's fundamental narratives disqualified one from full national membership even if one belonged ethnically.[31] It was therefore helpful if a Croatian ethnic biography included antagonism toward the previous regime: this was not difficult for those whose career had been damaged by supporting Croatian nationalism,[32] but was more problematic if one had served Yugoslavia in performance or publicly sympathized with Titoism's suspicion of ethnic particularism. Đorđe Novković, who had been Neda Ukraden's usual composer in 1985–89, could himself have been politically questionable, having composed numerous patriotic songs about Tito/Yugoslavia;[33] he later composed several more songs supporting the Croatian army and its war aims.

Participation in pro-Croatian activities let musicians support a cause they believed in amid national upheaval and sorrow but also supplied a suitable demonstration of loyalty. The official media did not criticize the previous affiliations of cooperative performers, although unofficial understandings were not always so forgiving:[34] officially-managed ethnic biographies did not always manage to get their content across, even though they remained necessary for individuals with sensitive connections. Those who played along nonetheless fared better than those who had not remained within Croatia's physical space. These others were automatically excluded from the media and became part of the troublesome Yugoslav past.[35]

"It's Time We Broke Up": Ukraden, Novković, and the Revision of Musical Memory

In 1990 Neda Ukraden was well integrated into show business in Croatia, but late in the year moved from Jugoton to Diskoton (Sarajevo), making her the third Jugoton star from Bosnia to switch there in two years. She explained that Serbian tariffs on Croatian goods were making her records more expensive, affecting her Serbian sales; to protect her market she had been "forced" to move to Diskoton, which did not attract the tariff. Ukraden explicitly called her decision economic, not political, and hoped that "records will circulate around our homeland again" soon,[36] yet a Croatian viewpoint could still have perceived a musician privileging her Serbian market above Croatia's interests.

Ukraden remained living in Sarajevo and working with Diskoton until April 1992, when conflict spread to Bosnia and she moved to Belgrade.[37] Moving to Belgrade (or Zagreb) in the early 1990s was interpreted, especially in Bosnia, as pledging allegiance to that regime and assigned an individual to that ethnicity. In Croatian and Bosnian discourse, Ukraden's Serb ethnicity, not her education in Sarajevo or birth in Imotski, was thus activated as the most salient thing about her, hence — as Ugrešić related — she "became . . . a Serb."[38] Neither Croatia nor Bosnia could accommodate personalities who had deliberately aligned themselves with Belgrade/Serbia/Serbdom, and Sarajevans (particularly Bosniaks) who stayed behind were often particularly affronted by them. Thus Safet Isović, a sevdah (Bosnian folk) singer in the Bosniak party SDA, complained of Ukraden "flee[ing] to Belgrade and 'marvel[ing]' from there that Croats and Muslims are under threat in Bosnia."[39] The reevaluation of the past according to present realities took place in all the societies affected by the Yugoslav wars.

Ukraden's personal unacceptability in Croatia was first confirmed by interviews with Sarajevan musicians in the Croatian press (while Bosniak and Croat forces/politicians were allied against Serb forces in BiH), suggesting that negative information about ex-Sarajevans was initially filtered through Bosnia. In 1993, Croatian media reports from Belgrade corroborated the dominant interpretation of the war by describing Serbian celebrities supporting Milošević and the Serbian aggression. A 1993 *Večernji list* article stated, "only two things are blossoming in Serbia — crime and newly composed folk music," and linked certain singers to extremist nationalism.[40] Another in 1994 maintained the linkage between organized crime, nationalist politics, folk singers, and a widespread village-populist mentality. Ukraden was again included in a list of pro-regime folk-singers, and accused of a manipulative self-presentation as "sometimes 'a Croat from Imotski,' sometimes 'a pure Serb who had everything burned down by the Croats in Imotski.'"[41] In 1996 she was still seen as an inimical Serb: the Zagreb nightclub-singer Dragica Brkić flatly refused to perform Ukraden's songs because "she had shown her true face well before the Serbian aggression against Croatia" — yet Brkić was happy to perform songs by Ceca Veličković (then married to the Serbian paramilitary Željko Ražnatović-Arkan) "because they are sexy, not fratricidal."[42]

VL never spelled out what Ukraden had done, even after the independent right-wing weekly *Slobodni tjednik* published much more detailed allegations. *ST*'s Belgrade correspondent first alleged that Ukraden had been publicly emphasizing her "Serbness," singing "an Orthodox schlager about Vidovdan [i.e., the Battle of Kosovo]" and criticizing Muslims (Bosniaks) and "her Sarajevan brothers and sisters."[43] Later on he secured a four-page interview with her (practically unprecedented length for an entertainment topic). This discussed Ukraden's controversial statement that she "wouldn't be safe in Sarajevo," her recording of *Vidovdan* for PGP-RTB in Belgrade, her unrest at Bosnia's apparent Islamicization ("I don't want my child to wear harem-pants [dimije], to kneel, to sing ilahije and kaside,[44] to go on the haj. . . . I want my child to wear a mini-skirt and speak English"), Serbs' (lack of) responsibility in the Bosnian conflict, and intolerance toward her Serb family in Imotski during World War II and more recently. Ukraden also expressed her sadness that not one ethnic group had accepted her, concluding that "my only sin was: being a Serb born in Croatia!"[45] If Ukraden was attempting to relate the Yugoslav past's complex ethno-biographical consequences, it was lost on a politically constructed Croatian community that demanded public performances of the correct ethnicity — impossible to do anyway in Milošević's Belgrade.

Ukraden's claim to a Serb identity and the resultant political connotations made her music unsuitable for broadcast or sale in early 1990s Croatia, even when Croatians had written it; yet her songs were usually acceptable when Croatians rerecorded them. The role of her Belgrade lyricist seemed unproblematic, and the lyrics' Croatian language prevailed. Both Ukraden's main Croatian composers had some of her songs rerecorded in 1992–93. Some of the Rajko Dujmić songs appeared on a 1992 Jasna Zlokić album, but Dolores (Višnja Prsa) drew more attention when her 1993 album — titled *Došlo doba da se rastajemo (It's time we broke up)* consisted almost entirely of

Novković/Ukraden hits. Radio Karlovac listeners apparently complained about it because they thought the DJ had actually been playing Ukraden,[46] and it was also hampered by the *Slobodni tjednik* interview. Dolores and Novković found themselves aligning their music within a narrative of loyalty to Croatia and resistance to Serbia/Serbdom, and Dolores vowed to erase Ukraden from Croatian memory: by "taking over her songs I have . . . killed Neda Ukraden," whom "[w]e all know . . . achieved everything at the expense of Croatia and her composers."[47] Novković still encountered difficulties advertising the project on HTV, suggesting that state ideology encompassed competing stances on cultural separation. When HTV refused the advertisement, Dolores accused HTV of *supporting* Ukraden by obstructing "our political action for Neda to be forgotten."[48]

Novković's own media presence in 1993–94, meanwhile, epitomized a suitable ethnic biography. Now-sensitive aspects of his professional life included his use of folk elements in pop, his associations with Tucaković and Ukraden, his compositions about Tito/Yugoslavia, and even his own uncertain ethnicity. Interviewed by *Večernji list*, he was most outspoken on Ukraden's move to Belgrade: "she should have decided to stay to live and sing where she was born — in Imotski. Had she done that, she would be one of the queens of Croatian show business today."[49] This representation matched the presidential narrative about Croatian Serbs (expecting them to associate themselves with the Croatian state not the Serb rebellion). Novković managed his personal complicity by stressing that all his music came from Croatia and was unconnected to Serbia's market or cultural space: his work was "mainly linked with the Mediterranean territory" and "99 percent of the singers [he] worked with came from Croatia." Even Ukraden "sold 80 percent of her recordings in Croatia" and sold out a Zagreb concert while leaving empty seats in Belgrade, apparently evidence that she and her songs did not belong to Serbia's "completely different musical mentality."[50] Novković did not spell out what this mentality amounted to, but his comments came after several years in which Serbia had been constructed as Croatia's ultimate cultural Other. By this point in Croatian public discourse, the difference was so commonsensical that it did not need spelling out.

Novković's cultural/political opinions were much clearer than his own biography. His birthplace and ethnicity were both uncertain: his beloved Sarajevo, where he grew up, was often given as his birthplace, but his biography on the Croatian Composers' Society website today states it as Šabac (Serbia).[51] Ethnically, one could only ascertain that he was not precisely Croat. His previous census-registration as a "Yugoslav" required explanation: he said he had chosen it in lieu of a geographical, nonethnic option for

"Bosnian [Bosanac]."[52] Elsewhere he once described himself as "by origin . . . a Montenegrin from Bijelo Polje."[53] In 2002 he explained that his two grandfathers were Serbs, one grandmother was a Sarajevan Croat, and the other was Volksdeutsch, adding that he had "never had a feeling of national belonging."[54] Gossip that Novković was actually a Serb continued to circulate until and after his death in May 2007.

The act of presenting an ethnic biography also involved a recontextualization of space, performing the work of newly constituting territory as national. Novković could describe Ukraden's songs as unambiguously Croatian by referring to the spatial origins of their folk elements — namely "'ojkanje' [singing] . . . from Imotski and Dalmatinska zagora,'" which "has little to do with newly composed Belgrade and Serbian folklore."[55] "Ojkanje" referred to the polyphonic singing of extended vowels that characterized folk music in the Dinaric regions of Croatia and Herzegovina.[56] Although many public narratives in 1990s (and 2000s) Croatia sought to constitute Dinara as part of the excluded Balkans and thus an unwelcome Other within the national whole of European Croatia, the geographical origins of "ojkanje" allowed Novković to distinguish it from what he attempted to construct as a narrower concept of "Serbian folklore" which was restricted to musical markers from the vicinity of Belgrade.

The meaning of Bosnia, meanwhile, seemed infinitely malleable in this re-presentation of space. On one hand, Bosnian victimhood and the siege of Sarajevo served to further "prove" Serbian aggression and barbarity (the entertainment media backed this up by foregrounding the suffering of Bosnian interviewees who had experienced the siege). Yet Sarajevo's significance as a cultural center was also regularly downplayed to contrast Croats' and Serbs' nations/cultures more directly. Novković's 1994 reconstruction of Ukraden's career lacked information that might complicate the simple Serbs-in-Croatia narrative — such as the fact she had actually lived in Bosnia since early childhood. To be ritually unmade as a Croat, she had to be made into a *potential* Croat.

The systematic minimization of Bosnia's contribution to ex-Yugoslav culture in the politicized early-1990s entertainment media added to the public impression of a binary, civilizational clash between European/western/ innocent Croats and Balkan/eastern/aggressive Serbs. This could only accommodate Bosnia as linguistically and historically part of the Croatian cultural area.[57] Alongside Bosnia's destruction as a cultural production center (musicians reestablished their careers abroad or gave up music altogether), the Bosnian contribution to what had become "Croatian" popular music was also downplayed: although particular Croatian musicians expressed personal nostalgia for 1980s Sarajevo or associated their music with the "Sarajevo school" of folklorized rock,[58] the standard Croatian critical repertoire (which strongly disapproved of folk) did not acknowledge the significant Bosnian input into it. Instead, critics focused on NCFM's status as "Serbian" and/or "eastern" and also transferred this framework to 1990s Croatian pop production, which echoed NCFM techniques or subject-matter: the oppositions of east/west, rural/urban, civilized/uncivilized, and European/Balkan had been constructed in the Yugoslav era,[59] but took on extra significance under the symbolic framework of Croatian nationalism.[60]

The need to align one's public persona with 1990s conceptions of Croatian cultural identity led some individuals to edit musical repertoires as well as ethnic biographies.[61] Hits compilations themselves were an effective site for revising public musical memory, at least in Croatia: songs about Yugoslav socialism/institutions or Tito were still routinely absent from Croatian compilations after Tuđman, and even non-Croatian Yugoslav toponyms might be frowned upon. However, the most effective revision of memory through compilations involved not issuing them at all. For some time this appeared the case with Ukraden: although Croatian and Serbian labels both had rights to her 1980s songs, it took a Ljubljana label to reissue them first. Slovenia was also where Ukraden held her first postwar concert outside Serbia/Montenegro (2001).[62] Slovenia's "inertial, traditional, 'nostalgic'"[63] approach to ex-Yugoslav cultural products made it arguably the most welcoming space for ex-Yugoslav performers of any ethnicity.

Reconstructing Musical Connections, 2000 to 2008

CROATIA

During the 1990s Ukraden recorded four albums in Serbia; late in 2000, after the fall of Milošević, she visited Zagreb to record with a Croatian team led by Franjo Valentić and Branimir Mihaljević. Ukraden presented this to a Croatian interviewer as "logical," adding that most of her career sales had been "in collaboration with Croatian authors."[64] The trip accorded Ukraden her first Croatian press interviews since 1993, although HTV management reportedly vetoed her appearance on the HTV2 talk-show *Metropolis*: Boris Homovec, who had invited her, blamed "editors who justified themselves by saying that, because of her past, she was still not acceptable for presence on state television."[65]

Ukraden recorded three albums in Croatia between 2001 and 2004, still occupying an ambiguous area between zabavna music and pop-folk. The Valentić/Mihaljević production emphasized darabuka drums, drum-machines, and folk wind instruments (panpipes [frule] and bagpipes [gajde]);

a rearranged *Zora je* replaced the 1985 version's frule with gajde played by the Croatian folk-musician Stjepan Večković. There was little sign of the most typically "Serbian" musical markers, accordions and trumpets (the accordion was associated with the Šumadija region in central Serbia and was typically used in Yugoslav NCFM; the trumpet came from Roma brass bands and became a symbol of an authentic Serbia through the annual Guča festival), although the 2002 album's title track sampled a čoček (Roma trumpet instrumental) by the Serbian folk/jazz trumpeter Boban Marković. All three albums were released by the Serbian folk label Grand, although Croatian labels (Croatia Records then Dallas) promoted the first two in Croatia.

Ukraden's first concert in post-Yugoslav Croatia was in Domašinec in 2003, and she first "returned" to Zagreb at The Best nightclub in 2005.[66] This low-key, limited reintegration still encountered obstacles, such as a 2005 talk-show where the host Alka Vuica challenged Ukraden about her apparent disregard for Croatian wartime suffering. A potential reentry route into Croatia appeared when she was included in several celebrations of Novković's life and work in 2007 to mark his fortieth anniversary in show business and his death. She thus appeared on Zlatan Zuhrić's talk show in April 2007, on a 2007 CR compilation of Novković songs, and in a February 2008 memorial concert by Novković's clients. In February 2008 CR also released a compilation of her hits, and in June 2008 she performed at a postwar Croatian pop festival (Hrvatski radijski festival) for the first time — as Hari Varešanović (a Bosniak who left BiH via Belgrade when war broke out) had done when successfully reentering the Croatian market in 2002. Another benchmark of star status, a solo hall/arena concert in Croatia, came in November 2008 when she performed at the Lisinski hall in Zagreb. At the time of writing, it was too early to tell whether these initiatives would have any lasting effect in the Croatian music market.

BOSNIA-HERZEGOVINA

During the war in Bosnia and siege of Sarajevo, the Sarajevan media and many private individuals considered those who had left for Belgrade to have abandoned their city and Bosnia.[67] Interviewers — such as Vuica (a Croatian whose own biography included happy memories of 1980s Sarajevo) — still bring up the issue with Ukraden herself, and Sarajevo loyalists still criticize Ukraden for her "disloyalty" to the city. In a 1994 Croatian interview the Bosniak sevdah singer Hanka Paldum (who had remained in Sarajevo and often performed for the Bosniak army) attacked Ukraden and others who had left, remembering that the two had been good friends until, three days before the shelling started, Ukraden left Sarajevo "when the most necessary thing [was] to stay in it and defend it."[68] In 2001 Paldum still condemned Ukraden and other singers (e.g., Zdravko Čolić, Goran Bregović) who had left rather than "defend this city of our birth" as Paldum had.[69] Paldum's narrative of her falling-out with Ukraden resembles the "former friends" discourse of the split between the actors Boris Dvornik and Bata Živojinović. However, the most significant relationship in Ukraden's wartime/postwar biography was between Bosnia (particularly Sarajevo) and Serbia, not Serbia and Croatia. Croatia figured in her post-2000 ethnic biography only on account of her new recordings with Croatian producers and her regrets about Đorđe Novković's comments about her in the mid-1990s, and she still did not adduce her birth in Imotski as relevant.

Ukraden's return to performing in Bosnia, as in Croatia, was low key. She performed in the Bosnian Serb entity at Banja Luka's Zlatni mikrofon festival in 2003, although the Muslim–Croat Federation's broadcaster reportedly edited her out of its recorded highlights.[70] She first performed in the Federation in May 2004 at a Sarajevo concert including various Serbian and Bosnian singers (of various ethnicities) such as Halid Bešlić, Seka Aleksić, and Hanka Paldum, and in Mostar at the Melodije Mostara festival (out of competition).[71] There is certainly evidence to suggest that Ukraden, like other individuals in this paper, has been complicit in the ethnocentric entertainment-media system of her country of residence,[72] and may also emphasize different aspects of her biography depending on her audience.[73] However, unlike a figure such as Novković (who helped shape the largest Croatian record label's editorial policy), Ukraden has not been significantly able to structure the systems she operates within. Instead, she has had to negotiate several neighboring markets that respect certain ethnic biographies and have been configured not to accommodate others.

Conclusion

During the 2001 Paldum/Ukraden exchange, Paldum's own criteria for respecting musicians reflected a public sphere in which ethnicity (produced and confirmed by political loyalty) continued to be one's primary identity:

> Lots of singers . . . were exceptionally nationalistically inclined during the war, but that doesn't bother me at all. Everyone has to be what they are. I appreciate and respect that more than those who are not anything.[74]

In Croatia as well as Paldum's postwar Bosnia, acceptability in the nationalizing state media depended on ethnic biography, which in turn entailed performers making and standing by a narrative of "what they were." The multiple possibilities of a mixed ethnic background had to be reduced to one. In 1989, Goran Bregović referred to his own ethno-biographical ambiguity: with a Croatian father and Serbian mother, if he married a Bosniak, his child "would have nothing else to be except — a Yugoslav," and what could be done with "so many Yugoslavs" if Yugoslavia disappeared?[75] The answer in both Croatia and Serbia was to integrate them into a system that required all public figures to perform the corresponding ethnicity, as Croats or Serbs. Even Bregović, despite his professed multiethnicity, seemingly "became a Serb" through moving to Belgrade and, possibly, through his connection to the 1995 Emir Kusturica film *Podzemlje* (*Underground*), which was attacked as Serbian propaganda in Croatia and Bosnia.[76]

When "show business in Croatia" became nationalized into "Croatian show business" and ethnic biography became a primary value in performers' public personas, Neda Ukraden could no longer be accommodated. Not present in post-independence Croatia to carry out the ritualized performances of ethnic identity that accompanied the restructuring of Croatian show business, she was categorized primarily through her Serb ethnicity, which set her outside the boundaries of a Croatian nation believed to be under attack by Serbs. Her move to Belgrade and attempt to continue her career there, within a similarly ethnicized and politicized mass-media system, compounded her unsuitability. As Dejan Jović argues, the "new official memories" promoted by the nationalist elites of Serbia, Croatia, and Bosnia could not accommodate "memories of Yugoslavs living together as good neighbours and in peace"[77] — nor memories of Yugoslavs failing to treat ethnicity as the most important thing about others. Personal biographies were revised so as not to acknowledge one's own implication in multiethnic Yugoslav life.[78]

Political change in Serbia/Croatia after 2000, following the fall of Milošević and death of Tuđman, removed the greatest barriers to Croatians/Serbians performing in each others' countries. The most successful musical returnee to Croatia was Zdravko Čolić, another Sarajevo Serb who had moved to Belgrade. His Croatian solo concerts in 2001 and 2004 were received without controversy and Croatia Records participated in his 2007 transnational album launch (qualifying it for "domestic" charts and airplay on the Croatian Music Channel). Meanwhile, despite Ukraden's absence from the Croatian market, the techniques Croatian composers developed with her in the 1980s — setting folk rhythms to zabavna arrangements, incorporating vocal trills into zabavna songs, and emphasizing wind instruments not the accordion or trumpet — came to characterize mainstream Croatian pop.[79] Even Novković's 1994 justification of Ukraden's pop-folk — its basis in Dalmatian-hinterland folklore — reappeared as a pop trend using musical markers from that region.[80]

A more recent Croatian pop-folk star, Severina Vučković, was involved in the highest-profile Croatian–Serbian–Bosnian pop project since the fall of Yugoslavia when she hired Goran Bregović to re-arrange her 2006 Eurovision Song Contest entry (written by Franjo Valentić and Novković's son Boris),[81] then recorded her 2008 album with Bregović and Tucaković. In the 1980s Yugoslav music industry, as indicated by the older Novković's work with Neda Ukraden, this professional structure of cross-border cooperation would have been routine rather than the polemic it became. Now that 1990s nationalist efforts to divide Yugoslav cultural space into separate entities defined by exclusive ethno-national belonging still structure today's music market, the relationships became a transnational controversy and/or selling-point. Perhaps, following Ukraden's increased Croatian activity in 2008, she might yet be reintegrated into Croatian show business as successfully as Zdravko Čolić; perhaps she was too ambiguous too early to be accommodated into an entertainment industry restructured along ethno-national lines.

Notes

The research for this paper was supported by the UK Arts and Humanities Research Council. Thanks to Wendy Bracewell, Alena Ledeneva, Jelena Obradović-Wochnik, Marina Simić, and two anonymous readers of this volume for comments on earlier versions.

   1. Dubravka Ugrešić, *The Culture of Lies: Anti-Political Essays,* trans. Celia Hawkesworth (London: Phoenix), 141–42.

   2. Dean Vuletić, "Generation Number One: Politics and Popular Music in Yugoslavia in the 1950s," *Nationalities Papers* 36, no. 5 (2008): 870–73.

   3. Catherine Baker, *Sounds of the Borderland: Popular Music, War and Nationalism in Croatia since 1991* (Farnham, UK: Ashgate, 2010), 1.

   4. Michael Billig, *Banal Nationalism* (London: Sage, 1995), 8.

   5. Tim Edensor, *National Identity, Popular Culture and Everyday Life* (Oxford: Berg, 2002).

   6. Michael Ignatieff, *Blood and Belonging: Journeys into the New Nationalism* (New York: Farrar, Strauss, and Giroux, 1993).

   7. Rogers Brubaker, *Ethnicity without Groups* (Cambridge, MA: Harvard University Press, 2004), 41.

   8. Brubaker, *Ethnicity without Groups,* 53.

   9. One, Vojislav Koštunica, would later become president of Serbia-Montenegro (2000–2003) then prime minister of Serbia (2004–2008).

   10. Another name, used in Serbia, is "the war in Croatia."

11. See Nenad Zakošek, "The Legitimation of War: Political Construction of a New Reality," in *Media and War*, ed. Nena Skopljanac Brunner et al. (Zagreb: Centre for Transition and Civil Society Research/Belgrade: Agency Argument, 2000), 109–16; Alex Bellamy, *The Formation of Croatian National Identity: A Centuries-Old Dream?* (Manchester, UK: Manchester University Press, 2003); Dunja Rihtman-Auguštin, "The Monument in the Main City Square: Constructing and Erasing Memory in Contemporary Croatia," in *Balkan Identities: Nation and Memory*, ed. Maria Todorova (London: Hurst, 2004), 180–96.

12. V. P. Gagnon Jr., *The Myth of Ethnic War: Serbia and Croatia in the 1990s* (Ithaca, NY: Cornell University Press, 2004), 25.

13. Gagnon, *Myth of Ethnic War*; Dubravka Žarkov, *The Body of War: Media, Ethnicity and Gender in the Break-Up of Yugoslavia* (Durham, NC: Duke University Press, 2007).

14. Žarkov, *Body of War*, 2.

15. Anthony Giddens, *Modernity and Self-Identity: Self and Society in the Late Modern Age* (Cambridge: Polity Press, 1991), 5.

16. Stef Jansen, "The Violence of Memories: Local Narratives of the Past after Ethnic Cleansing in Croatia," *Rethinking History* 6, no. 1 (2002): 82.

17. Asim Mujkić, "We, the Citizens of Ethnopolis," *Constellations* 14, no. 1 (2007):112–28.

18. New compositions using (particularly Serbian/Bosnian) folk music and/or lyrics.

19. "Zabavna" music derived from German schlager ("šlager" in ex-Yugoslav languages), Italian canzonetta and English-language rock-and-roll. On NCFM in the Yugoslav era, see Ljerka V. Rasmussen, *Newly Composed Folk Music of Yugoslavia* (London and New York: Routledge, 2002).

20. Rasmussen, *Newly Composed Folk Music*, 120. Brena came from Brčko (Bosnia–Herzegovina), but was managed in Belgrade. She produced big-budget videos and hyperrealistic musicals, with songs tending toward "folk-šlager," sometimes with explicit patriotic (pro-Yugoslav) messages.

21. Zrinko Tutić, another Croatian pop composer, sometimes wrote her lyrics. Arrangements were usually by Dujmić or another Croatian, Mate Došen.

22. The names indicate a vowel change.

23. Bosnian and Montenegrin emerged later as separate languages. See Robert D. Greenberg, *Language and Identity in the Balkans: Serbo-Croatian and Its Disintegration* (New York: Oxford University Press, 2004).

24. Sanja Pribić, "Narodnjaci protjerani zbog stida." One exception to this trend was another periodical, *Arena*. This show business and true-life magazine continued to cover Serbians and Bosnians in entertainment until September 1991.

25. "Ostvarena volja građana," *Večernji list*, June 26, 1991.

26. Mark Thompson, *Forging War: The Media in Serbia, Croatia and Bosnia-Herzegovina* (London: Article 19), 166.

27. See Slavenka Drakulić, *Café Europa: Life after Communism* (London: Abacus, 1996), 149–52.

28. Dunja Rihtman-Auguštin, *Ulice moga grada: Antropologija domaćeg terena* (Belgrade: Biblioteka XX vek, 2000), 41–48.

29. Anči Fabijanović, "Neki se vraćaju, drugi odlaze," *Večernji list* (January 3, 1990).

30. In public culture, perhaps the emblematic instance of Croat–Serb distancing was the falling-out of Bata Živojinović (Serbian) and Boris Dvornik (Croatian), actors who had starred in several films about Tito's Partisan movement — the Yugoslav state's legitimatizing myth. Dvornik publicly recalled their friendship and his sadness that Živojinović was now accusing Tito of persecuting the Serbs. See Boris Dvornik, "Lipa li si, Mare moja." *Večernji list* (July 6, 1991).

31. Gordana Uzelac, "Franjo Tudjman's Nationalist Ideology," *East European Quarterly* 31, no. 4 (1998): 4460–61.

32. Such as Vice Vukov, who had enthusiastically joined in the "Croatian Spring" mass movement in 1969–71. See Petar Luković, *Bolja prošlost: prizori iz mužičkog života Jugoslavije 1940–1989* (Belgrade: Mladost, 1989), 95.

33. Including one of the most famous, Zdravko Čolić's *Druže Tito, mi ti se kunemo* (*Comrade Tito, we swear to you*).

34. Another Novković client, Mišo Kovač, had been explicitly pro-Yugoslav/anti-particularist in the 1980s (Petar Luković, *Bolja prošlost: prizori iz mužičkog života Jugoslavije 1940–1989* [Belgrade: Mladost, 1989], 240–42), but supported the Croatian war effort in 1991 and performed a graphic song in sadness at massacres of Croatian civilians (Vladimir Tomić, "Sin mi je rođen kao princ, umro kao pas, a pokopan kao kralj!" *Globus* [October 16, 1992]). An anthropologist observing a Croat-Australian family watching Kovač's song on video still heard them comment that Kovač was "an Orthodox . . . not a Catholic" and mention his previous pledge to leave Croatia if it became independent (Dona Kolar-Panov, *Video, War and the Diasporic Imagination* [London: Routledge, 1997], 147).

35. E.g., Marina Perazić, a member of the Croatian 1980s duo Denis i Denis, who lived for some time in Belgrade — apparently enough to make her politically Serbian during the 1990s.

36. Pavle Pavlović, "Nedin visoki C," *Arena* (December 8, 1990).

37. According to a Croatian interview Ukraden gave in 2000, moving to Belgrade had been natural because she had bought a flat there in 1987 (Arsen Oremović, "Logično je da ja snimam u Zagrebu!" *Večernji list* [November 17, 2000]).

38. Ugrešić, *Culture of Lies*, 141.

39. Diana Kučinić, "Granata prekinula sevdalinke," *Večernji list* (November 26, 1992).

40. Ukraden was not linked to a particular party, but accused of nationalist statements/songs. Maroje Mihovilović, "Novokomponirani poziv u rat," *Večernji list* (August 22, 1993).

41. Milovan Nedeljkov, "Putuj Evropo, ne čekaj na nas," *Večernji list* (March 20, 1994).

42. Nevenka Mikac, "Ja sam kraljica hrvatskog turbo folka!" *Večernji list* (April 28, 1996).

43. Pero Zlatar, "Tko su poznati Hrvati u Beogradu? Što rade i kako žive?" *Slobodni tjednik* (January 8, 1993).

44. Muslim religious songs which connoted Bosniak ethnicity during the war (Mirjana Laušević, "Some Aspects of Music and Politics in Bosnia," in *Neighbors at War: Anthropological Perspectives on Yugoslav Ethnicity, Culture and History*, ed. Joel M. Halpern and David A. Kideckel [University Park: Pennsylvania State University Press, 2000], 289–302).

45. Pero Zlatar, "Neda Ukraden tuži Republiku Hrvatsku za 200.000 DEM!" *Slobodni tjednik* (April 16, 1993).

46. Ivo Pukanić, "Likvidirala sam Nedu Ukraden!" *Globus* (February 26, 1993).

47. Pukanić, "Likvidirala sam Nedu Ukraden!"

48. Mirela Kruhak, "Intimna sam s Duškom Lokinom samo kad je riječ o pjesmi," *Arena* (August 21, 1993).

49. Branko Vukšić, "Doživio sam uzvraćenu ljubav," *Večernji list* (August 12, 1994).

50. Vukšić, "Doživio sam uzvraćenu ljubav."

51. HDS — Croatian Composers' Society, www.hds.hr/member/clan. htm?CODE=513 (accessed 14 October 2008).

52. Mario Mihaljević, "Prestar sam i prekomotan da bih špijunirao izvođače." *Globus* (December 31, 1993).

53. Bojan Mušćet, "Skladao sam domoljubne pjesme i prije pobjede HDZ-a!" *Slobodni tjednik* (March 19, 1993).

54. Mirjana Dugundžija, "Hitmejker koji je Severinu pretvorio u megazvijezdu," *Nacional* (May 28, 2002).

55. Vukšić, "Doživio sam uzvraćenu ljubav."

56. See Joško Ćaleta, "Trends and Processes in the Musical Culture of the Dalmatian Hinterland," *Music and Anthropology* 6 (2001), www.fondazionelevi. org/ma/index/number6/caleta/jos_0.htm (accessed February 4, 2009). It was often accompanied by the "gusle," a bowed lyre which official culture in both Croatia and Serbia aimed to promote as a symbol of Serbian-ness during the 1990s — even though Croatian gusle players sang patriotic songs and considered themselves the

most authentic Croats of the lot. See Ivo Žanić, *Flag on the Mountain: A Political Anthropology of War in Croatia and Bosnia* (London: Saqi, 2007).

57. David Bruce MacDonald, "The Quest for Purity," *Slovo* (London) 15, no. 1 (2003): 17.

58. For example, Alka Vuica and Siniša Vuco.

59. Rasmussen, *Newly Composed Folk Music*, 152–53.

60. The Croatian composer most typically blamed for concocting ersatz NCFM after independence was the manager-entrepreneur Tonči Huljić, although he had also used folk rhythms in the 1980s (taking a lead from other composers) when there was no political imperative to replace NCFM with something Croatian. Dujmić and Novković, meanwhile, slipped out of the pop-folk critique as journalists closed on Huljić. In 1989 Dujmić had happily taken credit for introducing folk into pop through his songs with Ukraden (Luković, *Bolja prošlost*, 277), and he was perhaps the leading figure affected by the first major controversy about Croatian pop-folk (in 1993); even more strikingly, Novković's own folklorization of Croatian pop did not seem to figure at all in the anti-Huljić discourse, despite the 1980s pop-folk songs he had written for several performers including Ukraden. Even though Huljić himself once acknowledged the influence of the biggest Novković/Ukraden hit (*Zora je*) on his own preference for folk elements (Darko Hudelist, "Neda Ukraden otvorila mi je glazbene vidike," *Globus* [March 30, 2001]), Novković (and Ukraden) still remained largely absent from the Croatian pop-folk story. When Novković's 1999–2001 client Severina Vučković became another focus of anti-folk discourse (Ines Prica, "Na tlu trivijalnog: pismo iz trancizije," *Narodna umjetnost* 41, no. 2 [2004]: 141–56), critics debated Severina as a personality but not Novković's musical significance.

61. Doris Dragović, a 1980s rival of Ukraden, had ended up as the "queen of Croatian show business" herself: she appeared at wartime charity concerts and HDZ political rallies, and performed several patriotic songs in the role of a normative nationalist mother. Her 1980s music (by the Croatian composer Zrinko Tutić, lyrics by Tutić or Tucaković) had resembled Greek pop-laika, and she sang one song in honor of Yugoslavia, but her 1990s songs were largely romantic ballads (apart from two up-tempo albums in 1999–2000 — when she was also severely criticized for performing in Montenegro at New Year). After the Montenegro incident and another controversy over whether her 2000 album resembled Serbian turbo-folk, Dragović's next release (2001) was an extremely selective compilation almost entirely of love ballads. Her Greek-style hits remained excluded from her public persona — yet they were available on a Serbian compilation by Hi-Fi Centar, which had claimed Serbian rights to Jugoton's archive (Melisa Skender, "D Dvornik i ET pjevaju za Pale Records u piratskom izdanju," *Večernji list* [June 29, 1997]). Some of them finally appeared in Croatia on Dragović's next compila-

tion (2007) after Croatia Records' new management resolved to exploit its back catalog extensively.

62. Ukraden, "Publika u Hrvatskoj i Sloveniji se zaželela Nede Ukraden," *Balkanmedia*, (September 2001). www.balkanmedia.com/magazin/kolumne/30/30. html (accessed 23 October 2006). Now available at http://muzika14.tripod.com/ interwievs/id22.html (accessed 14 October 2008).

63. Mitja Velikonja, "Ex-Home 'Balkan Culture' in Slovenia after 1991," in *The Balkans in Focus: Cultural Boundaries in Europe*, ed. Barbara Törnquist-Plewa and Sanimir Resić (Lund: Nordic Academic Press, 2002), 195.

64. Oremović, "Logično je da ja snimam u Zagrebu!"

65. "Urednici pamte samo prošlost," *Glas javnosti* (November 26, 2000).

66. Dora Đuras, "Nedu su pet puta vraćali na binu," *Arena* (September 11, 2003); Ana Konta, "U Zagrebu pjevam slomljena srca," *Arena* (February 24, 2005).

67. Ivana Maček, "'Imitation of Life': Negotiating Normality in Sarajevo under Siege," in *The New Bosnian Mosaic: Identities, Memories and Moral Claims in a Post-War Society*, ed. Xavier Bougarel, Elissa Helms, and Ger Duijzings (Aldershot, UK: Ashgate, 2007), 39–57.

68. Željko Garmaz, "Uvijek sam bila žena borac pa mi Srbi zovi balijka s pendrekom!" *Globus* (April 1, 1994).

69. Hanka Paldum, "Ponosna sam što sam, za razliku od Nade Topčagić, ostala vjerna svom narodu." *Balkanmedia* (September 2001), http://muzika14 .tripod.com/interwievs/id33.html (accessed October 14, 2008); Hanka Paldum, "Razočarali su me Suzana Mančić, Miroslav Ilić, Neda Ukraden . . ." *Balkanmedia* (October 2001), http://muzika14.tripod.com/interwievs/id34.html (accessed October 14, 2008).

70. "Neda Ukraden nepoželjna u Gradiški," *Svet* (July 11, 2003).

71. "Sarajevo, gde je moja raja?" *Kurir* (May 6, 2004); "Postala sam zvezda preko noći," *Blic* (May 5, 2004).

72. For example, an article written for an online magazine after the 1999 vandalization of her café in Belgrade. She presented herself as even more un-ambiguously Serbian — "I'm sorry for everything that happened to the Shiptars [Albanians] in Kosovo, and for what happened to the Croats in Vukovar, but the hardest thing for me is what my Serbs experienced and survived" — although still stated that her "soul was in Bosnia" and she would go to Sarajevo as soon as she was offered a solo concert there. Neda Ukraden, "Beograd je za sve bolji osim za svoju decu i Srbe," *Balkanmedia*, www.balkanmedia.com/magazin/dzungla/7/ index.html (accessed 23 October 2006).

73. When relating to Serbian tabloids, Ukraden does appear to present herself (or is reported) as primarily Serbian. In February 2006 one Serbian tabloid questioned the apparent irreconcilability of this with her self-presentation on a

Croatian talk show: apparently she had given a different version of the Belgrade move that distanced her from Milošević, mentioned her many performances at overseas Croatian clubs, stated that she had "never said a single nasty word about President Tuđman," and spoken in ijekavica rather than ekavica, which in a political and exclusive definition of ethnicity all made one less of a Serb.

74. Paldum, "Ponosna sam što sam."

75. Luković, *Bolja prošlost*, 312.

76. See Dina Iordanova, *Cinema of Flames: Balkan Film, Culture and the Media* (London: BFI, 2001), 122–24.

77. Dejan Jović, "'Official Memories' in Post-Authoritarianism, an Analytical Framework," *Journal of Southern Europe and the Balkans* 6, no. 2 (2004): 102.

78. Jović, "'Official Memories' in Post-Authoritarianism," 103.

79. In 2001 Ukraden remarked that "some Croatian singers have taken up that style, which I built up for years, and have become well-known" (Ukraden, "Publika u Hrvatskoj").

80. That is, multipart "ojkanje" and "ganga" singing; diple pipes; the lijerica (a bowed lyre).

81. See Catherine Baker, "When Seve Met Bregović: Folklore, Turbofolk and the Boundaries of Croatian Musical Identity," *Nationalities Papers* 36, no. 4 (2008): 741–64.

CHAPTER THREE

Between the Lines

"Lili Marlene," Sexuality, and the Desert War

CHRISTINA BAADE

"Lili Marlene" was "the most bewitching, haunting, sentimental song of the war" in the words of the British Captain C. F. Milner, who was stationed in North Africa during the Second World War.[1] Although now closely associated with Marlene Dietrich, the song first became popular with Axis and Allied forces during the Desert War of 1941 and 1942. A nearly legendary level of mutual respect and the sparsely populated desert allowed what the German General Erwin Rommel famously labeled, "Krieg ohne Hass" ("war without hate"). Radio, with its ability to disseminate propaganda and to support troop morale, played a key role in the conflict. First broadcast by the Nazi-controlled Radio Belgrade and later by the British Broadcasting Corporation (BBC), "Lili Marlene" crossed and re-crossed the lines of combat, ultimately becoming the marching song of the British Eighth Army and, according to the 1944 collection *GI Songs*, nearly "*the song of this war*."[2] When the Allies finally triumphed in North Africa, the song was one of their "trophies," according to Humphrey Jennings's 1944 Ministry of Information film, *The True Story of Lili Marlene*.[3]

According to the film, the trophy of "Lili Marlene" was not merely its copyright; rather, it was the physical object of Lale Andersen's August 1939 recording of the song, the same version that Radio Belgrade broadcast daily from the summer of 1941.[4] The primacy that Jennings accorded to a German Electro disk of "Lili Marleen,"[5] which was captured in the Libyan desert in 1942, suggested the powerful role it played for listeners as musical surrogate, to borrow Carol Muller's term describing recording and broadcasting's function as replacements for absent performers.[6] Milner suggested the intimacies that Andersen's mechanically reproduced and broadcast voice offered:

> Perhaps you have not been away from the sound of a woman's voice for a year; for this voice was at once seductive and soothing, husky, intimate but mysteriously unattainable, reaching down to you as you lay in your blankets on the unsympathetic desert as though from the stars you were gazing at, longing for. *Yet somehow she was just beside your head.*[7]

Andersen's appealing aural persona vaulted her to stardom and the song to hit status throughout North Africa, the Mediterranean, and Occupied Europe, where Radio Belgrade was heard. Many of the thousands of letters sent to Radio Belgrade conflated Andersen with Lili Marleen, the subject of the song, who waited under a lantern outside the barracks to meet her soldier sweetheart.[8]

For German and British forces, Lili Marlene embodied the sweetheart waiting faithfully in the homeland, but she was also a woman who frequented the street by a barracks — and insinuated herself aurally into a soldier's desert bed. As John Bierman and Colin Smith argue, she was an ambivalent character, "that archetypal if clichéd male fantasy figure: Virgin and Whore."[9] The situation was more complicated, however: Lili Marlene and the voices of women who sang the song resonated with the phenomenon of the pinup girl, the term Americans coined (and the British adopted) for the glamorous star photographs and sexy illustrations believed to bolster military morale. While wartime love and sexuality were laced with fear — of unfaithfulness, venereal disease, and mechanized death — the unthreatening pinup reinforced the heterosexual masculinity of her consumer.[10] Cecil Madden, who directed overseas popular programming for the BBC, transferred the concept to radio, promoting numerous "radio girl-friends," including wholesome Anne Shelton, whom the BBC promoted "to counteract the Marlene idea for sex-starved troops."[11] Ruth Yorck encapsulated the transition of Lili Marlene from German seductress to Anglo-American pinup: "She has defied all rules; jumped over all boundaries. *Lili Marlene* is export goods."[12]

Lili Marlene dramatized the ambivalent roles that real women negotiated in the war. For Germans, she symbolized the power of romantic love in a culture where the Nazis instrumentalized marriage, sex, and women's bodies for building a master race.[13] In North Africa, Allied ideology and military policy were unified regarding "foreign" women: they were cast as exotic, sexually available, and potentially diseased. Servicemen could enjoy the benefits of both ostensibly faithful wives and sweethearts at home and tacit approval for sexual relations abroad, but the situation was more complicated for Anglo-American women. On the home front, the movement of women into employment and civic participation was accompanied by an obsession with their sexual morality.[14] Women who took pleasure-seeking too far were linked to the social problems of promiscuity, venereal disease, illegitimacy, and "amateur prostitution."[15] According to Marilyn Hegarty, such women were cast as deviant at the same time that "magazines, movies, posters, and other media covertly and overtly urged wartime women to provide sexualized support for the military in various types of public and private entertainment." Although broadcasting removed its female performers from the fraught terrain of physicality, they still had to negotiate this "complex sexualized border zone" in their performances as radio girl friends.[16]

At the same time that "Lili Marlene" embodied the sexual double standard for women in wartime, it dramatized the emotional double standard that male soldiers faced. While home ties were promoted as supportive of morale in the forces, authorities (particularly the British) worried that too much nostalgia and sentimentality would emasculate them and erode their fighting spirit. Although both the original German text and most English adaptations voiced a male soldier's perspective, the singers most assiduously promoted by broadcasters and to whom listeners were most receptive were women. Captain Milner argued, "['Lili Marlene'] is not . . . something for a man to tackle."[17] The insistence that cross-gender performance was the most appropriate choice (an argument continued by Carleton Jackson in his history of the song) suggested the dangers of men expressing too much sentimentally, longing, and nostalgia.

In the remainder of this chapter, I shall focus upon three key wartime performers of "Lili Marlene": Lale Andersen, Anne Shelton, and Marlene Dietrich. More specifically, I shall consider how they negotiated the ambivalent sexuality and sentiment of the song in live performance, broadcasting, and recording during the Desert War, as the "Lili Marlene" legend grew later in the war, and in the postwar period. All three operated in the border zones of nation, gender, and desire in their relationship with the song.

The Desert War and Lili Marleen

First broadcast by Radio Belgrade in April 1941, Lale Andersen's version of "Lili Marleen" reached German and British troops in the North African desert at an ideal time to make an impression: during the 242-day siege of Tobruk, which began in the same month. Between November 1941, when the British launched Operation Crusader to relieve Tobruk, and November 1942, when they finally triumphed at the second battle of Alamein, British and German forces engaged in a series of bloody tank, artillery, and infantry battles. In an environment of "growing mutual respect" and often confused battle conditions, in which a soldier's life depended as much upon military technology as upon bravery and tactics, "Lili Marleen" was heard nightly by both sides.[18] A German soldier wrote, "Soldiers can die, but an evening without Lili Marleen is unthinkable."[19]

While the song achieved an aura of inevitability through repeated broadcasts, it was not an instant hit. The poet and critic Hans Leip wrote the text in 1915 as a soldier during the First World War. Following its 1937 publication, two composers set it in radically different manners: Rudolf Zink set it as a through-composed waltz, while Norbert Schultze, who achieved infamy during the war with his song "Bomben auf England," set the song as a strophic march. Andersen initially performed Zink's setting, but she soon found its sophistication to be a liability, so in 1939, she adopted Schultze's version for her appearances at the Kabarett der Komiker, a fashionable Berlin nightclub.[20] She reflected, "Aesthetically perhaps, Zink's version was better . . . pragmatically, to suit the mood of the time, Schultze's version was realistic."[21] Schultze's lilting march was highly accessible. Harmonically straightforward, it rocked between tonic and dominant with a single foray into the subdominant. The simple melody moved largely through conjunct motion and sequences, punctuated by longing leaps and sighing appoggiaturas — particularly on the final words of each verse, "Wie einst, Lili Marleen (as once, Lili Marleen)."[22] Rather than a waltz, which carried associations with heterosexual pairing, desire, and nostalgia — emphasizing the relationship of Lili Marleen and the soldier — Schultze's march evoked the barracks setting and romance tempered by military responsibilities. In contrast to Zink's shifting major and minor modes and passages of recitative, which rewarded the individual interpretation of a cabaret artiste, Schultze's straightforward version invited a sing-along.

Ultimately, radio propelled "Lili Marleen" into becoming the iconic song of the Desert War. Andersen's August 1939 recording, the only version made at the time, sold only seven hundred disks, but in 1941 a copy was included in the paltry selection of recordings that the station director Lieutenant Reintgen obtained to broadcast over the newly acquired Radio Belgrade. Listening to the disks, he judged its bugle call introduction to be excellent "close-down music." Within a week of the song's first broadcast, the station received thousands of letters requesting it again, and "it became a fixture on Radio Belgrade" as "the last record of the night." From late 1941, the song could be heard thirty times daily on German-controlled stations.[23]

Andersen's recording was received enthusiastically, not only by German soldiers, but also by British forces. In May 1942, the *Daily Herald* reported that "Lili Marleen" was the most popular song with British soldiers in North Africa.[24] One officer observed, "This tune is really good and our boys hum and sing it too."[25] The arrangement did much to amplify the charms of Schultze's march setting: capitalizing on the line, "Schon rief der Posten: Sie blasen Zapfenstreich (In no time at all, the sentry called out, 'they are sounding curfew')," a snare roll and bugle call opened and closed the song, and the bugle heralded the verse containing the line.[26] Other military topoi in the refrains — a prominent bass drum and a male "soldiers'" chorus (which Bergmeier, Lotz, and Kühn suggested mitigated the cross-gender delivery of the soloist) — added further interest to the string and accordion accompaniment.[27]

The attraction resided not merely in the tune or accompaniment but in Andersen's voice and performance style. Reintgen regarded her voice as "sweet" while Leip described it as an endearing "Come kiss me" voice.[28] For British soldiers, her "husky, sensuous, nostalgic, sugar-sweet" voice was exotically appealing: "she put it over in a way we hadn't heard before with an accent lovably un-English," explained Milner.[29] In the 1939 recording, Andersen employed crisp diction while maintaining a conversational address. Her mostly straight-toned delivery was that of a singing actress, not an opera singer or crooner. Rather than a cabaret artiste's sophistication, the slight portamento at the ends of lines and her emotionally frank tone conveyed intimacy, sincerity, and charm.

The desire that Andersen's voice singing "Lili Marleen" elicited was not simply sexual; rather, it dramatized her listeners' longing for home. One German soldier wrote to Radio Belgrade,

Each day we go out in our tanks. In the evenings we are tired and weary and we are laboring under thirst. We want once more to wash up, and have something to see besides sand, horizon, and blue heaven. Then rings out on the radio a woman's voice. . . . This song has a real value — we laugh as though the radio was a small piece of home.[30]

"Lili Marleen," Jackson argued, played a key role in German messages programs.[31] Josef Goebbels regarded such programs, which blended sentimental favorites and new hits with "cheerful greetings" between soldiers and families, as critical to lightening the public mood, particularly with the opening of the Eastern Front in June 1941. Goebbels "disapproved" of "Lili Marleen," however. He described it as having a "cadaverous smell" — perhaps thinking of the final verse:

Aus dem stillen Raume,
aus der Erde Grund,

Hebt mich wie im Traume
dein verliebter Mund.
Wenn sich die spaeten Nebel drehn
Werd' ich bei der Laterne stehn
Wie einst Lili Marleen.

(From the quiet place,
from the earthly ground,
I rise as if in a dream
to your beloved lips.
When the evening mist swirls around itself
I will stand by the lantern
as once, Lili Marleen)."[32]

In contrast to party officials on the home front, who worried about its impact on military morale, Rommel liked the song and recognized it as "a unifying force among his men."[33]

For British officers in North Africa, the troops' infatuation with Andersen was more troubling. British soldiers knew the song primarily in its German form, but by August 1942, the BBC Monitoring Service reported that Nazi stations had begun broadcasting an English version — most likely the innocuous adaptation by the British defector Norman Baille-Stewart, which Andersen had recorded in June.[34] R. A. Foggin, a Squadron Leader at Air Headquarters, explained his concerns: "This broadcast . . . will possibly create a feeling that Germans who can produce such good music, etc. cannot be such bad chaps after all. . . . It arouses . . . thoughts of civilization and our own womankind at home." Apart from the song, the broadcasts had "little propaganda value" at the moment, "but again some day [they] may."[35]

By mid-July 1942, Foggin's letter circulated among BBC staff, who began formulating a response.[36] Cecil Madden, who headed the BBC's Empire Entertainments Unit, suggested that Walt Disney's "team of musical experts" be contracted to write a simple marching song, and continued,

> If you really want to counteract the Marlene idea for sex-starved troops, give us a time every day at the same time and let us put on a Glamour programme with say Four girls . . . say a Blonde, a Brunette, and a Redhead — and an American girl too, for the USA troops in the Middle East. Plenty of songs, Records, all sorts of changes.[37]

While Madden objectified women discursively, in practice he opened the airwaves to an unprecedented number of women producers, announcers, and performers. Like the Germans, the British broadcast numerous messages programs; Madden's innovation was to have women — or "radio girl friends" — host them.[38] He also favored female singers over male, explaining, "We invariably . . . cut out male 'crooners' or 'high tenors' and include bright girls, for whom there is a real demand by, say, Forces in the Desert. Male crooners are quite divorced from the reality of the times."[39]

Madden's "croonettes" carried out BBC propaganda objectives with a personal touch. *Parade*, a weekly magazine for forces in the Middle East, described how "the girls who sing from London . . . bring us London in their song."[40] Their intimate address to overseas forces enacted musical surrogacy, reinforced by their on-air personas, publicity photographs, and, sometimes, in-person appearances. Although the term "pinup girl" did not enter common usage until 1943, these women functioned as what Madden later called "pin-up personalities," combining girl-next-door charm with innocent sex appeal.[41]

Madden's ambitious brainstorm was soon reduced to a program featuring a single blonde, Anne Shelton, with an adaptation of "Lilli Marlene" as its signature tune. Only fifteen years old when war was declared, Shelton, within the space of a year, had been hired by the famous bandleader Ambrose and was launched into a solo career under his management; from the start, critics praised her low, strikingly mature voice and assured technique.[42] In June 1941, she began singing in the messages program *Calling the British Forces in Malta*, in which she acquired a reputation for versatility, singing sentimental ballads, comedy numbers, and bright marching tunes.[43] Thousands of letters attested to her popularity with forces throughout the Mediterranean and North Africa:

> Anne, Anne, Why must you do it? Here we are in the desert, war like, full of hate for the hun [*sic*], ready for war and you come and sing. . . . That voice of yours, really, well I can't say what it does to one but everything else goes into the background. Do you look like you sound? If you do you must be delicious.[44]

Shelton's visual mystery was unveiled when *Parade* featured her photograph, with BBC microphone, on its cover, transforming her from mysterious voice to pinup.[45]

To counteract "Lili Marleen," the BBC deployed Shelton in a star vehicle, patterned after *Sincerely Yours — Vera Lynn*. First airing on Sunday, 4 October 1942, *Introducing Anne* was broadcast simultaneously to the Middle East and the home front. Accompanied by the Ambrose Players, Shelton sang a range of old favorites, like "Begin the Beguine," and current hits. She also delivered the continuity talk, scripted by the producer David Miller in a conversational style.[46] As to "Lili Marlene," the signature tune, Shelton recalled that she thought it was awful but was told, "Well darling, it isn't whether you like it or not. You're being used to counteract the Nazi propaganda programme Goebbels is putting out."[47] The BBC's Programmes as Broadcast logs indicate clearly that Shelton did not sing the signature tune (no British lyrics yet existed); rather, the Ambrose Players performed it instrumentally at the start and close of each program.[48] The arrangement "was heavily and ornately orchestrated and . . . listeners would not be likely to recognize it distinctly and instantly as the German song."[49] *Introducing Anne* was weak counterpropaganda: it provided no convincing replacement for "Lili Marleen" while the instrumental arrangement failed to equip the song with English lyrics to supplant the German version. It offered Shelton, however, as a safe, British alternative to Andersen's dangerous appeal.

Nevertheless, Shelton's address to the forces in the program was still subject to concern. Alick Hayes, her *Calling Malta* producer, argued that Miller's continuity talk was turning Shelton into another sentimental Vera Lynn, undoing his depiction of her as "a cheerful and cheery personality: in fact as the sort of pleasant English girl whom a man serving overseas . . . would be glad to introduce to his wife or mother or sister or girl friend."[50] At the BBC in 1942, this was a serious criticism. As British forces experienced significant defeats and mass surrenders and prepared to retreat from Egypt, critics condemned sentimental popular music as having a demoralizing influence on the troops. In response, the BBC banned male crooners, overly sentimental female singers, and "slushy" songs.[51] Shelton's broadcasts were expected to offer troops an uplifting connection to home while avoiding excessive sentimentality.

While sentimental longing played a role in the morale threat of the Nazi's broadcasts of Andersen's "Lili Marleen," it also carried a more direct connection to fears of defeatism in the ranks. Foggin linked the song's role in humanizing the enemy with stories that the Germans treated their captives well, both of which encouraged surrender.[52] His fears were borne out by a British soldier's letter to Andersen after the war: "You captured something in that song that every serviceman feels . . . and the sound of your voice, as much as the words, pulled at the very strings of our hearts. . . . It made Germans and British friends together! The Afrika Korps sang it and their British prisoners joined in and vice versa."[53] Andersen's voice not only filled her listeners with nostalgia for home but with a sense of connection to their opponents, a connection that both reinforced the legendary qualities of the "war without hate" and threatened to undermine the will to fight — and kill — the enemy.

In July 1943, Morris Gilbert, a U.S. embassy official in London, thanked Madden for helping him assemble a brief on "Lili Marlene," observing, "Nothing about this song seems to make much sense, does it?"[54] Over the next year, "Lili Marlene" emerged into Anglo-American public awareness, with the publication and recording of English-language versions, the release of Jennings's *True Story*, and Marlene Dietrich's incorporation of the song into her repertory. The impetus for "Lili Marlene's" new visibility on the Anglo-American home front was the Allies' stunning victory in North Africa. November 1942 signaled the turning point, with both the Eighth Army's victory at Alamein and the launch of Operation Torch, in which Americans joined British forces in invading Vichy North Africa. On May 12, 1943, the Desert War finally ended, with the Allies taking 275,000 prisoners. Britain's public worries about forces morale were replaced by celebration of the Eighth Army.

Jennings's *True Story* tied "Lili Marlene" explicitly to the Allies' North African triumph. The film made striking use of combat footage — tanks firing in the desert night, U-boats at sea, and dead German soldiers on the Eastern Front — which Jennings interwove with (re)enactment, such as the song's central tryst under the lantern. Belying its title, the film was riddled with inaccuracies (e.g., it reported that Andersen was Swedish); however, it conveyed a coherent narrative of the "modern fairy tale," linking the song to the military fortunes of the belligerents. "Lili Marlene," the film recounted, became a German "smash hit" in 1941 with Wehrmacht victories and the opening of the Russian front. But the British captured the song, along with 800 miles of desert, when they triumphed in North Africa. Finally, with von Paulus's surrender at Stalingrad in February 1943, the Germans' pleasure in the song was silenced — literally, since Goebbels ordered a three-day cease of all entertainment to mourn the defeat (true) and Andersen was sent to a concentration camp (untrue). "Lili Marlene" exemplified love of home, although the Germans failed to recognize that others loved their homes, too; the Allies' victory demonstrated that their "home thoughts served them best." Ultimately, the song was not merely spoils; rather, in a peroration that, given the film's June 1944, post-D-Day release, must have resonated for audiences, it was a "reminder to sweep fascism from the face of the earth and to make it really the last war."

The film helped vindicate Andersen for Allied audiences by promoting the rumor that she was interned. At first, Nazi authorities had exploited her sudden popularity by sending her on tours of the Western front in 1941 and Germany in early 1942. Andersen was uneasy with the regime, however —

particularly after she saw the Warsaw Ghetto during her tours — and she expressed her desire to escape Germany in a letter that the Gestapo intercepted.[55] They put Andersen under house arrest and forbade her from performing publicly.[56] Goebbels also banned "Lili Marleen" in summer 1942, but the song's popularity rendered the ban ineffective, and German stations continued to broadcast it.[57]

While not in a concentration camp, Andersen credited the BBC propaganda broadcasts that initially spread the rumor with ensuring her freedom. Under house arrest, she had despaired and taken an overdose of sleeping tablets. Her "disappearance" while convalescing raised false alarms that she was incarcerated; to prove the lie of the BBC's announcement, the regime allowed her to record, broadcast, and perform again.[58] Although her voice was used almost entirely for propaganda against the Allies, until she slipped away in early 1945 to a North Sea island, her suffering at the hands of the Nazis, both real and rumored (not to mention the common belief that she was not German), rehabilitated her from enemy temptress to Nazi victim.[59]

Just as Andersen escaped being labeled a German propagandist, the figure of Lili Marleen needed to be rehabilitated in English translation. Jackson argued that well into 1944, British soldiers still sang the song in German and composed numerous, often risqué, English parodies.[60] British and, to a lesser extent (since the song became popular more slowly in the United States), American authorities regarded a good translation of the song as critical. Because "Lili Marleen" was under enemy copyright until the U.S. government seized it in May 1943, Anglo-American music publishers needed to negotiate the song's rights with the government. Chappell rose to the challenge first, with a "Lili Marlene," by Mack David and Phil Park (Schultze was unaccredited) that was first broadcast in the United States in June 1943. Peter Maurice issued its version in early 1944 with lyrics by the British songwriter Tommie Connor.

"Lili Marlene" particularly needed rehabilitation because of the reputation its title figure had acquired among English speakers. Although Leip defended Lili Marleen as a respectable girl, English listeners regarded her as a whore.[61] She embodied the "amateur prostitute," who figured so prominently in policy makers' classification of "loose" women as deviant — irresponsible, morale-sapping, and alien.[62] Connor asked, "Wasn't it all about a young prostitute who wanted to give as much for her country as the soldiers — so she gave her body? Can you imagine that in English?" To accord with censorship demands and commercial good sense, Connor needed "to write a song imagining the girl was a daughter, a mother, sister or sweetheart — a song that wouldn't offend the hearts and morals of people."[63] While still intimate, the song's affection was more chaste than in the

German version, with the soldier recalling simply in the second verse, "Darling, I'd caress you and press you to my heart. . . . I'd hold you tight, We'd kiss goodnight," rather than Leip's "unsere beide Schatten sah'n wie einer aus (our two shadows seemed like one)."[64] To avoid suggesting the soldier's demise in the final stanza, Connor placed him "resting in a billet, just behind the lines," where "Your sweet face seems to haunt my dreams." While unarguably sentimental and nostalgic, Connor's lyrics resonated with other wartime songs that sustained hope for future reunions.

Shelton's recording reinforced the sense of a virtuous "radio girl-friend" waiting for her sweetheart. The arrangement excised the military topoi of the Andersen recording: the tempo was about twenty beats per minute slower, the instrumentation featured the smooth strings and woodwinds of a commercial swing ballad, and the only echo of the bugle call (in music or text) occurred when a muted trumpet played the penultimate chorus. In contrast to Anderson's crisp diction and husky tone, Shelton conveyed the text with polished expressivity, played conservatively with the rhythm, and added tasteful ornaments.[65] Still, while Andersen's lighter voice underscored the cross-gender delivery, Shelton's contralto queerly elided it.[66] It was probably necessary to omit the second verse for timing, but its excision also precluded any non-heterosexual interpretations that might have arisen from lyrics involving caressing, pressing, and kissing. Without this verse, Shelton's "Marlene" became a song of chaste love and longing with only a mild frisson from her delivery of a man's point of view, which still avoided the dangers of a man envoicing the same degree of sentimental longing. The formula was extraordinarily popular: Connor claimed that her recording sold a million copies, and Shelton became closely identified with the song in the public's imagination.[67]

In contrast to Connor and Shelton's sentimental chastity, Marlene Dietrich offered a more carnal approach to the song, which likely helped reinscribe Lili Marlene's ambiguity for postwar American audiences. Since 1930, Dietrich and her exposed legs, cross dressing, and sultry accent embodied Continental decadence in Hollywood cinema. Nevertheless, she was an outspoken critic of the Nazis' rise in her homeland, becoming an American citizen in 1937 and playing an active role in the American war effort. In April 1944, she and her USO troupe flew overseas, where they entertained servicemen in North Africa and Italy. Her act built upon and expanded her star persona: she sang songs from her films and wore a "nude" dress, with spangles sewn onto flesh-colored cloth; she also played the musical saw, which necessitated hiking up her skirts so that she could position it between her thighs.[68] Soon after arriving in North Africa, Dietrich incorporated "Lili Marlene" into her act.

Dietrich sang her own translation of "Lili Marlene."[69] Using first-person singular extensively, her version focused more firmly upon the soldier-protagonist's perspective than other English-language translations. It also shifted the couple's roles: rather than Lili Marlene waiting patiently, here the soldier "[will] always stand and wait for you at night." Dietrich granted Lili Marlene further agency: the narrator acknowledged that when he left, "Surely tomorrow you'll feel blue, / but then will come a love that's new." Unlike Connor's chaste lyrics, Dietrich's version implied a consummated affair in which the soldier requested, "Bugler, tonight / don't play the call to arms. / I want another evening with her charms." Rather than resenting Lili Marlene's inconstancy, as authorities concerned with female sexual "deviance" feared, the soldier's love continued to sustain him: "When we are marching in the mud and cold, / and when my pack seems more than I can hold, / My love for you renews my might, / I'm warm again, my pack is light."

Dietrich's performance history of frank sexuality, theatricality, and gender-bending made it possible for her to embody both the narrator and his object of affection. Robert Peters explained in his GI memoir: "I was drawn to her throaty octaves and to her peculiar humor which, in the films, kept men at bay and was tinged with masculinity. . . . By appearing inaccessible, she could flaunt sexuality . . . and at the same time seem aloof from it."[70] In a September 1945 recording, Dietrich sang in her chest voice, declaiming the lyrics in a relaxed manner, ornamenting the melodic line with her distinctive scoops and fast vibrato. In the final verse, the tempo slowed significantly with the repetition of "My love for you renews my might," emphasizing the text's open-ended interpretation: the soldier's revival — or his escape through death.[71] Her responsive interpretation helped cement her close connection to the song: when she performed it at Paris in May 1945, its introduction "produced pandemonium. She stopped, bowed, and raised a white gloved arm to quiet the audience. Dietrich *was* Lili."[72]

In summer 1944 during a brief sojourn in New York, Dietrich recorded "Lili Marleen" in German for the Office of Strategic Services.[73] The oss used her recordings in propaganda broadcasts directed to German troops and civilians. In a 1951 remake, Dietrich crooned the German text, its meaning shifting from a declaration of love to a wistful lullaby.[74] In contrast to the newly composed text that the émigré actress Lucie Mannheim had declaimed so passionately in BBC propaganda broadcasts, enjoining listeners to "Hängt ihn an die Laterne! (Hang him [Hitler] from the lantern!)," Dietrich's rendition gained its impact through her expressive rendition of the original lyrics. Steven Bach, her biographer, explained, "Their power was all the greater for absence of rhetoric and for the *Weltschmerz* in her voice: a German making love to the Germans with German."[75] For an actress known for her emotional remove, the strength of her German-language performances was her sincerity. Indeed, Amy Lawrence argued that her support for the war effort was "described as a[n] . . . expression of her 'real' self," which she demonstrated by putting her body on the line, not only in her USO tours, but by the risk she took of being summarily executed as a traitor had she been captured. Dietrich's boundary crossing existed not only in areas of sexuality but of nationality: building on her cosmopolitan prewar persona, in wartime "she became professionally German, a native who speaks German on behalf of and at the behest of American."[76] In so doing, she personified "Lili Marlene" for many Americans.

Remembering Lili Marlene

In the immediate postwar period, "Lili Marlene" continued to circulate in a discourse of spoils. GI slang designated women in occupied Germany as "Lili Marleens," and a parody of the song drew upon familiar stereotypes (and desperate realities) of foreign women as sexually available for a price: "Vie Fiehl [sic], Lili Marlene? (How much, Lili Marlene?)"[77] The song also evoked the recent conflict more nostalgically; in the work of Andersen, Shelton, and Dietrich, it reinforced their connections to positive memories of the war, particularly for soldiers. In a period dominated by themes of domesticity for Anglo-American women and defeat for German women, the three performers drew upon wartime understandings of glamour, romantic love, and longing to forge successful careers for the Cold War era.

Andersen's well-publicized fall from favor with Goebbels spared her censure under denazification. Her fame with both sides helped her gain almost immediate postwar employment at Northwest German Radio in Hamburg and in entertaining occupying British and American troops.[78] In 1950, she toured the United Kingdom, prompted by an invitation to perform at the Eighth Army Veterans' Alamein Reunion. A letter from the Council of Victory (Ex-Services) Club registered her warm reception among British veterans, with its thanks for her "charming singing . . . posing again and again for photographs — and signing many autographs."[79] While still positioned as foreign, she was portrayed in the press as unthreatening: "She has blonde hair, laughing blue eyes, three children and a limited knowledge of English."[80]

Although she recorded other hit songs, Andersen maintained a close relationship with "Lili Marleen," recording it seven times between 1948 and 1964. Three Zurich recordings from the late 1940s offered different nostalgic approaches. A 1949 disk faithfully recreated her original 1939 recording, but the 1948 session featured sentimental reinterpretations of the song, with an accordion playing the opening bugle call; a slower tempo; and sweet strings, accordion, and low woodwinds supporting Andersen's close-miked voice as she crooned the lyrics in a sweetly intimate manner. One of the session's recordings was entirely in German, but the other combined Connor's first two romantic verses with the haunting final two strophes of Leip's text, embodying the shared experiences of soldiers on opposing sides.[81] An American soldier wrote to Andersen: "[I]t's wonderful to think that it's the song sung by all armies of WWII. . . . You are to me *Lili Marleen*."[82]

Andersen's embodiment of Lili Marleen continued in her biography. When she married the Swiss composer Artur Beul in June 1949, press around the world reported the marriage of "Lili Marleen," reminding readers of her wartime popularity and recounting her resistance to and victimization by the Nazis. The story represented a comforting resolution to the narrative of wartime romance: the dangerous sexuality of Lili Marleen was now contained in marriage — conveniently, to a man from a neutral country, leaving her safe in the nostalgic memory of both sides. According to Gisele Lehrke, it "was hardly a love match, though it was a good partnership that benefited both parties in turn."[83] The marriage helped Andersen gain the economic and political benefits of Swiss citizenship, providing a stable base for her singing career.

Shelton, whose persona was that of the respectable girl next door, negotiated the transition to her postwar career more easily. One of her most striking new hits was Connor's "The Wedding of Lilli Marlene," which he wrote two months after Andersen's marriage.[84] The text described Lilli Marlene's wedding as evoking "tender memories" for "men who'd march where the desert sands are burning / from Tobruk down the road to Alamein."[85] Although the original had hinted at the pain of war, the sentimental wash of the new song, particularly in Shelton's lush 1949 recording, obscured all but the most nostalgic memories.[86]

Shelton built a successful career around this nostalgia and her early appeal to the forces. Touring throughout Europe, the United States, and the Commonwealth, she had a significant following among veterans groups. Active as a performer until her death in 1994, Shelton participated in numerous events commemorating the Second World War, and she continued to be associated closely with "Lilli Marlene."[87] Many accounts, such as the program from the 1975 Glenn Miller Anniversary Concert at Albert Hall, erroneously identified *Introducing Anne* as the program in which she had introduced the song to counteract Nazi propaganda.[88]

Dietrich's postwar reputation rested on more than her wartime singing, but she had to contend with the effects of aging on her career and the decreasing availability of film roles.[89] She filled the gap by turning to her voice, recording albums and acting on radio. In 1953 at the Sahara Hotel in Las Vegas, Dietrich embarked upon a concert career, building upon her wartime USO performances. The press was fascinated by her costume, which Bach described as "the culminating expression of the 'nude dresses' she had worn . . . all through the war."[90] She performed standards, songs from her films, and of course "Lili Marlene." In a 1954 recording, not released until the 1990s, Dietrich declaimed her English translation in a full, deep voice, with a pronounced use of portamento that seemed almost a parody of her style.[91] She toured worldwide until 1975, cementing the relationship between the song and her own legend as "passionately distant, sincerely ironic . . . the deeply German American patriot, the aging and ageless 'Marlene Dietrich.'"[92]

The 1961 film *Judgment at Nuremberg* drew upon Dietrich's close relationship with the song. Made at the height of the Cold War, when the Berlin Wall was being constructed, the film revisited the Nuremberg trials in 1948, when the Allies were addressing the complicity of ordinary Germans with Nazi crimes against humanity. Dominated by courtroom scenes, the film also traced the muted romance between Spencer Tracy's American judge and Dietrich's Madame Bertholt, whose field marshal husband was executed for his role in the Final Solution. Escorting her home after a concert, they hear "Lili Marleen" emanating from a pub. Bertholt/Dietrich hums along for half a verse and then remarks, "I wish you understood German. The words are very beautiful, very sad — much sadder than the English words. The German soldier knows he's going to lose his girl and his life."[93]

Unlike Andersen and Shelton's legacy with the song, which carried in its boundary crossing the hope of mutual understanding — Dietrich's scene pointed to the limits of translation and understanding. During the war, the song expressed romantic longing while also embodying the ambivalence that underlay women's sexualized patriotism. For military authorities, it threatened their forces, not only with its sentimentality, but also with its ability to foster commonality with the enemy, thus humanizing him. As "The Wedding of Lilli Marlene" implied, postwar nostalgia embraced the Desert War precisely because, in a total war that affected both soldiers and civilians, in air raids as well as in genocide, it was a "clean" conflict. "Lili Marlene," as a trophy of that conflict and as wartime romance, helped embody the Second World War in cultural memory as a "good" war.

Notes

I delivered versions of this paper at the 2009 meeting of the Canadian Chapter of the International Association for the Study of Popular Music in Halifax, the Twisted Covers Symposium at the University of Western Ontario, and the 2010 meeting of the Society for American Music in Ottawa, where I received many helpful responses. My thanks to Susan Fast, Kip Pegley, Alana Hudson, and the anonymous reviewers of this volume for their valuable feedback on earlier drafts of this essay. Many thanks as well to that remarkable resource, the BBC Written Archives Centre in Caversham, especially the head archivist Jacquie Kavanagh, for permission to reprint BBC copyright material in this article.

1. Capt. C. F. Milner, Letter to the Editor, Radio Newsreel (copy), September 13, [1942], BBC WAC (British Broadcasting Corporation Written Archives Centre) R27/178.

2. Edgar A. Palmer, ed., *GI Songs: Written, Composed and/or Collected by Men in the Service* (New York: Sheridan House, 1944), 101.

3. Humphrey Jennings (dir.), *The True Story of Lili Marlene* (Ministry of Information, 1944).

4. Johann Holzem, *Der lange Weg zum Ruhm: Lili Marleen und Belgrade 1941* (Meckenheim: Warlich Verlag, 1997), 7; and Carlton Jackson, *The Great Lili* (San Francisco: Strawberry Hill Press, 1979), 86.

5. In Hans Leip's original German, the title was "Lili Marleen," but the spelling was anglicized to "Lili Marlene" or "Lilli Marlene." Here, I will shift the spelling depending on the context.

6. See Carol Muller, "American Musical Surrogacy: A View from Post–World War II South Africa," *Safundi* 7, no. 3 (July 2006): 1–18.

7. Milner, Letter to the Editor (emphasis added).

8. Jackson, *The Great Lili*, 17, 22; see also Gisela Lehrke, *Wie Einst Lili Marleen: Das Leben der Lale Andersen* (Berlin: Henschel Verlag, 2002), 72, 76.

9. John Bierman and Colin Smith, *War without Hate: The Desert Campaign of 1940–1943* (New York: Penguin Books, 2004), 84.

10. See Susan Gubar, "This Is My Rifle, This Is My Gun: World War II and the Blitz on Women," in *Behind the Lines: Gender and the Two World Wars*, ed. Margaret Randolph Higonnet (New Haven, CT: Yale University Press, 1987), 227–59.

11. "Lilli Marlene," BBC Internal Circulating Memorandum (ICM) from Mr. Cecil Madden, Criterion, to DEP, August 8, 1942, BBC WAC R27/178.

12. Ruth Yorck, *Lili Marlene: An Intimate Diary* (New York: Reader's Press, 1945), quoted in Jackson, *The Great Lili*, 36.

13. See Gabriele Czarnowski, "Hereditary and Racial Welfare (*Erb- und Rassenpflege*): The Politics of Sexuality and Reproduction in Nazi Germany," *Social Politics* (Spring 1997): 114–35.

14. Sonya O. Rose, *Which People's War? National Identity and Citizenship in Britain 1939–1945* (Oxford: Oxford University Press, 2003), 90.

15. Rose, *Which People's War?* 79–83.

16. Marilyn E. Hegarty, "Patriot or Prostitute? Sexual Discourses, Print Media, and American Women during World War II." *Journal of Women's History* 10, no. 2 (Summer 1998): 112–36.

17. Milner, Letter to the Editor.

18. Holzem, *Der lange Weg zum Ruhm*, 53; and Bierman and Smith, *War without Hate*, 83–84, 102. According to Holzem, the song was broadcast nightly from May 29, was banned briefly in July by the station director Lieutenant Reintgen, and was brought back on air in a regular program on August 18, following protests from listeners.

19. Quoted in Jackson, *The Great Lili*, 23.

20. Horst J. P. Bergmeier and Ranier E. Lotz, *Hitler's Airwaves: The Inside Story of Nazi Radio Broadcasting and Propaganda Swing* (New Haven, CT: Yale University Press, 1997), 246, n. 5.

21. Jackson, *The Great Lili*, 21.

22. Leip's lyrics and a translation by Frank Petersohn may be viewed at Gordon Brock, "The Official Lili Marleen Page," *20,000 Volkslieder, German and Other Folksongs*, edited by Frank Petersohn, http://ingeb.org/Lieder/lilimarl.html (accessed April 30, 2009).

23. Bergmeier and Lotz, *Hitler's Airwaves*, 187–88; Holzem, *Der lange Weg zum Ruhm*, 53; and Derek Jewell, "Lilli Marlene: A Song for All Armies," in *Alamein and the Desert War*, ed. Derek Jewell (London: Sphere Books, 1967), 148–49.

24. Horst Bergmeier, Ranier Lotz, and Volker Kühn, Liner notes to *Lili Marleen an Allen Fronten: Das Lied, seine Zeit, seine Interpreten, seine Botschaften* (Bear Family Records, BCD 16022 GL, 2005), 44.

25. R. A. Foggin, Letter to W. J. Brown, BBC WAC R27/178.

26. A more literal translation of "schon" would be "already" or "by this time"; the context suggests the intrusion of real time into the romantic idyll between the two sweethearts. "Zapfenstreich" (literally "strike tap," relating to the practice at military camps of sealing up liquor barrels in the evening) can be translated numerous ways, including "taps" and "tattoo." Essentially, it was a series of bugle calls and drum rolls indicating when soldiers were required to return to their barracks. A song evoking Zapfenstreich was highly appropriate for ending Radio Belgrade's broadcasting day. D. J. S. Murray, "Tattoo," *Grove Music Online, Oxford Music Online*, www.oxfordmusiconline.com (accessed April 30, 2009).

27. Lale Andersen, dir. Bruno Seidler-Winkler, "Lied eines jungen Wacht-postens (Lili Marleen)," Electrola EG 6993, 1939 (reissued on compact disc 1 of *Lili Marleen*); and Bergmeier, Lotz, and Kühn, liner notes to *Lili Marleen*, 13. This recording may be heard at "Lale Andersen — Lied eines jungen Wachtpostens

(Lili Marlen)," www.youtube.com/watch?v=r9hW7dMWqjs (accessed April 24, 2009).

28. Quoted by Jackson, *The Great Lili*, 22, 31.

29. Fitzroy Maclean quoted by Bierman and Smith, *War without Hate*, 84; and Milner, Letter to the Editor.

30. Quoted by Jackson, *The Great Lili*, 23.

31. Jackson, *The Great Lili*, 23.

32. Much of the ambiguity seems rooted in the preposition "aus," which can mean "out of" or "from" — meanings that have very different implications in relation to the ground. Is the soldier rising from his bedroll or out of a grave? Bergmeier and Lotz, *Hitler's Airwaves*, 141–43, 188.

33. Jackson, *The Great Lili*, 26.

34. "Lilli Marlene," BBC ICM from African Service Director (J. Grenfell-Williams) to Mr. Godfrey Adams, September 1, 1942, BBC WAC R27/178.

35. Foggin, Letter to Brown.

36. "Attached Letter from Squadron Leader Foggin," BBC ICM from Director of Empire Programmes (S. J. de Lotbiniere) to Mr. Davenport, July 18, 1942, BBC WAC R27/178.

37. "Lilli Marlene," Madden to DEP.

38. "Forces Like the Radio 'Girl Friends,'" *The Evening News* (January 16, 1942), BBC WAC press clippings.

39. "Anti Flabby Entertainment in Empire Programmes," BBC ICM from Mr. Cecil Madden, Criterion, to DEP, March 11, 1942, BBC WAC S24/14.

40. "Sing a Song from London," *Parade* 7, no. 81, Cairo (February 28, 1942): 16.

41. Cecil Madden, "AEF PROGRAMS do something EXTRA for the Boys," BBC WAC S24/54/23.

42. "Pick-Up," "Novel Discs for Your Shelter," *Melody Maker* (September 28, 1940): 9.

43. Madden memoir, BBC WAC S24/54/21; and Christina Baade, *Victory through Harmony: The BBC and Popular Music in World War II* (New York: Oxford University Press, 2012), 160–61.

44. Captain W. M. Mair, Chopel Sultania Infantry, MEF, Letter to Anne Shelton, August 13, 1941, BBC WAC S24/54/9.

45. "Hullo Troops," *Parade* (April 18, 1942): 1, 3.

46. *Introducing Anne*, undated [October 4, 1942], BBC WAC R19/1153/1.

47. Mavis Nicholson, *What Did You Do in the War, Mummy? Women in World War II* (London: Chatto & Windus, 1995), 12.

48. Forces Programmes as Broadcast, October 18, 1942, BBC WAC.

49. "Lili Marlene," Letter from Morris Gilbert to Thomas H. Eliot, June 11, 1943, BBC WAC R27/178.

50. "Anne Shelton," BBC ICM from Mr. Alick Hayes to DEP, October 7, 1942, BBC WAC R19/1153/1.

51. For a fuller discussion of the "crooner ban," see Baade, *Victory through Harmony*, 131–52.

52. Foggin, Letter to Brown.

53. Quoted by Jackson, *The Great Lili*, 77.

54. "Lilli Marlene," BBC ICM from Mr. Gilbert to Mr. Cecil Madden, July 28, 1943, BBC WAC R27/178.

55. According to Lehrke, Andersen also smuggled letters out of the Warsaw Ghetto. Jackson, *The Great Lili*, 29–30; and Lehrke, *Wie Einst Lili Marleen*, 76, 85–89.

56. Bergmeier, Lotz, and Kühn, Liner notes to *Lili Marleen*, 45–46.

57. Bergmeier and Lotz, *Hitler's Airwaves*, 188.

58. Jewell, "Lilli Marlene: A Song for All Armies," 154; and Lehrke, *Wie Einst Lili Marleen*, 93–95.

59. Lehrke, *Wie Einst Lili Marleen*, 96.

60. Jackson, *The Great Lili*, 45, 47.

61. Jackson, *The Great Lili*, 11.

62. Rose, *Which People's War?* 79–80.

63. Quoted by Jewell, "Lilli Marlene: A Song for All Armies," 150.

64. Connor's lyrics may be viewed at Brock, "The Official Lili Marleen Page," http://ingeb.org/Lieder/lilimarl.html (accessed April 30, 2009).

65. Anne Shelton, dir. Stanley Black, "Lilli Marlene," Decca F 8434, 1944 (reissued on compact disc 2 of *Lili Marleen*). This recording may be heard at "Lilli Marlene by Anne Shelton," www.youtube.com/watch?v=7gBCWMseKw8 (accessed August 12, 2011).

66. My thinking here is influenced by Elizabeth Wood's brilliant essay on operatic voices and lesbian desire. See Elizabeth Wood, "Sapphonics," in *Queering the Pitch: The New Gay and Lesbian Musicology*, eds. Philip Brett, Elizabeth Wood, and Gary C. Thomas (New York: Routledge, 1994), 27–66.

67. Jewell, "Lilli Marlene: A Song for All Armies," 150.

68. Steven Bach, *Marlene Dietrich: Life and Legend* (New York: William Morrow, 1992), 290–91.

69. Dietrich's lyrics may be viewed at "Lili Marlene," *International Lyrics Playground*, http://lyricsplayground.com (accessed April 30, 2009).

70. Robert Peters, *For You, Lili Marlene: A Memoir of World War II* (Madison: University of Wisconsin Press, 1995), 65–66.

71. Marlene Dietrich, dir. Charles Magnante, "Lili Marlene," Decca 23456, 1945 (reissued on compact disc 2 of *Lili Marleen*). A much faster-tempo version, sung by Dietrich on a radio program, may be heard at "Marlene Dietrich Lili Marlene

USO Camp," July 16, 1944, www.youtube.com/watch?v=0RxR7e2c2L0 (accessed April 24, 2009).

72. Peters, *For You, Lili Marlene*, 66–67.

73. Central Intelligence Agency, "A Look Back . . . Marlene Dietrich: Singing for a Cause," www.cia.gov/news-information/featured-story-archive/marlene -dietrich.html (accessed December 1, 2008).

74. Marlene Dietrich, dir. Jimmy Carroll, "Lilli Marleen," *Marlene Dietrich Overseas*, Columbia GL 105, 1951 (reissued on compact disc 1 of *Lili Marleen*). This recording may be heard at "Lili Marlene," www.youtube.com/watch?v =MOolUXnAs-U (accessed September 12, 2011).

75. Bach, *Marlene Dietrich: Life and Legend*, 294.

76. Amy Lawrence, "Marlene Dietrich: The Voice as Mask," in *Dietrich Icon*, ed. Gerd Gemünden and Mary R. Desjardins (Durham, NC: Duke University Press, 2007), 85.

77. Jackson, *The Great Lili*, 79, 75.

78. Bergmeier, Lotz, and Kühn, Liner notes to *Lili Marleen*, 102.

79. Major General FHN Davidson, Director of Appeals, Council of Victory (Ex-Services) Club, Letter to Lale Andersen, March 23, 1950, reproduced in ibid., 39.

80. "'Lili Marlene' is here with a song and a mission," *Daily Graphic* ([undated] 1950), reproduced in ibid., 38.

81. Lale Andersen, dir. Walter Baumgartner, "Lili Marleen," Telefunken A 10862, 1949 (reissued on compact disc 1 of *Lili Marleen*); Lale Andersen, dir. Michael Jary, "Lili Marleen," Decca F 49076, 1948 (reissued on compact disc 1 of *Lili Marleen*); and Lale Andersen, dir. Jary, "Lili Marlene," Decca C 16027, 1948 (reissued on compact disc 3 of *Lili Marleen*).

82. Quoted in Jackson, *The Great Lili*, 77.

83. Lehrke, *Wie Einst Lili Marleen*, 100–101, 104. "Eine Liebesheirat war es sicher nicht, aber eine gute Partnerschaft, von der beide zeitweilig profitierten."

84. Lehrke, *Wie Einst Lili Marleen*, 100.

85. The lyrics may be viewed at "The Wedding of Lili Marlene," *International Lyrics Playground*, http://lyricsplayground.com (accessed April 30, 2009).

86. Anne Shelton, dir. Paul Fenoulhet, "The Wedding of Lilli Marlene," Decca F 9148, 1949 (reissued on compact disc 5 of *Lili Marleen*).

87. "Biography," *The Official Anne Shelton Website*, www.anne-shelton.co.uk (accessed December 2, 2008).

88. Program, Glenn Miller Anniversary Concert 1975 at Royal Albert Hall, Tuesday, December 16, 7:30 PM, BBC WAC S24/54/26.

89. Lawrence, "Marlene Dietrich: The Voice as Mask," 95.

90. Bach, *Marlene Dietrich: Life and Legend*, 368.

91. Marlene Dietrich, "Lili Marlene," Columbia/Legacy CK 53209, 1993 (1954) (reissued on compact disc 7 of *Lili Marleen*).

92. Lawrence, "Marlene Dietrich: The Voice as Mask," 98.

93. Stanley Kramer (dir.), *Judgment at Nuremberg* (United Artists, 1961). The scene may be viewed by searching "Marlene Dietrich singing Lili Marlene on Judgment at Nuremberg" on *YouTube.com*.

CHAPTER FOUR

The Changing Sounds of War

Television News Music and Armed Conflicts from Vietnam to Iraq

≫≋≪

JAMES DEAVILLE

It is no longer a matter, as previously, of a tele-audition (the Second World War)
or of a tele-vision (the Vietnam War), but indeed of a true tele-action . . . , the
establishing of the interactivity of the partners in war: those actually making
the war, and those watching it *at the same time as their counterparts.*
— Paul Virilio, *Desert Screen*[1]

Indeed, the constant projection of war scenarios could have created a desire for
war to resolve the situation or to relieve the tension built up by the frenzied
reporting which, especially in CNN's 'Crisis in the Gulf,' merged reports, military
statistics, speculation, music, and images of war into a nightly spectacle that
normalized, and perhaps created a desire for, war.
— Douglas Kellner, *The Persian Gulf TV War*[2]

From their earliest days, moving images have served as the privileged medium for the public representation of armed conflict, from the Spanish-American War of 1898 to the countless military skirmishes and wars of the early twenty-first century. As Paul Virilio has pointedly observed, "war is cinema and cinema is war."[3] That moving images of war are eminently newsworthy as well has repeatedly proven itself in American media over the past century, from newsreel applications of the journalistic dictum "if it bleeds, it leads" to CNN's meteoric rise to preeminence in the field of television news through its slick reporting of the Persian Gulf War of 1991.[4] When we add the sonorous realm — sound effects, music — to the visual representations, a new level of experience results in the audio-viewer:[5] In his classic text *The Theory of Film* from 1960, Siegfried Kracauer makes the following perceptive observation about the addition of aurality to film images:

> Supposing shrill screams or the blasts of an explosion are synchronized with images of their source and/or its environment; much as they will leave their imprint on the spectator's mind, it is unlikely that they will prevent him [*sic*] from taking in the images; rather, they may prompt him to scrutinize the latter in a mood which increases his susceptibility to their multiple meanings.[6]

Unlike Douglas Kellner, Kracauer does not invoke music here as a further enhancement to the audio-viewer's susceptibility to the messages of the moving images. Gilles Deleuze does, however, in his *Cinema 2: The Time-Image* (1985): "All the sound elements, including music, including silence, form a continuum as something which belongs to the visual image [of cinema]."[7]

It is this continuum of sound elements that has figured so prominently in American cinematic and televisual reporting about war since the introduction of sound-on-film technique in the late 1920s (newsreel footage of World War I, for example, was generally not accompanied by sounds other than those of live photoplay music in movie theatres).[8] Theatrical newsreels were able to capture the entire range of diegetic sound and nondiegetic music for World War II; however, by the time of the Korean War, television in the United States had begun to create competition in the "screen" news market. Indeed, for the Truman inauguration in 1949, the "television industry was able to scoop its motion picture competition by a number of hours from New York to Chicago, and with considerably more coverage."[9] Television may not have been ready for the Korean War, but by the time of the Vietnam War, American television news had come of age, whereby historian Daniel Hallin could call Vietnam "the first televised war"[10] and Michael Arlen could use the title *Living Room War* for his early study of the conflict.[11] However, American audio-viewers of today, accustomed to high-concept Hollywood entertainment values in war coverage, tend to find newscast footage from the Vietnam War as "painfully" direct and stark. Obviously, media coverage of war in particular, and newscasting in general, underwent a radical transformation in the years between 1975 and the "first virtual war," the Persian Gulf War of 1991, which — through the coordination on CNN of all production elements in the newscast (titles, graphics, still and moving images, music, diegetic sound, narration, live broadcasting) — created an audio-visual spectacle for the news consumer. This is the hyper-mediated news program that televiewers of the late twentieth and early twenty-first centuries have come to expect in reportage of armed conflict, whether 9/11 and the "War on Terror" (2001) or the "Invasion of Iraq" (2003).

At the time of Vietnam, music had not yet become a partner in the tele-visual reporting of news about war (indeed, about any breaking event), whereas the Persian Gulf War brought music front-and-center into the mediation of conflict in television news. Looking at the national network coverage of these two wars explains and illustrates how music served as a primary agent for the transformation of the American living room into the site for war's "virtual reality," as conceptualized by Virilio.

Early History of Television News Music

Television news began its life in the late 1940s as a transference of the the-atrical newsreel to the small screen. The ten-minute NBC *Camel Newsreel Theater* of 1948 presented Movietone newsreels on television — it was suc-ceeded in 1949 by the fifteen-minute prime-time *Camel News Caravan*, which featured its own stories rather than newsreel footage. These short news programs, as well as comparable programs on CBS, ABC, and Du-Mont networks, involved the use of music for news items in the manner of the theatrical newsreel. Music played less of a role in CBS news of the 1950s, and the arrival of Richard S. Salant as president of the CBS News division in 1961 spelled the end of the practice. The guiding figure behind CBS News until 1979, Salant banned the use of music and sound effects from their news programs, with the intention of keeping the news free from elements of entertainment and thereby maintaining its credibility. This policy was so entrenched that the *CBS Evening News* did not feature a musical theme until 1987, possibly in response to the success of the John Williams theme airing on NBC since 1985. Walter Cronkite's newscasts did exploit the authoritative sound of the teletype, which NBC news producer Reuven Frank pointedly described as "music . . . [that is] no less artificial than the music we were using."[12]

Newsreel-style music also disappeared from ABC and NBC during the late 1950s, with the professionalization of the news during the early 1960s, as marked by the move to a half-hour format in 1963 — the major US television networks barely featured music for their news during the 1960s. The nota-ble exception was NBC, which with its half-hour national newscast begin-ning on September 9, 1963, closed its evening newscast with the first bars from the Scherzo of Beethoven's Ninth Symphony, a decision by network news producer Reuven Frank[13] — this theme remained in use until 1970, when Chet Huntley retired and the network replaced the *Huntley-Brinkley*

Report with the *NBC Nightly News*. ABC's first news theme dates from 1975, and NBC commissioned Henry Mancini in 1977 for an original theme. In general, we can observe that television news directors of the 1960s and early 1970s were skeptical of adding music to the news, fearful of adding "unwelcome emotion and feeling"[14] to what they regarded as the objective reporting of the day's events.

DATES FOR NETWORK ADOPTION OF MAJOR THEMES

ABC: 1975–76, "ABC News Theme" (KPM Music); 1978–98, "World News Tonight Theme" (Bob Israel); 1998–, "World News Tonight" (Edd Kalehoff)

CBS: 1987–91, "Evening News Theme" (Trivers, Myers, Pasqua); 1991–2006, "Evening News Theme" (Patterson, Walz, Fox Music); 2006–2011, "Evening News Theme" (James Horner); 2011–present, "Evening News Theme from 1987–91

CNN: 1983–, "CNN Theme" (Bob Israel)

NBC: 1963–77, "Evening News Close" (Beethoven); 1977–82, "Nightly News Theme" (Mancini); 1985–, "Nightly News Theme" (Williams)

Music and News Coverage of the "First Living Room War"

Andrew Hoskins convincingly argues that structural factors in the frame of news broadcasting at the time were responsible for the character of daily coverage of the "first living room war," the Vietnam War:[15]

> *The "reordering" of the images of war* produced a version that fitted the predominant televisual network form of evening news of 22-and-a-half-minutes. *The news-cycles of this* era were geared around recorded reports edited and simplified to fit a couple of minutes of air time.

Virilio likewise refers to the technologies of television news when he observes how the effect of Vietnam "depended solely upon televised news programmes in deferred time," as compared to the immediacy and twenty-four-hour reporting of news from the operational theatre of the Persian Gulf War in 1991.[16]

Thus the context was not yet right for the "artificial" insertion of music into the diegesis of the evening newscast. Accordingly, we could assert that the entire conflict in Vietnam (between 1959 and 1975) played out in living rooms across North America by and large without the support of music. However, it would be inaccurate to comment that news coverage of the Vietnam War from the 1960s was devoid of all musical underscoring: the Universal Newsreels, which had such an impact on American perceptions of World War II, musically set moving images and narration from the conflict in Southeast Asia until it ceased operations in 1967. The stock music used for their Vietnam coverage harkens back to the style and affect of the music for World War II — both the narration by Ed Herlihy (who began working for Universal Newsreels in the 1940s) and the music itself strike the modern audio-viewer as outdated and excessively dramatic.[17]

For example, the Universal Newsreel from February 28, 1967 — the first item entitled "Viet Sweep — Troops Take Cong Stronghold" — begins with ominous fanfare-like brass and swirling string music under the title, which continues into the report.[18] As we see and hear about the efforts of American soldiers in routing the Viet Cong, the music takes on a more march-like character. This continuous cue of stock martial music accompanies a round-up of Viet Cong sympathizers, the "necessary" burning of the village and the rescuing of innocent women and children, "tragic figures trapped by war." Interestingly, just as Herlihy narrates those final words, the music reaches a triumphant conclusion, as if to underscore the humanitarianism and moral correctness of the American position in the war.

As the Universal Newsreels stopped production later in 1967, so did the sounds of music as nonstop accompaniment for moving images from the Vietnam War. It is necessary to remember that this type of scoring for Vietnam was the only musical setting for news about war that would have been familiar to the American public of the time. Newsreel specialist Raymond Fielding may assert that the newsreels from the mid-1960s had little cinematic presence, but 1,700 theaters in the United States were still showing them as late as 1967.[19]

If Vietnam was the first television war, as repeatedly asserted by media historians, the American audience for television news about that conflict was consuming a product that did not glamorize the conflict. Specialists are unanimous in countering the Pentagon-inspired myth that the media "lost the war," with studies establishing journalistic coverage of Vietnam as following popular opinion and not the reverse,[20] yet in 1967, an estimated 42,850,000 Americans — 20 percent of the total population at the time — saw and heard reports from Vietnam on a nightly basis from the three national networks.

NETWORK EVENING NEWS VIEWERS IN 1967

NBC (Huntley-Brinkley), 200 stations: 18,540,000

CBS (Walter Cronkite), 200 stations: 16,730,000

ABC (Peter Jennings), 160 stations: 7,580,000

Total: 42,850,000[21]

With the half hour in the evening serving as their only source of national television news, audiences were less needful of high-concept entertainment values for them to remain in front of their television sets: with regard to Vietnam, this was the American public's first experience of war on television, and the immediacy and intensity of the report in the evening news (compared with radio and newspaper journalism) helped "bring the audience 'close' to events [of the war]," as Vietnam media historian Daniel Hallin has emphasized.[22] It is true that the television coverage was not the nightly deluge of horrifying images that some observers asserted after the war: actual battle scenes did not appear on any regular basis. However, the very absence of music and other high-concept framing production elements, coupled with reporters' free access to the war arena, lent a liveness and directness to the reporting of troop movements and minor skirmishes.[23] This sense of liveness, of "you-are-there-ness," was aided by the diegetic sounds of war, which might not always include the explosions of weapon fire and bombing raids, but in reports from the field or Saigon would index the reality of battle through the noises of war machinery (tanks, transport trucks, etc.).

This may seem to contradict Virilio's hypothesis about the limitations of (American) televisual coverage of the Vietnam War, playing itself out in "deferred time" and within a rigid structural framework. It is true that news footage from Vietnam experienced time delays because the film needed to be flown to New York or — in the case of urgent news after 1967 — was taken to Tokyo for satellite transmission to New York.[24] However, theory and practice do not always coincide, and in the case of the Vietnam War in American living rooms, audio-viewers were not aware of the mediation behind the reportage from Southeast Asia, which leads Jaramillo to recognize the "relative immediacy of Vietnam War coverage" in comparison with Korea and Iraq.[25] As Rick Berg observes, in comparing radio reporting of World War II and television coverage of Vietnam, "unlike radio, it [i.e., television] did not so much report the war or even dramatize it; rather, TV witnessed the event actually happening."[26]

Given the absence of music in television news during the 1960s, the introduction of music to network coverage of Vietnam on any regular basis might have alienated the visually oriented television news consumers of the late 1960s and early 1970s. For them, photography and television "were seen as having the ability to faithfully reproduce reality, providing a one-to-one correspondence between an event in the world and that event's photographic or filmic depiction,"[27] as observed by sociologist Robert Nideffer. The sense of reality was heightened through the use of hand-held, 16 mm film cameras with sound technology that — according to television historians Donovan and Scherer — "vividly captured conflict."[28] In an extended explanation of how the public could be made to believe the "reality" of the mediated news coverage of Vietnam, Berg also identifies the (moving) image as crucial:

> The photographer's *cinéma vérité* style effaces its technology and intervention, thus translating the production of the "real," the real production, into a "capturing of reality." By means of this TV magic (which conjured up and transmitted the "real" war to the "world"), Vietnam, the war, and the country became for the American viewer a set of transparent signs, signifying at one and the same time "reality" and "Vietnam." They were interlocked, especially when TV's master authorized each evening's fare with his signature — "and that's the way it was."[29]

Inasmuch as network producers privileged the visual in creating the illusion of reality and masking the mediation of the conflict for living room "consumers" of Vietnam, it should not surprise the researcher that music did not figure in newscasting about the war — it had yet to come into its own as an integral component of network news.

In an interesting inversion of early twenty-first-century, Hollywood-mediated expectations of news programming, however, Vietnam-related reports from the home front did regularly feature music, to the extent that the televised reports covered public protests of the war. Americans audio-viewed their evening news with a regular dose of protest songs, whether "Give Peace a Chance," "Where Have All the Flowers Gone?" or even the chant "Hell, No, We Won't Go."[30] Perhaps the most extensive panoply of protest music in Vietnam-era newscasting occurred on the day of the "Moratorium to End the War in Vietnam," October 15, 1969, which was a nationwide day of protest. The entire *NBC Evening News* broadcast consisted of brief reports from fifteen locations across the United States, featuring crowds singing "Give Peace a Chance," "We Shall Overcome," "Let the Sun Shine In" and "Now Peace" in Chicago and suburbs; "Get Together" and "Give Peace a Chance" in Cleveland; and "Now Peace" in New York City. Protesters and networks were both aware of the power of music in the diegesis of the television screen, at a time when, in late 1967, CBS censored Pete Seeger's performance of his song "Waist Deep in the Big Muddy" from the *Smothers Brothers Comedy Hour*.[31] However, at the same time, on-screen singing or chanting lent credibility to newscasts from sites of protest, captured audio-viewers' interest as a departure from the typical "talking heads" of reporting, and served as a tangible manifestation of a protesting group's collective power and agency. Thus it was in the networks' and protesters' interest for the music of dissent (and occasional assent) to resonate — briefly — during the evening news, even though news consumers of the late 1960s may have come to associate music with the peace movement.[32]

To illustrate the sonic realm in television newscasting from the arena of combat, Vietnam, it is worthwhile to examine coverage of the American invasion of Cambodia in April and May of 1970, which bears comparison with that of the Persian Gulf War at the beginning of 1991: this was a breaking news item about a military incursion that was to be "surgical." On April 29, President Nixon authorized the U.S. move into Cambodia — called "Operation Total Victory" — which accounted for about the first ten minutes of the half-hour evening news on ABC, CBS, and NBC (in the same program, they had to cover the findings of the Mary Jo Kopechne inquest, new developments in the Egyptian-Israeli conflict, and escalating student protests).

We can take the coverage on the *NBC Nightly News* program as representative of what the American television news public viewed and heard that evening. The newscast opens with John Chancellor in the studio (no music, or a "cold open"), with the following reports almost exclusively from the studio or Washington, D.C., the news media having been kept in the dark to that point. The coverage of Cambodia consists of seven discrete reports, extending to over eight minutes before the first commercial break, which then introduces the first music into the newscast. Chancellor narrates the news about the invasion in front of a map as the only graphic (a superimposed arrow points to the place where the attack began) — in other words, we observe a straightforward, ostensibly factual reporting that focuses on content. Confronted with this new war front, the American public was required to interpret the development on the basis of what they would perceive as hard news, regardless of the mediation behind it.

For the invasion of Cambodia, there were no special reports, no interruption of commercial breaks, although each network provided a brief analysis of Nixon's broadcast speech on April 30. As Hoskins observed, the principal vehicle for presenting news items — even important breaking news — remained the evening newscast, functioning within its traditional frame for that era: four to six increasingly briefer news segments, alternating with commercial breaks and moving from leading hard news items to commentary and "soft" news at the end. This structure has proven quite durable, persisting up to the present in network evening newscasts — it has provided a sense of normalcy to news consumers, who are unsettled when the sights and sounds of commercials yield to twenty-four-hour coverage for major news events like 9/11 or the onset of the War in Iraq.

When reports from the studio or field did feature images supported by the diegetic sounds of war, they enhanced the experience of the Vietnam War's reality for the audience, creating an alternate soundtrack to the omnipresent spoken word. As Jaramillo posits, "semiotic analysis underscores the signifying powers of visuals *and* sounds — powers that claim an intimate relationship with reality on television news. . . . Diegetic sounds in television news are the keys to journalistic fidelity . . . effectively legitimizing the narrative by making it sound real."[33] John Ellis observed in 1982, shortly after the end of the Vietnam War, that although the televisual image is "simple and straightforward," the news requires sound "as the major carrier of information."[34] Vietnam reportage foregrounded the verisimilitude resulting from the sonic realm by momentarily pausing the narration of anchor or reporter for the diegetic sounds of war. Thus during the *NBC Evening News* on September 12, 1968, Liz Trotta reported from Tay Ninh about military actions against the Viet Cong, pausing during her narration for the audio-viewer to see and hear the sounds of bombers and exploding napalm. This one example multiplies itself over the years of Vietnam coverage, and a recent blog by Adele M. Stan (posted July 19, 2006, on *Tapped: Group Blog of the American Prospect*) well articulates the powerful effect of diegetic sound in making the war come alive in the living rooms of Americans: "Back in the day, we watched the Vietnam War on television, with only the sounds of war to accompany the image. And the heart of a nation was moved."[35]

Since diegetic and nondiegetic music rarely figured in the news from Vietnam, those occasions when it did merit special consideration stand out for audio-viewers of the twenty-first century through the emotional poignancy the musical soundtrack adds. Nondiegetic music accompanied photo or video montages as underscore, while diegetic music was featured in stories about music and the war. The following table lists the most prominent occurrences of music during the later years of the war.[36]

PROMINENT MUSIC IN NETWORK EVENING NEWS REPORTS
FROM VIETNAM, 1968–1975

ABC, December 23, 1968, Saigon, Vietnamese children sing "Silent Night" over images of battle, soldiers

ABC, February 12, 1969, banned Vietnamese pop singer sings protest songs over images of life in Vietnam

CBS, June 19, 1969, Saigon, South Vietnamese government bans sale and playing of illegal (banned) songs

NBC, April 29, 1970, Phnom Penh, funeral for government officials with Cambodian funeral music

CBS, January 20, 1971, Hanoi, film shot by Japanese at "Hanoi Hilton," with POWs singing traditional sacred songs

CBS, February 25, 1971, Saigon, American helicopter pilot writes and sings song for greater military support

ABC, April 6, 1971, Saigon, "Battle Hymn of Lieutenant Calley"

NBC, April 22, 1971, Saigon, Vo Min (cameraman) shows images from Vietnam over traditional music

NBC, April 26, 1971, Saigon, Vietnamese soldier sings popular song over images of war

NBC, May 31, 1971, Saigon, rock concert staged by South Vietnamese army

CBS, October 13, 1971, Binh Dinh Province, South Vietnam musical group sings about war and its destruction

ABC, January 20, 1972, song about POWs written with support of White House

NBC, March 6, 1973, Clark AFB, POW choir sings song

ABC, June 4, 1975, Camp Pendleton, Marine band plays for Vietnamese refugees

Returning to the sonic realm of the invasion of Cambodia, particularly telling is the news report listed above from April 29, 1970, the outbreak of the incursion. NBC correspondent Richard Hunt reported from Phnom Penh about a recent funeral of three Cambodian health workers who were killed by the Viet Cong: we see the procession and ceremony throughout the report, over which Hunt narrates. Remarkable was the news editor's decision to let the sralai (oboe-like instrument) and the suspended barrel drum (the "klang khek") funereal ensemble of Buddhist monks serve as a ghostly underscore,[37] which — in the context of the musical silence of the diegesis at the time — must have been effective in bringing home the human cost of war. Equally powerful are the montages of images from the war or the Vietnamese landscape, which tend to occupy the final position in the newscast that is reserved for human interest stories, so-called "soft news" items.[38] This understated use of diegetic/nondiegetic music to add "heart" to a news report from the Vietnam conflict functions quite differently from the composed war themes and stingers of the Persian Gulf War and the War in Iraq, which sanitized and even glamorized the dark realities of military action, as we shall directly observe.

From Vietnam to the Persian Gulf: Music Enters Newscasting

Virilio, Jaramillo, media observer Danny Schechter,[39] and other commentators on the production elements of television newscasting regard the CNN coverage of the Persian Gulf War of 1991 as the point of initiation for high-concept values in television news during war.[40] A closer look at the evidence from individual newscasts reveals, however, that even as high-concept films emerged in the mid-1970s, so did entertainment values in television news. To that extent, then, Schechter falls into oversimplification when he notes, "It started with the Gulf War — the packaging of news, the graphics, the music, the classification of stories."[41] Examination of network newscasts between 1975 and 1991 reveals that a relatively gradual shift took place over those years, with the news product continually enhanced and refined through the incorporation of "infotainment" features, including effective music, authentic sounds, authoritative voice-overs, eye-popping graphics, riveting still and moving images, quick-paced film edits, and urgent live reporting. It took an enterprising network to put them together in the coverage of a large-scale event, in other words a war, which happened with CNN in 1991 (see below).

A crucial turning point for bringing entertainment values into the evening news occurred in 1985, when NBC hired the quintessential high-concept film composer John Williams to create a signature package of orchestral cues for their evening news. He composed hundreds of cues — from promo beds and bumpers to stingers for various types of news events — in a package called "The Mission," which the network has been mining ever since.[42] The resulting unity among musical elements gave the network's news programs structural coherence, while the consistency over time has helped to create one of the most recognizable brands of news products. Indeed, Williams's traditional, stately theme, replete with the requisite brass fanfares to establish authority and scurrying strings to emulate the teletype and the busy news office, set a standard for ABC, CBS and — above all — CNN.

Music and the Persian Gulf War

With their own music in place by the late 1980s, the four American networks were well along the path toward fully embracing high-concept values in their national newscasts. The Persian Gulf War of 1991 provided the opportunity for CNN to take the final step, which would involve coordinating all production elements — titles, graphics, still and moving images, music, diegetic sound, narration, live broadcasting — around the crisis to create a spectacle that tapped into the audience's experiences with film (and video games).[43]

Indeed, media analysts have tended to compare the CNN coverage of the Persian Gulf War and its coordinated deployment of production elements with such staged forms of entertainment as theatre and cinema — the literature is rife with terms like "spectacle," "staging," and "Hollywood." As Douglas Kellner observed one year after the war's conclusion, CNN coverage "merged reports, military statistics, speculation, music, and images of war into a nightly spectacle."[44] The network's staging of the Persian Gulf War inspired Jean Baudrillard to analyze the unfolding drama in three articles, which he extended in the notorious book *The Gulf War Did Not Take Place* (first published in May 1991).[45] Baudrillard theorized how televisual news outlets like CNN exploited high-concept values in its war coverage to convey "a sense of unreality as we recognised the elements of a Hollywood script which had preceded the real."[46] CNN's twenty-four-hour coverage from the war's outset immersed its enormous base of audio-viewers — its audience increased by 271 percent the night before the war broke out[47] — into Virilio's virtual reality, played out on the television screens of America. In an interview recorded on the eve of "Desert Storm" (January 14, 1991), Virilio recognizes Ted Turner as "constructing the theatre of 'real time,' of the live broadcast that causes us to take as true that which we see live."[48] The audio-viewers of CNN may have interpreted the liveness as true or real, but they were consuming anything but reality: it was infotainment, with a dual purpose beneath the surface rationale of providing a lively news product. On the one hand, public engagement through the exploitation of familiar, high-concept entertainment values ensured CNN remarkable ratings throughout the war, whereby the network emerged as the undisputed leader among television news providers. On the other hand, the CNN package supported a position on the war that marched in lockstep with the Bush administration and the Pentagon.[49] They used the media in general "to mobilize support for the war," revealing themselves as "able to control the flow of images and discourses and thus to manage the TV spectacle of the Gulf War."[50] However CNN's coordinated infotainment practices made it particularly well suited for the possibility of sedating and persuading the American public,[51] for — as Kellner notes — the network "normalized, and perhaps created a desire for, war."[52]

In order to accomplish the goals of establishing its preeminence among news networks and having an influence upon the American (and global) public, CNN's high-concept elements — including effective "war themes" — had to work hard to maintain audio-viewer interest at the war's outset. The Pentagon's initial tight restrictions over media access to the arena of war resulted in what one observer described as "TV war coverage dominated by talking heads: network anchors, correspondents, and a succession of military analysts endlessly discussing the action that could not be shown."[53] This helps to explain why CNN's televisual frame drew such special attention from media observers and cultural theorists, since it was the network that most effectively overcame those limitations of access. After all, "CNN had cameras and reporters in Baghdad throughout the war, a large crew in Israel, and live coverage of all U.S. military and government press conferences. Thus its images, discourses, and material tended to shape global coverage of the event."[54]

The other networks simply could not compete, since they had neither the field reporters nor the available air time to satisfy the American public. Moreover, CNN already had an edge long before the first bombing raids: within two weeks of Iraq's invasion of Kuwait on August 2, 1990, the network began a nightly one-hour special report at 7:00 PM replete with music, graphics, and live reporting under the logo "Crisis in the Gulf." It was this daily news feature that gave CNN the advantage later on, for already the American public was being regaled with a steady stream of military images and accompanying graphics, supported by music. By September the program fell into a consistent format, opening with images of marching American and Iraqi soldiers accompanied by a martial theme with chimes, and often closing with shots of Saddam Hussein and Iraqi soldiers marching to military music. Such parting sounds and images "left the spectators with a notion of the threat to 'the American way of life' posed by the Iraqi army."[55]

Thus the production elements of CNN's staging of the Persian Gulf War were significantly aided by music that was carefully chosen for its effect.[56] Music's suasive potential was tapped as it was made complicit in the public relations campaign of media, government, and military: each network had special music in place for its newscasts that aired once the hostilities began on January 16, 1991. The three established American networks — ABC, CBS, NBC — used "militarized" variants of their branding themes throughout the intervention, but only in sporadic special reports rather than in the evening news itself. In contrast, CNN featured striking, newly composed music as an integral part of its multimedia mix — this aspect of its coverage is so important that Kellner, who almost never mentions music in his own analyses of the 1991 war, had to recognize its role in CNN's engagement of the American news audience: "The Gulf war was packaged as an aesthetic spectacle, with CNN utilizing powerful drum music to introduce their news segments, superimposing images of the U.S. flag over American troops, and employing up-beat martial music between breaks. The audience was thus invited to participate in a dazzling war spectacle by its media presentation."[57]

CNN was only able to use selected musical production elements, due to its twenty-four-hour, commercial-free war coverage — they had no need for bumpers, for example. However, the "war themes" and stingers of CNN are striking, clearly crafted to produce the greatest effectiveness. Investigative reports and reviews of music critics may not exist for the music of the

Persian Gulf War like they do for the 2003 War in Iraq,[58] yet at least the researcher can access the specific CNN newscasts and their production elements for musical analysis.[59]

One CNN war stinger — probably by noted production element composer Bob Israel[60] — stands out in particular. Initially aired on January 18, this five-second, music-text-image production element subliminally communicates the message that everyone wanted to hear at that time: we can win this war and exorcise the demons of Vietnam.[61] In that stinger, we experience a timpani triplet anacrusis (not coincidentally reminiscent of the opening of Beethoven's Fifth Symphony) against the graphic of the CNN logo, which morphs into the title "War in the Gulf" over a decrescendo timpani roll. The very simplicity of the music creates a believable conflict, which we win through CNN with an authentic cadence. These four notes, in that particular rhythmic pattern, melodic contour, and timbre, tap into what Philip Tagg would call the "martial" synoptic classification.[62] In other words, the audio-viewer would decode this specific phrase, working in conjunction with the image and graphic, as a representation of military action, based upon a lifetime of associations from music and film/television. The news consumer would not have to identify the music as specifically alluding to the World War II appropriation of the first four notes of Beethoven's Fifth Symphony in order for it to have its effect:[63] a more general recognition of the music's "martiality" would suffice when observed with the other production elements. Indeed, Tagg (among others) regards music in film and television as inseparably connected to its communicative function.[64] In the case of the CNN stinger, this means that identifying the music as sounding warlike and as arriving at a satisfying close (V–I cadence), against the words "War in the Gulf" that come into focus, could lead to the perception of the stinger as signifying armed victory over Iraq. As Kellner argues, networks exploited such identifications to mobilize pro-war consensus[65] — and the "invisible" music enabled this to occur without making the audio-viewer aware of any manipulation.[66]

At times the attempts at persuasion were not so subtle. For example, on February 15, 1991, CNN aired a favorable story about the "new patriotism" during the 6:00 and 10:00 PM newscasts. The feature showed images of flags flying across America superimposed over portraits of George H. W. Bush, accompanied by the 1988 campaign song for the Republican Party, "This Land Is Your Land" by (socialist) Woody Guthrie. Here again music is complicit in selling the news story and CNN's particular take on it to a compliant American public, who are encouraged to believe that supporting the war is their patriotic duty. In a curious inversion of normal practice, the song more precisely articulates the meanings of the images, making clear the connection between the display of flags and the country: support of the war effort and of the soldiers is an act of upholding American liberties. Moreover, the musical reference to George Bush and the Republican Party adds a further layer of signification, inviting — perhaps even compelling — the news consumer to associate him (and his war) with American patriotism. The logic behind these linkages may be thoroughly flawed, yet seeing and hearing is believing, especially when the public has already been immersed for one month in the virtual reality of war for a "just cause."

The traditional networks (ABC, CBS, and NBC) were caught "with their music down" in 1991, at least in comparison with the wildly successful upstart CNN, but they would all be set for another major military crisis. Since the four-day bombing raid on Iraq in December 1998 (Operation Desert Fox) did not escalate, one could say that the networks anticipated the outbreak of true and prolonged war in Iraq in late March 2003, to test out the music they had commissioned weeks or months earlier. The disturbing comments of news producers and production element composers certainly make it clear that they intended for the war music to tap into a mood of hostility within the American public.[67]

Final Remarks

In her 1994 essay "Kicking the Vietnam Syndrome: CNN's and CBS's Video Narratives of the Persian Gulf War," Michelle Kendrick analyzes the CNN documentary video *Desert Storm: The Victory* (released on May 15, 1991), which introduced news footage from the Vietnam War in response to Norman Schwarzkopf's (in)famous dictum of January 1991 that "this [i.e., the Persian Gulf War] is not going to be another Vietnam." She observes,

> The nightmarish quality of the grainy black-and-white footage [from Vietnam], further enhanced in slow motion, sharply contrasts with the bright, sunlit expanses of the Persian Gulf War footage. . . . In fact, this particular scene, accompanied by somber music, portrays the Vietnam War . . . as an utterly mysterious event, which was the site for physical pain and existential anguish. The viewer can then juxtapose these images with the clarity of the Persian Gulf War, as it is exemplified both rhetorically, in the video reiterations of the allies' clear, morally unambiguous purpose for fighting, and aesthetically, in the splendor and beauty of the sunlit desert scene.[68]

Here we again encounter Virilio's distinction between a "tele-vision" (Vietnam) and a "true tele-action" (Persian Gulf War), as played out by the media. Of course, CNN's representation of the earlier armed conflict is intended to demonstrate not only advances in media's improved ability to report on war, but also to herald America's "improved" moral position in the Gulf War, with music/sound exploited to do its surreptitious work for both conflicts (the sunlit desert scene is not without its own appropriate soundscape). It stands to reason that the "documentary" would render the network's own position invisible in its sanitized restaging of the Gulf War, as did the war retrospective of CBS, ominously titled *Desert Triumph* (1991).

It is clear that music's role in reporting war exponentially developed from the "silence of the frames" in Vietnam coverage, from the extraordinary, humanizing agent in television broadcasting of conflict, to the normalized, dehumanizing component of newscasting in armed engagements, beginning with the Persian Gulf War. We observed how the mobilization of music in wartime news helped change the reality of war in our living rooms into a perverse spectacle for the eye and ear. This simulation has played itself out in homes across the country in ever greater sophistication for the coverage of 9/11, the War in Iraq, and the ongoing War in Afghanistan, as news networks have introduced more advanced technologies — for increasing "reality" — in order to maintain market share. Still, although traditional network newscasting has begun to lose its audience to alternative news programming on television (e.g., *Countdown with Keith Olbermann*, *The Daily Show*, *The Colbert Report*) and to news websites (including those for the networks), it seems likely that television, with the increasing dimensions of screens and the improving quality of images and sound, will remain the chosen medium for war. The improved realism afforded by technological innovations applied to news reporting can always be further enhanced for news consumers to "enjoy"/consume what Edmund Burke and others have described as "the horrid sublimity of war."[69] One potential example would involve soldiers broadcasting video and sound from actual battlefields with added music tracks, which is not unlike the daily experiences of millions of gamers through such conflict-based screen entertainment as *Red Alert* or *World of Warcraft*.

Much work remains to be undertaken regarding the function of music in media representations of armed conflict. In his groundbreaking study *Sound Targets: American Soldiers and Music in the Iraq War*, Jonathan Pieslak conducted an ethnographic investigation of listening and performing practices among soldiers, which includes a detailed examination of recruiting videos from both sides of the conflict.[70] Comparing such videos and their overt reliance upon ideology-driven music with televisual war reportage that also features nondiegetic music/diegetic sound (special reports, ads for war coverage, and the like) would help to uncover technological and psychological mechanisms for music's complicity in media propaganda. At the same time, controlled testing of audio-viewers regarding the efficacy of network war themes would assist in identifying the actual responses to and effects of music used in television's coverage of armed conflict. Other topics for further study include music used for war reporting by local television stations, the possible interconnections with radio coverage of conflict, and the influence of video games upon all of this.[71] Working with this material may well depress the scholar, and yet as Philip Tagg has observed, one of our responsibilities is "to diminish the risks of musical manipulation."[72] If we can accomplish that for our colleagues, students, and (hopefully) the general public with regard to the subliminal messages of wartime news music, we may just have some impact upon the cause of peace.

Glossary of Terms for Musical Production Elements in Television[73]

Opens, Closes, Titles, Themes, Jingles: Longer theme that identifies the newscast and provides musical material for the rest of the broadcast. Typically fanfare-like, quick, syncopated in brass and strings, over a driving beat. Establishes impression of dynamic newsroom and authority of the newscast.

Stinger, Tease: Very brief musical and visual marker for an important, long-term news item. Announces item to follow and helps create attitude about item within viewer. Image and music closely correspond. The most original and freest musical production element.

(Promo) Beds: Framing and background music for extensions of opens. Loops are used to accommodate texts and images of variable lengths.

Bumpers: Musical lead-ins to and lead-outs from commercials. Create mood and attitude for upcoming news item. Widely differ within one broadcast.

Lazers, Sparkles, Sweeps, Whooshes: Descriptive names for special sound effects used in production music elements.

Notes

I am grateful to the Social Sciences and Humanities Research Council of Canada for a seed grant (administered through Carleton University), which has supported this research. For their insights and comments along the way, I especially thank Kathy McKinley (Carleton University), Martin Daughtry (New York University), Jonathan Pieslak (City University of New York), Kip Pegley (Queen's University), Susan Fast (McMaster University) and James Buhler (University of Texas). The Television News Archive at Vanderbilt University and its director, John Lynch, have been extremely helpful by allowing me to search and copy relevant network news footage.

1. Paul Virilio, *Desert Screen: War at the Speed of Light*, trans. Michael Degener (London: Continuum, 2002), 56.

2. Douglas Kellner, *The Persian Gulf TV War* (Boulder, CO: Westview Press, 1992), 88.

3. Paul Virilio, *War and Cinema: The Logistics of Perception*, trans. Patrick Camiller (London: Verso, 1989), 26.

4. It should be noted that this progression played itself out specifically in the news media of the United States, which is the focus of this essay. The move toward news as "infotainment" could only have taken place in America of the twentieth century, as a result of the powerful influences from Hollywood and from corporate interests upon all media in the United States. See Bonnie M. Anderson, *News Flash: Journalism, Infotainment and the Bottom-Line Business of Broadcast News* (San Francisco: Jossey-Bass, 2004), for a detailed historical account of the corporatization of American network newscasting.

5. Michel Chion introduced the terms "audio-vision" and "audio-viewer" to the discussion of film music — I find them eminently suitable for describing the consumption of television music as well. See Michel Chion, *Audio-Vision: Sound on Screen*, trans. Claudia Gorbman (New York: Columbia University Press, 1994), passim.

6. Siegfried Kracauer, *Theory of Film: The Redemption of Physical Reality* (New York: Oxford University Press, 1960), 127–28.

7. Gilles Deleuze, *Cinema 2: The Time-Image*, trans. Hugh Tomlinson and Robert Galeta (London: Continuum, 2005), 231.

8. See Raymond Fielding, *The American Newsreel: A Complete History, 1911–1967*, 2nd ed. (Jefferson, NC: McFarland and Company, 2006), 63–76, for an extended account of newsreels during the First World War.

9. Fielding, *The American Newsreel*, 192.

10. Daniel C. Hallin, *The "Uncensored War": The Media and Vietnam* (New York: Oxford University Press, 1986), 6

11. Michael J. Arlen, *Living-Room War* (New York: Viking, 1969). Arlen was the television critic for the *New Yorker*, and this book is a collection of his contributions to the magazine from the 1960s.

12. Nicholas Engstrom, "The Soundtrack for War," *Columbia Journalism Review* 42, no. 1 (2003): 45.

13. Engstrom, "The Soundtrack for War," 45. The network used the Beethoven theme into the 2000s on MSNBC, especially in the opening music to *Countdown with Keith Olbermann* (since 2003).

14. Deborah Lynn Jaramillo, "Ugly War, Pretty Package: How the Cable News Network and the Fox News Channel Made the 2003 Invasion of Iraq High

Concept" (PhD diss., University of Texas, 2006), 150. Jaramillo condensed her dissertation in preparing it for publication, thereby omitting or rewriting certain passages.

15. During the Korean War, television was still in its infancy and news programming was limited to the aforementioned newsreel-style reports, which had the subliminal effect of bringing the televisual audio-viewer into the movie theatre.

16. Virilio, *Desert Screen*, 52.

17. The literature about newsreels consistently establishes how important entertainment values were for bringing the news within the context of the cinematic theatre. See, for example, Ray Edmondson, "The Voice of Australia: *Cinesound Review." Metro: Media & Education Magazine* 137 (2003): 138–40.

18. "Viet Sweep. Troops Take Cong Stronghold, 1967/02/28 (1967)." The newsreel is available online in the Internet Archive collection of Universal Newsreels at www.archive.org/details/1967-02-28_Viet_Sweep (accessed February 7, 2009).

19. Fielding, *The American Newsreel*, 193.

20. See above all Hallin, *The "Uncensored War*," which was the first academic study to challenge those assertions. Other scholars who have confirmed Hallin's findings include William M. Hammond, *Reporting Vietnam: Media and Military at War* (Lawrence: University Press of Kansas, 1998), and Melvin Small, *Covering Dissent: The Media and the Anti-Vietnam War Movement* (New Brunswick, NJ: Rutgers University Press, 1994).

21. William A. Wood, *Electronic Journalism* (New York: Columbia University Press, 1967), 36.

22. Hallin, *The "Uncensored War*," 196.

23. Television networks and stations boldly trumpeted their "embedded reporters" during the first days of the 2003 War in Iraq, yet the practice of having reporters accompany soldiers on missions began in Vietnam, with television journalists like Dan Rather and Liz Trotta.

24. Jaramillo, "Ugly War, Pretty Package," 21–22.

25. Jaramillo, "Ugly War, Pretty Package," 22.

26. Rick Berg, "Losing Vietnam: Covering the War in an Age of Technology," in *The Vietnam War and American Culture*, eds. John Carlos Rowe and Rick Berg (New York: Columbia University Press, 1999), 118.

27. Robert Nideffer, "Bodies, No-bodies, and Anti-bodies at War: Operation Desert Storm and the Politics of the 'Real'" (PhD diss., University of California at Santa Barbara, 1994), http://proxy.arts.uci.edu/~nideffer/BNAatWAR/ (accessed February 7, 2009). The Vietnam War generated a number of photographic images that seemed to symbolize the war and its realities, whether the self-immolation of Buddhist monk Thich Quang Doc (1963), or South Vietnamese General Nguyen Ngoc Loan executing a Viet Cong prisoner (1968), or ten-year-old Phan Thim

Kim Phuc running in terror from a village after a napalm attack (1972). See Andrew Wiest, *Rolling Thunder in a Gentle Land: The Vietnam War Revisited* (New York: Osprey Publishing, 2006), for reproductions of these and other iconic images from Vietnam, some of which won awards for the photographers.

28. Robert J. Donovan and Ray Scherer, *Unsilent Revolution: Television News and American Public Life, 1948–1991* (Cambridge: Cambridge University Press, 1992), 86.

29. Berg, "Losing Vietnam," 119.

30. For a brief introduction to these and other such songs, see H. Ben Auslander, "'If Ya Wanna End War and Stuff, You Gotta Sing Loud': A Survey of Vietnam-Related Protest Music," in *American Popular Music: Readings from the Popular Press*, Volume 2: *The Age of Rock*, ed. Timothy Scheurer (Madison, WI: Popular Press, 1990), 179–84.

31. Public reaction was so strong that CBS allowed Seeger to sing it on the show in January of 1968. See Bert Spector, "A Clash of Cultures: The Smothers Brothers vs. CBS Television," in *American History, American Television*, ed. John E. O'Connor (New York: Frederick Ungar, 1983) and Aniko Bodroghkozy, "*The Smothers Brothers Comedy Hour* and the Youth Rebellion," in *The Revolution Wasn't Televised: Sixties Television and Social Conflict*, ed. Lynn Spigel and Michael Curtin (New York: Routledge, 1997), 201–20.

32. This speculation about the American public's association of music with peace in the late 1960s, as reinforced if not established by daily newscasts, merits further investigation.

33. Jaramillo, "Ugly War, Pretty Package," 148, 158.

34. John Ellis, "Broadcast TV as Sound and Image," (1982) in *Film Theory and Criticism: Introductory Readings*, ed. Leo Braudy and Marshall Cohen, 5th ed. (New York: Oxford University Press, 1999), 386–87.

35. Adele M. Stan, "War Porn with a Beat," *Tapped: The Group Blog of the American Prospect* (July 19, 2006) www.prospect.org (accessed February 7, 2009).

36. The Vanderbilt Television News Archive maintains virtually complete videotapes or digital files for the three daily network newscasts from September 1968 through the end of the war in 1975.

37. I am grateful to Kathy McKinley of Carleton University — specialist for Cambodian music — who helped me with identifying the style and instruments.

38. It is interesting to observe the prominence assigned to music in the 1970 Christmas video from the "Hanoi Hilton." The role of music in videos that attempt to humanize the portrayed conditions of prisoners, whether in Hanoi or in Tehran (December 1979), awaits investigation.

39. See especially Schechter's books that analyzed the media coverage of the 2003 Invasion of Iraq: *Embedded: Weapons of Mass Deception: How the Media Failed to Cover the War in Iraq* (Amherst, NY: Prometheus Books, 2003); *Media Wars:*

News at a Time of Terror (Lanham, MD: Rowman & Littlefield, 2003), and *When News Lies: Media Complicity and the Iraq War* (New York: Select Books, 2006).

40. "High-concept" here refers to a cinematic style and marketing strategy that have been associated with "blockbuster" films since the mid-1970s. See Jaramillo, "Ugly War, Pretty Package," 22–26, for an extended discussion of the components of high-concept film.

41. Interview with Danny Schechter, cited by Janny Scott, "The President Under Fire: The Media; A Media Race Enters Waters Still Uncharted," *New York Times*, February 1, 1998, Late Edition — Final, Section 1:1, www.nytimes.com (accessed February 7, 2009).

42. Over the intervening years, NBC and Williams have made some modifications to the theme and other elements of the package, also changing their positions and roles within the newscasts, but the musical substance has remained the same.

43. The connection between video games and television coverage of war has not been established in any definitive manner, whether through theoretical or empirical studies, but James Der Derian does make an attempt in *Virtuous War: Mapping the Military-Industrial-Media-Entertainment Network* (Boulder, CO: Westview Press, 2001).

44. Kellner, *The Persian Gulf TV War*, 88.

45. The three articles appeared at different stages of the war: before — "La Guerre du Golfe n'aura pas eu lieu," *Libération* (January 4, 1991): 5; during — "La Guerre du Golfe a-t-elle vraiment lieu?" *Libération* (February 6, 1991): 10; and after — "La Guerre du Golfe n'a pas eu lieu," *Libération* (March 29, 1991): 6. The book itself was entitled after the final article: *La Guerre du Golfe n'a pas eu lieu* (Paris: Galilée, 1991).

46. Baudrillard, *The Gulf War Did Not Take Place*, trans. Paul Patton (Bloomington: Indiana University Press, 1995), 2.

47. Kellner, *The Persian Gulf TV War*, 141.

48. Virilio, *Desert Screen*, 41.

49. Kellner presents CNN as adopting a pro-war position from August of 1990, illustrating for example how Wolf Blitzer "emerged . . . as the most compliant and naïve Pentagon disinformation tool among the military reporters" (*The Persian Gulf TV War*, 118).

50. Douglas Kellner, "The Persian Gulf War Revisited" (long version). http://pages.gseis.ucla.edu/faculty/kellner/papers/gulfwarrevisited.htm (accessed February 7, 2009).

51. See Daya Kishan Thussu, *News as Entertainment: The Rise of Global Infotainment* (London: Sage, 2007), for a discussion of the propaganda uses of infotainment. Particularly valuable is his elaboration of Jacques Ellul's "propaganda of integration."

52. Kellner, *The Persian Gulf TV War*, 88.

53. Ken Tucker, "Talk, Then Action: Summing Up the Persian Gulf War Coverage," *Entertainment Weekly* 57 (March 15, 1991). www.ew.com/ew/article/0,,313645,00.html (accessed February 7, 2009). The ground war did not begin until February 24, so the only combat action on television screens for the first month was the air campaign, which significantly limited the television sights and sounds of the early days of the conflict.

54. Douglas Kellner, "The Persian Gulf War Revisited," in Reporting War: Journalism in Wartime, ed. Stuart Allan and Barbie Zelizer (New York: Routledge, 2004), 136. The editors must have rather severely edited the essay for publication, for Kellner's personal website features a substantially longer version (without comment). See "The Persian Gulf War Revisited" (long version).

55. Kellner, *The Persian Gulf TV War*, 87.

56. Information regarding the composers of special music for the Persian Gulf War has not surfaced as it has for the War in Iraq of 2003, even though the intervention of January 1991 was long anticipated (at least since Iraq's invasion of Kuwait in August of 1990).

57. Kellner, "The Persian Gulf War Revisited" (long version).

58. See James Deaville, "Selling the War in Iraq: Television News Music and the Shaping of American Public Opinion." *Echo: A Music-Centered Journal* 8 no. 1 (2006) www.echo.ucla.edu/Volume8-Issue1/roundtable/deaville.html (accessed February 7, 2009) for an investigation of the reviews and reports about the media (mis)appropriation of music to support their positions about the 2003 conflict. This interest in the "musicality" of news coverage of the war — primarily in print sources (newspapers, journals) — may have resulted from a heightened awareness of high-concept war reporting after the many studies of the media and the Persian Gulf War.

59. In the early 1990s, the Television News Archive did not yet tape CNN on any regular basis except for a crisis situation like the Persian Gulf War, for which the archive preserved the twenty-four-hour coverage from January 16 through March 4, 1991.

60. Writing in *Slate*, Adam Baer implies that Bob Israel and his Score Productions composed war themes for CNN. See Baer, "The Sounds of War: Rating the Networks' Theme Music," *Slate* (April 17, 2003), www.slate.com/id/2081608 (accessed February 7, 2009).

61. Among other authors, Douglas Kellner juxtaposes the Vietnam War and Persian Gulf War under the sign of postmodernity, in his insightful essay "From Vietnam to the Gulf: Postmodern Wars?" in *The Vietnam War and Postmodernity*, ed. Michael Bibby, (Amherst: University of Massachusetts Press, 2000), 173–98.

62. Philip Tagg, "An Anthropology of Stereotypes in TV Music?" *Svensk Tidskrift för Musikforskning* 71 (1989): 24–25.

63. The Morse code rhythmic pattern for the letter "V" (for victory) is the same as the first four notes of Beethoven's Fifth Symphony: the musical motive was appropriated by the Allies during World War II to symbolize victory.

64. Philip Tagg, "Music, Moving Images, Semiotics, and the Democratic Right to Know," in *Music and Manipulation: On the Social Uses and Social Control of Music*, ed. Steven Brown and Ulrik Volgsten (New York: Berghahn Books, 2006), 171.

65. Kellner, "The Persian Gulf War Revisited" (long version).

66. Kellner, "The Persian Gulf War Revisited" (long version), passim.

67. Deaville, "Selling the War in Iraq."

68. Michelle Kendrick, "Kicking the Vietnam Syndrome: CNN's and CBS's Video Narratives of the Persian Gulf War," in *Seeing through the Media: The Persian Gulf War*, ed. Susan Jeffords and Lauren Rabinovitz (New Brunswick, NJ: Rutgers University Press, 1994), 66.

69. James Dack, "Sacred Music," in *The Cambridge Companion to Haydn*, ed. Caryl Clark (Cambridge: Cambridge University Press, 2005), 148.

70. Pieslak, *Sound Targets: American Soldiers and Music in the Iraq War* (Bloomington: Indiana University Press, 2009), 16–44 and 58–77.

71. Pieslak himself devotes only one page (39) to the possible role of video games in shaping soldier listening practices.

72. Tagg, "Music, Moving Images," 183.

73. The glossary presents the most standard descriptions for the terms, but alternate definitions do exist for them as well.

PART II

≫

Violence and

Reconciliation

≫

In chapter 5, David McDonald introduces us to the second theme of the book: music, violence, and reconciliation. McDonald analyzes the music of several influential Palestinian performers from the time of the al-Aqsa intifada (2002–2006) and reveals the complex and diverse strategies that allowed artists to challenge the oppression of occupation and imagine new ways of what it means to be Palestinian. Importantly, McDonald challenges seeing identity as static, or homogeneous, inviting us instead to see it as multifaceted and complex. His interest in disarticulating their voices "leads to a more nuanced understanding of Palestinian identity, in effect, empowering diverse voices, experiences, and beliefs against rampant Orientalist and Islamophobic depictions of Arabic culture in mainstream corporate media." Indeed, this homogenization of Arabs is not only particular to corporate media (and, in turn, internalized by the viewing public) but is also a significant problem within the realm of the political. Since 9/11, for instance, the homogenization of Arabs — to say nothing of the inaccurate conflation of "Arab" with "Muslim" — has been particularly rampant within the U.S. military. A 2004 article in *The Guardian*, for instance, reported that Raphael Patai's text *The Arab Mind* (1973) is "probably the single most popular and widely read book on Arabs in the US military." Moreover, this "bible of the neocons on Arab behavior"[1] is also used as a textbook for officers at the warfare school at Fort Bragg, North Carolina. [2] While this text has been heavily criticized for its overt racism, its use within the American military, author Brian Whitaker explains, is in part due to its lack of academic jargon, its simple and readily digested (read: ugly) stereotypes, and sexualized material (this latter content was used as background reading on how to effectively torture Iraqi prisoners). That such a reductionist text of Arabs is used as a reference book by the world's most powerful military force increases the importance of writings like McDonald's that allow readers to learn about Palestinians' complex and changing identities through their heterogeneous — and sometimes internally dissonant — cultural articulations.

In chapter 6, Victor Vicente explores how the musical, poetic, and ritualistic practices of Islamic mysticism are being used to help bridge relations between Muslim and Western worlds. By exploring three Sufi performance practices in Turkey, an Islamic country that desires stronger connections with the European Union, Vicente argues that collective trancing, dancing, and music making serve as a reconciliatory gesture between Islam and the West. Like the Palestinian artists that McDonald describes in the previous chapter, however, Vicente here too exposes a community — similarly viewed by the West as undifferentiated and militant — to be heterogeneous, moderate, and with the internal struggles over self-definition that are faced by most communities.

In chapter 7, Kevin Miller explores how, in 2005, during Fiji's inter-coup period (2000–2006), the government strove to present Fiji as a harmonious nation, ideal for foreign consumption. Accordingly, two groups — long stereotyped as factions unfriendly toward one another — were presented as culturally cooperative: the Indigenous Fijians, who comprise a slight majority of the country's peoples, and the Indo-Fijians, who descended from nineteenth- and twentieth-century laborers brought to the country from India. In order to make their new partnership palatable for tourist consumption, the government offered cooperative and peaceful "multicultural" dance performances, which, as Miller shows on closer reading, served once again to perpetuate symbolic violence by reinforcing Fijian dominance and authority. Far from the spotlight and the public eye, however, Miller documents a second representation of Fijian musicality that contests the first: Indigenous Fijian crossover singers who specialize in Indo-Fijian Hindi folksongs. Unlike Baker's earlier example of Croatians rerecording songs made famous by Croatians-turned-Serbs in an attempt to sever ties with Serbian identity, here Indigenous Fijians reach toward their alienated cohort in a form of grassroots reconciliation, giving a new — and more genuine — notion of cultural exchange.

Notes

1. Seymour Hersh, "The Gray Zone: How a Secret Pentagon Program Came to Abu Ghraib," *New Yorker*, May 24, 2004, www.newyorker.com.

2. Brian Whitaker, "'Its Best Use Is as a Doorstop,'" *Guardian*, May 24, 2004, www.guardian.co.uk (accessed November 20, 2011).

CHAPTER FIVE

Revivals and New Arrivals

Protest Song in the Al-Aqsa Intifada

DAVID A. MCDONALD

I will plant a rose for you [Jenin] in my heart, and my blood will be its water. . . .
I will keep my word. I am a wave, and your stones are the sea of my tides.
— "We Are Not Afraid of You, Occupier," as performed by Mais Shalash

Operation Defensive Shield, Jenin 2002

Tanks and troops had begun to arrive around 7:00 PM, April 2, 2002, posi-
tioning themselves adjacent to Jenin's Arabeh and Salem neighborhoods.
By 2:00 AM the shelling began. Tanks and heavy artillery bombarded the
city from the north, south, and west, while Israeli ground troops entered
from the east, taking up tactical positions among the houses, apartment
buildings, and mosques. This massive and thoroughly planned military offensive, named Operation Defensive Shield (ODS), came in response to the
March 27 Hamas-directed suicide bombing of Netanya's Park Hotel, which
resulted in the deaths of twenty-eight Israelis celebrating their Passover
meal. Emboldened by the highly publicized suicide attack, then prime minister Ariel Sharon oversaw the invasion of every major city, refugee camp,
and village in the West Bank. While the cities of Ramallah, Bethlehem, and
Nablus were each placed under prolonged curfew, the most intense fighting took place in Jenin, considered to be the center of the West Bank resistance movement.

Within seventy-two hours the city was secured, with all access in and out
of the refugee camp blocked. Attack helicopters then provided cover as a
dozen heavily armored Caterpillar D-9 bulldozers set to work leveling Jurit

129

al-Dahab, Sumran, Damaj, Sahah, and Hawashin neighborhoods, leaving an estimated four thousand residents immediately homeless.[1] Reports quickly emerged that the demolishing of these neighborhoods was undertaken without regard to the many residents still inside.[2] Entire families were reported missing, assumed buried underneath their demolished homes. House-to-house fighting then continued for nearly two weeks, as residents who were able to escape reported a "massacre" of decomposing bodies and wounded left in the streets, prevented from receiving medical care.[3]

With aid workers, journalists, and international observers prohibited from entering the camp following the end of the invasion, precise data on the full extent of the destruction (deaths, injuries, and property damage) has been impossible to credibly ascertain. Official Israeli government reports list fifty-six Palestinians and twenty-three Israeli soldiers dead. However, camp residents and international aid workers estimate the number to be much higher. In the aftermath, the United Nations, Amnesty International, Human Rights Watch, and a host of other independent humanitarian organizations have each presented findings on the invasion, some accusing Israel of war crimes and a wanton disregard for human life in their two-week bombardment of the refugee camp.[4]

Upon my initial arrival in Jordan in May 2002 the echoes of the Jenin invasion, and the larger Operation Defensive Shield of which it was a central part, reverberated throughout the region. Scenes of horrific devastation and human loss broadcast continuously across the Arab mediascape for months following the invasion, eliciting a powerful cultural response. In Jordan, where a large majority of its 5.5 million inhabitants are Palestinian refugees and/or their descendants, nationalist activity reached a fever pitch. Throughout its many diverse neighborhoods signs of the intifada flooded the city. Downtown shopkeepers, customers, and passersby would huddle tightly around small television sets in myriad coffee shops and businesses, anxious to hear the latest updates. Local community leaders and political pundits filled the radio waves, actively calling for justice and an end to the siege. Taxicabs and buses would blast twenty-year-old recordings of intifada songs, while Palestinian kaffiyas (black-and-white checkered headscarves) adorned businesses, homes, and bodies. University students organized consumer boycotts against Israeli- and American-made products, as cultural organizations sponsored myriad performances (concerts, poetry readings, lectures, art exhibits, etc.) and demonstrations denouncing the occupation and the failure of the international community to protect civilian life.

And while popular sentiment for Palestinian causes reverberated across the region, within its calls for the amelioration of suffering and an end to the occupation emerged a new public sphere for debate over fundamental issues of identity, nationalism, politics, and religion. Embedded within ubiquitous performances of national solidarity arose a poetic terrain upon which competing and contrasting elements of Palestinian identity were actively negotiated. Thrust into the traumas of violence and sociocultural instability, Palestinians both under siege and in exile were compelled to navigate deep-seated questions of what it means to be Palestinian, how the nation ought to be defined, and who most effectively represents the people in their struggle for self-determination.

In an attempt to better understand this profound moment of intense national sentiment and collective empathy, in this chapter I examine the interactive poetics of Palestinian identity from within the fields of performative and expressive media (music, dance, poetry, etc.). Drawing on recent contributions in the fields of gender, subaltern, and performance studies, I focus particularly on the ways in which Palestinian ideational strategies are embodied, performed, acted out, from within various politico-nationalist frames.[5] Moving outward from an ethnographic analysis of individual performances and events, I then locate these ideational strategies within the larger spectrum of nationalist politics. In this endeavor I proceed from the position that the complex interactions between performative and political spheres provide a unique site for scholarly investigation, revealing the discursive tactics through which nations may be imagined and articulated. In this formulation, performative and expressive media are not epiphenomenal to larger social, political, and economic forces, but rather they are constitutive of those forces.[6] Music, dance, poetry, graffiti, and the like do not merely *reflect* popular sentiment. They in fact *generate* popular sentiment, shaping national and political identities and affiliations, and providing performative spaces for subverting and reinforcing entrenched power structures.[7]

By interrogating the ways in which performative media shape popular sentiment, I move against the analytical tendency to view identity and culture as primordial, stable, natural, homogeneous, and internally unconflicted. Rather, my analysis begins from an understanding of Palestinian culture as a performative construct, as an ongoing process of identity formation shaped within a diverse field of social forces. These forces differentially affect individuals and subgroups along myriad axes of power and influence. To interpret Palestinian identity as inherently processual, contingent, and performative does not in any way mitigate the nationalist project, nor the legitimacy of the Palestinian cause for self-determination. Rather, such an approach, I believe, leads to a more nuanced understanding of Palestinian identity, in effect, empowering diverse voices, experiences, and beliefs against rampant Orientalist and Islamophobic depictions of Arab culture in mainstream corporate media. My analysis is therefore situated in the lives and personal experiences of several influential intifada artists active during the height of the al-Aqsa intifada (2002–2006). In myriad performative devices (rhythm, melody, dress, gesture, instrumentation, etc.) each of these artists embodied a particular imagining of Palestinian identity, nationalism, and politics. By charting the aesthetic boundaries between these various performance repertoires, I strive for a better understanding of the diverse ways in which Palestinians both under occupation and in exile have confronted the occupation, negotiating contrasting and conflicting interpretations of violence, resistance, and sociocultural trauma.

Palestinian Protest Song (2000–2008)

Not unlike the major periods of resistance that preceded it, the escalation of the al-Aqsa intifada in 2002 marked a new era in Palestinian expressive culture in which contrasting aesthetic repertoires interacted, both in competition and collaboration, across the public sphere. In performance, production, and consumption this field of expressive media was dominated by four broadly defined aesthetic formations, or genres. Initially, multinational Arab pop stars, seeking to raise awareness for Palestinian issues, flooded the marketplace with a panoply of humanitarian pop anthems, calling for redemption and solidarity with Palestinian issues. More widespread in the near diaspora than in Gaza and the West Bank, this new wave of stylish "pop intifadiana" has been effectively interpreted as a revival of sorts, drawing inspiration from the ostentatious performances of pan-Arabism emanating from Egypt in the 1950s to 1960s.[8] A more local revival of a different sort occurred simultaneously from within Palestinian communities, as once famous resistance singers of the 1970s and 1980s found themselves thrust back into the public spotlight performing their repertoires of twenty- to thirty-year-old protest songs before a new generation of audiences. These performers inspired a revival of indigenous Palestinian folksong and dance in public spaces, and reinforced the entrenched secular nationalist leadership of the resistance moment. Alongside this revival of past political song emerged the arrival of a new generation of nationalist performers born of contemporary social and political issues. Foremost among these were young Islamist artists performing new hybridized repertoires of religious song, or *anashīd*, interwoven with indigenous musical elements and contemporary sound drama. The dominant presence of contemporary anashīd, and other Islamic-inspired popular culture in the mainstream marketplace, fueled the ascendance of political Islamism more generally in the public sphere, allowing for new ways of imagining the nationalist movement. And finally, amid these repertories of Palestinian resistance song emerged a wave of locally produced hip-hop. As a counterbalance to the performative Islamism embodied in the anashīd, the arrival of Palestinian hip-hop propelled new ways of conceptualizing Palestinian identity by linking it with transnational discourses of racial dispossession and urban empowerment in the global pop music marketplace.

Arab Pop "Intifadiana"

In the two years prior to Operation Defensive Shield musical expressions of solidarity with Palestinian issues had been dominated by a series of transnational Arab pop anthems recognizing Palestinian suffering and calling for an end to the occupation. Arab pop stars, anxious to throw their celebrity behind the cause of Palestinian self-determination, dominated the charts with empathetic ballads and calls for peace and redemption. Foremost of these was "Al-Ḥilm Al-'Arabī" (The Arab Dream). Although initially released in 1998, it was subsequently revived in October 2000 and again in April 2002 immediately following the Jenin invasion.[9] Directed by Ahmed Al-Arian and composed by Hilmi Bakr, this pop collaboration featured the talents of twenty-three pop stars from across the Arab world, in an attempt to reimagine Arab unity through the lenses of Palestinian suffering. Throughout the song strategic musical and textual signs reinforced a poetics of pan-Arabism by alternating between solo verses, sung in thick native dialects, and ensemble choruses, where local accents blended together into melodic singularity. Musical markers of place, performed through language (accent), vocal timbre, and ornamentation continuously alternated between the national identity of the soloist and the pan-Arab identity of the ensemble. The lyrics further reinforced the notion of pan-Arab solidarity in the face of international conflict.

> Min āy makān fī al-arḍ
> Nāṭaq bilasān al-ḍād
> Wa ba'alā al-ṣawt wa al-nabaḍ
> Banaqūl al-waḥda mīlād
> Aṭfālnā fī kul makān
> Ḍaya' 'ayūn al-awṭān
> Al-ḥaq al-ḥub al-khayr
> Rasālatnā fī kul zamān
>
> Wa al-ghanūa batalghī ḥadūd
> Wa waṭanhā hūa al-qalb
> Wa mā dām 'āyshīn ḥanaghanī
> Wa mā dām qādrīn ḥanḥubb

Ḥilminā wa fī kul zamān
Waḥda kul al-awṭān
Kul al-khalāfāt ḥatazūl
Wa kafāya innak insān

From anywhere on earth we speak with an opposing tongue (Arabic),
With the loudest voice we have, we say unity.
Our children everywhere are the light of our nation.
Right, love, good is our message throughout time.

A song cancels national borders,
And its homeland is the heart.
As long as we live we will sing,
As long as we are able we will love.

Our dream has always been,
The unity of all nations.
All disagreements will disappear.
It is enough that you are a human being.[10]

Although packaged with graphic imagery of Palestinian suffering, "Al-Ḥilm Al-ʿArabī" perpetuated a theme of unity through very abstract depictions of place. Keyboard-laden orchestrations, heavy bass, and synthesized pop rhythms signified the larger repertory of Arab pop rather than localized Palestinian song. Ironically, while "Al-Ḥilm Al-ʿArabī" was a testament to Palestinian suffering, nowhere in it are Palestinians ever mentioned. Nor were any Palestinian artists asked to participate in its production or performance. The song focused on the redemption of the presumed Palestinian people through love, perseverance, unity, and hope for a better tomorrow.

In the fall of 2000 a second star-studded collaboration surfaced, "Al-Quds Hatarjaʿ Lina" (Jerusalem Will Return to Us), featuring the combined talents of thirty-six pop stars, actors, and other celebrities representative of virtually every Arab country (except Palestine). This star-studded collaboration went into production less than two weeks after the televised death of Mohammad al-Durra and the outbreak of the al-Aqsa intifada, and was subsequently revived in response to Operation Defensive Shield in the spring of 2002. In similar fashion this pop ballad contrasted themes of pan-Arab solidarity amid cultural and linguistic diversity. What distinguished this pop anthem from its predecessor, however, was a more combative call for Palestinian liberation. Lyrics spoke of unending violence and terror, while the accompanying video presented graphic images of Palestinian suffering, beatings, and funeral processions. The dream of peace and solidarity was replaced by a collective message of shock, mourning, and a call to action. Singing of the twelve-year-old victim of Israeli violence, Mohammad al-Durra, the chorus laments:

> *Kān shāyal aluwānhu kān rāyaḥ madrasthū*
> *Wa yaḥlam bahaṣānhu wa bilʿabhu wa ṭayārathu*
> *Wa li-mā anṭalaq al-ghadar wa mawt ḥatā barā ʾthu*
> *Sāl al-dam al-ṭāhar ʿalā karāsathu*

> *Abū mad bakhūfhu aydīhu*
> *Yaḥmī biʿamrhu ḍānhu*
> *Wa li-mā artaʿash al-jasad al-ṭifal*
> *Wa baqā fī aydīn Allah*

> *Kulnā banaqūl arḍinā*
> *Arḍinā damnā aminā*
> *Wa ann māt milāyyīn minnā*
> *Al-Quds ḥatarja ʿlinā*

He was carrying his crayons, he was going to school.
Dreaming of his horse, his toys, his plane.
And when the treachery occurred, it killed his innocence.
His pure blood was spilled across his notebook.

A fearful father reached with his arms,
Protecting the life of his child.
And when the child's body twitched,
He became in God's hands.

We all say our land.
Our land, Our blood, Our nation.
And even if millions die,
Jerusalem will return to us.

The video for "Al-Quds Hatarjaʿ Linā" presents the artists defiantly assembled in front of a picture of the Dome of the Rock wrapped in barbed wire.[11] Dressed in black they collectively mourn the death of the young child (al-Durra) walking home from school carrying his "crayons and his notebook." Several of the artists weep openly during their solos, while others angrily gesticulate toward the camera. The underlying message of outrage, lost innocence, and pervasive suffering is further indexed as the artists stand united with a collection of young children (dressed in white) assembled at the front of the stage. Graphic depictions of violence, martyrdom, and death are then juxtaposed with the "pure" images of the young children and the holy sites of Jerusalem.

Not unlike the pan-Arabist songs of the late 1950s, these two pop productions drew from the same stock repertory of musical and linguistic signs of Arab unity and a shared cultural-religious identity. A humanitarian crisis, a foreign colonial threat, and a common Arab (and Islamic) cause became the foundation for transcending cultural difference in the service of pan-Arab unity. And while each of these songs made a considerable impact in the transnational Arab pop marketplace, raising awareness and generating substantial public empathy for the intifada, among Palestinians both under occupation and in exile such songs quickly faded from public view. As the violence continued to escalate across the West Bank and Gaza Strip with little international response, these transnational pop songs did little to articulate explicitly Palestinian experiences. Their soft idealist rhetoric, infectious melodies, and cosmopolitan orchestrations failed to fully address the severity of the violence and the poetics of Palestinian life under occupation. Daily images of violence on the streets of Jenin, Gaza, Nablus, and Tulkaram rendered such songs politically innocuous. As Palestinian protest singer Kamal Khalil would often say:

> These are merely crying songs. They [Arab pop stars] don't know what it is like for us [Palestinians]. What will crying get us? We are done crying. What we need are fighting songs that tell the world what is really going on, and demand freedom.[12]

While this new wave of transnational Arab pop intifadiana (music, videos, graphic design, T-shirts, bumper stickers, key chains, and other paraphernalia) was immediately popular throughout the region, among many Palestinians such media had little sociocultural impact.[13] For while the outpouring of Palestinian-themed popular culture elicited a much-needed empathy for Palestinian suffering, it did so at the expense of explicitly Palestinian voices, experiences, and poetics. After watching the video to "Al-Quds Hatarja' Linā" Palestinian protest singer Adnan Odeh quipped, "who is the 'we' they are talking about? Arabs? If they want al-Quds [to return to the Arabs], why aren't they helping us [Palestinians] in Jenin right now?" Quite simply, these were songs *for* Palestine, and not necessarily songs *of* Palestine.[14]

On another level, pop intifadiana failed to have a lasting impact on the national movement primarily because Palestinians could not reconcile popular support for political issues with the overtly cosmopolitan lifestyles and aesthetics of the artists themselves. While many of these transnational Arab pop stars sang in support of Palestinian self-determination, they did so from the comfort of their recording studios in Cairo, Paris, or Beirut. What is more, many of their international tours were sponsored by multinational corporations with problematic relationships with both American and Israeli governments. The many transnational pop songs in support of Palestinian issues were neither explicitly political nor did they articulate with the embedded discourse of Palestinian resistance. Empty slogans for peace and understanding held little meaning for besieged communities forced to navigate the occupation in their daily lives.

Intifada Revivals: Firqat Aghani Al-'Ashiqin

It was this sense of alienation that led many Palestinians to seek out repertories of resistance song from previous generations. Artists and ensembles that had largely disappeared from public life or disbanded were suddenly lured back into the public sphere as Palestinian society reverted back to its "intifada mode" of the past. Syrian singer Samih Shaqir returned to performing nationalist protest songs at political rallies. In Jordan, Kamal Khalil was literally pulled away from his day job as a construction worker in order to perform at a political rally in the summer of 2002. Marcel Khalife, Mustapha al-Kord, Abu Arab, Firqat al-Markaziya (The Central Ensemble), Firqat al-Quds (The Jerusalem Ensemble), Firqat al-Baysan (The Baysān Ensemble), Firqat al-Yarmuk (The Yarmūk Ensemble), and many others each found their twenty-year-old recordings back on the shelves of street kiosks in urban centers and refugee camps throughout Balād al-Shām (the combined area of Jordan, Syria, Lebanon, Israel/Palestine). Soon requests for public performances brought many of the remaining members of these ensembles back together to perform for cultural societies, political parties, labor syndicates, and other social organizations. Among all of these, however, Firqat Aghani al-'Ashiqin (The Songs of the Beloved Ones) mounted the most ambitious comeback, embarking on a regional tour that included several large venues in Syria, Jordan, and the United Arab Emirates.

Since its founding in 1976 al-'Ashiqin has been widely considered the most influential Palestinian resistance ensemble throughout the region. Their early studio recordings, *Min Sijin 'Akkā (From 'Akka Prison)* and *Hubbat al-Nar (The Fire Swelled)*, although originally released in the refugee camps of Lebanon, very quickly spread among Palestinian communities throughout the near diaspora such that by the time the group disbanded in 1985 their cassettes had come to dominate the field of Palestinian protest song.[15] As was true of many resistance ensembles in the 1970s, al-'Ashiqin was founded and developed under the supervision of the Palestinian Liberation Organization's (PLO) general council, specifically linked to Fatah.[16] In the early years the group functioned as part of the PLO's cultural operations, generating grassroots support for Fatah party leadership through performances at political rallies, cultural festivals, and national meetings.

Although the ensemble was officially linked to secular nationalist causes and organizations, al-ʿAshiqin was quite successful at mobilizing a diverse social and political spectrum around a core set of common goals and themes in their performances. In song, dance, and gesture al-ʿAshiqin forged performative spaces for the articulation of various political ideologies encompassed within the PLO: secular nationalist, socialist, and communist. Much of their success can be attributed to founding composer and artistic director of the group, Hussein Nazak, who was credited with developing a style of composition whereby indigenous Palestinian *dabke* (circle line-dancing) and *zeffa* (wedding processional) songs were reset with contemporary nationalist lyrics and messages.[17] These *shaʿbī* ("of the people," indigenous) protest songs were then juxtaposed with contemporary *thawrī* (revolutionary) martial hymns and marches, creating a unique form of creative indexing of various cultural and political elements.

Immediately following the Jenin invasion in the Spring of 2002 al-ʿAshiqin's famed lead-singer, Hussein Munther (Abu Ali), and oudist Adnan Odeh set to work on the group's revival. Working from Beirut and Damascus they assembled an ad hoc collection of musicians too young to have ever heard al-ʿAshiqin perform live. Much to the dismay of several of the original members of the group now scattered across the region, Abu Ali advertised this new ensemble as a revival of the original al-ʿAshiqin, and devoted nearly the entire set list to the group's famous past hits. After only two week's rehearsal the newly reconstituted al-ʿAshiqin debuted at Amman's Private University on November 25, 2003. The boisterous crowd consisted of a diverse audience of older men and women, seeking to relive al-ʿAshiqin's famous repertory of resistance songs (seated at the peripheries of the arena), and a new generation of youth (filling the floor of the arena), anxious to experience al-ʿAshiqin live for the first time. Politically, the audience was equally diverse, as sections of the arena were quartered off by flags, banners, and posters representative of various political organizations: Fatah, the Popular Front for the Liberation of Palestine (PFLP), Hamas, and the Palestinian Islamic Jihad (PIJ).

Throughout the evening, competing factions would engage one another through chanting, singing, dancing, and outright physical fighting. As these competing groups were each vying for control of the arena, a collective negotiation of sorts emerged. In their raucous assertions of political allegiance these youth were in many ways advancing an ideational strategy of how the nation should be defined, who is best equipped to lead it, and what types of tactics should be employed. As young men would attempt to tear down a competing group's banners or posters, a brawl would often ensue. Islamists carrying posters of Sheikh Ahmed Yassin and Hamas confronted secular nationalists, displaying posters of Yasser Arafat and flags of Fatah. The red banners of the PFLP, and its populist/socialist agenda, clashed (literally and figuratively) with the green and yellow banners of the PIJ and Hezbollah. More than merely politics, such confrontations were imbricated with strategic assertions of national and religious identity.

During one particularly powerful moment in the concert Samer Khadar, one of al-'Ashiqin's backup singers, recited a poem that ended in the ubiquitous chant, "By spirit, by blood, I sacrifice for you, oh Palestine." In a moment of collective protest a crowd of Hamas supporters joined in, changing the last word to "Yassin." Raising posters of the spiritual leader of Hamas, Sheikh Ahmed Yassin, segments of the crowd momentarily recognized the new waves of support for Islamist politics and its most recent wave of suicide operations against Israeli targets. The performative and political shift in the arena was fleeting, but it nevertheless caused a large reaction. Seeking the opportunity to retake control of the performance space Abu Ali then directed the group through a set of indigenous folksongs and dances (*mūsīqā al-sha'bīya*) reset with verses of famous resistance poetry.[18] He did this to reinforce the secular nationalist politics of the PLO, and the unquestioned leadership of Yasser Arafat. Speaking after the performance he commented:

> I didn't want it [the concert] to be taken over by *those fundamentalists* [*mata'ṣabīn*] with their posters of Yassin, and their beards. So, we made sure to play many dabke folksongs [*dabke sha'bīya*] to keep everyone dancing. *Dabke* is of the Palestinian people [*sha'b*], the nation [*waṭan*], and not from religion [*mesh min al-dīn*]. I wasn't going to let them [Islamists] turn it [the concert] into some kind of religious celebration [*mawlid*].

In fact, each of these songs was carefully selected backstage to reinforce the group's political message of support for the PLO (and by extension Fatah) and its secular nationalist politics. The first of these songs, "Qīdī yā Nār al-Thawra" (Ignite, Oh Fires of the Revolution), offers an excellent example of how al-'Ashiqin very successfully operationalized indigenous folksong in the service of this particular political ideology.

Based on a simple processional chant commonly performed at wedding celebrations (*zeffa*), Hussein Nazak arranged "Qīdī yā Nār al-Thawra" with an expanded melody, reset with verses of contemporary resistance poetry. Maintaining the original rhythmic structure (*malfūf*) and call and response format, Nazak preserved the participatory aspect of this processional while layering it with new politicized meanings. The result was a powerful articulation of indigenous Palestinian lifeways and militarized resistance.

Qīdī yā nār al-thawra wa ḍawī bi-l-dār
Wa jamara batūlʿ jamara wa batishab al-nār
Ṭalʿanā min damūʿ al-faqarā wa zind al-falāḥ
ʿĀlaynā al-rayāa al-ḥurra wa jaynā thuwār

Qīdī yā thawra qīdī wa daqī al-jarās
Al-thawra al-thawra āntalaqat wa rafaʿnā al-rās
Taslam āydak yā mujāhid zūd al-ʿayār
Ṣār raṣaṣak ghanīyya taʿyūn al-nās

Ignite, oh fires of revolution
And be a light upon the houses.
Embers reproduce and the fire spreads.
We arose from the tears of the poor
And the bracelets of the villagers.
We raised the banners of freedom
And came as revolutionaries.

Ignite, oh revolution and ring the bell.
The revolution began and we raised our head.
Peace be upon your hands, oh freedom fighter.
Increase your intensity.
Your bullets became a song upon the eyes of the people.

This style of "creative indexing," whereby familiar rhythms and melodies are layered with contemporary political messages and imagery, fused together powerful associations of past and present, the primordial nation and the contemporary nationalist movement.[19] "The *fires* of revolution," "the *light* of freedom," and *bullets* becoming a "song in the eyes of the people" are all very common signifiers of the PLO and its *fidāʿiyīn* (freedom fighters) movement of the 1970s and 1980s. In al-ʿAshiqin performances men wear military fatigues, identifying themselves with the *fidāʿiyīn,* while women wear traditionally embroidered dresses.[20] Here the resistance (and the music) is framed as a paramilitary struggle for liberation, imagined in the fires of revolution and arising "from the tears of the poor and the bracelets of the villagers." This reference locates the Palestinian nation among the "folk" (*fallāḥīn*), the rural poor masses. The strategic use of a wedding song (an indexical sign of rural Palestinian lifeways), as the carrier for this message, further reinforces this relationship, locating the nation and the nationalist movement within the poetics of the "folk" and the secular nationalist leadership of the PLO.[21]

New Arrivals: Mais Shalash, the "Voice of Freedom"

On the streets, the young singer was often known simply as "*al-ṭifla*" (the child) or "*al-ṣawt al-ḥurrīya*" (the voice of freedom), yet among musicians, activists, and artists familiar with her work, Mais Shalash was a rising star in the nationalist movement. Her highly acclaimed debut albums, *Al-Ṣawt Al-Ḥurrīya* (The Voice of Freedom) and *Istūra al-Jenīn* (The Legend of Jenin), were released in the summer and fall of 2002, and quickly spread among Palestinian communities throughout the region.[22] Although only twelve years old at the time, Mais Shalash had already spent several years performing anashīd in refugee camps, hospitals, and cultural organizations throughout Jordan, Kuwait, and the United Arab Emirates. And while anashīd and other Islamic musics have served an important, though often neglected, component of the nationalist movement for many years, *Al-Ṣawt al-Ḥurrīya* marked the arrival of a new style of anashīd born of a unique mixture of sha'bī rhythms, Islamic poetry, and contemporary sound drama.[23] The juxtaposition of these various musical elements combined into a unique form of protest song illustrative of contemporary poetics, political debates, and ideology. Especially among disgruntled communities seeking a new direction in the entrenched nationalist leadership, Mais Shalash gave voice to an alternative national identity formation. She offered a performative space within which audiences could imagine a new path to self-determination beyond the corruption of the PLO, advocating a return to local grassroots resistance based in core religious values, simultaneously nationalist and Islamist.

Due to local laws governing Islamist activities in Jordan, Mais Shalash performed primarily at informal community meetings, labor syndicates, university campuses, and other cultural events beyond the gaze of government censors. In contrast to al-'Ashiqin, Mais preferred to perform before smaller more intimate audiences. Nested between political speeches, religious sermons, and reports from the West Bank and Gaza Strip, Mais would take the stage armed with a collection of songs directly linked to the immediacy of the occupation. As firsthand reports of the Jenin invasion emerged, for example, she would incorporate those testimonials into her lyrics, emphasizing the voices and experiences of those currently under siege. Among her audiences, this gave her music a profound sense of immediacy and authenticity to the struggle, locality in experience, and loyalty to cultural-religious jurisprudence.

Speaking with Mais's father and chief composer Saud Shalash in 2002, he explained the importance of her music in the new resistance.

When people hear Mais, they hear the voice of every Palestinian child. She is their daughter; her voice has become the voice of all children suffering under occupation. In this new intifada, we see children homeless, orphaned. They are the real victims. When Mais sings we hear the voices of those children.

Given that media representations of the intifada were focused primarily on the plight of suffering children, dominated by images of Mohammad al-Durra, Mais's stature as a young child was an essential element to her music, and effectively articulated with a discourse of humanitarian suffering and martyrdom central to the nationalist movement. Yet to fully understand her impact within the field of Palestinian music it is equally important to emphasize her embodiment of the very core religious principles she sings about. Wearing a beautifully ornamented *thawb* (ankle-length Islamic gown) and *ḥijāb* (headscarf), standing motionless on stage, the adolescent Mais personified the engendered image of the innocent, pure, vulnerable Palestinian nation in need of defense and collective sacrifice. In performance her body and childlike voice simultaneously called forth the cultural imperatives of protection and steadfastness to core Islamic principles (modesty, justice, integrity). Amid a field of cosmopolitan pop stars selling their bodies and products on billboards, and a dysfunctional corrupt national leadership bending to international will, for her audiences Mais Shalash presented an alternative Palestinian identity formation rooted in an uncompromising devotion to Islamic values and ideals. She offered a counterbalance to history and the status quo, advocating for a new direction in the performative politics of the nationalist movement.

Mais Shalash's second album, *Istūra al-Jenīn* provided a powerful musical response to the Jenin invasion of 2002. Moreover, this album is an excellent example of Islamist poetics in Palestinian protest song. The album begins with the eerie sounds of gunfire, explosions, and helicopter blades over a synthesized drone. Emerging from within these dramatic sounds of violence, a collage of voices give testimony to their experiences of survival in the Jenin invasion.

> "The first time I entered Jenin, it was such a shock and surprise for me. Corpses left on the doorways of the houses."
>
> "Destruction of entire neighborhoods of the Jenin refugee camp."
>
> "Indescribable, seeing is believing."
>
> "Displacement."
>
> "The tanks and the airplanes . . ."
>
> "The whole world was shaking, there was something, it was not an earthquake, an earthquake lasts for only a second . . ."

Amid thundering explosions the voice of the young singer emerges.

Li-zara'lak wa rada fi qalbi
Wa asqayhā min damī
Yā Jenīn al-āghlā
Wa āghlā min abuī wa immī

Wa aqlak ba'adī 'alā 'ahadī
Anā mawjhu 'alā ṣakhrak madī
Madī bashūqak aydak madī
Wa baḥabak dafīnī

I will plant a rose for you in my heart,
And my blood will be its water.
Oh, Jenin you are the most precious,
More dear to me than my father and mother.

And I tell you, I will keep my word.
I am a wave and your stones are the sea of my tides.
Raise your hand with love, raise it
And warm me with your love.

In contrast to the sha'bī folksongs of al-'Ashiqin, Mais Shalash's repertory of nationalist anashīd musically embodied a call to Islamist principles.
The meanings of her lyrics were intended to index Islamist thought and
practice. For example, she routinely emphasized the *promise* of the people,
the *obligation* of redeeming the Holy Land, and the *precious* character of the
land, all intertextual references to Islamic doctrine of poetry. Later in the
song, following a second round of testimonials, she sings of the attack on
Jenin within the larger Islamic history of the region.

Yā Jenīn ḍalā 'alā 'ahadak
Khalī tārīkhak yan'ād
Kam mast'amar marr b'rḍak bi-l-hazīma wa al-lū'āt?

Anta al-'azah 'a-kul jabīn
Wa anta al-ḥurra illī batadāfa'a
Mīn kiān yaṣdaq, mīn?
Al-Ḥijāra batahazam madāfa'a

Ṣabāra wa ahlak ṣābrīn
Istūra wa asmak Jenīn
Wa nūr al-shams ba'aynak sāta'a
Damak khayṭ al-fajar al-ṭāla'a

Oh Jenin, keep your promise
Let history repeat itself
How many colonizers have passed through your lands,
And left with defeat and hardship?
You are the pride of everyone
And you are the free one who defends its land
Who would believe? Who?
That stones can defeat tanks?

You are patient and your people are patient too
You are the legend, your name is Jenin
The light of the sun shines bright in your eyes
Your blood is the coming dawn

Whereas *sha'bī* singers often sing of the power of the *ḥajr* (stone) against
foreign occupation, Islamist singers typically prefer the word *ṣakhra* (stone)
instead. "I am a wave, and your *stones* are the sea of my tides." This usage of
the word has powerful religious connotations, as it often refers specifically
to the rock (*al-ṣakhra*) upon which the Prophet ascended to heaven from
Jerusalem. In singing of patience, and the long history of foreign occupation, Mais draws together powerful imagery of Islamic conquest, martyrdom, and collective sacrifice going back to the Crusades. "The light of the
sun shines bright in your eyes" references the light of God (*al-nūr*) and the
promise of freedom in "the coming dawn" (*al-fajar al-ṭāla'a*). In her music
the nation is located specifically among the Islamic nation (*umma*), and the
cause for self-determination is one of religious obligation and redemption.

Mais Shalash's performances also follow a very strict pattern. She begins
each song with an unmetered extemporization of several verses of poetry,
rendered with little ornamentation. Following this initial introduction, a
collection of frame drums (*daffāt*) establish a rhythmic time-cycle upon
which she sings the remainder of the verses. Between lines of text a unison
male chorus, singing in a deep resonant chest voice, accompanies her by
repeating the ending phrases of each line of text. At times, she will enlist the
efforts of a keyboardist to provide melodic ornamentation and accompaniment, as well as to perform various sound effects (chimes, winds, etc.). Yet,
in every performance she follows the standard practices of Islamic anashīd,
where participatory singing and dancing is discouraged so as to maintain a
sense of religious jurisprudence and propriety toward the subject of the
event. With the revitalization of Islamist politics in mainstream Palestinian
society, marked by the widespread election of Islamist candidates in the
Palestinian free elections of 2005, this style of nationalist anashād provided
an important forum for debate on fundamental issues of religion, politics,

and violence. Mais Shalash, the young "voice of freedom," became a reflection of and contributor to this political shift, giving voice to the new waves of popular support for Islamist organizations.

New Arrivals: DAM and Palestinian Hip-hop

If the Islamist poetics of Mais Shalash's contemporary anashīd advocated for a reimagining of Palestinian identity through the introspective revival of core religious values, the development of locally produced hip-hop sought to establish ideational linkages with the transnational mediascape. In particular, the ascendance of hip-hop crews DAM (Da Arab MCs), PR (Palestinian Rappers), Ramallah Underground, Arapeyat, Sabreena Da Witch, Mahmoud Shalabi, and many others has revealed a new nationalist strategy that seeks to align local Palestinian experiences of dispossession with a larger discourse of racial trauma. In drawing from an established lexicon of hip-hop these artists have situated the Palestinian struggle for self-determination with the African American plight for racial empowerment using contemporary pop culture conduits of production and consumption. In this sense, hip-hop has presented a discursively neutral space where audiences (Palestinian and non-Palestinian) might engage each other outside of the rigid discourses of religion and the nation-state. But most importantly, the ascendance of local hip-hop at the height of the al-Aqsa intifada has served to challenge essentialist representations of Palestinian culture and society, opening new discursive spaces for representing and interpreting the conflict.

Many of these observations became apparent as I was touring with Palestinian hip-hop crew DAM in the summers of 2004 and 2005. Moving with DAM between performances in Israel and in the West Bank it was fascinating to observe the various levels of code switching that took place as they attempted to engage with Israeli Jewish and Palestinian audiences. Linguistically, the group fluidly shifted between dialects of English, Hebrew, and Arabic. Musically, the group folded together sampling from Arab, Israeli, and American pop sources. On stage the group presented itself as cultural arbiters between the local and transnational world. Yet, among nationalist audiences, DAM was often accused of abandoning their Palestinian identity (huwīya) in favor of a cruel American (or worse, Israeli) substitute. At many of their earlier performances in the West Bank, crowds of angry youth were incredulous, angrily chanting politicized slogans that challenged their very identity as "real" Palestinians. Living as citizens of Israel, growing up in Israeli schools, fluent in Hebrew and Israeli national culture, these young rappers were viewed as Judaized (bityūhid), Americanized (bitammrak), potential traitors (khawān) to the cause.

Against these criticisms, DAM's leader Tamer Nafar, would often present his blue identification card as evidence of his Palestinian identity, speaking eloquently of his personal experiences living as a marginalized, racially maligned citizen of Israel.[24] In one of our conversations he addressed the issue, stating that hip-hop best represented his experiences growing up in the urban ghettos of Israel, far more so than folkloric songs of the past. Referencing the sha'bī protest songs of artists like al-'Ashiqin, he once stated to me:

> So for me to be Palestinian I have to sing wedding songs about olive trees or farming or goats? What does that have to do with my life here and now? What do songs about goats and trees have to do with my life? Look out that window. Do you see any trees or goats? I grew up in Lyd, we don't have any trees.[25]

Rather than seeking to preserve an artificial Palestinian experience rooted in "folk" rural practices (sarcastically imagined in the form of trees and goats), Tamer Nafar unapologetically offered hip-hop as a powerful means of being Palestinian today in the "here and now." Based on their increasing popularity, it seems that they were not alone. For example, at a performance in Ramallah in the summer of 2005 a group of young fans approached the stage and asked if they might perform some of their break-dancing, or B-boy, moves. Never having had the opportunity to perform this style of dance in public the boys were welcomed up on stage to demonstrate their skills before an audience of their friends and classmates. Other youth in the audience stated that they had been listening to hip-hop for years, but never had the opportunity to hear it live in their native language, to dance it, and act it out: "To feel Palestinian in rap" (*biḥiss filisṭīnī bi-l-rab*), as one young girl commented. Among their audiences DAM provided a unique space wherein assertions of Palestinian identity and politics need not be restricted to rigid nationalist or religious definitions. Rather, such assertions of national identity could serve as a performative means of transcending political and ideational boundaries between East and West.

Conclusion

Refracted through the lenses of the Jenin invasion and Operation Defensive Shield, the field of Palestinian protest song constitutes a unique sphere for public debate and the negotiation of fundamental elements of identity, religion, and politics. In an effort to understand the various ways in which Palestinians have attempted to engage the violence of the intifada, I have examined four interrelated sites of public performance. Each of these sites may be interpreted as unique spaces of interactive poetics: spaces where embodied and performed acts may generate, record, and transmit cultural knowledge. Melodies, rhythms, timbres, instrumentation, accent, dress, and dance, are all mnemonic reserves, or residual moments, indexically linked to various political structures and ideologies.[26] In these spaces music performance offers the possibility of challenge, of ideational intervention into a political situation overdetermined by violence and trauma. These performative interventions then act as conduits for the reflection, transmission, and creation of new ways of *being* Palestinian. Coming to grips with the traumas of the occupation and a resurgence of nationalist activity Palestinians both under occupation and in exile were compelled to navigate a wide spectrum of nationalist politics. How should the nation be determined? Who should lead the people? And what tactics would most effectively accomplish these goals? Performative and expressive media created a space wherein these fundamental issues of national identity were negotiated and performed, giving voice to diverse experiences, each uniquely constitutive of the Palestinian nation.

Notes

1. Ida Audeh, "Narratives of Siege: Eye-Witness Testimonies from Jenin, Bethlehem, and Nablus," *Journal of Palestine Studies* 31 (2002): 13–14.

2. On May 31, 2002, the Israeli Newspaper *Yediot Aharonot* published an interview with one of the bulldozer drivers, Moshe Nissim. Nicknamed the "Kurdi Bear," Nissim proudly admitted to operating the D-9 for seventy-five consecutive hours, drinking whiskey to remain alert. Asked about whether the homes he demolished were still inhabited he answered, "I didn't see, with my own eyes, people dying under the blade of the D-9. And I didn't see houses falling down on live people, but if there were any, I wouldn't care at all." The *Guardian* reported, several days after the invasion had ended, several eyewitness testimonies of families trapped in their basements as bulldozers toppled their homes, citing deaths nearing a thousand. See Peter Beaumont, "Ten-Day Ordeal in Crucible of Jenin," *Guardian*, April 14, 2002, for further information, www.guardian.co.uk/world/2002/apr/14/israel (accessed July 14, 2010).

3. Ramzy Baroud, *Searching Jenin: Eyewitness Accounts of the Israeli Invasion, 2002* (Seattle, WA: Cune Press, 2003), 16–32.

4. In its study of the invasion, Human Rights Watch stopped short of labeling the invasion a "massacre," but did accuse the Israeli government of war crimes. See Paul Wood, "'No Jenin Massacre' Says Rights Group," British Broadcasting Corporation, May 3, 2002, http://news.bbc.co.uk/2/hi/middle_east/1965471.stm (accessed July 14, 2010). Similar findings by Amnesty International are summa-

rized by Joel Greenberg, "Amnesty Accuses Israeli Forces of War Crimes," *New York Times*, November 4, 2002, www.nytimes.com (accessed July 14, 2010).

5. Diana Taylor, *The Archive and the Repertoire: Performing Cultural Memory in the Americas* (Durham, NC: Duke University Press, 2003); Judith Butler, *Precarious Life: The Powers of Mourning and Violence* (New York: Verso Press, 2006).

6. Martin Stokes, "Introduction: Ethnicity, Identity, and Music" in *Ethnicity, Identity, and Music: The Musical Construction of Place*, ed. Martin Stokes (Oxford: Berg, 1994), 1–33; Bonnie C. Wade, *Imaging Sound: An Ethnomusicological Study of Music, Art, and Culture in Mughal, India* (Chicago: University of Chicago Press, 1998); Thomas Turino, *Nationalists, Cosmopolitans, and Popular Music* (Chicago: University of Chicago Press, 2000); Taylor, *The Archive and the Repertoire*.

7. David A. McDonald, "Poetics and the Performance of Violence in Israel/ Palestine," *Ethnomusicology* 53 (2009): 58–85

8. Elliott Colla, "Sentimentality and Redemption: The Rhetoric of Egyptian Pop Culture Intifada Solidarity," in *Palestine, Israel, and the Politics of Popular Culture*, ed. Ted Swedenburg and Rebecca L. Stein (Durham: Duke University Press, 2005) 340; David McDonald, "My Voice Is My Weapon: Music, Nationalism, and the Poetics of Palestinian Resistance" (PhD diss., University of Illinois, 2006). The term "pop intifadiana" is borrowed from Elliot Colla's engaging analysis of pop intifada material culture emanating from and within Egypt at this time.

9. Recordings of this highly influential song are freely available on the Internet via video-sharing sites such as YouTube.

10. Song texts were collected, transcribed, and translated by the author from live performances and recordings of live performances.

11. This video is freely available on the Internet via video-sharing sites such as YouTube.

12. All interviews for this study were conducted in Arabic, and are here provided in my translation.

13. Colla, "Sentimentality and Redemption."

14. McDonald, "My Voice Is My Weapon," 150.

15. Al-'Ashiqin's dominance in the field of Palestinian nationalist music continued well into 2002 when I first arrived in the field. Their cassettes were the most popular in public spaces, and their core repertory of songs was commonly known and sung among Palestinian musicians more so than any other ensemble.

16. Abu Sha'ira, *Dalil Lil-Aghaniya Al-Wataniya Al-Filistiniya: Fakr wa Maqawma [Guide to Palestinian Nationalist Songs: Conception and Resistance]* (Damascus: Dar Al-Shajara Lil-Nashr, 2004), 255.

17. Abu Sha'ira, *Dalil Lil-Aghaniya Al-Wataniya Al-Filistiniya*, 255.

18. McDonald, "My Voice Is My Weapon."

19. McDonald, "Poetics and the Performance." Creative indexing is a term that I borrow from the discussion of music and political movements in Thomas

Turino, *Music as Social Life: The Politics of Participation* (Chicago: University of Chicago Press, 2008), 208.

20. In addition, female members of the group were prohibited from wearing their *ḥijub* (pl: headscarves) on stage in an attempt to distance the group from any particular religious associations.

21. Ethnographic video footage of this performance will be available in the fall of 2012 via the Ethnographic Video for Instruction and Analysis (EVIA) website, http://www.eviada.org.

22. Despite strong censorship I very easily found bootleg copies of these recordings in Jordan, Syria, and the West Bank from 2002 to 2005.

23. Anne M. Oliver and Paul Steinberg, "Popular Music of the Intifada," in *Garland Encyclopedia of World Music: The Middle East*, vol. 6, ed. Virginia Danielson, Scott L. Marcus, and Dwight Reynolds (New York: Garland. 2002), 635–38.

24. Palestinian citizens of Israel are issued blue identification cards. Palestinians living in areas of Israeli occupation are issued green identification cards. While blue identification card holders are granted far more freedom of mobility, the collective practice of being legally defined by the Israeli state with these cards is a powerful means of national identification and resistance among Palestinian communities.

25. McDonald, "My Voice Is My Weapon," 271.

26. Joseph Roach, *Cities of the Dead: Circum-Atlantic Performance* (New York: Columbia University Press, 1996), 26; Taylor, *The Archive and the Repertoire*, 5.

CHAPTER SIX

Pax Mevlana

Mevlevi Sufi Music and the Reconciliation of Islam and the West

> ⋙

VICTOR A. VICENTE

A Call for Cooperation

The best known and most commonly cited poem in the Islamic mystical tradition today can be translated from the Persian more or less as follows:[1]

> Come, come, whoever you are.
> Wanderer, idolater,[2] worshipper of fire,[3] come even though you have broken
> your vows a thousand times,
> Come, and come yet again. Ours is not a caravan of despair.

This quatrain is reprinted often in anthologies of Persian or sacred texts[4] and is turned into living culture by its adornment of innumerable Internet blogs and websites as well as its frequent intoning over instrumental musical accompaniment at sacred and semi-sacred gatherings in many corners of the world. Popularly attributed to the thirteenth-century mystic Mevlana Celal ed-Din Rumi,[5] even though it cannot be found in the earliest manuscripts of his writings, it has come to represent the philosophies not only of the great master, but also of Islamic mysticism, termed Sufism, as a whole. It is also popularly invoked, like so many other poems of its ilk, as an open invitation to confraternity, a call for cooperation in healing the wounds of cultural division, namely those of what is not unproblematically described as the increasing "rift" between the Muslim world and the West.[6]

In this chapter, I explore the roles that Sufi poetry, music, and ritual currently play in this mending of fences. My focus is specifically on how the music of Mevlana Rumi's followers, especially that of the legally banned, but furtively promoted Mevlevi Order from Turkey, serves as a locus where conflicting Western and Islamic cultural, religious, and political ideologies are negotiated and reconciled. After presenting the historical and contemporary contexts of the tensions between Islam and the West and describing the state of Sufism in Turkey, I examine the nature of reconciliation in three principal areas of Sufi music making: public state-sponsored *sema* whirling shows, private *zikr* ceremonies, and performances of popular music incorporating Sufi themes and sounds. Importantly, I am also careful to pinpoint moments when reconciliation is not fully possible and when the musical acts of reconciliation themselves create new tensions, not only between Islam and the West, but also within Sufism proper.

Contexts for Conflict and Transcendence

Tensions between Islam[7] and the West long predate the tragic events of recent history; yet even in the darkest of times there has always been a strong compulsion to transcend difference and work toward peaceful coexistence. Indeed, the earliest traces of acrimony, as well as amity, date back to the first century of Islam when beginning in the early 630s Muslim Arab armies swept through Christian territories in West Asia, North Africa, and Western Europe. Many turned to Islam voluntarily, but there were also many who were forced into conversion despite the Qur'anic injunction stipulating that Jews and Christians be treated as "people of the covenant of protection" (*ahl al-dhimmi*).[8] As "people of the book" (*ahl al-kitab*), those who did not convert were nevertheless able to live in relative peace under Islamic rule and jurisprudence. Such tolerance would for centuries prove to be a cornerstone of Islamic civilization in the Mediterranean Basin. Themes of tolerance and coexistence were thus much in evidence, and even celebrated, in the music of al-Andalus (Medieval Iberia)[9] as well as in the musical life of the Ottoman court;[10] two contexts, incidentally, in which Sufism was, at times, exceptionally prominent.

Be this as it may, Bernard Lewis does caution against conjuring up the image of "an interfaith, interracial utopia, in which men and women belonging to different races, professing different creeds, lived side by side in a golden age of unbroken harmony, enjoying equality of rights and of opportunities, and toiling together for the advancement of civilization."[11] He asserts that understanding Islam's concept of tolerance necessitates comparison with other religions and civilizations and involves the consideration of such facets of coexistence as discrimination, persecution, and egalitarianism, among others.[12] He points out that Islamic law in fact not only set out, but indeed managed basic inequalities between masters and slaves, men and women, and believers and unbelievers.[13] The ways in which these relationships were legally and socially recognized and handled, of course, depended on the politics and circumstances at hand.

The generally stable, if not always conciliatory, relationship that Muslim powers managed with the Christian West were most substantively undermined by the retaliatory and bloody enterprises of the crusades, the *reconquistas*, and, beginning in the nineteenth century, the colonial dismantling of the Ottoman Empire along ethnic-religious lines. More recent strains, including the ongoing crisis in the Palestinian territories, the attacks of September 11, 2001, and the subsequent U.S.-led war in Iraq, have only worked to widen the gulf. Voicing the sentiments of many around the world, the Turkish rock group Bulutsuzluk Özlemi (The Longing for Uncloudiness) ask in "Bağdat Kafe" ("Baghdad Cafe"), a fragile and uncertain Iraq War ballad from their 2005 album *Felluce* (*Fallujah*), "Where is the end of the road?"

The sense of frustration and growing rupture between Islam and the West has indeed become all too profound in Turkey, a country that literally encompasses the crossroads between East and West. As a strategic ally of the United States and an aspiring member of the European Union, Turkey has long sought to resolve this "clash of civilizations,"[14] but recently it has begun to question its Western aspirations. A BBC poll conducted in 2006, for example, found that only one third of the Turkish population favored membership in the E.U., as opposed to 66 percent in the previous year.[15] The military incursions into Iraq and Afghanistan in the "International War on Terror" undoubtedly further antagonized the public, which already harbored long-standing resentment over European and American pressure for Turkey to declare its massacre of Armenians at the end of World War I as genocide and to grant greater cultural autonomy to its Kurdish population. In my own research trips to Turkey since 2002, I have observed with much concern how widespread public sympathy for the September 11 attacks and a longing to unite with Europe have transformed into angry debates, threats of boycotts, and open protests.

I have also observed with considerable amazement, though, that it is in this very context of escalating political and cultural tension that Sufism and Sufi music, conversely, have begun to experience a renaissance and now thrive not only in Turkey, but in the West as well.[16] In 1997, for example, the *Christian Science Monitor* reported to much surprise not only in Turkey and Iran, but in the United States as well, that Mevlana Celel ed-Din Rumi had become the best-selling poet in the United States.[17] Seeming to connect Rumi's messages of peace, love, and forgiveness with recent world events, Coleman Barks, Rumi translator and lucky recipient of his newfound popularity, explains,

His presence and his poetry was, and is, inclusive, allied with the impulse to praise and recognize every being and every moment as sacred. *Interfaith* hardly reaches the depth of his connecting. Rumi speaks for *the clear bead at the center*. . . . Surely someday we will quit killing each other over [religious differences]. . . . [Yet even without this,] his place among world religions is as a dissolver of boundaries.[18]

Sufism, sometimes described as a heterodox form of Islam, first emerged in the eighth century as an alternative to the mainstream Orthodoxy, stressing spiritualism and personal connections with Allah and His creation through a variety of means including asceticism, esotericism, meditation, and ecstatic worship. Unlike Orthodox Muslims who often consider music to be a distraction from worship, most Sufis believe that music, on the contrary, provides the only direct means of communing with the Divine.[19] Thus, Sufis have been among the greatest purveyors of music in the Islamic world, and they have cultivated music to a rich degree both to facilitate trancing[20] and to accompany *sema*, a distinctive counterclockwise turning motion practiced by some Sufi orders (*tarikats*) and often misidentified as a dance. At the core of the prayers, gestures, and music of their ritual are the themes of peace, love, self-renunciation, and acceptance so well summarized in the rhymed couplets (*gazels*) of such figures as Mevlana Celal ed-Din Rumi:

> Reconciling to myself, I emerge into the world
> bare of all thought, clear love in which
> the sun on my doorstep dances to your drum
> The ant walking into it is no less than you[21]

Commonly believed to have been born on September 30, 1207, in Balkh, Afghanistan,[22] Rumi wrote such verses in an age when the Muslim world faced the ravages of the Mongols from the east and no less than five crusades from the West; an age that for Islam was strikingly comparable to that of today in terms of bloodshed. Although he did not personally experience the atrocities and mass killings of his era, having migrated westward in advance of the devastation and eventually settling in the sanctuary Turkish city of Konya, he advocated a path that transcended violence and retribution to his followers:

> In fact, every enemy is your medicine,
> Who is your beneficial alchemy and heart healing[23]

> Dance, when you're broken open
> Dance, if you've torn the bandage off.

Dance in the middle of the fighting.
Dance in your blood.[24]

Undoubtedly, such wisdom and forbearance brought solace to many, as it still does today,[25] and it surely accounts for the rapid growth of his cult upon his death on the evening of December 17, 1273.

While many Sufi tarikats lay claim to Mevlana Rumi as a spiritual guide, he remains most deeply associated with the Mevlevi Order, which was founded by his son Sultan Veled. Rising to power during the Ottoman period, the Mevlevi not only came to dominate the musical life of the royal court, they eventually ruled over the whole empire under several Mevlevi sultans who were also poets, musicians, and composers. After the fall of the Ottoman Empire, however, the Mevlevi, along with all other Sufi tarikats in Turkey, were officially banned on December 13, 1925 by the staunchly secular government of the new Republic of Turkey, in large part to curtail their influence in public life. Mevlana Rumi was, consequently, demoted from a saint to a poet and his shrine in Konya was officially reconstituted as a museum. Even today, performances of all Sufi rituals and sacred music remain illicit as manifestations of religious devotion and are allowed only under a technicality that permits displays of Turkish cultural heritage.

Despite the ban, however, Mevlevi Sufi thought, ritual, and music have gained tremendous popularity over the course of the past three decades, and not only in the sales of the large collection (*divan*) of Rumi's poems, which serve as the spiritual and textual nucleus of Mevlevi ritual and music. The rebirth can be said to have commenced, ironically, with the commemorations of the seven hundredth anniversary of Rumi's death in 1973. In that year, proclaimed by UNESCO as the international Year of Rumi, the Turkish government permitted and oversaw the reintroduction of Mevlevi practices, especially the sema ceremony (discussed below) into the public sphere, a process that had actually been slowly underway since the 1950s.[26] Recognizing the many opportunities that Sufism offers in the post-9/11 world, the Turkish government seized upon a second UNESCO Year of Rumi, commemorating his eight hundredth birthday, in 2007 with unprecedented vigor and thereby further stimulated the Sufi renaissance, but without lifting the ban. Among the more unusual initiatives implemented under the aegis of the Year of Rumi and complementing countless sanctioned performances of sema have been the establishment of a Mevlana Peace Prize, the founding of a "living" Mevlevi museum, the sponsoring of a Rumi chess tournament, and the reintroduction of a forgotten Mevlevi dessert.[27]

This Rumi craze can indeed be seen and heard almost everywhere in Turkey today. Bookstores prominently display anthologies of his poems along with the *Mesnevi*, his six-volume magnum opus, in their front windows. Figurines, posters, puppets, and even snow globes of Mevlana and whirling dervishes abound in the bazaars of all the major cities. Sounds of reed flute improvisations (ney *taksims*) waft over the din on the main pedestrian street of the upscale shopping area of Taksim in Istanbul, luring patrons into the record shops, where recordings of Mevlevi music do good business. In fact, many music stores, including the one at Atatürk International Airport in Istanbul now have separate, specially designated sections just for Mevlevi and other Sufi music, where before they went unmarked. Available on CD are several historical and contemporary recordings of Mevlevi *ayins*, numerous selections of taksims and programmatic pieces by prominent ney players, New Age Sufi music fusions, and even the occasional foreign import field recording of local *zikr* ceremonies (see below).[28] Meanwhile in the video section, DVD documentaries on the life of Rumi and VCDs on the Mevlevi rite can be readily found.

Following suit, the Ministry of Culture and Tourism has also been keen to promote Mevlana Rumi and the Mevlevi both domestically and abroad. Despite the legal ban that remains in force, the ministry has made Mevlevi Sufism the liberal face of Turkey and the tolerant, moderate branch of Islam, and it has actually turned the Mevlevi dervish, whirling in sema, into an outright icon of the nation. In a recently televised tourism advertisement entitled *Istanbul: Love of Two Continents*, for instance, one of many endorsed by the ministry, a pair of lovers (apparently compelled by their natural and inviolate affinity) hurl themselves across the Bosphorus Straight (which divides Europe from Asia) and leap onto such supporting objects of Anatolian heritage as a Hittite sistrum and the Trojan Horse. At the climax of the ad, our protagonists soar into each other's embrace from the outstretched arms of two whirling dervishes. The theme of love here operates on multiples levels as it does in Sufi poetry, though in far more obvious ways. The ad not only plainly depicts romantic union and spiritual devotion, but, in the context of contemporary East-West politics, evidently also the reconciliation of Christian and Muslim civilizations. Such advertisements, when combined with the host of other recent developments surrounding the Year of Rumi, clearly illustrate the critical role that Mevlevi Sufism now plays in mediating Turkish relations with the West; but as we shall see, such developments have also provoked important questions and concerns about the nature of this reconciliation.

The Mevlevi Sema and the Politics of Peace

Winegar, with reference to both the 2007 Year of Rumi and sema performances, has articulated important critiques of the use of Sufism in brokering international and interfaith peace. She notes that official presentations of Sufi music, although often purportedly apolitical on the surface, are in fact ideologically consonant with and financially aided by governments and agencies (like the United States and UNESCO) that have specific agendas of promoting particular forms of Islam that are religiously and politically moderate. In essence, they work by either erasing all connections with Islam or by resisting or attacking "bad," that is, radical or fundamentalist, interpretations of Islam.[29]

Hence, Rumi and his Mevlevi associates currently have many advocates in the Turkish political establishment. Undoubtedly the most prominent and potent is none other than Prime Minister Recep Tayyip Erdoğan. A religious conservative strongly campaigning for Turkey's accession into the E.U., Erdoğan is ostensibly an enormous admirer of Rumi's. Erdoğan has himself called for reconciliation between Islam and the West in interviews in which he emphasizes the rich history of tolerant philosophy shared by both civilizations, exemplified, as he sees it, in Turkey by Mevlana of Konya and in the West by Erasmus of Rotterdam. For his efforts, the Rumi Forum, an academic organization based in Washington, D.C., created to foster interfaith and intercultural dialogue, awarded the Rumi Peace and Dialogue Award jointly to Erdoğan and his Spanish counterpart, José Luis Rodríguez Zapatero, for their work, carried out under the auspices of the United Nations, on intercivilization cooperation. At the awards ceremony in March 2007, their collaboration was celebrated with a performance by a Mevlevi group from Istanbul of sema, the characteristic Mevlevi trancing ceremony that has become the international symbol of Islamic openness and tolerance.

As I have explained, such politicization of Mevlana Rumi and the Mevlevi sema has facilitated the reinstatement and revitalization of Sufi culture in Turkey today, but it has also opened up the discourse to include concerns over authenticity and questions about the spiritual essence (*tasavvuf*) of the tradition. Already in 1967, Resuhi Baykara, a Mevlevi *postnişin* (officiating sheikh), created a schism in the community when he became offended by the presence of journalists and paparazzi at a public ceremony and declared it inauthentic. Barred from participating in later years by the Ministry of Culture for implying that such public events were somehow sacred, he went on to form his own Sufi group in London.[30] Indeed, by the time I had arrived in Turkey in 2004 to conduct my research, I was informed by many that the Mevlevi no longer existed; that there was no longer any tasavvuf in Mevlevi music, only tourism.

Such impressions are understandable given that the typical officially sanctioned public Mevlevi ceremony today in many ways resembles more a concert than a ritual. Many performances take place in restored Mevlevi lodges, such as the Mevlevihane in Galata, or at newly constructed halls like that at the large Mevlana Cultural Center in Konya, but they are also commonly held in such evocative tourist locales as old caravanserais, castles, and the Şirkeci train station in Istanbul; still more commercialized ceremonies take place in restaurants, airports, and outdoor pavilions. Termed "whirling shows" by some, they break from tradition in their adoption of Western staging conventions and concert etiquette[31] as well as in their periodic inclusion of laser lights displays, concerts of folk music, and other entertainment.

Despite some contextual changes to the ceremony, however, the basic ritual and music, at least of the popular performances at the Galata Mevlevihane and the Mevlana Center in Konya, remain genuine and are in keeping with traditional Ottoman Mevlevi practice. The music played in these venues, for example, is exclusively drawn from a somewhat closed repertory of around sixty-five lengthy multi-movement suites called *ayin-i şerif*-s that were mostly compiled from the oral tradition by Mevlevi musicologist and theorist Rauf Yekta Bey in the 1930s.[32] The majority of these works were composed in the eighteenth and nineteenth centuries, but a few may date back as far as the sixteenth century.[33] They are performed in full along with Qur'anic recitations, prayers, and other chants according to the liturgical order. The ayins, performed by sizeable ensembles of classical Mevlevi instruments and choirs of singers, specifically accompany the presentation of sema, which is sometimes performed by as many as thirty or more *semazens* (whirlers). For the octocentennial in 2007, for example, a staggering three hundred semazens whirled in a gargantuan ceremony held simultaneously in Konya and in thirty-two other cities across Turkey.[34] Although such large performing forces create enormous spectacles that are not in keeping with the standard practice of the Ottoman period, the actual music, sema whirling, and ritual are essentially authentic.

Nevertheless, many foreign and some local spectators attending these performances, including the larger ones that proliferate in December as commemorations of Rumi's death, experience them as "touristy" and "commercialized." This is the case even though there is usually little to no overt advertisement or corporate sponsorship mentioned in printed programs or incorporated into the performance proceedings of even the most touristic of whirling shows. In fact, performance organizers usually work diligently to ensure that sema is presented in as respectful and sacral an atmosphere as possible. What really calls the spiritual authenticity of such events into question is the fact that many Sufi music troupes employ musicians and semazens who are professionally trained performers, but may or may not be actual Sufi adherents.

Yet many local Turkish audience members do in fact experience whirling shows as religious events, as do some foreign tourists. The mass appetite for whirling shows is not grounded solely in the aesthetic appeal and mechanics of the performances, nor do the tourism ads attract only culturally curious dabblers. A great deal of what we might term Mevlana tourism could in fact be more correctly identified as Mevlana pilgrimage. For example, the Mevlana Museum in Konya received over two million visitors in 2007, and officials expect as many as ten million in the next few years.[35] Although officially a secular public space, the museum, which houses Rumi's tomb and was formerly a mosque-shrine complex, is very much treated as a sacred space by visitors, many of whom drink from the healing waters of the main fountain in the courtyard and pray at every tomb and relic. Most of these pilgrims are domestic, but an increasing number also come from Europe and the western coast of North America from British Columbia to California, where the Mevlevi Order is in many ways far stronger and more active than in Turkey.

For these visitors to Konya and elsewhere, attending a sema performance is nearly inevitable, and their involvement as spectators can vary from simple reverence to open prayer or even trancing. Although ecstatic worship as well as interfaith collaboration are typically somewhat limited by the rigid sequence of the ceremony and the performance conventions borrowed from the European concert hall, the dim lighting, performer-audience separation, and the mandate for respectful reverence does create a contemplative atmosphere reminiscent of a mosque or a church. This encourages quiet prayer and is in keeping with the Mevlevi tradition of achieving ecstasy through meditative audition or listening (samaʿ). The integration of readings of poems by Rumi in Turkish and English translation as well as recitations from the Qur'an into the programs further enhance the meditative experience of the whirling shows for both Western and Muslim audiences alike.

In the politics of sema, however, the ever-larger shows and the growing numbers of tourists, even when they are pilgrims, are regarded by some traditionalists as diluting the spiritual, that is to say Islamic, nature of Sufism. Some, fearing a secularist usurpation of Islamic Sufi ideals, even perceive the government's leniency toward and promotion of Mevlana and the Mevlevi as a way to further minimize the limited influence and autonomy of the country's many Sufi tarikats. Thus, while the Mevlevi sema ceremony and its music are synonymous with the messages of peace, love, and tolerance that abound in Mevlana's writings and still very much function as potent sites for mediating East-West tensions, their politicization by the government has also rendered them controversial loci of competing interests.

Forgetting and Not-Forgetting:
The Zikr as a Communal Experience

In marked contrast to the somewhat controversial public spectacles sponsored by the Turkish Ministry of Culture and Tourism are the many private ceremonies called *zikrs* (Arabic, *dhikr*) that take place clandestinely throughout Sufi communities in Turkey and more openly across the world. The term *zikr* is commonly translated as "remembrance," but is more accurately understood as "not-forgetting" or "anamnesis" in English.[36] It refers to a host of meditative and ritual practices all aimed at helping the devotee not forget the name and place of Allah in daily life. Sufi varieties of zikr range from meditating on *tespih* beads and listening to music (*sama'*) to mass rituals involving collective trancing and the reiteration of Allah's name.[37]

Different Sufi tarikats developed their own idiosyncratic forms of collective zikr. The more sober Mevlevi zikr, for instance, involves whirling counterclockwise with outstretched arms to the accompaniment of sophisticated vocal and instrumental music, which I have termed the sema ceremony here. Most other Sufi sects practice a more raucous ceremony that may include a combination of loud drumming, semi-classical and folk music, and the continuous rhythmic chanting of the word "Allah" and other verbal formulas. Historically, distinctions between tarikats were always rather fluid, as dervishes could belong to more than one order at a time. Today, we find that the sema is not the sole property of the Mevlevi and that some Mevlevi also regularly participate in the pan-Sufi zikr. Thus, it is not uncommon to find zikr séances that involve the musical and gestural elements of both rites.

Unlike the public sema ceremony, the private zikr is a flexible sequence of prayers, chants, hymns, odes, and instrumental music that requires participation from all congregants present. The inclusive, communal experience of zikr is forged not only through collective singing, chanting, and drumming, but also through group movement best described as a front-to-back, and sometimes up-and-down, rocking that is performed in a seated, or sometimes standing, position. The perpetual repetition of these motions as well as the incessant reiteration of the chanted formulas not only create a spirit of communitas among congregants, but also induce ecstatic trancing, often manifest in the form of convulsions and involuntary spastic fits. Because of the religious fervor they inspire, zikr sessions are usually held in secret in Turkey so as not to provoke authorities. In order to preserve this secrecy and anonymity, I will not dwell too deeply on the zikr in this chapter. I cite here briefly and anecdotally just two examples I have documented elsewhere[38] that I feel strongly elucidate our understanding of the ways Sufi music and performance enable cross-cultural dialogue and reconciliation.

The first took place in 2004 at a carpet shop in Konya not too far from Rumi's shrine on the evening before his Şeb-i Arûs, the grand ceremony commemorating his death in 1273. The participants in the zikr included a core of local musicians who played a mixture of folk and classical Turkish instruments and were associated with one of the nearby *tekkes* (lodges). The tekke attracts a wide congregation throughout the year and is frequented by Mevlevis and other Sufis as well as by pilgrims and tourists visiting from every corner of Turkey and from all over the world. For a variety of reasons, the evening's zikr was not held in the tekke but at a carpet shop that could accommodate the thirty or so who eventually showed up. The majority of the congregants were internationals from Afghanistan, France, India, Israel, the United States, and elsewhere. They included dervishes and sheikhs as well as tourists and invited guests.

As a ritual, the zikr met every qualification of liminality, with all personal, social, and national divisions subverted by more than three hours of communal chanting, whirling, eating, and camaraderie. The two invited middle-class women from Istanbul were novices to Sufism and were visibly anxious, but the two French tourists cycling across Asia could not have been more thrilled. The Israeli, who had been training for some time, performed sema, as did one of the Turkish kudüm (small kettledrum) players who spontaneously abandoned his instrument in a moment of elation. Forgetting that their countries were at war, the Afghan rebab player repeatedly invoked the name of Allah along with the American at his side, even as twenty-eight soldiers were about to perish in Helmand Province. Meanwhile, the modest young Indian woman erupted frequently throughout into loud, ecstatic outbursts, her hair frazzled and her voice hoarse from "not forgetting." The ceremony proper lasted only about an hour, but the participants stayed on well into the early hours of the night, immersed in talk about Mevlana, sema, music, cultural differences, cultural similarities, and about how drinking rose-flavored tea could be interpreted not just as a Sufi symbol, but as zikr itself. The departing goodbyes were as prolonged as the promises of meeting the next day were sincere.

Such feelings of concordance and brotherhood were common at the zikr gatherings I attended at the tekke, as were moments of spiritual transcendence. The weekly zikrs hosted by the sheikh at the tekke follow the liturgy of the standard zikr, but they also include an open section in which congregants are invited to perform music or read poetry at will. In fact any visitor is normally afforded the opportunity to recite poetry, perform sema, sing, or play with the ensemble of musicians during the course of the ceremony.

A few days prior to the gathering I just described, I participated in a zikr dominated by pilgrims from Iran, Belgium, and the Netherlands. The session had been especially exuberant because the Iranian contingent was both quite pious and impassioned; the chanting had been extremely vigorous and the displays of trancing were so frequent they bordered on the competitive. After the main ritual but before the closing prayers, in the period when congregants cool down from the intensity of the zikr and the floor is opened up for free expression, a Dutch woman, still in a state of elation and with her eyes closed and her hands on her heart, began singing a Latin Sanctus in a high, moving voice. Asked to translate, she struggled at first, but eventually exclaimed, "It means Allahu Akbar," which garnered enthusiastic approval from the sheikh and others Turkish congregants.

A third example I would like to include here is only partly related to the zikr, but it took place during the same week of festivities as the others and involves many of the same individuals I have been discussing. It also problematizes, somewhat, the way zikr functions as a means of establishing amity between Muslims and Westerners in the same way that I will discuss in the following section. Namely, it raises the related questions of intention and what exactly is meant by the term "Sufi music."

In the week or two preceding Mevlana's Şeb-i Arûs, the anniversary of his death on the night of December 17, the city of Konya hosts the Mevlana Festival, which in recent years has grown to incorporate a number of side festivals and programs. For the Şeb-i Arûs in 2004, the Konya Ministry of Culture established the concurrent International Mystic Music Festival, and, in the spirit of Mevlana and universal brotherhood, invited performers from Turkey, Azerbaijan, Iran, Pakistan, and France to perform. The French group, a gospel choir named The Gospel Legend Singers, was unequivocally the most unexpected and, therefore, the most memorable act.

Comprised of Afro-French and Francophone Africans, the choir was founded in Paris in 1995 by Jackson Mpongo, an émigré from the Belgian Congo. The choir performs mainly American gospel songs and spirituals in English and French, though occasionally songs will have texts in Zulu or other African languages. The recital had been quite lively, but Mpongo, wanting a bit more interaction with the audience, initiated a dance motion during the song "Freedom Is Coming" that a group of European Sufi pilgrims sitting in the front immediately interpreted as the rocking motions of the zikr. Led by an Italian sheikh, the joyful pilgrims transformed the Christian hymn, much like the Sanctus discussed previously, into an occasion for a short Sufi zikr, much to the amusement of the more reserved Turkish audience. It would appear on the surface that what we have here is an honest two-way musical dialogue on the question of interfaith reconciliation. In interviews with some of the choir members afterward, however, most admitted that they had no idea who Rumi was, and that they had come mainly to visit Turkey and preach the Gospel.

Pop and the Probabilities for Peace

During my time in Konya, I was told repeatedly that Sufism is "all-loving" and that the devotees of Mevlana welcome all people: women, Christians, Jews, Hindus, gays, lesbians, and even atheists. Yet, I have found that this tolerance is in many ways challenged not only by the previous example, but also, as we have seen, by the commercialization of the Mevlevi sema and the periodic mass influx of tourists, pilgrims, admirers, and opportunists. The greater test for Sufism in Turkey today, however, comes from the way mystical Islamic concepts, sounds, and images are being incorporated into pop culture and popular music.

Sufi popular music, as it were, has yet to develop into a full-fledged genre of its own. It is sometimes awkwardly and inappropriately subsumed within the broader category of so-called *"yeşil* pop" (green pop), a term now commonly used to describe the influential Islamic Turkish popular music movement that developed in the 1990s at around the same time as the growth of the more mainstream, "secular" pop industry and the privatization of the national airwaves. Sufi pop examples are far fewer in number, less prominent, and are not as stylistically uniform as yeşil pop. Rather, they exist as one-off experiments, occasional one-hit-wonders, and the idiosyncratic endeavors of individual artists. The purveyors of Sufi pop must not only deal with these issues of style and genre, but they must also contend with the broader questions that plague the popularization of Sufism in general, especially those of commercialization, dilution, and spiritual authenticity.

At the crest of the Sufi pop wave, as well as at the undertow of its controversies, is Mercan Dede, a Turkish-born Canadian DJ who blends Turkish, Persian, and Indian Sufi music with ambient techno and various world music forms. Born Arkın Ilıcalı, Mercan Dede is trained in the traditions of several Sufi tarikats, including those of the Mevlevi, and is a proficient player of the ney, the diagonally blown reed flute characteristic of the Mevlevi, and the bendir, the ubiquitous frame drum of the communal zikr. In his quest to bridge the divide between Islam and West through music, he has readily adopted Rumi's messages of peace and tolerance and infused them into his rather diverse and sizeable corpus of works.

All of Mercan Dede's albums, for example, are informed by Sufi themes and imagery. These include the as of yet unfinished cycle on the four elements — *Nar (Fire,* 2002), *Su (Water,* 2003), *Nefes (Air,* 2007), and *Toprak*

(*Earth*) — as well as a series of albums inspired by the Sufi tradition of ascetic wandering, including *Journeys of a Dervish* (1999), *Seyahatname* (*Book of Travels*, 2001), and *Sufi Traveler* (2004). His most recent album, entitled *800*, was released in 2007 in commemoration of Mevlana's birth (see below). Mercan Dede's works are often sonically evocative of the zikr (e.g., "Dreams of Sufi Saints" from *Sufi Dreams*, 1998) or explore such core Sufi concepts as mystical love (*aşk*). Iconographically, his music videos, promotional art, and live performances often include important Sufi symbols such as spirals and the name of the Prophet Mohammad, as well as more internationally recognized indices of peace and spirituality, such as doves, angels, and candles.[39] Though used sparingly, his lyrics and vocal samples, usually in a variety of languages, are either inspired by or directly quote Mevlana Rumi and other Sufi poets.

In the spirit of mitigating cultural difference, Mercan Dede commonly collaborates with artists from an array of backgrounds working in a plurality of styles. Among these have been the British Tamil singer Susheela Raman, the Iranian Sufi musician Azam Ali, the Canadian violinist Hugh Marsh, and the Turkish rapper Ceza. His performances have also often starred the whirling of the Canadian dancer and semazen Mira Burke (now Hunter). As a result, his music can be described as a fusion of techno with a variety of styles, including jazz, rap, Turkish arabesk, Anatolian folk music, gypsy music, and Western, Turkish, Persian, and Indian classical music. Likewise, it features a large assortment of instrumentation including ney, kanun, ud, bağlama, tar, sitar, electric violin, double bass, flugelhorn, clarinet, didgeridoo, tabla, dholak, and other sundry percussion.

Although Ilıcalı eschews the fame his music has afforded him by performing under a variety of stage names, of which Mercan Dede is his most well known, his popularity has steadily grown over the past decade and especially since September 11, 2001. Among his successes are the album *Su*, which occupied the top spot on the European World Music charts for two months after its release, and *800*, which was declared the Best World Music album for 2008 by WOMEX (World Music Expo). His appeal in fact comes very much from his global sensibilities as well as from his philosophical and musical desire to heal the wounds of division between Islam and the West, a task that was facilitated by the Turkish Ministry of Culture in 2004 when he was appointed an official worldwide representative of Turkish culture and arts. With this official sanction, Mercan Dede gave a huge performance in 2005 in the city of Izmir on the occasion of the Universiade, a prominent international sporting competition hosted annually by the universities of a chosen city. The highlight of the festivities involved Mercan Dede playing ney for a large number of semazens whirling on a patchwork of flags and pictures of Rumi. He has also used his international prominence to more forcefully push for political change, denouncing the American "occupation" of Iraq at concerts in the United States and refusing to perform in Israel, despite several invitations, on account of Israeli settlement on what he believes is Palestinian land.[40]

Despite his good intentions and praise from the international community, he is often regarded in Turkey, especially among traditionally minded Sufis, as exploiting, diluting, and trivializing Islamic mysticism. His performances with Mira Hunter in particular have garnered quite a bit of disapproval. Although the daughter of a sheikh in Vancouver, Hunter has been criticized not only for being a female whirler, but also for performing sema in a non-standard, free-form manner and for lining her tunic with glow sticks in some shows. Mercan Dede, for his part, is denounced in more conservative areas of Turkey for his unorthodox hairstyles and attire and for assuming the high Sufi honorific title of *dede* as a stage name. More significantly, detractors reject his works as Sufi music because they have little in common with traditional forms and are not used in authentic ritual contexts. Specifically, they regard the hybridization of musical styles as a dilution of Sufi tradition.

Mercan Dede has usually responded to such deprecation by invoking conciliatory Mevlana-like aphorisms or by turning the criticism into optimism, as Mevlana suggested. His 2004 album *Fusion Monster*, for example, responds to the attacks of hybridization by embracing them full on; the album title was taken directly from a negative critique in the Turkish press.[41] He also did not perform for any of the commemorations of Mevlana's birth in 2007 so as not to be seen as taking advantage of the Rumi craze.[42] In fact, despite his conspicuous outward appearance, he very much avoids the limelight, typically performing behind a wall of computers and turntables. Moreover, although not usually attended by committed Sufi devotees, Mercan Dede's performances, behind the techno rave veneer, at times do bear some resemblance to more traditional Sufi forms of ritual worship. His music creates meditative environments that blend the more inactive experience of the sema concert with the participatory nature of the zikr; indeed, the back-and-forth, up-and-down dancing performed by some of Mercan Dede's audiences can be directly compared to the ritual movements of the traditional zikr rite.[43] In addition, I have been informed by some Sufi enthusiasts that recordings of Mercan Dede's music have been used by Sufis in the United States to accompany zikr worship, though I have been unable to verify the claims. If true, such cases would very much complicate and challenge traditional notions of Sufi music and ritual even further.

Jean During has written that Sufi music is essentially any music that is performed with or interpreted as having "mystical essence" or tasavvuf.[44]

Using this expanded definition, there is certainly nothing that would preclude gospel music, techno, or even a Sanctus from serving as "Sufi music"; certainly there are more ecstatic manifestations of tasavvuf at these performances than at the generally more staid presentations of the classical Ottoman Mevlevi ceremony. Yet even During, with such a broad interpretation, was quick to dismiss popular music as being devotionally viable. Indeed, many traditionalists perceive the rapid changes in context, ritual, and sound brought by popular Sufi artists like Mercan Dede, as well as by the commercialization of the Mevlevi rite and by the preponderance of tourists at zikrs, as diminishing the Sufi way of life. Such developments, it would seem, are creating division and conflict within the Sufi community, even as they, ironically, appear to be advancing international movements calling for interreligious dialogue, peace, and reconciliation. Nevertheless there remains tremendous opportunity in this era of the Mevlana renaissance for the Sufi community itself to reconcile the demands of tradition with the global desire to connect with Sufism more deeply. As Mercan Dede has submitted, "Counterfeit gold points to real gold. The one that is not genuine is like a soap bubble and is thus temporary. Time will eliminate it."[45]

Postscripts: Whirling to Oneness

On September 11, 2007, just a couple of weeks shy of Mevlana Rumi's eight hundredth birthday, Dr. Hasan Ali Yurtsever, president of the Rumi Forum, the Turkish-American think tank referred to earlier in connection to the Rumi Peace and Dialogue Award, proclaimed that "9/11 was not only against the U.S., but also against Islam."[46] Yurtsever echoed the sentiments of many in the Muslim world, including those who disapproved of the tone and rhetoric of the subsequent "War on Terror" and despised the wars in Iraq and Afghanistan as perceived revenge for 9/11. In an effort to promote peace and bridge the divide between Islam and the West that had long existed, but had been exposed and widened by the 9/11 terrorist attacks, many on both sides turned to Sufism. They found in Sufi writings, music, and ritual not only a refuge, but also a viable means of transmuting discord into harmony and forging a path toward coexistence.

If we overlook the complex negotiations that securing such coveted endorsement entails,[47] we can see that UNESCO, in recognizing 2007 as the Year of Rumi, initiated what can only be regarded as an extremely successful campaign furthering intercultural understanding and collaboration. In the years leading up to the worldwide festivities, and even well after, Mevlana's writings, which are the core of his teachings on peace and spiritual transcendence, gained a wider global readership than ever before. In the literary world, this spawned a flurry of activity in translation of Sufi poetry, Sufi-themed creative writing, and other postscripts.

In music, as we have seen, the "Pax Mevlana" has involved not only a tremendous growth of interest in older forms like the Mevlevi ayin-i şerif, the sema, and the zikr ceremony, but also the creation of new music by such artists as Mercan Dede which, in all its fusions and hybridities, bears witness to the present-day yearning to integrate Islam and the West with one another as well as with the rest of the world. The performance of Sufi music in churches,[48] the elaborate greeting of *görüşmek* that opens some zikr gatherings,[49] and the worldwide presentation of sema are also all further enactments of the Mevlevi Sufi doctrine of whirling to oneness.[50] While this process has become fraught with contention over the issues of spiritual authenticity, commercialization, and misunderstanding, issues that may yet prove to be intractable obstacles to fuller Sufi musical reconciliation between East and West, it has, for the time being, also championed more moderate alternatives to the radicalized versions of Islam presented in the international media.

Notes

1. Among the many existing variants, perhaps the most satisfying English translation, given here, can be found in Amin Malak, *Muslim Narratives and the Discourse of English* (Albany: State University of New York Press, 2005), 151.

2. The reference here is to Christians and pre-Islamic pagans who venerate icons and idols during religious worship.

3. This reference is to Zoroastrians, who revere and pray in the presence of fire (*atar*) or some other source of light.

4. See for instance the Unitarian Universalist Hymnal, *Singing the Living Tradition*.

5. As I deal primarily with Sufism in connection with contemporary Turkey in this chapter, I use the modern Turkish version of his name throughout. Other common transliterations from the Persian include Mawlana Jalaluddin Rumi and Maulana Djelaluddin, among seemingly countless permutations. In modern Turkish, his full name is Melvana Hüdavendigâr Celal ed-Din Muhammad ibn Muhammad al-Balkhi al-Rumi.

6. A 2007 Gallup poll conducted in twenty-one countries demonstrated that tensions between Muslim and Western nations were more nuanced than is generally portrayed in the popular media. While a majority of respondents in the United States, Israel, and Turkey believed tensions were worsening, only a minority felt the same in Saudi Arabia and Pakistan. The poll also indicated significant ranges of opinion within the European and North American countries

of the West and the various Asian nations of the Muslim World. "Islam-West Rift Widens, Poll Says," *BBC News*, January 21, 2008, http://news.bbc.co.uk/2/hi/europe/7200514.stm (accessed January 23, 2008).

7. The term "Islam" (and also "Muslim") derives from the Semitic root s-l-m which bears a cluster of meanings ranging from "wholeness" and "joining" to "safety" or "security." It is frequently translated as "submission," as in giving up of the self to Allah (the Arabic word for God), to the teachings of the Prophet Mohammad, and to the community, and is equated with the term *salam* (peace). Thus, Islam is often said to be literally a religion of peace.

8. See Jonathan Berkey's sensitive treatment of the question of forced conversions in *The Formation of Islam: Religion and Society in the Near East, 600–1800* (Cambridge: Cambridge University Press, 2003), 162ff.

9. Amnon Shiloah, "The Meeting of Christian, Jewish, and Muslim Musical Cultures on the Iberian Peninsula (before 1492)," *Acta Musicologica* 64, no. 1 (1991): 14–20. For a more populist account of the cultural climate of al-Andaluz see Menocal, *The Ornament of the World*.

10. Walter Feldman, *Music of the Ottoman Court: Makam, Composition and Early Ottoman Instrumental Repertoire* (Berlin, Germany: Verlag für Wissenschaft und Bildung, 1996).

11. Bernard Lewis, *The Jews of Islam* (Princeton, NJ: Princeton University Press, 1984), 3.

12. Lewis, *The Jews of Islam*, 6ff.

13. Lewis, *The Jews of Islam*, 8–9.

14. The term appears to have been first used in the context of Western and Muslim societies by Bernard Lewis in "The Roots of Muslim Rage," *Atlantic Monthly* 266, no. 3 (1990): 47–60.

15. William Horsley, "Turks Cool Towards 'Unfaithful' Europe," *BBC News*, November 6, 2006, http://news.bbc.co.uk/2/hi/europe/6121106.stm (accessed November 6, 2006).

16. For a fuller discussion of this rebirth of Sufi music and culture see Victor Vicente, "The Aesthetics of Motion in Musics for the Mevlana Celal Ed-Din Rumi" (PhD diss., University of Maryland, 2007).

17. Alexandra Marks, "Persian Poet Top Seller in America," *Christian Science Monitor* (November 25, 1997).

18. Coleman Barks, et al., *The Essential Rumi*, 2nd ed. (New York: Harper-Collins, 2004), xvii (italics in the original).

19. For discussion of what has been termed the *sama'* debate see Amnon Shiloah, *Music in the Islamic World: A Socio-Cultural Study* (Detroit: Wayne State University Press, 1995); and Seyyed Hossein Nasr, "Islam and Music: The Legal and the Spiritual Dimensions," in *Enchanting Powers: Music in the World's Religions*, ed. Lawrence E. Sullivan (Cambridge, MA: Harvard University Press, 1997),

219–35. For an alternative perspective see Dane Kusić, "Positivity of Music and Religion in Turkey," *Narodna umjetnost: Hrvatski časopis za etnologiju i folkloristiku* 34, no. 1 (1997): 147–78.

20. I use the verb "trancing" instead of "trance state" to better describe the processual nature of the experience as suggested in Judith Becker, *Deep Listeners: Music, Emotion, and Trancing* (Bloomington: Indiana University Press, 2004).

21. Attributed to Rumi by a blogger identified as "Nick" on The Gaiam Blog, http://blog.gaiam.com/quotes/topics/reconciliation (accessed October 12, 2007). I have been unable to locate the original published source of this citation.

22. Recent research argues that his birthplace was most likely in Vakhsh, in what is today Tajikistan. See Franklin D. Lewis, *Rumi, Past and Present, East and West: The Life, Teaching and Poetry of Jalâl al-Din* (Oxford: Oneworld Publications, 2000), 92.

23. Majid Naini, *Mysteries of the Universe and Rumi's Discoveries on the Path of Love* (Delray Beach, FL: Universal Vision Research, 2002), 220.

24. Barks, et al., *The Essential Rumi*, 281.

25. See Jonathan Curiel, "Can Rumi Save Us Now? Life and Words of the Popular 13th-Century Persian Poet Have Special Meaning for a 21st-Century World Torn by War, Genocide and Hatred," *San Francisco Chronicle*, April 1, 2007.

26. See Vicente, "The Aesthetics of Motion," 147ff, for a fuller reconstruction of the history.

27. For a more thorough listing of such commemorations see Vicente, "The Aesthetics of Motion," 316ff.

28. This open support for Sufi music is part of a larger trend in which the Turkish music industry, purportedly in the spirit of national and interfaith reconciliation, has reclaimed the music of the Ottoman past and promoted the musics of the country's various ethnic minorities. Recordings of gypsy, Jewish, and Laz music are now as abundant as those of classical compositions by Ottoman Armenian, Greek, and women court composers.

29. Jessica Winegar, "The Humanity Game: Art, Islam, and the War on Terror." *Anthropological Quarterly* 81, no. 3 (2008): 665–67.

30. Shems Friedlander, *The Whirling Dervishes: Being an Account of the Sufi Order, Known as the Mevlevis, and Its Founder, the Poet and Mystic, Mevlana Jalalu'ddin Rumi* (New York: Macmillan, 1975), 120; Metin And, "The Mevlana Ceremony," *Drama Review* 21, no. 3 (1977): 84; Kudsi Ergüner, *Journeys of a Sufi Musician*, trans. Annette Courtney Mayers (London: SAQI, 2005), 47–48.

31. Jonathan H. Shannon, "Sultans of Spin: Syrian Sacred Music on the World Stage," *American Anthropologist* 105, no. 2 (2003): 266–77.

32. Raouf Yekta Bey, *Mevlevî Ayînleri* (Istanbul: Istanbul).

33. Feldman, *Music of the Ottoman Court*, 85–99.

34. "Turkey to Celebrate Rumi's Birthday with a Giant Sema Performance," *Hürriyet Daily News and Economic Review*, September 28, 2007, www.hurriyet dailynews.com (accessed September 30, 2007).

35. "Mevlana Museum Expects Record Numbers of Tourists," *Hürriyet Daily News and Economic Review*, October 10, 2007, www.hurriyetdailynews.com (accessed October 12, 2007); "Konya Targets 10 Mln Tourists in 2013," *Hürriyet Daily News and Economic Review*, November 1, 2008, www.hurriyetdailynews.com (accessed December 3, 2008).

36. Muhammad Isa Waley, "Contemplative Disciplines in Early Persian Sufism," in *Classical Persian Sufism: From Its Origins to Rumi*, Vol. 1 of *The Heritage of Sufism*, ed. Leonard Lewisohn (Oxford: Oneworld Publications, 1999), 507.

37. Walter Feldman, "Musical Genres and Zikr of the Sunni Tarikats of Istanbul," in *The Dervish Lodge: Architecture, Art, and Sufism in Ottoman Turkey*, ed. Raymond Lifchez (Berkeley: University of California Press, 1992), 187–202; Christian Poche, "Zikr and Musicology," *The World of Music* 20, no. 1 (1978): 59–71; Daniel A. Sonneborn, "Music and Meaning in American Sufism: The Ritual of Dhikr at Sami Mahal, A Chishtiyya-Derived Sufi Center" (PhD diss., University of California, Los Angeles, 1995).

38. Vicente, "The Aesthetics of Motion."

39. See the "Artwork" and "Media" sections on the official website: Arkın Ilıcalı, *Mercan Dede — Arkin Allen*, www.mercandede.com.

40. Ali Pektaş, "Mercan Dede: We Need Tolerance More Than Ever," *Today's Zaman*, November 9, 2007, www.todayszaman.com (accessed December 1, 2007).

41. Yvonne Mitton, "Mercan Dede, The Visual DJ," January 15, 2006, *World Music Central.org*, http://worldmusiccentral.org/2006/01/15/mercan-dede-the-visual-dj/ (accessed December 1, 2007).

42. Pektaş, "Mercan Dede."

43. For fuller documentation see Vicente, "The Aesthetics of Motion," 276–77 and Vicente, "Sounds Like Sufi Spirit: Sufism in Popular Music and Culture," in *İzmir Ulusal Müzik Sempozyumu Bildiriler Kitabı*, ed. Paolo Susanni and Uzay Bora (Izmir, Turkey: Yaşar University, 2010), 5–6. http://izmirulusalmuziksem pozyumu.yasar.edu.tr/ulmusebk.pdf (accessed December 1, 2007).

44. Jean During, "What Is Sufi Music?," in *The Legacy of Medieval Persian Sufism (1150–1500)*, Vol. 2 of *The Heritage of Sufism*, ed. Leonard Lewisohn (Oxford: Oneworld Publications, 1999), 277–87.

45. Pektaş, "Mercan Dede."

46. "9/11 Was Not Only Against USA, But Also Against Islam," *The Rumi Forum*, www.rumiforum.org (accessed October 23, 2007).

47. See for instance, "Karagöz Not Turkish, Greek Minister Says," *Hürriyet Daily News and Economic Review*, July 15, 2010, www.hurriyetdailynews.com (accessed July 15, 2010).

48. Mustafa Ercan, "Sufi Music Concert at Church," *Hürriyet Daily News and Economic Review*, May 17, 2010, www.hurriyetdailynews.com (accessed May 17, 2010).

49. Vicente, "The Aesthetics of Motion," 190.

50. Başak Güneş Başat, "Whirl to Achieve Oneness," *Hürriyet Daily News and Economic Review*, April 15, 2008, www.hurriyetdailynews.com (accessed May 17, 2010).

CHAPTER SEVEN

Choreographing (against) Coup Culture

Reconciliation and Cross-Cultural Performance in the Fiji Islands

≥≈≋

KEVIN C. MILLER

The island nation of Fiji, a former sugar colony of the British Empire, is unique among its Pacific neighbors for its particular postcolonial predicament. This scattering of over 300 tropical islands in the South Pacific is today shared between two previously disparate ethnic groups brought together by the machinations of colonial-era capitalism. Indigenous Fijians, who, although phenotypically Melanesian, follow cultural patterns associated more with Polynesia, compose approximately 55 percent of the total population, while Indo-Fijians, the majority of whom descend from indentured laborers brought from India during the late nineteenth and early twentieth centuries, now compose about 37 percent of the population. Tensions between these two ethnic groups have contributed to Fiji's volatile political history, which includes four relatively bloodless coups d'état within the last two decades. Although the coups of 1987 (May and September) and 2000 (May) arose from various catalysts, the dominant narrative described the "reclaiming" of indigenous Fijian political power from the hands of elected governments perceived to be "Indian-dominated." By the time the military executed Fiji's fourth coup on December 5, 2006, observers both within and outside of Fiji had begun to speak of a "coup culture" that threatened the stability of democracy in the South Pacific.

The narrative of Fiji as a bicultural state is typically articulated in terms of mutual alienation — an inventory of *difference* engendered and sustained through a collusion of historical and social forces. Yet the tenacity of social segregation, while both anecdotally significant and empirically measurable, masks a second, less-explored narrative of cultural sharing and mutual amity accomplished through the micro-interactions of indigenous Fijian and Indo-Fijian individuals and organizations. As detailed in this chapter, the performance of music and dance, whether ethnically marked or deliberately cross-cultural, is a critical site for nation making in Fiji, particularly in the representative contexts of the tourist industry and government-sponsored events. The following analysis is based on two case studies of cross-cultural performance situated historically during Fiji's recent inter-coup period (2000–2006), an era characterized by the political ascent of the Soqosoqo Duavata ni Lewenivanua (SDL) party. In particular, these case studies highlight the important role that both official and "grassroots" cross-cultural performance played in reifying or challenging the SDL government's prescribed vision of Fijian nationhood.

I documented both case studies in Fiji during the year prior to the 2006 coup, during which the doomed SDL government launched a campaign of "reconciliation" and "unity" designed to portray Fiji as a harmonious multi-ethnic nation.[1] Specifically, I analyze the government's appropriation for this purpose of an emergent "fusion" performance genre that combines classical Indian dance with indigenous Fijian dance and music. I then contrast this public, politicized convergence of nationalism and cultural performance with an analysis of a very different case study: indigenous Fijian singers who specialize in the Indo-Fijian repertoire of Hindi folksongs and Hindu devotional music. This "crossover" phenomenon occurs far from the national spotlight, often in the rural sugarcane areas of Fiji where the two major ethnic groups coexist. Still, a fundamental point of both examples is that such collaborations remain rare even after nearly 130 years of cohabitation. In the context of Fiji's "coup culture," both case studies speak to issues of ethnic identity as they demonstrate the symbolic and generative power of cross-cultural performance in bicultural states.

Ethnic Relations in Contemporary Fiji

A host of persistent mutually held ethnic stereotypes underpin the often-uneasy relationship between indigenous Fijians and Indo-Fijians. For example, there is a common but quietly held view among indigenous Fijians that Indo-Fijians are untrustworthy, individualistic, and materialistic. But the indigenous Fijian's central complaint is that Indo-Fijians make no effort to understand the Fijian "traditional way of life" (*vakavanua*) or adhere to Fijian "customs of respect" (*vakaturaga*). In the broadest conception, indigenous Fijians see themselves as *taukei* ("owners of the land") and Indo-Fijians as *vulagi* ("visitors" or "perpetual foreigners"). The Indo-Fijian perception of indigenous Fijians is, likewise, often negative. Stemming from the indenture period, an underlying sense persists that indigenous Fijians are "primitive" and "dirty" (*maila*), only a century removed from cannibalism. Indo-Fijians may bolster this critique through recourse to their own "superior" culture rooted in the antiquity of a classical, literate, and spiritual Indian past. Additionally, the perception persists that indigenous Fijians are "lazy," "unmotivated," and occasionally "dangerous."

This mutual ethnic stereotyping, although certainly bleak, is constantly challenged by the everyday actions of indigenous Fijians and Indo-Fijians, who generally — I hasten to add — demonstrate amicable and cooperative relations. Less clear, however, is the *depth* of these relationships and the mutual impact these daily interactions have on the lives of two ethnic groups divided by a chasm of difference. As is often claimed, the social division of indigenous Fijians and Indo-Fijians stems, in part, from the colonial legacy of divide and rule, as several features of British governance were enshrined in Fiji's postcolonial constitutions. For example, the British insured that indigenous Fijians retained ownership of more than 83 percent of the land, relegating Indo-Fijians to the role of tenants, and established a race-based system of representation that translated into postindependence political parties divided along lines of ethnicity.

Multiple cultural and social barriers inhibit significant, transformative interactions between indigenous Fijians and Indo-Fijians, including traditional social hierarchies, kinship obligations, and social etiquette, but the most entrenched are language use, educational patterns, and religious practice. English is the primary *lingua franca* for ethnic groups in Fiji, but the natal languages of indigenous Fijians and Indo-Fijians remain, respectively, Fijian and Fiji Hindi. Despite the government's longstanding commitment to multicultural policies in education, the majority of primary and secondary schools in Fiji are either uniracial or dominated by one or the other ethnic group in terms of student body and staff. It is perhaps not surprising to find that the rate of interethnic marriage between indigenous Fijians and Indo-Fijians remains very low.[2] While Christianity is a fundamental, deeply cherished aspect of indigenous Fijian identity, only 6 percent of the Indo-Fijian population identify as Christian. The majority of Indo-Fijians identify either as Muslim (16 percent) or Hindu (76 percent). Regarding the latter, most practice the *bhakti* doctrine of Hinduism, which emphasizes a personal relationship with God through devotion.

Such is the social context for cross-cultural performance in contemporary Fiji: a divisive colonial heritage, an educational system that remains largely segregated, and an inventory of difference (often exploited by political figures) that includes natal languages, religious practices, social customs, and cultural values. As discussed below, the state responded to this uniquely postcolonial ethnic dilemma through recourse to the discourse of multiculturalism.

Ethnicity and the State:
The Discourse of Multiculturalism in Fiji

The literature on nationalism, dominated in recent decades by the tropes of "invented traditions" and "imagined communities" — as articulated by Eric Hobsbawm (1983) and Benedict Anderson (1991), respectively — has increasingly engaged issues of performance, representation, and power.[3] We must ask, as Kelly Askew does in her ethnography *Performing the Nation*, just *who* does the "inventing" of a tradition or the "imagining" of a nation.[4] Askew, following other scholars such as Akhil Gupta (1995), examines the nation-state in terms of (1) its official discourses and representations, and (2) the everyday, *lived* practices of individuals, and — importantly — the co-implication of both phenomena. Whether termed the "state" and the "citizenry," "macro" and "micro," or "top-down" and "bottom-up," she suggests that the dialectic between the two is not exclusively in the hands of the political or economic elite; rather, the performative practices of "ordinary citizens" have the potential to contest, construct, and thus represent the (ever fluid) identity of the nation. To escape the finality implied by imagined communities, Askew offers "national imaginaries," a term that captures the "multiple and often contradictory layers and fragments of ideology that underlie continually shifting conceptions of any given nation."[5]

The confluence of these phenomena in the particular process of "making" the nation of Fiji has prompted a prolific and ever-expanding body of academic literature. Of particular note is John D. Kelly and Martha Kaplan's provocative monograph *Represented Communities*. Writing against Anderson's "imagined communities," the authors contend that nation making in colonial and postcolonial states is primarily a matter of controlling the representations, both semiotic and political, that ultimately shape communal identities.

> While it is wiser, as has been endlessly reiterated in Anderson's wake, to depict communities, national and otherwise, as imagined rather than actually organically primordial, this insight does not explain the mechanisms that make some "imaginaries" more foundational than others, nor how alternative representa-

tions gain the substance to change things. Actual regimes of representation, routines legal and otherwise, constitute the communities represented.[6]

Kelly and Kaplan's point is that "top down" representations, such as the "Fijian" and "Indian" racial categories imposed upon the citizenry by colonial officials, are often resisted by the heterogeneous subjects they represent who, in turn, counter with their own self-generated representations.

In sum, recent scholarship depicts the process of nation making as a contest between multiple national imaginaries originating from both top-down (the state) and bottom-up (the citizenry) sources of agency and propagated through intertextual representations, of which cultural performance is a primary and particularly efficacious example. Confronted with an array of internal and irreversible postcolonial differences, efforts to represent Fiji as a cohesive nation-state have taken various forms, yet the most persistent invoke the discourse of multiculturalism. British officials sowed the seeds of multiculturalism in Fiji during the postwar period, at which time policy shifted to encourage cross-racial political cooperation in preparation for decolonization. Following independence, "multiracialism" became the cornerstone of the Alliance Party administration headed by the iconic Ratu Sir Kamisese Mara, successfully suppressing both the Indo-Fijian political vision of a "national citizenry" purportedly achievable through common roll voting and the ethnonationalist agenda of the indigenous Fijian political fringe, whose banner read, "Fiji for the Fijians." The 1970 Independence Constitution enshrined the multiracial paradigm through communal voting and the race-based allotment of House seats while taking careful measures to ensure indigenous Fijian paramountcy. A period of indigenous Fijian (Christian) nationalism ushered in by the 1987 military coups temporarily abandoned the political experiment of multiracialism. However, after former coup leader Sitiveni Rabuka returned to power (more legitimately) as prime minister, he appeared on national television calling for "an achieving nation, rich in diversity . . . a nation of several spiritual values, a nation dancing to many cultural forms."[7] The restorative 1997 Constitution revived the multiracial paradigm (now updated to "multicultural" or "multiethnic"), and the official recognition and accommodation of "discrete" ethnic populations with unique cultural differences persevered into the twenty-first century.

Fiji's brand of multiculturalism, as elaborated below, most closely resembles the "cultural mosaic" model — first articulated in Canada — and is likewise subject to its critique. Eva Mackey, among others, points out that multicultural policies often mask social, economic, and political asymmetries and ultimately serve hegemony, not through the erasure of difference, but through the "proper management" of a hierarchy of cultures within a unified project.[8] Furthermore, the ethnic communities that constitute the cultural mosaic are rendered "multicultural" only in relation to the dominant core culture, which has the additional effect of leveling minority groups with differing claims of influence, visibility, and historical importance in the national project.[9] The corollary to Fiji's multiculturalism, however, is that the dominant culture cohering the mosaic is not the white, unmarked core cultures of European, North American, and Australian multiculturalisms, but the ethnically marked and sacrosanct culture of indigenous Fijians.

Reconciliation and Collaborative Performance: The "Fusion Dance" Phenomenon

It is a critical fact of history that at the time of Fiji's independence in 1970 the Indo-Fijian population demonstrated a clear and relatively stable majority over the indigenous Fijian population (approximately 50 percent to 43 percent).[10] With the exit of "Europeans" from governance, the analogy of Fiji as a "three-legged stool" gave way to the postcolonial reality that Fiji was, politically, a bicultural state. In this sense, Mara's policy of "multiracialism" appears to gloss the inconvenient fact of Indo-Fijian numerical dominance. Nation making required new national rituals with space allocated for cultural performances representing each "discrete" ethnic group.[11] The performing arts selected and honed to represent Indo-Fijian culture were of the "classical" type: Hindustani vocal and instrumental music and classical dance styles such as *kathak* and *bharata natyam*. As Fiji's first decade of independence progressed, however, a minority of Indo-Fijian academics and artists began to question the appropriateness of these choices. For example, the Indo-Fijian writer Raymond Pillai proposed a search for folk-based forms of cultural expression reflective of the local Indo-Fijian experience that, he suggested, would enable cultural liaisons with other communities.[12] Despite such appeals, the public cultures of indigenous Fijians and Indo-Fijians remained largely discrete as the former drew on precolonial forms of song and dance (particularly *meke*) and the latter continued to emphasize the classical performing arts.

The emergence of the "fusion dance" phenomenon, the first of two case studies discussed herein, occurred during the inter-coup years (2000–2006), a period defined by the legal, ethical, and political aftermath of George Speight's attempted coup, the first in Fiji's history to fail. Dominated by the mutually contentious tropes of "justice" and "reconciliation," the return to normalcy deteriorated into a protracted war of words between the Republic of Fiji Military Forces (RFMF) commanded by Commodore Voreqe "Frank"

Bainimarama and the ruling SDL government headed by Prime Minister Laisenia Qarase. With a history marked by three coups d'état in less than twenty years — and the prospect of a fourth on the horizon — Fiji's claim to model "the way the world should be" had gradually given way to the reality of a "coup culture" that threatened the viability of democracy in the South Pacific. As discussed below, the hallmark of coup culture in Fiji includes the threat of physical violence but more often evokes a type of "symbolic violence" enacted through the discourses of coup perpetrators and hidden in the policies of the governments they bring to power.

Accordingly, the SDL government sought a counter-narrative to "coup culture" emphasizing national unity, multiculturalism, and reconciliation to be enacted both through actual legislation and, importantly, cultural representations. To this end, the government appropriated an emergent, collaborative dance genre loosely referred to as "fusion dance" that combines indigenous Fijian meke with classical Indian dance. The act of "fusing" these previously discrete, ethnically marked dance styles — which had served as the standard-bearers of cultural representation during the Mara era of multiculturalism — provided the ideal symbol for the SDL government's reconciliation campaign. Critics of the government, particularly Bainimarama, countered that the SDL government's celebration of ethnic diversity and national unity was merely a smokescreen intended to divert attention away from its own ethnically divisive legislative agenda.

Sometimes called "multicultural dance" or "fusion dance," the collaborative dance genre is defined by the deliberate combining of indigenous Fijian and Indo-Fijian dance styles, costumes, and musics into a single choreographed piece. This typically occurs in one of two ways. The more common involves a dance troupe of a single ethnicity (usually Indo-Fijian) adopting or incorporating dance elements or styles understood to be representational of another ethnic group (usually indigenous Fijian). An example of this type would be an Indo-Fijian dance troupe performing the indigenous Fijian meke, dressed in traditional *masi* (barkcloth, similar to Polynesian *tapa*) costumes, to prerecorded Fijian music. Meke, as described further below, is a broad term referring to "traditional" indigenous Fijian ensemble dance styles with musical accompaniment and a sung narrative verse. The second type of "fusion dance," less common than the first, features the actual collaboration of performers from two or more ethnic groups. The following case study, a collaboration between Indo-Fijian choreographer Shobna Chanel and the meke ensemble of the Republic of Fiji Military Forces (RFMF), fits this latter type of cross-cultural performance.

Chanel, like other choreographers of the collaborative dance genre, describes the motivation behind her work in terms of cross-cultural education designed to encourage her own indigenous Fijian and Indo-Fijian students to develop new perspectives and relationships through cultural sharing.[13] Her business card advertises the Shobna Chanel Dance Group as "promoting racial harmony through dance and music." Chanel explains her group's crossover success: "I think a lot of the locals — the natives here — respect us a lot for the fusion dances. It's like we've made a breakthrough. Even for Fijian functions, they invite us to come and perform. . . . It truly unites people who come to watch."[14] Although the popularity of the "fusion dance" genre is spreading, Chanel's group is the troupe most closely associated with the phenomenon. As such, they have received numerous invitations to perform at official events around Fiji and have repeatedly represented their country abroad.

The particular performance analyzed here took place on January 6, 2006, a full eleven months before the military-led coup that would follow in December. The occasion was the arrival of the Queen's Baton in Fiji, the Commonwealth Games' equivalent to the Olympic torch. The Shobna Chanel Dance Group, in collaboration with the RFMF Meke Group, performed on the expansive lawn of the Government House in Suva before a private audience that included Prime Minister Qarase, other members of government, and foreign dignitaries. Qarase's ministers had specifically requested Chanel's group — and particularly their "fusion dance" — for this occasion, as they had several times previously for other state functions.

The performance featured a tight set of five choreographed, seamlessly linked dance sequences lasting a total of approximately sixteen minutes. Once Prime Minister Qarase took his seat, the performance began with four young women from Chanel's group attired in black with traditional *magimagi* (coconut fiber rope) tied around their waists. The dancers performed in unison, emphasizing arm movements that derived equally from Indian classical dance and Hawaiian hula.[15] The music, played through PA speakers, was the Tokelauan-language hit "Pate Pate" by the popular Auckland-based band Te Vaka, an eclectic group of Pacific Islanders. As the piece concluded, the Army Band launched into "Bula Maleya," a widely known example of *sere ni cumu*, a guitar and ukulele-based popular song genre. Six indigenous Fijian male members of the RFMF Meke Group entered the performance space. Dressed in typical meke dance attire — bare-chested with *salusalus* (garlands) and long pandanus-leaf skirts — the dancers fit the postcard image of the Pacific as they performed the vigorous *meke iri* (fan dance). In two staggered rows, the men held palm leaf fans and moved with an athletic agility in the manner of traditional meke, in which synchronous movements "emphasize collective excellence, rather than individual achievement."[16] Midway through the meke, the men were joined by

Members of the Chanel-RFMF meke group perform "fusion dance" at the Government House, Suva, Fiji, 2006. *Photo by K. Miller*

the original four female dancers whose delicate Indian/hula movements provided a striking contrast to the vigor of the men's performance (see figure 7.1).

The third piece featured one of Chanel's students in a brief solo performance of *kuchipudi*, a classical dance style associated with Telugu-speaking South India. She wore the traditional sari-style dance attire, but a traditional Fijian masi pattern adorned the fabric of her *pallu* and pleats. The piece, performed to prerecorded Karnatak (South Indian classical) music, emphasized *nrtta*, or abstract, nonnarrative movements. Upon her exit, three Indo-Fijian female dancers reappeared with large strips of brown masi added to their costumes. The music transitioned to "Meda Butu," a neotraditional meke song by Black Rose, as the women performed a piece in unison with movements derived from women's meke and Indian dance styles, such as *kathak*. The women had learned these meke dance movements from the male RFMF dancers. Finally, the men of the RFMF Meke Group sprinted back into the performance space, forming two lines roughly parallel with the Indo-Fijian dancers, and the kuchipudi dancer returned as well. In an unexpected twist, the prerecorded music for the finale was the "world percussion"-dominated techno hit of 2000, "Played-A-Live (the Bongo Song)" by the Danish pair Safri Duo. As the men launched into a synchronized meke iri, the Indo-Fijian dancers — joined by the kuchipudi dancer —

Fijian masi patterns displayed on the pallu of this kuchipudi performer
in Chanel's group, Suva, Fiji, 2006. *Photo by K. Miller*

moved in formation among them, keeping a discreet distance. The effect
was visually harmonious, but emphasized a type of harmony born of com-
plement rather than union. At the close of the performance, the audience
responded with an appreciative applause before returning to tea and conversation.

Upon close analysis of this particular performance as a representative
example of the "fusion dance" genre, it appears that "fusion," as used here,
is a misnomer, or at least misleading. Although the indigenous Fijian and
Indo-Fijian dancers share the performance space, their interaction is limited, and rather than blending, the culturally marked aspects of the choreography remain relatively discrete. Importantly, Chanel's students *do* embody aspects of indigenous Fijian culture through their costuming and
dance movements, yet these details are largely overpowered by the inescap-
able presence of the dancers' own ethnicities carried on their "racialized"
bodies. There are at least two factors in this particular performance that
preserve the correlative relationship between a dancer and the representation of his or her ethnicity. The first is that the RFMF Meke Group dancers
do not make any gestures toward Indo-Fijian culture: their costuming and
choreography remain exclusively representative of indigenous Fijian tradi-

tions. The second factor is that the ethnic integrity of each group of dancers is underscored by their gender: all of Chanel's Indo-Fijian dancers are female, while all of the RFMF Meke Group dancers are male.

In this regard, it is interesting to note that both of the "sources" for this collaboration — Indian dance styles and indigenous Fijian meke — have their own respective histories of gender-segregated performance: neither folk nor classical forms of Indian dance tend to intermix the sexes, and indigenous Fijian meke is typically divided into men's and women's genres. In this sense, the collaborative dance represents each ethnicity as gendered — the gentle, feminine (and "refined") Indo-Fijian, and the vigorous, masculine (and "coarse") indigenous Fijian — and the lack of mutual engagement between the two in the choreography reflects the gendered performance history of each group. Still, the gender-ethnicity correlation in this example invests the cross-cultural impact of the choreography with a particular salience. Indigenous Fijian *men* and Indo-Fijian *women* are, generally, the "culture bearers" of their respective groups, and the matrimonial union of this pairing is far rarer than that between an Indo-Fijian man and an indigenous Fijian woman.[17] In this sense, the combination of indigenous Fijian men and Indo-Fijian women in cross-cultural performance carries the greatest potential to challenge existing concepts of ethnic relations.[18]

Finally, the music that accompanies the dance sequence positions both sets of dancers against various culture-localities. The Karnatak piece and the meke song ("Meda Butu") represent Indo-Fijian and indigenous Fijian cultures respectively at their most traditional, while the sere ni cumu ("Bula Maleya") suggests a postcolonial Fijian culture interconnected with tourism.[19] The choice of "Pate Pate" reflects a broader identification with Oceania or, more specifically, Polynesia, while the concluding selection of the "Bongo Song" remix provides an ethnically neutral and globally modern sonic finale, save for the prominent "tribal drums" that index indigeneity. In essence, the Chanel–RFMF collaborative dance is, in many ways, an innovative and creative piece of choreography, but its representation of indigenous Fijian and Indo-Fijian relations ultimately emphasizes coexistence over integration — a vision easily compatible with state's conception of multiculturalism.

Choreographing (against) Coup Culture

The state's recruitment of the collaborative dance genre for the work of nation making dates back to the traumatic events of May 2000 when Speight's civilian-led coup deposed Fiji's first Indo-Fijian prime minister, Mahendra Chaudhry, and his administration. Although the coup was put down by

Bainimarama and declared illegal, Chaudhry was forced into snap elections in 2001 against Qarase, the head of the caretaker government. Qarase's SDL party won the election and took the reigns of government for the five years that followed. Qarase, himself a moderate ethnonationalist, launched a campaign of "reconciliation" based, in part, on indigenous Fijian rituals of apology (*matanigasau*) and conflict resolution (*veisorosorovi*) and buttressed by an explicitly Christian concept of "unconditional forgiveness." In 2004, the weeklong Fiji independence celebration — dubbed "Reconciliation Week" by Qarase — culminated with a public *matanigasau* ceremony in Albert Park, Suva. In an apparent act of contrition, figures under investigation for involvement in the 2000 coup — or their relatives or representatives — offered a public apology to those victimized by the actions of Speight and his supporters; none of the aggrieved Members of Parliament attended, however, and Indo-Fijians showed little interest in the spectacle.[20] Undeterred, Qarase declared 2005 to be the "Year of Forgiveness" and launched a series of Ministry for Multiethnic Affairs–sponsored educational workshops targeting the Indo-Fijian community.

In 2005, the campaign culminated with the drafting of the controversial Promotion of Reconciliation, Tolerance, and Unity Bill (RTU Bill), which sought to promote national (that is to say, ethnic) reconciliation through the principles of restorative justice. Modeled partly on the South African Truth and Reconciliation Commission, the bill contained provisions for the amnesty of coup perpetrators as part of a formula summed up by Qarase as "justice plus forgiveness and reconciliation, equals peace."[21] Although Qarase steadfastly denied that the bill would provide blanket amnesty, Indo-Fijian religious, professional, and political organizations broadly condemned the proposed legislation. Chaudhry, then Leader of the Opposition in Parliament, summed up the counter position in his year-end message printed in the *Fiji Times*: "The government's determination to push through the highly controversial Amnesty Bill has created deep divisions within the nation, and leaves behind indelible impressions of an administration that backs lawless elements in society."[22] More critically, the introduction of the RTU Bill exacerbated tensions between the government and the military forces, as the latter claimed that the amnesty provisions threatened their ongoing prosecution of coup supporters and financers.[23]

Therefore, the "fusion dance" genre with its explicit juxtaposition of indigenous Fijian and Indo-Fijian cultural symbols (and actual bodies) provided the SDL government with a visible embodiment of national reconciliation and a timely counter-representation for those who accused Qarase of fueling the nation's ethnic divide. As media coverage of Chanel's group increased, SDL ministers were often quoted in praise of the cross-cultural choreography. For example, Konisi Yabaki said of the group, "They are a perfect example that, while we can maintain our respective cultural and traditional ways, there are ways of incorporating them, allowing us the best of both worlds."[24] As the contentious RTU Bill stalled in Parliament (along with other bills intended to increase indigenous Fijian control of land and fishing waters), the government directly encouraged cross-cultural collaboration through the influence of its Ministry of Multiethnic Affairs, and "fusion dance" became a staple item at state-sponsored events. Simultaneously, through performances in the tourist industry and abroad, "fusion dance" projected the image of a harmonious, multiethnic Fiji to the international community.

But the wheels of history were already turning. Just three days prior to the performance described above, military Commander Bainimarama issued his first call for Qarase's resignation, claiming that the SDL government was delaying the prosecution of coup participants and dividing the nation through its proposed ethnonationalist legislation. Following the SDL's reelection in May 2006, Bainimarama's threats grew more dire until, on December 5, he initiated the military's "clean-up campaign," took over government, and subsequently assumed the position of interim prime minister. Unlike the previous coups, which sought to enshrine indigenous Fijian paramountcy, this coup claimed to topple a corrupt government whose policies threatened to exacerbate ethnic tensions. For the first time, the indigenous Fijian-dominated military had ousted an indigenous Fijian-dominated government, and the Indo-Fijian community remained largely on the sidelines.

During his address to the nation on the day of the military takeover, Bainimarama claimed that Qarase had "already conducted a *silent coup* through bribery, corruption and the introduction of controversial bills."[25] In September 2007, Bainimarama attempted to justify his actions to the international community at the United Nations General Assembly in New York. "Fiji has a *coup culture*," he explained, "a history of civilian or military coups executed in the interests of a few, and based on nationalism, racism and greed. To remove this coup culture and to commit to democracy and the rule of law, policies which promote *racial supremacy* and further the interests of economic and social elites must be removed once and for all."[26]

If we follow the claims of Bainimarama's discourse, Qarase's appropriation of the "fusion dance" genre for the purposes of national reconciliation appears as a disingenuous smokescreen, an act of symbolic violence in the sense suggested by Pierre Bourdieu: a "gentle, invisible violence, unrecognized as such, chosen as much as undergone."[27] From this perspective, a representation of ethnic relations in the form of cross-cultural performance generated by the citizenry (in this case, individual choreographers) for the purposes of cultural education was co-opted by the state to serve its own agenda and extend its own political life. It was, in the end, too little, too late.

Qarase's response to ethnic unrest spurred by the 2000 coup was to combine a concept of reconciliation, informed by Christian principles and "Fijian custom," with Mara's vision of multiculturalism based on the rhetoric of "accommodation." There were two consequences of this synthesis. First, Qarase and his administration couched the terms of reconciliation within the context of the *taukei-vulagi* relationship: the Indo-Fijians were the (often ungrateful) "guests" and the indigenous Fijians the tolerant, accommodating "hosts."[28] Second, the "multiculturalism" that Qarase sought to promote was inherently asymmetrical and predicated on an implied (and constitutionally reinforced) indigenous Fijian paramountcy. In this light, the discourse of multiculturalism successfully masked the numeric, economic, and political importance of Indo-Fijians by relegating them to a cultural mosaic shared by a multitude of numerically less significant ethnic groups. In other words, the propagation of the *multiculturalism* discourse tempered the threat of *biculturalism* in Fiji.[29]

In this respect, Qarase found the collaborative dance genre to be congruous with his vision of multiculturalism. Although the choreography was often called a work of "fusion," the government embraced it because it was not. The indigenous Fijian meke dancers performed side by side with the Indo-Fijian dancers but made no choreographic concessions to the latter's culture. It was the Indo-Fijian dancers who adopted the cultural symbols of indigenous Fijian culture, although, as explained above, the overall effect was one of coexistence, not integration. Knowing that nation making requires the control of principal representations, Qarase and the SDL government were quick to seize the collaborative dance and redirect its meaning. The singular image of Fiji thus projected was one of multiethnic harmony cohered by an assumed indigenous Fijian cultural and political dominance.

Crossing the River: Indigenous Fijian Singers of the Hindi Repertoire

Critics of the multicultural paradigm, particularly as conceived and practiced in Fiji, caution against the overemphasis of immutable, primordial cultural differences and the concomitant neglect of other socioeconomic factors affecting group conflict. Furthermore, multicultural policies, they claim, tend to focus on the easily identifiable, superficial aspects of culture. For example, Steven Ratuva describes multiculturalism in postindependence

Fiji as "a thin layer of film to camouflage the increasing ethnic segregation and deepening socio-economic disparity."[30] I heard similar statements from my field consultants, including Satvik Dass, a retired music educator and accomplished musician:

> Today, what they call multicultural promotion is very superficial. . . . I think that right from scratch, at the grassroots level, Fijians should be taught the Indian language, and Indians should be taught the Fijian language. And if the Fijians are able to sing a Hindi song or perform a Hindi dance, and likewise, the Indians perform the meke [Indigenous dance] — that is true multicultural promotion; that is what you could call national reconciliation.[31]

In this regard, my second case study, indigenous Fijians who perform the Hindi repertoire of folk and devotional music, stands to challenge the superficial, compartmentalized conception of multiculturalism through performances that reveal a deep embrace of Indo-Fijian culture. Although I heard of only a handful of such individuals during the course of my fieldwork, several had achieved a relatively high profile on the local circuit of Hindi singing competitions and in the Fiji-based Hindi music industry. Despite their negligible numbers, I argue that an ethnographic focus on these individuals reveals important insights into the broader social relationships of indigenous Fijians and Indo-Fijians. A key point here is that their interest in Indo-Fijian music and culture stems from their amiable, lifelong "grassroots" interactions with Indo-Fijians in the periphery of their Fijian villages or in the cities.

The areas of Fiji with the greatest potential for grassroots, cross-cultural micro-interactions between indigenous Fijians and Indo-Fijians are the sugarcane districts of central Vanua Levu and western Viti Levu. In these areas, a decades-long history of cooperation and mutual exchange between the two major ethnic groups has fostered relationships that resist the ebb and flow of Fiji's racialized national politics. Cohabitation in these areas has cultivated a mutual respect for and curiosity about the religious practices and cultural histories of the other. Many indigenous Fijians in these areas speak Fiji Hindi in addition to Fijian, enjoy watching Hindi films, and eat Indian curry at home. The concept of a Hindu indigenous Fijian in the national imagination is, at best, embryonic, and isolated images of indigenous Fijians taking part in a Hindu *puja* (worship service) or fire-walking ceremony surface occasionally in the media as curiosities. During his research in the early 1970s, Ian K. Somerville noted indigenous Fijian participation in several Hindu *mandalis* (singing groups) in western Viti Levu. In at least one case, the young men were praised by the group's leader for showing "a great deal more enthusiasm than the Indians."[32]

Juniya Noah is an up-and-coming indigenous Fijian *bhajaniya*, or singer of Hindu devotional songs. I first heard Noah sing at a Krishna Janmashtami (Krishna's birthday) celebration in a suburb of Lautoka in western Fiji. A group of devotees formed a tight circle and began singing *kirtans* (hymns) in praise of Krishna; Noah was among them. Indo-Fijian folk and devotional music is participatory and typically performed loudly, employing a core ensemble of harmonium (portable hand-pumped organ), *dholak* (double-headed barrel drum), and various idiophones. Noah delighted his fellow devotees by singing a kirtan to the tune of "*Dafli Wale Dafli Baja*," a popular Hindi film song from the late 1970s, before singing a second kirtan in a more traditional style. Following requests for a third song, Noah launched into a *hori*, a genre normally associated with the Holi season. Noah's hori drew on the theme of Shiva's flower garden, a rich metaphoric terrain in which different types of flowers stand in for various human characteristics:

Cello dekh ai bhola ki phul bagiya
Bela bhi boya camela bhi boya
Ek nahi boya anarkali

Come, let's see Shiva's flower garden
He has planted (zambac) jasmine and also (grandiflorum) jasmine
But he did not plant any pomegranate!

Noah performed this *hori* in a leader-chorus style, much like the kirtan format, and the devotees sitting around him raised their voices with the contagious felicity characteristic of Holi. From behind the harmonium, Noah encouraged a young man to rise and perform a brief, improvised folk dance, which he executed in a mock-*filmi* style that elicited howls of laughter. As he sang, Noah revealed a comfortable command of the Indo-Fijian folk aesthetic, particularly in terms of vocal timbre. Whereas indigenous Fijian vocal timbre tends to be open and relaxed, Noah has mastered the preferred "Indian" vocal timbre, which is constricted and nasal. As Noah would explain to me later, "If you put me on cassette and played it for an Indian guy, he'd never know that a Fijian guy was singing."[33]

Noah represents a vanguard minority of well-known indigenous Fijian singers of the Hindu repertoire that also includes Iliaisa Seru and Male Sadhu. These singers follow an earlier generation of indigenous Fijian performers who moved between Fijian, Hindi, and English repertoires and often recorded bilingual or trilingual cassettes for release in the local music industry. For example, Saimone Vuatalevu, one of Fiji's most successful

Noah Juniya performs a Hindu devotional song, Lautoka,
Fiji, 2006. *Photo by K. Miller*

songwriter-musicians, stunned the local Indo-Fijian community in 1973 by
winning the Fiji Sangeet Sitara (a talent contest in Indian music) for his
rendition of a popular Hindi film song. He followed this achievement by
dedicating six months in 1976 to the study of Hindi in New Delhi, India.[34]
Yet contemporary crossover singers such as Noah, Seru, and Sadhu distinguish themselves from their predecessors by moving beyond the secular,
romantic themes of the Bollywood repertoire to become specialists of the
Hindu *bhakti* repertoire of *bhajans* and kirtans. As such, they tend to self-
identify as Hindus, study the epic and Puranic literature, follow Hindu
dietary restrictions, and worship at pujas where they fraternize with other
(Indo-Fijian) devotees. The local music industry actively promotes these
indigenous Fijian *bhajaniyas* through recordings and the sponsorship of
bhajan muqablas (live, competitive stage shows). The spectacle of two indigenous Fijian singers in a bhajan competition has proven to be extremely
popular in the Indo-Fijian community.

A brief biographical sketch of Noah based on my interviews suggests that
the phenomenon of indigenous Fijian crossover singers may satisfy critics
of multiculturalism in Fiji, who seek cross-cultural exchange at the "organic," grassroots level of micro-interactions among the citizenry. Noah, a
tall, slender, soft-spoken young man in his mid-twenties, identifies himself

as Hindu, speaks Fiji Hindi fluently, and is literate in Standard Hindi. He grew up in a small Fijian village situated in the sugarcane district to the east of Labasa on Vanua Levu. From about the age of seven on his own initiative, Noah began to attend the weekly recital of the Ramayana epic held in the neighboring Indian settlement. He said of his natal village, "This was a small village, and there were seventy-two Indians right around. We had good relations with them; they would come to our house; we would go there. There was no problem there." Through participating in the mandali, Noah learned to sing the epic's verses in addition to the kirtans that followed the recital. As he grew older, Noah taught himself to play the harmonium and expanded his repertoire through the meticulous study of recordings available through the local cassette industry. At the time I met him, Noah had participated in over twenty singing competitions, holding his own against the most revered Indo-Fijian singers. While Noah is popular among the Indo-Fijian community, he reports a degree of support from the indigenous Fijian community as well, including his own Christian family members. "My family supports me," he said, "whenever I'm in competition, they always come and listen to me. . . . I travel all over and the Fijians come and support me. If one or two are there, soon the whole *koro* [village] will be there. They are very happy that I can sing that kind of song."

Therefore, in the context of nation making, Noah's command of the Hindu song repertoire represents a type of cross-cultural performance generated "from below": a "natural" outcome of intersecting ethnically defined social networks in spaces beyond the reach of the state. Unlike the choreographers of the collaborative dance genre discussed above, the indigenous Fijian bhajaniyas did not deliberately set out to model an alternative vision of ethnic relations in Fiji. Nonetheless, the symbolic impact of an indigenous Fijian singer not only adopting, but mastering the language, aesthetics, and performance style of Indo-Fijian devotional music poses a serious challenge to the vision of multiculturalism championed by the state in which race corresponds directly to cultural expression. Furthermore, although indigenous Fijian bhajaniyas "cross cultures," they do *not* create a new "cross-cultural genre" — Noah brings nothing "Fijian" to his performance of a hori or bhajan apart from his racialized body. An ethnonationalist government, such as Qarase's SDL, would find very little to exploit in this form of cross-cultural performance, which is, in essence, a complete transference. On the contrary, it raises old fears of Indo-Fijian political and cultural domination, the same fears that fueled the coups of 1987 and 2000. It is, ultimately, not the government, but the local music industry that promotes these indigenous Fijian singers, and the motivation is not political, but economic.

Conclusion

As demonstrated in this chapter, cross-cultural performance in Fiji highlights the interplay between the "top-down" and "bottom-up" forces that shape national imaginaries, that is to say, the sometimes-competing and sometimes-complementary efforts of the state and its citizenry to author national identity. My particular questions regarding the two case studies analyzed above are political and ask how the nation-state is represented and by whom: Why, during a particular historical moment, did the SDL government seize upon one form of cross-cultural performance but not the other? And what does the state's appropriation of this performance genre reveal about the vision of nationhood that the SDL government was attempting to propagate? Since Fiji's independence, the state has responded to its internal and often unruly ethnic divide by promoting multiculturalism, initially as evidence that Fijian leadership was ready to self-govern, and later as a counter-narrative to "coup culture." And yet Fiji's concept of multiculturalism has always demonstrated internal asymmetries that guarantee cultural and political indigenous Fijian paramountcy, both by implication and constitutional decree. In this respect the collaborative dance genre, in order to live up to its "fusion" epithet, must break from the compartmentalizing narrative of multiculturalism. In my analysis, the collaborative dance genre fails to complete this break, instead reifying a vision of ethnic relations that emphasizes harmonic coexistence over integration.

For Qarase's SDL government, the appeal (and the safety) of the "fusion dance" genre was specifically that it was *not* a fusion: each ethnic group remains relatively discrete in the choreography and each has its place. In this way, the dance is congruous with the Fijian nationalist paradigm of multiculturalism that assumes the dominance of an "unadulterated" Indigenous Fijian culture. Under pressure from the military, the government appropriated the "bottom-up" vision of reconciliation developed by individual choreographers for its own official, "top-down" national imaginary, which it wielded, allegedly, as symbolic violence. Meanwhile, the second case study, the indigenous Fijian "crossover" singers — another bottom-up, grassroots phenomenon — offers a serious challenge to the multicultural paradigm by rupturing (completely) the correlative relationship between the ethnically marked performer and the "culture" that he or she represents through performance. Furthermore, the superseding culture in this case is decidedly Indo-Fijian, so it comes as no surprise that the SDL government would have very little to gain through association with these singers. Although no new "cross-cultural genre" is actually created through this cross-cultural performance (since the indigenous Fijian singers simply reproduce existing Indo-

Fijian performance styles and genres), these singers may be the conduits of a different sort of reconciliation, a grassroots reconciliation long delayed in Fiji based on genuine cultural exchange through micro-interactions.

Notes

1. This chapter is based on my dissertation research conducted over a period of fourteen months in 2004 and 2005–06. See Kevin C. Miller, "A Community of Sentiment: Indo-Fijian Music and Identity Discourse in Fiji and its Diaspora" (PhD diss., University of California, Los Angeles, 2008). The ethnographic focus of my research was the Indo-Fijian community.

2. Indigenous Fijian and Indo-Fijian unions made up less than 1 percent of the total number of recorded marriages in the 1996 census. According to Portia Richmond's analysis, the majority involved an Indo-Fijian husband and an indigenous Fijian wife, occurred most often between Christians, and took place in the Ba province in western Viti Levu followed closely by the Suva-Rewa area. See Portia Richmond, "Never the Twain Shall Meet? Causal Factors in Fijian-Indian Intermarriage" (MA thesis, University of Hawaii, 2003), 102–3.

3. Benedict Anderson, *Imagined Communities: Reflections on the Origin and Spread of Nationalism*, 2nd ed. (London: Verso, 1991).

4. Kelly M. Askew, *Performing the Nation: Swahili Music and Cultural Politics in Tanzania* (Chicago: The University of Chicago Press, 2002), 14.

5. Askew, *Performing the Nation*, 270, 273.

6. John D. Kelly and Martha Kaplan, *Represented Communities: Fiji and World Decolonization* (Chicago: University of Chicago Press, 2001), 99.

7. Robert Norton, "Reconciling Ethnicity and Nation: Contending Discourses in Fiji's Constitutional Reform," *The Contemporary Pacific* 12, no. 1 (2000): 87.

8. Eva Mackey, *The House of Difference: Cultural Politics and National Identity in Canada* (London: Routledge, 1999), 151.

9. Kogila Moodley, "Canadian Multiculturalism as Ideology," *Ethnic and Racial Studies* 6, no. 3 (1983): 320–31.

10. Based on a comparison of the 1966 census and 1976 census, both provided by Brij V. Lal, *Broken Waves: A History of the Fiji Islands in the Twentieth Century* (Honolulu: University of Hawaii Press, 1992), 336–37.

11. Regarding the 1970 independence ceremonies, which were jointly planned by British colonial officers and prominent European, indigenous Fijian, and Indo-Fijian locals, Kaplan observed, "In representing Fiji through new national rituals, for the first time Indian rituals were included as part of official ceremonial. In fact, there was a full-scale, self-conscious attempt to give equal time to Fijian and Indian ceremonies and entertainment" (Kelly and Kaplan, *Represented Communities*, 131).

12. Raymond C. Pillai, "Culture and the Fiji Indian," Transcript of Radio Fiji Program, "In My View," (1978), 1–3.

13. Cross-cultural dance experiments have occurred in schools and cultural institutes throughout the independence period as a means of cultural education, but the frequency and consistency was never enough to qualify as a phenomenon, and these dances — usually of the monoethnic type — rarely achieved national visibility.

14. Interview by author with Shobna Chanel. December 8, 2005, Suva, Fiji.

15. Hula, of course, has a pan-Pacific appeal, and it is a popular item in Fiji's cultural centers and schools.

16. David Goldsworthy "Fijian Music," in *The Garland Encyclopedia of World Music, Volume 9: Australia and the Pacific Islands,* ed. Adrienne Kaeppler and J. W. Love (New York: Garland Publishing, 1998), 774. There are multiple types of meke genres, usually divided between men's and women's repertoires, in which the dance is only one aspect of a performance centered on a narrative text. In this sense, dancing meke to sere ni cumu is untypical. Meke songs are usually accompanied by a small ensemble of *lali ni meke* (a small "slit drum" idiophone), *derua* (bamboo stamping tubes), and body percussion. Meke remains a fixture of "traditional" ceremonies of exchange and social interaction, but performance contexts have expanded to include church events, school programs, tourist shows, and a variety of official occasions ranging from sporting events to government meetings. From Kaye Glamuzina, "Melanesia: Fiji," in *Grove Music Online*, ed. L. Macy. 2007, www.grovemusic.com (accessed December 11, 2007).

17. Richmond, "Never the Twain Shall Meet?" 102.

18. I bracket here what could be an extensive gender analysis of this piece because the correlation between gender and ethnicity — present in this performance — is not a consistent feature of the "fusion dance" genre in general. I saw other collaborative performances in which Indo-Fijian male dancers performed folk dances amid a group that also included female indigenous Fijians performing women's meke.

19. A staple of the guitar-ukulele band repertoire, "Bula Maleya" is a song of welcome that often greets tourists as they arrive at the airport or their resorts.

20. Mosmi Bhim, "The Impact of the Promotion of Reconciliation, Tolerance and Unity Bill on the 2006 Election," in *From Election to Coup in Fiji: The 2006 Campaign and its Aftermath*, ed. Jon Fraenkel and Stewart Firth (Canberra: Australian National University E Press and Asia Pacific Press, 2007), 114.

21. This quote is from Qarase's speech in Parliament during the second reading of the RTU Bill on June 2, 2005. The text was reproduced in "A Plea for Restorative Justice," Fijilive, June 17, 2005, www.fijilive.com (accessed October 12, 2007).

22. Mahendra Chaudhry, paid advertisement, "Taking stock of 2005 and looking to the future," *Fiji Times*, December 31, 2005. Note his deliberate gloss of the RTU Bill as the "Amnesty Bill."

23. The RFMF's official submission to the parliamentary select committee read, in part, "The Bill is ill conceived and is a recipe for internal conflict, unrest and violence. It is discriminatory and will breed ethno-nationalism . . . bring about despair, hopelessness and insecurity amongst the people as well as promote greater racial division" (Bhim, *From Election to Coup*, 127).

24. Matelita Ragogo, "Dance Could Bring Harmony to Ethnically Divided Pacific Nation," *Agence France Presse* (July 22, 2002).

25. "Voreqe Bainimarama's Press Statement," December 5, 2006, www.fiji times.com/extras/TakeOverAddress.pdf (emphasis mine) (accessed December 5, 2006).

26. Voreqe Bainimarama, address to the United Nations General Assembly, September 28, 2007. Excerpt of full transcript from *Pacific Islands Report* (online): http://pidp.eastwestcenter.org (emphasis mine) (accessed October 16, 2007).

27. Pierre Bourdieu, *The Logic of Practice*, trans. Richard Nice (Stanford: Stanford University Press, 1990 [1980]), 127.

28. For example, Qarase gave this response in Parliament to a comment by an Indo-Fijian MP who disparaged the Fijian-dominated government: "To me and the Government, that remark is a gross and provocative insult. It was a racist attack on a community, which has been *tolerant* and *accommodating* toward the needs of those who came to Fiji over 120 years ago in search of a better life. . . . When insensitive remarks and gross insults are thrown at us as the 'i taukei' and landowners, we will, as we must, take a stand and say enough is enough." In Ganeshwar Chand, *Papers on Racial Discrimination, Volume 1: The CERD Papers* (Lautoka: Fiji Institute of Applied Studies, 2005), 241 (his emphasis).

29. According to the 2007 census, the population of Fiji is primarily divided between indigenous Fijians (57.3 percent) and Indo-Fijians (37.6 percent), with a small remainder of other ethnic groups, including Chinese, European, and other Pacific Islanders (5 percent). Fiji Island Bureau of Statistics, 2007 Census, Fiji Government, www.statsfiji.gov.fj (accessed November 12, 2007).

30. Steven Ratuva, "Towards Multiculturalism and Affirmative Action: A Case for Fiji," in *Educating for Multiculturalism*, ed. Jill Cottrell (Suva, Fiji: Citizens' Constitutional Forum, 1998), 67.

31. Interview by author with Satvik Dass. December 14, 2005, Nadi, Fiji.

32. Ian Keith Somerville, "The Ramayan Mandli Movement: Popular Hindu Theism in Fiji, 1879–1979" (MA thesis, University of Sydney, 1986), 144. I focus here on Hindu indigenous Fijians at the expense of analyzing the "reverse" scenario: Christian Indo-Fijians. I have made this choice for several reasons. Although they are a much larger group — over 20,000 in number or 6 percent of the Indo-Fijian population — Christian Indo-Fijians often worship in "Indian churches" separate from indigenous Fijian devotees of the same faith. The practice

of Christianity, therefore, does not always challenge entrenched patterns of ethnic segregation.

33. Here and below: interview by author with Juniya Noah. August 29, 2006, Lautoka, Fiji.

34. Anendra Singh, "Making It Big on the Local Music Scene," *Fiji Times* (September 10, 1986).

PART III

⚡

Musical
Memorializations
of Violent Pasts

⚡

In the final section of the book we turn to explore ways in which music helps us remember acts of subjective and objective violence. Through these articles we are reminded that commemoration shapes our experience both in terms of what we are summoned to remember as well as what we are encouraged to forget. In chapter 8, Jonathan Ritter compares two narratives of remembrance: The first is a state-sanctioned narrative forwarded by the Peruvian Truth and Reconciliation Commission (2001–2003), a body formed to uncover and examine abuses — including "disappearances," massacres, and other human rights violations — from the 1980s and 1990s. The second narrative from those same traumatic years, meanwhile, was embedded in the lyrics of a large repertoire of musical pieces called "testimonial songs." In his comparison of these "official" and "unofficial" discourses respectively, Ritter invites us to ponder how emblematic memory — discussed in the introduction to this book through a brief analysis of the Montréal Massacre — has both disadvantages and advantages. For instance, Peruvian President Alberto Fujimori's administration (1990–2000) represented their 1992 capture of a guerrilla leader as emblematic of their positive efforts to eradicate the violence that had plagued Peru. By enforcing a "savior" narrative, the government subsequently thwarted oppositional narratives that were critical of their regime. In other words, this capture — seen by many citizens as a positive step toward eradicating uncontrolled subjective violence — was memorialized in such a way that it silenced those who objected to the government's brutality. But emblematic memory is not always restrictive: Ritter argues that by the mid-1990s, as the immediacy of Peruvian violence waned, the testimonial song repertoire also declined. Yet the power of song remained: instead of a vibrant, ever-expanding repertoire, fewer songs took on greater meaning, becoming "intertextual" as they referenced multiple violent events, allowing one incident or another to be fore-grounded within each performance context. Such emblematic practices, in turn, permit a smaller number of songs to speak to generations of current (and future) listeners, many of whom will not have experienced the event when it happened, but will nonetheless participate in making and remaking its meaning through ongoing musical memorializations.

In chapter 9, Amy Wlodarski examines the unanticipated meanings of a musical composition when it is appropriated by two competing political entities to extend and strengthen their sovereign power. Originally con-ceived as a response to anti-Semitic uprisings in the late 1950s, the work included collaborative input from both East and West German composers whose intention was to promote a shared humanistic understanding of their history. Indeed, reviews after its premiere suggested that the composers' efforts were successful. But, as Wlodarski illustrates, this is only the begin-ning of the *Chronik*'s complex story: it subsequently was used by both East and West Germany to advance "counter-memories" about the Holocaust —perpetuating further symbolic violence — thus precluding the work's po-tential for realizing a genuine reconciliation. Through its extensive appro-priation, Wlodarski argues, the work ultimately became less about the Holocaust and more about the current Cold War. This echoes what Barbie Zelizer has written about places of commemoration: designed to create new collective memories, they are a graphing "of the past as it is used for present aims . . . and woven into the present and future."[1] By tracing the *Jüdische Chronik*'s immediate afterlife as well as its postmemorial life (for those in the succeeding generations), the music is shown to contribute to violence we might not yet be able to envision in the moment of production or initial reception, violence that might only become visible years or even decades after the event.

Notes

1. Barbie Zelizer, "Reading against the Grain: The Shape of Memory Studies," *Critical Studies in Mass Communication* 12, no. 2 (1995): 217

CHAPTER EIGHT

Complementary Discourses of Truth and Memory

The Peruvian Truth Commission and the Canción Social Ayacuchana

≫≈≪

JONATHAN RITTER

On December 21, 1982, in the city of Ayacucho, Peru, two Shining Path guerrillas entered the regional office of the National Institute of Culture (INC) and shot and killed its director, Walter Wong. As was typical of many Shining Path assassinations, no communiqué or other public statement was issued by the guerrillas to justify the killing, leaving the public to ponder the exact reasons behind his murder. Beyond a bureaucratic association with the state, and perhaps more obliquely, his promotion of "folklore" that stood in opposition to the Maoist party's Cultural Revolution–inspired dictums on such matters, Wong did not appear to have committed any specific infractions against the Shining Path.[1] Rather, his was simply the latest in a string of "selective assassinations" — the third in the city of Ayacucho that week alone — meant to "decapitate" the government at the local level and leave a power vacuum that would be filled by the guerrillas.

For the administration of President Fernando Belaúnde, the assassination of Wong marked a significant turning point in the government's response to the insurgency. After two and a half years of increasingly brazen and effective attacks on local authorities and infrastructure, the killing of this minor official of cultural affairs was the final straw, prompting the reluctant Belaúnde to at last place the Ayacucho region under military control.[2] Within weeks, deaths, disappearances and other human rights violations skyrocketed, as both the military and the guerrillas ratcheted up their campaigns of violence and terror. The death toll increased tenfold in the following year, and Ayacucho was soon immersed in a bloody and protracted conflict that would persist for more than a decade, claiming nearly 70,000 lives and uprooting much of the local population.[3]

In the midst of the explosion of violence in 1983, one of Wong's colleagues, a fellow cultural activist, veteran folk musician, and later director of that same regional office of the INC, Carlos Falconí, penned a song simply titled "Ofrenda" ("The Offering") that also marked an important milestone in the war. Written in Quechua and composed in the regional, guitar-based style of the mestizo *wayno*,[4] the song quickly gained a wide audience through local performances by Falconí, as well as recordings in the following year by two prominent artists within the national folk music circuit, Nelly Munguía and Manuelcha Prado. In contrast to the typically romantic, forlorn, or nostalgic lyrics to mestizo waynos from the region, the opening lyrics to "Ofrenda" painted a bleak scene of death, devastation, and wanton abuse:

Huamanga plazapi	In the plaza of Huamanga[5]
bumbacha tuqyachkan	bombs are exploding
Huamanga kallipi	In the streets of Huamanga
balalla parachkan	it is raining bullets
Karsil wasichapi	In the little jail
inusinti llakichkan	the innocent are weeping
Huamangallay barriu	the barrios of Huamanga
yawarta waqachkan	are weeping blood
Huamanga llaqtaypi	In my town of Huamanga
sinchi sinchi llaki	there is tremendous suffering
Huamanga llaqtapi	In the town of Huamanga
hatun hatun llaki	there is a great sadness
Muru pacha runa	The soldiers
wirayakullachkan	are getting fat
Kantinakunapi	In the cantinas
warmita rantichkan	they are buying women

"Ofrenda" was the first in a body of new songs in urban and rural folkloric styles, collectively referred to today as *canciones testimoniales* ("testimonial songs") or as the *canción social ayacuchana* ("Ayacuchan social song"), that were written explicitly in response to the events of Peru's internal war.[6] By the end of the 1980s, this testimonial repertoire comprised literally hundreds of such songs, all bearing witness to the traumatic experiences of the war and creating, through live performances and recordings, a needed and often singular social space for political protest, social commentary, and collective remembrance of those lost in the violence. It was, and remains to this day, one of the most dramatic and powerful artistic movements in modern Peruvian history.

The canción social repertoire is not alone today, however, on the public stage of representing the violent past in Peru. Exactly twenty years after "Ofrenda" was written, and more than a decade after the capture of Shining Path leader Abimael Guzman that signaled the beginning of the end of the war, on August 29, 2003, Carlos Falconí performed his song again, this time on a large stage set up in the very plaza referred to in its first line.[7] The poetic economy of the lyrics, evoking a now-past world of violent experience, resistance, and the hope of vindication, as well as the reconfigured space of the performance, from site of trauma to site of memory, were made all the more poignant by the occasion that prompted the concert. Earlier that day, the Peruvian Truth and Reconciliation Commission (CVR, in its Spanish acronym) had presented its final report in the municipal hall just off the plaza, concluding more than a year and a half of work investigating and analyzing the causes and events of the violence of the 1980s and 1990s.

Though Falconí and other musicians that night viewed their performances, billed as the last in a series of "Concerts for Memory," as a fitting conclusion to the Commission's work, public reactions to the Commission itself were decidedly mixed and overshadowed the sense of bittersweet celebration that might otherwise have been present that evening. Protesters marched against the Commission for much of the afternoon, contesting its conclusions and demanding attention to other concerns, while a media smear campaign, orchestrated primarily by political parties that were implicated in the violence and thus sought to suppress its findings, had already robbed the CVR of a portion of its public support and legitimacy.[8] Despite the controversy, for members of the Commission and hundreds of fans that evening, the concert marked a moment of closure, the end of one chapter in the ongoing struggle to come to terms with the violent past.

In this chapter, I offer some preliminary comparative thoughts on the narratives and discourses of remembrance presented within these two sites of memory[9] — the work of the Truth Commission, and the world of the canción social ayacuchana — that were so closely juxtaposed on that day. I am interested particularly in the rhetoric of what might be called "public speakability" that obtains to each, by which I mean the role that the very *possibility* of making public political statements about the violence played in how each was rationalized, and how "speaking the unspeakable" thus came to form a sort of mantra and mandate in the discourse surrounding each. The very similarity of those discourses raises interesting questions about the nature and value of their interventions in the public sphere. If the Truth

Commission justified its mission in large part on the need to "speak" what had previously been "silenced," it did so in seeming contradiction of nearly twenty years' worth of songwriting, musical performances, and recordings that had regularly raised a public voice of protest and commemoration. Given that Commission members were certainly aware of — and several, in fact, were known fans of — testimonial music about the war, how then are we to account for this apparent disparity in the relative power of music versus more "official" public discourses to bear witness to the violence of the past? What truths were each telling, and to whom?

To be clear, my intent here is neither to laud nor criticize the work of the Commission, which carried out, in my opinion, a sincere and moderately successful effort to clarify the events of the past and move the country toward a more just future. Nor do I wish to promote testimonial songs as a sort of utopian alternative to the complex legal, juridical, investigative, and commemorative work done by the Commission. Testimonial songs cannot bear the full weight and responsibility of national memory, though I would argue that it is clearly impoverished without them. Rather, I see both, in their similarities and distinctions, as unequal partners and complementary resources in a common and ongoing struggle to carve out a sustainable social space for collective remembrance of the years of violence in Peru.

The Peruvian Truth and Reconciliation Commission

In the late twentieth century, the model of the "truth commission" emerged in a number of places in the world as a new outlet for addressing the difficulties of transition from a period of crisis, usually involving extreme and sustained political violence, to a new, more democratic, integrated and peaceful future.[10] Though each of the more than twenty truth commissions formed thus far has come about within a very particular set of national, political, and social circumstances that has determined its mandate and limitations, the model for all "truth commissions" is based on two key, often contradictory assumptions: first, that in the wake of crisis, a more thorough and "truthful" account of the past is needed to counter previous acts of distortion, silencing and omission; and second, that this truthful knowledge can serve as the foundation for national reconciliation and the construction of that new, collectively imagined future.[11] Every commission has had to struggle with finding its own, locally-appropriate balance between these goals, weighing the need for justice and redress with the dream of forgiveness and reconciliation.

Peru's Truth Commission did not come about as the organic result of a sustained popular outcry and a public demand for a new accountability to the past, but rather as the result of sudden and largely unforeseen political conjuncture, a fact that may help to explain some of the ambivalence many Peruvians felt and continue to feel about it. Throughout the 1990s, the country had lived under the quasi-dictatorship of Alberto Fujimori, a one-time Japanese-Peruvian agronomist turned classic Latin American *caudillo* ("strongman"). After being elected as a political outsider in 1990, Fujimori staged an *autogolpe* ("self-coup") in April of 1992, disbanding Congress and the judiciary, and rewriting the constitution to give the executive branch greater power and allow himself the opportunity to run for office again. These steps were necessary, he argued, in order to more effectively "combat terrorism" in the country, a claim that was bolstered in the public eye by the capture of Guzman in September 1992.[12]

As Peruvian anthropologist and Truth Commission member Carlos Iván Degregori has argued, the capture of Guzman permitted the regime to "impose a certain narrative about the years of violence," promoting a "savior memory" in which Fujimori and his administration appeared as the heroes, solely responsible for finally putting an end to the violence that had wracked the country for more than a decade.[13] The "savior memory" and the absolutist logic that accompanied it — a Peruvian equivalent to "you're either with us or against us" — also served to discourage the expression of other versions of the past and/or dissent against the Fujimori administration in the public sphere.[14]

This climate of repression persisted until the fall of 2000, when the corruption of the regime was exposed in a series of videotapes showing Fujimori's chief of intelligence, Vladimiro Montesinos, paying off members of the main opposition parties. In December of that year, Fujimori fled into exile in Japan, where he remained until November 2005, and an interim government headed by centrist politician Valentín Paniagua was appointed by the Peruvian Congress to oversee the transition back to democracy. It was during Paniagua's brief term in office in early 2001 that the first mention of a truth commission surfaced, and by the end of that year, under newly elected president Alejandro Toledo, the Peruvian Truth and Reconciliation Commission had become a reality. Beyond investigating the crimes of the Fujimori era, the Commission's mandate was also expanded to encompass the entire history of the war. Specifically, the CVR was asked to "clarify the processes, acts and responsibilities of terrorist violence and the violation of human rights occurring between May 1980 and November 2000, investigating terrorist organizations as well as agents of the state, and propose initiatives destined to affirm peace and agreement among Peruvians."[15]

Of the many tasks initially undertaken by the CVR, including everything from forensic identification and exhumation of mass graves to determining

Poster advertising the formation of a Truth Commission in Peru. Ayacucho, December 2001. *Photo by Jonathan Ritter.*

feasible and just guidelines for reparations to be paid to victims and their families, two activities stand out for their contribution to the work of collective and private remembrance.[16] First was the collection and recording of nearly 17,000 individual *testimonios* ("testimonies") about the years of violence, the majority of them personal stories of loss and abuse related by indigenous *campesinos*, or peasants. The Commission itself reiterated the central role of these testimonios in its final report:

> The collection of testimonios has been perhaps the most important work undertaken by the Truth Commission, not only for the volume of personal histories that we have gathered, but also because in this activity we have accomplished a deliberate goal of the Commission, arising from the moral aspect of our mandate: to recover, first and foremost, the voice of the victims.[17]

In the work of the Commission, testimonios functioned essentially as legal depositions, turning orally transmitted memories into the transcribed documents of history — in Diana Taylor's terms, turning the "repertoire" of memory, the living active present of the past, into the "archive" of the state.[18] Edited, analyzed, and re-presented, these testimonios would in turn form the foundation of the Commission's final report, a mediating process for the "voice of the victims" not unlike that associated with the eponymous Latin American literary genre.[19]

The second task meriting our attention here was the Commission's staging of public, nationally televised hearings in several of the cities most affected by the violence, a tactic borrowed from the earlier South African Truth Commission. As Human Rights Watch noted: "These hearings . . . the first public hearings ever held by a truth commission in the Americas . . . [were] not meant to serve an investigative or judicial purpose. Rather, they serve, in the commission's words, 'as an act of dignifying and healing for the victims and those who can identify with the cases brought up.'"[20] Put in different terms, the purpose and power of the hearings lay in their very *performativity*. Distinct from the legalistic and private testimonio recordings, they offered a chance for the public rehearsal of traumatic memories in a way that would, ideally, offer both catharsis for the victims doing the telling as well as elicit sympathy from others in the country, who would hear in the most dramatic fashion possible about the unknown horrors and tragedies of the war.[21] The power of such testimonial performances was undeniable. As Albie Sachs has noted about the South African hearings upon which the Peruvian versions were modeled:

> The strength of . . . [the] Truth Commission lay not so much in its microscopic truths, in its source of detail. It lay in that experiential dimension: the tears of those who suffered; the stiff body language of former police, their little mustaches trying to find a way of saying sorry. . . . It was a whole different kind of setting, where the human being with human emotions was at the core of everything. We could identify with somebody or another in the interaction. And that's what drew the nation in. And that's what gave it its power, its strength, and its lasting impact. . . . It's not enough simply to have a commission of experts [looking] into what happened in the past. You need the tears, the anger, the emotion, the songs, the feeling."[22]

In Peru, building a shared sense of loss and empathy across regional, class, and ethnic lines was crucial to forwarding the ultimate goal of national reconciliation. The fact that many of those who spoke at the hearings did so in Quechua, which had to be translated into Spanish for much of the rest of the country watching on television, underscored how distant that goal of "national" unity remained. Throughout the process, then, both the hearings and the collection of recorded testimonios constituted a powerful interjection of forgotten, erased, and suppressed memories into the national consciousness, a victory in itself over the enforced silences of the Fujimori era.

This, at least, was the dominant narrative that framed the work of the Truth Commission: a discourse of rupture and "breaking-through" the silences of the past, laying bare the atrocities committed by the military forces and guerrillas alike. This narrative relies, however, on a very particular notion of the public sphere, one limited to official statements, government decrees, and only the most prominent (and conservative) news media. Without denying the limited nature of discourse previously available through those powerful channels, or in any way denigrating the very real power of the moments of private and public testimony that were sponsored and enabled by the CVR, I do however want to call into question this absolute rhetoric of "rupturing silence" that permeated and was used to justify its work. Too great an emphasis on such a rupture ignores or, at best, marginalizes the many alternate forms of narrative and testimony that were used throughout the violence to mediate the experience of trauma and commemoration for indigenous peoples, Ayacuchanos, and Peruvians more generally, and it risks overemphasizing the impact of the CVR along these same lines.[23] Though music was not the only such "alternate form" of testimony and remembrance, the kind of public intervention that it made via live performance and mass-mediated dissemination warrants special consideration, particularly in light of the preceding arguments about the otherwise limited nature of such public discourse.

The Canción Social Ayacuchana

The argument that narratives about past violence take many forms beyond official discourses is hardly a new one.[24] Decades of research on "resistance" in the social sciences and cultural studies have documented the myriad ways in which people seek to bear witness to their suffering in ways that contest official or otherwise dominant narratives. Music occupies a uniquely powerful niche within the realm of possible acts of resistance, incorporating the creativity and personal recollections or experiences of individual composers, the expressive power and performance frame chosen by performers and producers, the potential for widespread dissemination of critical ideas via recordings and the mass media, and the ever-present ability of audiences (live or mediated) to interpret and re-frame what they are listening to. Music's status as event-in-time is also potentially one of its greatest strengths in advocating dissent or a particular narrative about the past, allowing for the real-time creation of a palpable community of listeners to engage with a given composition's message each time it is performed, broadcast, or played back. Political opinion and understanding of that message need not be uniform in such listening communities, but copresence with other audience members, together with the pleasurable or otherwise emotional experience of the music itself, certainly combine for powerful effect in shaping how such messages are heard and internalized.

Bearing this in mind and returning our attention to the canción social ayacuchana, I want to argue here for a much less "silent" history of remembrance and resistance in Peru than that surrounding the CVR, one that recognizes the profound contributions made within an alternate discursive realm of musical composition, performance, and listening. Following upon the heels of Carlos Falconí's song "Ofrenda," the latter half of the 1980s witnessed a tremendous outpouring of Ayacuchan testimonial music. During a period when so-called "Andean folklore" was in decline in the rest of Peru — the historic coliseums of Lima's Andean migrant community shuttered, and the wayno itself challenged by the popularity of *chicha* and other forms of contemporary popular music[25] — waynos reemerged among Ayacuchanos as a popular genre among audiences of all ages. Old songs about pain, loss, and migration were given new meaning, and literally hundreds of new songs about the war, some full of oblique metaphor and others as direct as a gunshot, were written and many recorded. As Falconí remembers:

> The wayno, the "testimonial song," emerged from the grass roots. Almost everyone from Ayacucho, almost everyone from the highlands, saw someone die, someone from their family, especially in the center-south of the country. As a result, there was this effervescence, on one side out of fear, and on the other out of indignation for everything that one had seen. That is why these songs began to spread. The work of the composers was to put a song on the lips of all of the people — for catharsis, on the one hand, or as a massive social protest, on the other.[26]

When I asked Falconí why he and so many others wrote and performed these songs, especially given that doing so put a number of them in mortal danger on more than one occasion, his response was simple. "It was the only space we had to talk about the terrible things happening in our lives" — a statement that acknowledges both the climate of silencing and fear that permeated the public sphere in Peru, and the singular importance of music in repeatedly rupturing that silence.

Though recourse to music as vehicle for resistance as well as solace in times of violence is a widespread phenomenon, it is not universal; protest song movements do not simply spring forth from difficult circumstances or emerge "naturally" in times of oppression. Beyond the desire for a social space in which "to talk about the terrible things [that were] happening," other conjunctural factors played a catalytic role in spurring the Ayacuchan testimonial song phenomenon and deserve at least cursory mention here. First was the deep history of social commentary in Andean musical and other performative traditions that the canción social built upon. Carnivalesque inversions of the social order during civic-religious festivals, masked troupes and other popular dance-dramas critically depicting historical events or portraying current class and ethnic conflicts, and song traditions full of barbed commentary on current events constitute well-established aspects of Andean popular culture.[27]

The wayno song genre in particular bore a special reputation for critical social commentary by the time of the violence in the 1980s, due to the popularity of so-called "protest" waynos in the 1970s such as Ranulfo Fuentes's "El Hombre," Ricardo Dolorier's "Flor de Retama" (discussed later), and various works by the Ancashino wayno star "Jilguero de Huasacarán" (Ernesto Sánchez Fajardo). Consequently, though the canción social ayacuchana movement in the 1980s and 90s marked a qualitative and quantitative shift in the critical commentary offered by Ayacuchan waynos, it did so well within an established tradition that was generally acknowledged and built upon by its practitioners. That tradition was also easily recognized by listeners due to the relatively conservative musical language chosen by canción testimonial composers and performers in the 1980s, who, with very few exceptions, maintained the characteristic musical features of the mestizo wayno from Ayacucho.[28]

A second key development in the canción social movement's success was the development of new performance spaces and opportunities for the messages of its songs to be heard. Principal among these, particularly for the role it played in encouraging composers to write new material, was the song contest or *concurso*. Though such contests were not a recent invention, dating back at least to the 1920s and the first folklore festivals held in Amancaes that were sponsored by the Leguía administration,[29] the prominence and the prestige such contests offered among Ayacuchanos in the 1980s marked a qualitatively new moment in their history, and thus offered a significant platform from which to engage in social critique and public remembrance of the violence.

Perhaps the most interesting and surprising aspect of these politicized spaces for testimonial performance was the variety of entities who sponsored them, ranging from migrant associations in Lima's shantytowns to the Peruvian state itself. Of the dozens of such contests that were held at the local, regional, and national level in those years, one in particular was frequently cited to me by Ayacuchanos as an important moment in the history of testimonial music. Responding in part to criticism of a "national" music festival sponsored by the Alan Garcia regime in 1986 that featured primarily urban *criollo* (white, coastal, upper-class) and foreign Latin American musics,[30] in 1987 Garcia opted to host a song contest for traditional music (*música vernacular*) from Peru. Officially entitled the "Festival de Autores y Compositores del Perú" (Festival of Peruvian Authors and Composers), the contest was known more popularly as the Urpicha de Oro, or "Golden Dove," the use of a Quechua title indicative of the political aspirations of the festival. According to one of the judges of the contest, more than a thousand entries were received from Ayacucho in the festival's first two years (1987–88), vastly outnumbering submissions from other areas, and the majority of these songs addressed themes related to the war.[31] Furthermore, Ayacuchan composers nearly swept the awards in the categories for which they were eligible, and their songs are prominently featured in the LPs released by the government-run IEMPSA label documenting the festival. Given the overwhelming criticism of the government and military contained in these songs, not surprisingly, the Garcia administration cancelled the contest after just two years.

A third factor in the spread and importance of this music in the late 1980s was the popularization of cheap cassette technology in Peru, and the subsequent diversification of the national recording industry. While the few major labels left in Peru by this time largely refused to record political or controversial material,[32] a fact reiterated to me by many musicians, a host of micro-labels had emerged by late in the decade to fill the gap. Recording on relatively primitive, portable equipment, producing only cheap cassettes, and selling their wares through ambulant street vendors or in working class markets, many such micro-labels succeeded in turning a small profit in Peru's substantial "gray market" while also avoiding problems with the authorities over the content of such cassettes. Coupled with rampant piracy, which continues to plague the Peruvian music industry today, canción testimonial recordings received a much wider circulation than would likely have been possible just a decade earlier.

This informal music industry and its promotion of the cancion testimonial movement was sustained in part by its symbiotic relationship with live performance. In addition to sales by street vendors and in markets like Lima's Mesa Redonda district, wayno singers and other musicians sold cassettes of and at their own performances. The most famous such recording is of a 1987 concert by wayno singer Martina Portocarrero in Lima's Teatro Municipal. This concert, taking place at the height of the violence, in one of the country's most storied venues, by arguably the most popular and politicized wayno singer of the time, marked a high point for the Ayacuchan testimonial song movement, and live recordings of the event have been in circulation ever since.

The recent decision by Dolly J.R. Producciones — one of the most successful and important labels to emerge in the 1980s, in large part due to its promotion of the Ayacuchan cancion testimonial repertoire — to invest in remastering the original recording and rerelease it on CD offers some indi-

CD cover of Dolly J.R. Producciones' 2005
re-release of Martina Portocarrero's live recording
from a 1987 concert in Lima's Teatro Municipal.
Image courtesy of Dolby J. R. Producciones.

cation not only of the concert's historic importance as an event *during* the war, but also of the continued popularity and broad demand for testimonial song recordings well *after* the period of violence, a point to which I will return in a moment.[33]

Protest, Testimony, and Bearing Witness: *The Cancion Social Message(s)*

What, then, did these songs actually have to say? Within the ample public sphere created by song contests, recordings, and limited live performances, the emergent repertoire of canciones testimoniales in the late 1980s offered a number of perspectives on the violence itself. Most, such as Falconí's "Ofrenda," delivered a combination of lament and implicit outrage at the atrocities taking place, particularly those wrought by the army, though without offering detail on individual events. Indeed, drawing and building on the literary conventions of the wayno genre, poetic imagery and the frequent use of metaphor characterize the vast majority of songs, rather than blunt description or narrative. Martina Portocarrero's wayno "Mamacha de las Mercedes" ("Virgin of Mercy"), contained on the aforementioned recording, is typical in this regard:

Penas que arrastran mi alma	Grief that drags down my soul
Me están matando	They are killing me
Mamacha de las Mercedes	Virgin of Mercy
¿Qúe es lo que pasa aquí?	What is happening here?
Unos a otros se matan	Killing one another
Sin compasión	without compassion
Mamacha de las Mercedes	Virgin of Mercy
¿Qúe es lo que pasa aquí?	What is happening here?
Unos son hierba del campo	Some are country weeds[34]
Otros quien diablos serán	Others, what devils could they be?
Mamacha de las Mercedes	Virgin of Mercy
¿Qúe es lo que pasa aquí?	What is happening here?

Other songs such as Carlos Falconí's "¡Viva la Patria!" were more explicit in their references to abuses perpetrated by the Peruvian military, but again eschewed narrative in favor of poetic rumination. Falconí, by his own admission, wrote the song in response to a well-known army massacre that took place in 1983 at a wedding party in the small town of Soccos, near the city of Ayacucho.[35] Soccos, however, is not mentioned in the lyrics; rather, two other Ayacuchan towns that were also the site of army incursions are mentioned in passing,[36] while the *fuga* or "coda" presents a bitter, satirical indictment of army behavior more generally in Ayacucho.

Takichum takisqay, wiqichum wiqillay	Can my song continue to be sung
Warmachakunapa ñawichallampi	when the eyes of children
Chiqnikuy huntaptin	fill with hate?
Takichum takisqay, wiqichum wiqillay	Can my tears still be shed?
Vinchus viudalla asirillanmanchu	Can the widow in Vinchos still laugh?
Cangallu viuda kusiri	Is the widow in Cangallo still capable
Cangalu viuda kusirikunmanchu	of happiness?
Allqupa churinta unanchallanmanchu	Could she treat that son of a bitch as her own?
Pimanraq kutinqa sapan paloma	Who will help the lonely dove,
Quru sacha hina mana piniyuq	with no one, like a dying tree?
Sipillawaptimpas sayarimusaqmi	I will rise up, even if they kill me
Chakiytawiptimpas sayarimusaqmi	I will stand up, even if they cut off my feet
Makichallaykita haywa	Lend me your hand in solidarity, we
Makichallaykita haywaykullaway	have to walk quickly

Utqaymi purinay qamllama allinlla	Until later, I hope you will be alright
Huamanga del alma hatarillasunmi	Ayacucho of my soul, we must rise up

FUGA	CODA
Vacaytaqa nakankutaq	They cut off my cow's head
Radiuytaqa apankutaq	They steal my radio
"Concha tu madre" niwankutaq	They say my mother's a whore
"Viva la patria" niwankutaq	And they still say "Long live the Fatherland!"

There is more here, however, than simple outrage. The lyrics in the third verse allude to the Andean myth of the *Inkarrí* or "Inca King," whose body it is believed was dismembered and buried centuries ago by the conquering Spanish; when his body regrows or is rejoined underground, according to the myth, he will rise again. Falconí's valorization of Andean cultural/spiritual beliefs here is deliberately linked to a call for solidarity, for people to band together and "rise up" in defense of their lives and their identities as indigenous people, as peasants, and as Ayacuchanos.[37] This tie between cultural identity and political resistance is a frequent trope in the testimonial song repertoire, one also reinforced by the deliberate use of the Quechua language.[38]

Resistance, nonetheless, had its limits. Protests against abuses committed by the Shining Path, for instance, were almost nonexistent among urban *canciones testimoniales* in the 1980s and 90s. There are several reasons for this discrepancy. First, virtually everyone associated with the canción social movement retained a deep distrust of the Peruvian armed forces after the dictatorship of the 1970s, and the explosion of violence in 1983 (when the military entered the war) and subsequent persecution of a number of musicians and composers only confirmed that distrust. Second, though the Truth Commission would much later assign blame for more than half of the deaths and disappearances of the 1980s and 1990s to the Shining Path, during much of the conflict itself, the full extent of Shining Path violence and who it was directed against remained unclear for most observers.[39] Last, though singers and songwriters who publicly identified with the Shining Path were rare, for obvious reasons, many came from the same leftist university student social circles that the guerrillas did and held at least some degree of sympathy for their project, if not always their means. Indeed, a few explicitly Shining Path songs became well known in the 1980s thanks to performances by leftist performers. One, "Hierba Silvestre" ("Wild Weed"), a poem by the martyred Shining Path guerrilla Edith Lagos, set to music by

Martina Portocarrero, became one of the most popular waynos of the 1980s, and is still widely available on recordings today.

In sum, popular recordings that received wide circulation; prizes awarded for testimonial songs in contests at the local, regional, and national level; and concerts in some of the major theaters and concert halls in Lima all lend credence to the argument that the canción social phenomenon opened an important and widespread social space for protest and later commemoration of the years of violence. This fact is all the more remarkable given the inhibiting factors that *did* exist to curtail freedom of expression in this unconventional political arena. Many artists took substantial risks in composing and performing songs that could be interpreted as critical of the military or sympathetic to the Shining Path. For that reason, few of the nationally prominent musicians or composers associated with the canción social phenomenon lived in Ayacucho, where police and military presence under the state of emergency made it simply too dangerous to perform such songs outside of the occasional, officially sanctioned *concurso*. Carlos Falconí was one of the few such nationally known artists to continue living there throughout the 1980s and 1990s, a fact for which he paid by having to go into hiding for more than a year while being targeted by a paramilitary death squad.[40]

Even among those living and working in Lima, persecution by state authorities was common. Numerous musicians recalled in interviews with me concerts that were cancelled by the army, or occasions when they were taken into custody and questioned after publicly performing testimonial songs. Several of the most critical and prominent canción social performers, including Martina Portocarrero and guitarist Julio Humala, spent time in exile to avoid further police persecution, while Julio's brother and musical partner Walter Humala was imprisoned three times during the war, the last time in the mid-1990s explicitly for *apología de terrorismo* (being an "apologist" for "terrorism"), with the lyrics to his songs used as legal evidence against him.[41]

After the Violence: The Cancion Social Legacy

The flourishing of testimonial song composition in the late 1980s slowed in the early 1990s and, interestingly, ceased almost entirely by the middle of the decade, suggesting that the act of writing such songs was closely related to the immediacy of the experience of violence. Performing and listening to such songs did not, however, end with the conflict. Unlike most topical songs in the Andes, such as those composed for carnival, many of the testimonial songs written in the 1980s persisted in the performance repertoire of Ayacuchan singers and artists well into the 1990s, and several remain popular today, re-signified now as acts of memory, audible cues for the visceral recollection of past experiences.

By way of illustration, one of the most compelling and complex examples of this process of re-signification is contained on a 2001 recording of the song "Flor de Retama." Written by Ricardo Dolorier, a poet, professor, and teacher's union activist, "Flor de Retama" was composed in the early 1970s as a response to a 1969 massacre of students and peasants in Huanta, Ayacucho, more than a decade before the Shining Path war began:

Vengan, todos, a ver	Come, everyone, to see
Ay, vamos a ver	Ay, we are going to see
En la plazuela de Huanta	In the plaza of Huanta
Amarillito flor de retama	The little yellow *retama* flower
Amarillito, amarillando, flor de retama	Bright little yellow *retama* flower
Por cinco esquinas están	They are at Five Corners[42]
Los sinchis entrando están	The National Guard soldiers are entering
Van a matar estudiantes (campesinos)	They are going to kill students (peasants)
Huantinos de corazón	Huantinos at heart
Amarillito, amarillando, flor de retama	Bright little yellow *retama* flower
Donde la sangre del pueblo	Oh, where the blood of the people
Ay, se derrama	spilled over
Ahí mismito florece	Right there flowers
Amarillito flor de retama	The little yellow *retama* flower
Amarillito, amarillando, flor de retama	Bright little yellow *retama* flower
La sangre del pueblo tiene rico perfume	The blood of the people has a rich perfume
Huele a jazmines, violetas	It smells of jasmine, of violets,
Geranios y margaritas	Geraniums and daisies
A pólvora y dinamita, ¡carajo!	Of gunpowder and dynamite, damn it!
A pólvora y dinamita	Of gunpowder and dynamite

The song has become a veritable palimpsest of Ayacuchan memories of violence today, recalling several generations of meanings and associations. What began as a protest song focused on the specific 1969 event treated in its lyrics reemerged as a popular song of resistance to the military regime among radicalized workers, students, and migrants living in Lima in the late 1970s. It then became an unofficial anthem of the Shining Path guerrilla movement itself in the 1980s, and its public performance during the years

CD cover of debut album *Wistu Vida* by Dúo Retama
(Lima:Producciones Musicales Apu-Rimac, 2001).
Image courtesy of Producciones Musicales Apu-Rimac.

of violence was consequently a highly charged political act. By the mid-1990s, it had shed some of the specific associations with the guerrillas and had instead become a popular expression of Ayacuchan identity in general, yoking notions of "Ayacuchan-ness" to a thirty-year history of violence and resistance in the region. It has been recorded dozens of times, by a wide variety of wayno recording artists, and remains a staple in the repertoire of most mestizo musicians from the region.[43]

In this 2001 recording, the lead track on the debut album of the Duo Retama (named for the song), musicians Kramer Rojas and Erick Betalluz recontextualize the tune with references linked particularly to the Shining Path era, including a long voice-over "intro" and "outro" that paraphrase and reference the lyrics to Carlos Falconí's "Viva la Patria":

(Sung/crying; from "Flor de Retama")

Amarillito flor de retama	The little yellow *retama* flower
Amarillito, amarillando, flor de retama	Bright little yellow *retama* flower

(Spoken in Quechua; paraphrase/reference to "Viva la Patria")

Qomer pacha runakuna	Green earth people [soldiers]
Llaqtanchikman yaykuramunku	You come into our towns

"Cholo concha tu madre" niwaspanku	you say to us
Manchakullataña cheqarachispa	Spreading fear
Llaqtamasinchikta chinkarachinku	You "disappear" our neighbors
Imachay kunatapas suwaspa	You steal everything and anything
tukuramunku	

(Song: "Flor de Retama")

Vengan todos a ver . . .	Come everyone to see . . .

(Spoken "outro"; paraphrase/reference to "Viva la Patria")

Viva la patria qaparkachaspa	You shout "Long live the fatherland!"
Wañuyllataña aparamunku	But you come bringing death
Chaynam usiasun,	Leaving us to rot
chulla uchkupi pampaykusqa	Buried in a hole in the earth
wawanchanchikpas wakchalla	While our children walk along in
purikamunqa	poverty.

The intertextual references here, between not only different experiences of violence but also different well-known songs about those experiences, point to a certain self-referentiality within the testimonial song tradition today, allowing meanings to stack upon meanings, remembrances upon remembrances, to accrue and sediment to particular texts and songs such as "Flor de Retama." Indeed, the combination of "Flor de Retama" with a textual paraphrase of Falconí's "Viva la Patria," performed in the more pop-oriented style of Ayacuchan wayno at the turn of the millennium, draws together three different eras spread over thirty years into a single narrative, one that could be said to define Ayacucho today as a place of past violence and current reimaginings of self and the future.[44]

Conclusion

What, then, do these examples tell us about the kind of remembrance offered by the canción social ayacuchana? Or to pose the question as stated earlier, what truths do they tell, and to whom? First, it seems clear to me that the canción testimonial has formed its own discursive realm of commemoration and protest, residing and resonating within the media and entertainment circuits of middle- and working-class civil society in Peru, and thus quite separate from official or otherwise public forms of remembrance and commentary. Though the "Concerts for Memory" held during the Truth Commission process brought these two sets of discourses together for a brief period, literally sharing the same stage on occasion, the prior existence and continued viability of the canción social phenomenon indicate that the memory work it accomplishes is not contingent upon its promotion or legitimization by the state. To the contrary, it is frequently heard and experienced as legitimate by Peruvian and specifically Ayacuchan audiences precisely in its *opposition* to the state. The Truth Commission, on the other hand, despite its concerted effort to collect and (re)present the "voices of the victims" and civil society more generally, was by its very existence an act and an extension *of* the government, and was consequently experienced and regarded as such by many Peruvian citizens.[45]

Second, the generalized themes of lament and protest in most testimonial songs, rather than narratives of specific events or atrocities, were a crucial part of their appeal and their continued viability as vehicles for commemoration and social memory. The singular history of "Flor de Retama," a song that *does* narrate the events of a particular tragedy but whose specificity has repeatedly been re-signified and challenged by Ayacuchan audiences over several decades, offers a sort of exception that proves the rule — an "anti-emblematic" emblematic text. This dynamism, the constant renovation of song texts, meanings, and memories through performance and new recordings, is a vital aspect of the canción social tradition today, and one that distinguishes it in important ways from the kind of static "memory" necessarily contained in documents like the Truth Commission report. Argentine sociologist Elizabeth Jelin, though sympathetic to the project of truth commissions, and the Peruvian version in particular, has warned precisely against this latter sort of hardening and institutionalization of social memory, noting that in post-trauma social situations, "the processes of expressing and making public the interpretations and meanings of those pasts are extremely dynamic, as these interpretations and meanings are never fixed once and for all"[46] — a dynamism perfectly reflected in the shifting yet emotionally rich experience of listening to or performing testimonial songs.

Extending this argument still farther, Eduardo Gonzalez, writing on the globalization of what he calls the "right to truth," has argued that this sort of flexibility is in fact essential for acts of public remembrance — there cannot be a single, unitary national memory in the wake of mass violence. Rather, "what there can be, what is desirable, is a permanent and inclusive public forum where we all recognize ourselves as equals and submit our different memories with the goal of becoming citizens within a truth-under-construction."[47] The creation of such a forum was one of the major goals of the Truth Commission in Peru, and one that was, perhaps, fleetingly accomplished in the moment of its hearings. As I have argued in this chapter, however, the CVR was not the first or only such forum, as it was preceded nearly two decades earlier by the first stirrings of a testimonial song movement that flourished in the late 1980s and persists in the performance repertoire of contemporary wayno performers from Ayacucho today.

Far from supplanting the established social space for remembrance through musical performance, the Truth Commission offered compelling evidence of the differences between their discursive domains, despite similarities in the rhetoric — of "speaking the unspeakable" and "rupturing silence" — that is often used to justify each. John McDowell has usefully labeled these competing domains as "informative" and "commemorative" discourse.[48] The former, in McDowell's model, refers to expository prose and explanation, and could be used here to describe the kind of discourse produced by the Truth Commission in its final report — legal facts, timelines, written statements, and all the dry, necessary minutiae of official records that had been missing prior to the work of the CVR. These contrast in important ways with "commemorative" forms of oral performance that, particularly through differences in tone and a poetic economy of text, may have a more profoundly emotional impact on their audiences.[49] In this sense, testimonial music during and after the war might be most fruitfully compared with the CVR public hearings — as performative acts or events that create communities of listeners who engage with particular ways of knowing, experiencing, and narrating the violent past.

As the Commission's recommendations languish today in the desks of a hostile government, and the hearings recede into memory, the need for a public, enduring social space in which the war's trauma is acknowledged and recognized remains a crucial one. The continued performance of the canción social repertoire, more than a decade after the inconclusive end of the violence itself, and years after the publication of the CVR's final report, speaks to both this need for public remembrance and the ability of song to at least partially fulfill it. As before the Truth Commission, music once again appears to be one of "the only places," returning to Carlos Falconí's earlier assessment, "in which to talk about the terrible things" that so many in the country endured.

Notes

My initial research on testimonial music was carried out in Ayacucho, Peru, between 2000 and 2002 under the auspices of a Fulbright grant (IIE), a dissertation research fellowship from the Wenner-Gren Foundation for Anthropological Research, and support from the UCLA International Studies Overseas Program. Many singers, songwriters, and activists in Peru opened their homes, hearts, and lives to me during the years of this project, and no acknowledgment here can adequately express my gratitude and admiration to and for all of them, though

Carlos Falconí deserves special mention and thanks in this regard. I also wish to thank Raúl Romero, Gisela Cánepa, and the staff of the Instituto de Etnomusicología in Lima for their consistent support and feedback on my work while in Peru, as well as Martin Daughtry, Heidi Feldman, Javier León, Fernando Rios, and Joshua Tucker for their expert commentary on earlier versions of material contained in this paper. All errors in fact or interpretation are, of course, my own.

1. A matter that I have discussed at more length elsewhere, Jonathan Ritter, "Siren Songs: Ritual and Revolution in the Peruvian Andes," *British Journal of Ethnomusicology* 11, no. 1 (2002): 25–28.

2. Gustavo Gorriti narrates a more complete version of these events in his excellent history of the early years of the internal war, *The Shining Path: A History of the Millenarian War in Peru*, trans. Robin Kirk (Chapel Hill: University of North Carolina Press, 1999), 260.

3. The most comprehensive study of the war, appropriately enough, is found in the final report of the Peruvian Truth and Reconciliation Commission, which concluded that nearly 70,000 people were killed by political violence within the country between 1980 and 2000, a majority of them indigenous peasants from the Andean and Amazonian regions of the country. Comisión de la Verdad y Reconciliación (CVR). *Informe Final de la Comisión de la Verdad y Reconciliación* (Lima: CVR, 2003).

4. The *wayno* is the most widespread genre of music and dance in the Peruvian Andes. Though marked by significant regional variations in instrumentation and stylistic features, all waynos are based on a characteristic duple meter rhythm (an eighth note followed by two sixteenth notes), paired musical phrases (usually AABB), and strophic form.

5. "Huamanga" was the colonial name for the city of Ayacucho, and it remains the name of the province that the city lies in today. It is often used in everyday parlance to refer to the city, and differentiate it from the department (state) also known as Ayacucho.

6. For a recent analysis of this song and its articulations with the violence in Ayacucho at the moment of its composition, see Abilio Vergara's musical biography of Carlos Falconí, *La Tierra Que Duele de Carlos Falconí* (Ayacucho, Peru: Universidad Nacional de San Cristóbal de Huamanga, 2010), 170–77.

7. I would like to thank Kairos Marquardt, Cynthia Milton, Ponciano del Pino, Carlos Falconí, Nelly Munguía, and Manuelcha Prado for sharing their eyewitness accounts of the concert discussed in the introduction, and other events associated with the work of the Truth Commission. For a much more detailed account and analysis of the concert and other events in Ayacucho that day, see Cynthia Milton, "Public Spaces for the Discussion of Peru's Recent Past." *Antípoda* 5 (2007): 143–68.

8. For more on the reception of the CVR nationally, see Carlos Iván Degregori, "Heridas abiertas, derechos esquivos: Reflexiones sobre la Comisión de la Verdad

y Reconciliación," in *Memorias en conflicto: Aspectos de la violencia politica contemporanea*, ed. Raynald Belay et al. (Lima: Embajada de Francia en el Perú, Instituto de Estudios Peruanos, Instituto Francés de Estudios Peruanos, and Red Para el Desarrollo de las Ciencias Sociales en el Perú, 2003), 84–85. Kimberly Theidon, *Entre prójimos: El conflicto armado interno y la política de la reconciliación en el Perú* (Lima: Instituto de Estudios Peruanos, 2004); Wendy Coxshall, "From the Peruvian Reconciliation Commission to Ethnography: Narrative, Relatedness, and Silence," *Political and Legal Anthropology Review* 28, no. 2 (2005): 203–22; and Caroline Yezer, "Who Wants to Know? Rumors, Suspicions, and Opposition to Truth-Telling in Ayacucho," *Latin American and Caribbean Ethnic Studies* 3, no. 3 (2008): 271–89, provide excellent discussions of how the CVR was perceived in rural areas of Ayacucho.

9. I take the phrase "site of memory" here from the work of Pierre Nora, "Between Memory and History: Les Lieux de Mémoire," *Representations* 26 (1989): 7–24. Nora coined the term to highlight the self-conscious character of many past-oriented, explicitly commemorative places and events in the present, such as those under discussion here. I am less concerned than Nora, however, in drawing too fine a distinction between what he calls the *lieux* ("sites") and the *milieux* ("real environments") of memory, particularly in light of the deep roots of the *canción social* in Andean musical practices and traditions.

10. The study of truth commissions has become an interdisciplinary subfield of its own in the last decade, approached from perspectives across the social sciences. For more on the specific literature that has influenced this essay regarding the expanding "globalization of the right to truth," as Eduardo González has called it, "La globalización del derecho a la verdad," in Belay et al., *Memorias en conflicto*, 181–92, see Priscilla Hayner, *Unspeakable Truths: Confronting State Terror and Atrocities* (New York: Routledge, 2002); Sandrine LeFranc, "¿Cómo acabar con el desacuerdo? Las Comisiones de la Verdad como lugar de construcción disensual de la historia," in Belay et al., *Memorias en conflicto*, 193–223; Richard Wilson, *The Politics of Truth and Reconciliation in South Africa: Legitimizing the Post-Apartheid State* (Cambridge: Cambridge University Press, 2001); and Bronwyn Leebaw, *Judging State-Sponsored Violence, Imagining Political Change* (New York: Cambridge University Press, 2011); as well as Greg Grandin and Thomas Miller Klublock, eds., *Truth Commissions: State Terror, History, and Memory*, Special issue of *Radical History Review* 97 (2007).

11. LeFranc, "¿Cómo acabar con el desacuerdo?"; Tristan Anne Borer, "Truth Telling as a Peace-Building Activity: A Theoretical Overview," in *Telling the Truths: Truth Telling and Peace Building in Post-Conflict Societies*, ed. Tristan Anne Borer (Notre Dame, IN: University of Notre Dame Press, 2006), 1–57.; Leigh Payne, *Unsettling Accounts: Neither Truth nor Reconciliation in Confessions of State Violence* (Durham, NC: Duke University Press, 2008).

12. How much credit Fujimori can legitimately claim for the capture of Guzman is a matter of debate; the latter's arrest was largely the result of long-term investigative police work by DINCOTE, the counterterrorism police intelligence force, which had little to do with Fujimori's hard-line policies that came to the fore with the *autogolpe* ("self-coup") in 1992.

13. The original Spanish: "Pero se había impuesto, más bien, una cierta narrativa sobre los años de violencia política, [u]na 'memoria salvadora' en la que los protagonistas centrales de la gesta pacificadora eran Alberto Fujimori y Vladimiro Montesinos" (Degregori, "Heridas abiertas, derechos esquivos," 75–77).

14. Ann Kaneko's documentary, *Against the Grain: An Artist's Survival Guide to Peru* (2008), powerfully illustrates the extent of the Fujimori regime's efforts to control public discourse about politics and political violence within the country. Jo-Marie Burt's book *Political Violence and the Authoritarian State in Peru* (New York: Palgrave Macmillan, 2007) also offers a compelling and chilling analysis of the instrumental use of fear by the Fujimori regime.

15. The original Spanish: "esclarecer el proceso, los hechos y responsabilidades de la violencia terrorista y de la violación de los derechos humanos producidos desde mayo de 1980 hasta noviembre de 2000, imputables tanto a las organizaciones terroristas como a los agentes del Estado, así como proponer iniciativas destinadas a afirmar la paz y la concordia entre los peruanos." Decreto Supremo n. 065-2001-PCM, Articulo 1, quoted in Degregori, "Heridas abiertas, derechos esquivos," 75.

16. For a complete list of projects and investigative tasks undertaken by the CVR, see www.cverdad.org.pe/ingles/lacomision/balance/index.php.

17. The original Spanish: "El recojo de testimonios ha sido quizá la tarea más importante desarrollada por la comisión de la verdad, no sólo por el volumen de historias personales que hemos acopiado, sino también porque en esta actividad se expresa una opción deliberada de la comisión, que se desprende de la interpretación moral de nuestro mandato: recoger la voz de las víctimas en primer lugar." This portion of the Final Report is published online at www.cverdad.org.pe/ingles/lacomision/balance/index.php.

18. Diana Taylor, *The Archive and the Repertoire: Performing Cultural Memory in the Americas* (Durham, NC: Duke University Press, 2003).

19. Degregori, "Heridas abiertas, derechos esquivos,": 75–77.

20. Sebastian Brett, *Peru Confronts a Violent Past: The Truth Commission Hearings in Ayacucho* (New York: Human Rights Watch, 2003), 3.

21. The performative aspects of truth commissions and their work has also come under scholarly scrutiny in recent years, particularly with regard to the powerful role that staged hearings play in shaping public perceptions of such commissions' work and findings. See Tanya Goodman, *Staging Solidarity: Truth and Reconciliation in a New South Africa* (Herndon, VA: Paradigm Publishers,

2007; and Catherine Cole, *Performing South Africa's Truth Commission: Stages of Transition* (Bloomington: Indiana University Press, 2010).

22. Albie Sachs, "What Is Truth? South Africa's Truth and Reconciliation Commission." Public lecture given at the Chautauqua Institution, Chautauqua, New York, on June 26, 2002.

23. See in particular Coxshall, "From the Peruvian Reconciliation Commission," and Yezer, "Who Wants to Know?" on this issue.

24. Jay Winter and Emmanual Sivan, eds., *War and Remembrance in the Twentieth Century* (Cambridge: Cambridge University Press, 1999); Ksenua Bilbija et al., *The Art of Truth-Telling about Authoritarian Rule* (Madison: University of Wisconsin Press, 2005).

25. See Thomas Turino, "The Music of Andean Migrants in Lima, Peru: Demographics, Social Power, and Style." *Latin American Music Review* 9, no. 2 (1988): 127–50.

26. The original Spanish, from an interview with Falconí on April 16–17, 2000: "El wayno, la canción testimonial . . . surge de las bases. Casi todos los ayacuchanos, casi todos los serranos han visto morir a alguien, de su familia, especialmente en el centro sur del país de tal suerte que hay una efervescencia, por un lado miedo y por otra indignación por todo lo que sus ojos veían. Y es por eso que se comienzan a difundir las canciones, y el labor de los compositores es poner una canción en los labios de toda la gente, para que sirviera como catarsis por un lado, o como una gran protesta social masiva."

27. Rodrigo Montoya et al., *Urqukunapa Yawarnin: La Sangre de los Cerros* (Lima: CEPES, Mosca Azul Editores, and UNMSM, 1987); Raúl Romero, *Música, Danzas, y Mascaras en los Andes* (Lima: Pontificía Universidad Católica del Perú 1993); Gisela Cánepa Koch, ed., *Identidades representadas: Performance, experiencia, y memoria en los Andes* (Lima: Pontificía Universidad Católica del Perú, 2001).

28. While virtually all testimonial music in the 1980s remained faithful to traditional wayno instrumentation (guitar duos, in the case of the Ayacuchan mestizo wayno, or small ensembles including harp, violin, guitar, mandolin, or accordion), a more pop-oriented sound for Ayacuchan music emerged in the 1990s, in part due to the popularity of the testimonial repertoire. For a deeper discussion of *musica ayacuchana* in the 1990s, see Joshua Tucker, "Mediating Sentiment and Shaping Publics: Recording Practice and the Articulation of Social Change in Andean Lima," *Popular Music and Society* 33, no. 2 (2010): 141–62.

29. Thomas Turino, "The State and Andean Musical Production in Peru." In Joel Sherzer and Greg Urban, eds., *The Nation-State and Indian in Latin America* (Austin: University of Texas Press, 1991), 270–71; Zoila Mendoza, *Creating Our Own: Folklore, Performance, and Identity in Cuzco, Peru* (Durham, NC: Duke University Press, 2008), 44–46.

30. The polemics aroused by the 1986 festival are discussed in Thomas Turino, *Moving Away from Silence: Music of the Peruvian Altiplano and the Experience of Urban Migration* (Chicago: University of Chicago Press 1993), 226–27.

31. Chalena Vasquez, personal communication, April 2000. These rough numbers were reiterated to me by several of the singer/songwriters who participated in the contests. Unfortunately but perhaps not surprisingly, these song submissions were not archived by the government organizers of the contest.

32. This point is powerfully illustrated in John Cohen's documentary about wayno singers in Peru, *Dancing with the Incas* (1991), in which he interviews a number of prominent performers about the politics of recording testimonial or "protest" songs.

33. The advent of compact disc and video compact disc (VCD) recordings of Ayacuchan music since the turn of the millennium have gradually supplanted the cassette as preferred mediums, but this move has also reinforced the continued circulation and popularity of the cancion social repertoire. Tellingly, Dolly (originally "Dolby J.R. Producciones") issued the first CDs of Ayacuchan music in the year 2000, with a sampler of testimonial waynos as one of their first releases (*Ayacucho en el Corazón de Todos*, Dolby CD 006, 2000). Dolby/Dolly also played a crucial role in the development of a more pop-oriented sound for *musica ayacuchana* ("Ayacuchan music") in the 1990s, beyond the testimonial repertoire, which contributed to its massive popularity throughout the country. See Tucker, "Mediating Sentiment and Shaping Publics."

34. The reference here to a "country weed" (*hierba del campo*) is an early example of a now well-established tradition of intertextual references in testimonial songs. In this case, the reference is to "Hierba Silvestre" ("Wild Weed"), another testimonial song performed and arranged by Portocarrero, discussed later in this article.

35. Interview with Carlos Falconí, April 16–17, 2000. The incident in Soccos is also treated in quasi-fictionalized form in Francisco Lombardi's feature film *La Boca del Lobo* (1988).

36. Vinchos and Cangallo.

37. Personal communication from Carlos Falconí, February 2006. These songs are also discussed by Vergara, *La Tierra Que Duele*, 177–83.

38. Martina Portocarrero's decision to dress in the clothing of a rural, Ayacuchan peasant woman for her 1987 concert in Lima (previously discussed) offers another compelling example of the links testimonial singers often made between indigeneity and resistance.

39. This characterization was certainly true in the mid-1980s, during the formative stage of the cancion social phenomenon and at a time when reliable information about guerrilla activity in rural areas remained scarce, in part due to the Shining Path's own penchant for secrecy. By the end of the decade, however,

the shift in guerrilla strategy from rural actions to terrorist acts in urban areas left few delusions among Peruvian observers regarding the Shining Path's capacity for bloodshed.

40. Interview with Carlos Falconí, April 16, 2000.

41. Interview with Walter Humala, May 26, 2008.

42. "Five Corners" is, as it sounds, a five-cornered intersection in the town of Huanta.

43. In perhaps the most interesting re-signification of the song, a number of wayno singers mentioned to me occasions beginning in the 1990s in which they were asked by military personnel to perform "Flor de Retama," for whom it had become a sonic reminder of their undoubtedly intense years serving in the "emergency zone" of Ayacucho.

44. Further confirming this interpretation, multiple versions of "Flor de Retama" now exist on YouTube, including several by the Duo Retama, virtually all of which make textual, sonic, or visual references to the violence of the 1980s, but set within the instrumental format of the new *musica ayacuchana* style popularized in the 1990s.

45. See Coxshall, "From the Peruvian Reconciliation Commission."

46. Elizabeth Jelin, *State Repression and the Labors of Memory*, translated by Judy Rein and Marcial Godoy-Anativa (Minneapolis: University of Minnesota Press, 2003), 51.

47. González, "La globalización del derecho a la verdad," 181; see also LeFranc, "¿Cómo acabar con el desacuerdo?" The original Spanish: "No hay una memoria nacional; lo que puede haber, lo que es deseable que haya, es un foro público permanente e inclusivo donde todos nos reconozcamos como iguales y sometamos nuestras distintas memorias con el fin de ejercer ciudadanía alrededor de una verdad en construcción" (192).

48. John McDowell, "Folklore as Commemorative Discourse." *The Journal of American Folklore* 105, no. 418 (1992): 403–23.

49. McDowell, "Folklore as Commemorative Discourse," 403–23.

CHAPTER NINE

National Identity
after National Socialism

German Receptions of the
Holocaust Cantata, *Jüdische Chronik*
(1960/1961)

➳✂

AMY LYNN WLODARSKI

The tracing of collective memory in postwar Germany has proven difficult for scholars of all disciplines due to the division of the state into the Federal Republic of Germany (FRG) and the German Democratic Republic (GDR). Historian Jeffrey Herf argues that the writing of new postwar historiographies created a binary division of political memory along the East-West axis and "requires [scholars] to place [official memories] in the historical context of the ideologies and experiences . . . of the Cold War."[1] Regarding the Jewish Question, the task becomes even more arduous in that the Holocaust did not occupy congruent positions in the constructed narratives of either state. Instead, it became one of the principal issues upon which the two Germanys based their ideological differentiation. As a result, the Holocaust functions not as a binational issue but a contested one. During the Cold War, the FRG struggled to find the proper rhetoric for its public atonement, while the GDR argued for its own postwar victim status and avoided political mention of the Holocaust.

Recently, Joy Calico has countered that Herf's "binary model devised for high politics is not entirely adequate when extended to art and culture" in that collaborative artworks transcended such dichotomies to form a "pan-German third space for commemoration" between "the official programs of the FRG and the GDR."[2] As evidence, she cites *Jüdische Chronik*, a Holocaust memorial cantata composed in 1960/61 by a conglomerate of composers from both the FRG and the GDR, and argues that it provided "important common ground" during a time of intense political division.[3] She extends this spirit of collectivity to the work's critical reception, suggesting that reviews of its 1966 premiere articulate the existence of a shared cultural space between two nations: "West German critics for *Melos* and the *Frankfurter Allgemeine Zeitung* commended the moral call of the work . . . while GDR critics . . . lauded the collaborative effort to prevent the recurrence of Nazi atrocities."[4] Calico's account ends with this redemptive moment, in which East and West German journalists, laying aside their ideological divisions in the name of national cohesion, celebrate the *Chronik*'s musical protest of anti-Semitic violence.

Where Calico's narrative stops, however, the tale of *Jüdische Chronik*'s divided reception history begins, and its various manifestations in the GDR during the 1960s and 1980s suggest that its meaning was neither shared nor monolithic. Indeed, when one considers its memorial use over a longer period of time, the evidence seems to contradict — or, at the very least, soften — reconciliatory claims for the work.[5] Brief moments of social cohesion gave way to bitter and divisive rhetoric that pitted the musical culture and values of the GDR against that of the FRG, producing a cultural interface that demands contextualization of the *Chronik*'s genesis and reception. This essay traces the memorial afterlife of *Jüdische Chronik* and explores its postmemorial impact within the GDR, focusing on how its appropriation in East German political and cultural propaganda created a counterimage of both the West and the Holocaust that fortified the invented nationalist myths promoted by the state.

An Artistic "Five-Year Plan": 1960–1965

In the late 1950s, the FRG suffered a noticeable resurgence of anti-Semitic activity, including the December 1959 defacement of the newly reopened Cologne synagogue, which vandals covered with swastikas before overturning gravestones in the neighboring Jewish cemetery.[6] Reports of this sabotage troubled East German composer Paul Dessau, who himself had fled the Nazi terror. Unwilling to remain silent, Dessau organized the composition of *Jüdische Chronik* as a form of social protest and commentary. Political compositions on contemporary themes were common for Dessau, who considered composing his "political work" and joked that he had an "[artistic] Five Year Plan" to contribute to the socialist state.[7]

Dessau considered the *Chronik*'s humanistic message to be universal and therefore invited composers from both German states to collaborate on the work. He specifically sought out composers proficient in modernist idioms who were advocates of *engagierte Musik*, a catch-phrase for postwar musical works that addressed political themes with the intent to affect social or political change.[8] From the GDR, he invited composer Rudolf Wagner-Régeny and asked lyricist Jens Gerlach to write the libretto. Assembling the FRG team required more effort, and Dessau first contacted his friend, Boris Blacher, who graciously accepted. With Blacher's participation confirmed, Dessau then persuaded Hans Werner Henze and Karl Amadeus Hartmann to contribute movements.[9] Dessau's roster constituted his attempt to create a compositional team reflective of postwar German demographics, including the minority status of German Jews (Dessau was the sole Jew), the generational gap (a thirty-two-year range in age), and the wide range of wartime experiences including exile, unemployment, "inner emigration," Nazi collaboration, and military service.[10] In this manner, the project celebrated political union and national cohesion while the makeup of its participants subtly exposed the social fragmentation of the postwar German population.

The story of *Jüdische Chronik* unfolds in five movements. The work begins with a two-part prologue that juxtaposes recent examples of vandalism (such as the defiled Cologne synagogue) with anti-Semitic cries commonly heard at Nazi party rallies during the 1930s and references to the Wannsee Conference. In movement three, Gerlach writes a mournful lament of Jewish suffering in Treblinka, followed by a portrayal of the Warsaw Ghetto Uprising in the fourth movement, "Aufstand." The cantata ends with an epilogue in which the narrator warns the audience about "the acute danger of sliding back into . . . Nazi-fascism" and implores them to "remain watchful" for signs of fascist violence and discrimination.[11]

Once the libretto was completed, Dessau assigned each composer a section — Prologue (Blacher/Wagner-Régeny); Ghetto (Hartmann); Aufstand (Henze);[12] and Epilogue (Dessau) — and arranged a dual premiere of the work that would take place in October 1961 in Leipzig and Cologne.[13] Preparations for the concerts were underway when internal support for the project deteriorated among the West German composers. The sudden construction of the Berlin Wall on August 13, 1961, coupled with the heightened international focus on Germany's war crimes due to the April 1961 trial of Adolf Eichmann, caused Blacher, Hartmann, and Henze concern. As Daniela Reinhold notes, they feared that officials might misinterpret the *Chronik* as a harsh critique and their participation as a show of support for the recently constructed wall rather than a pan-Germanic protest against anti-Semitism.[14] After two weeks of debate, Hartmann telegraphed Dessau to request that "the current premiere of the Jewish cantata be abandoned" for a later date.[15]

The telegram shocked Dessau, who suspected that the Western composers had withdrawn their support in order to distance themselves from both its political statement and his communist affiliations. In an attempt to rectify the situation, he turned to Blacher, his closest friend among the West German composers: "I cannot bring myself to believe that you would want our piece (which denounces anti-Semitism and the horrors of the 20th century) not to be . . . performed only because I live in East Germany and am a communist! . . . I always had the impression that we understood each other well despite [my communist beliefs]."[16]

Blacher responded with a personal letter that recast the objections in a friendlier tone. "Let us wait for a more peaceful time," he wrote, "and hope that this comes soon."[17] Frustrated, Dessau pleaded his case one final time:

> I understand if you feel that [the premiere] would [be perceived] as an aggravation of the August 13th division of Germany. But, dear Blacher, what did our *Chronik* have to do with that?!? We FIVE [composers] stand by the public message that we delivered through this work. In no way was our stand against anti-Semitism an avowal of communism. . . . Dearest Blacher! The *Chronik* was not written in "peaceful times." We wrote it [in the hopes] that peaceful times could occur.[18]

Dessau's appeal fell on deaf ears, however. His artistic "Five Year Plan" would expire before he heard the *Chronik* performed.

Of Politics and Premieres: 1966

Jüdische Chronik's premiere finally occurred in Cologne on January 14, 1966, under the direction of Christoph von Dohnanyi. Dessau and Blacher both attended the premiere (Hartmann had died in 1963; Wagner-Régeny was seriously ill; Henze was inexplicably absent) and Gerlach contributed to the evening's program notes, in which he presented the work's heavy-handed political agenda:

> "For the millions of men who were murdered, there is no means of compensation. For those who live today, however, the obligation falls upon them to prevent the reoccurrence of such horror." So wrote Jens Gerlach in a letter to the West-German Rundfunk. He regards *Jüdische Chronik* . . . as a personal fulfillment of this obligation [and] . . . openly hopes that the rebellion will end with a victory for mankind.[19]

The program also made explicit the cantata's *engagierte* roots, noting its potential to incite social change and calling on the audience to "Be watchful! Be Vigilant! Consider the Past! The images of today and tomorrow's world bear your face!"[20] Dessau's recollection of the premiere in his diary the following day reflected his optimism and enthusiasm for the collective project: "The premiere of *Jüdische Chronik* in Cologne [made a] huge impression! The performance, in particular the chorus and orchestra (v. Dohnanyi), were very good."[21] The *Chronik*'s antifascist message had finally reached its target audience in the FRG.

Unfortunately, Dessau had not anticipated the degree to which Western appraisals of Holocaust art had advanced between 1961 and 1966, an oversight that failed to prepare him for the critical onslaught that ensued. During the 1950s, the FRG had quietly avoided questions of culpability vis-à-vis the Holocaust and generically mourned war casualties rather than specifically atoning for the genocide.[22] In 1959, this rhetoric faced criticism from Theodor Adorno, who accused Germans of circumventing true reconciliation: "The phrase 'Coming to Terms with the Past' does not imply a serious working through of the past, the breaking of its spell through an act of clear consciousness. It suggests, rather, wishing to turn the page and, if possible, wiping it from memory."[23] Shortly thereafter, Germany faced an intense period of judicial scrutiny during which several international tribunals investigated the scope of Nazi war crimes.[24] As Lynn Rapaport argues, the televising of these hearings "rendered the Holocaust a painful reality" and caused it to be a "dominant [cultural image] in the public sphere."[25] The judicial tone of these proceedings infiltrated West German newspaper culture, later finding voice in artistic creations ranging from memorials and monuments to plays and poetry.[26] German artists ultimately played a significant role in refocusing postwar consciousness from "questions of burdened guilt and avoidance to an examination of the German perpetrators," and theatrical productions such as Peter Weiss's *Die Ermittlung* (1965) spawned a memorial phase founded upon "critical appraisals of the past."[27]

In conjunction with these later memorial trends arose a more confrontational brand of Holocaust criticism that questioned the limitations of art and interrogated the ethical problems associated with representing the unimaginable "after Auschwitz." In a series of essays, Adorno responded to these artistic representations with a degree of judicial accusation. The philosopher's earlier concern that the Holocaust had engendered a cultural silence was now replaced with a new fear that the Holocaust had become common cultural capital that risked devaluation. In *Negative Dialectics* his rhetoric reached its most acerbic level when the philosopher declared post-Auschwitz culture and "its urgent critique" to be nothing more than "aesthetic garbage."[28]

Adorno's critique influenced West German reviews of the *Chronik*, which ranged from positive affirmations of the work's sociopolitical value to vehement condemnations of its artistic content. In general, progressive music journals and newspapers glossed over the work's disunity, a result of the uncoordinated and differing musical styles used by each composer in their respective movements, in favor of the *Chronik*'s collaborative nature. Most of these reviews reproduced Gerlach's program notes almost verbatim and provided basic information about the concert rather than interpretive reflections. Others, such as the music journal *Melos*, took Adorno to task, rejecting his theory of poetic nihilism outright:

> [*Jüdische Chronik*] proves that [Adorno's] fashionable witticism . . . that there would be no poetry after Auschwitz, or that the amount of suffering is meaningless, remains absolutely implausible. In this cantata, there is poetry in both word and tone. . . . One wishes the work many performances so that it can fulfill its primary mission — to keep people consciously alert.[29]

Conversely, the conservative papers adopted Adorno's harsher tone. In Adorno's local paper, the *Frankfurter Allgemeine Zeitung*, Gerhard Koch cited the philosopher directly in his review: "Engaged Art has become almost a slogan these days. . . . [*Jüdische Chronik*] seems to prove that engaged artwork — which is so sincere and human — is condemned to fail because its aesthetic level does not approach a radical nor truly advanced handling of the material (Adorno)."[30] The *Kölner Stadtanzeiger* concurred, arguing that "the attempt was so emphatic, so naked, that hardly any room remained for art and creative composition."[31] The most scathing review, however, was Rudolf Heinemann's "Can Music Represent Mass Murder?" (*Die Welt*), which mocked the composers' naiveté:

> Did they seriously believe that the monstrosity of Nazi crimes was possibly representable in the sublime sphere of music? Did they really accept that [actions such as] torture and the murder of millions could find a sonic equivalent in finely channeled structures (Blacher) and melodramatic gestures (Wagner-Régeny), in the sorrowful melody of an oboe (Hartmann), in skilled operatic theatrics (Henze), and in expressionistic passion (Dessau)?
>
> No — this *Jüdische Chronik* showed that it doesn't work that way. . . . One has to recognize that artistic expression has its limits. . . . A musical piece that does not respect these limits degrades the event and [reduces] the state of affairs to sniveling and banality.[32]

Heinemann's insistence that events of the Holocaust could not find adequate representation in the "music of the times" paralleled Adorno's rejection of representational poetry after Auschwitz.

Aesthetic critiques of this nature were rare in the GDR, where the "Jewish Question was largely ignored [or] formulated into an abstract anti-fascist question emphasizing the heroism of anti-fascist resistance."[33] In the 1950s, the state actively promoted a "myth of anti-fascism" which posited the FRG as the sole inheritor of the Nazi legacy and emphasized East Germany's socialist roots and heritage.[34] Party slogans such as "Before we unite, we have to differentiate ourselves!" soon became common propaganda and, characterizing the FRG as the inheritor of the Nazi legacy, one of the GDR's most prevalent means of distinguishing itself from its Western neighbor. Historians were advised to "abandon the misery concept of German history . . . and emphasize revolutionary moments" that would legitimize the GDR. Similarly, the Socialist Unity Party (SED) chose to observe annual anniversaries of socialist-themed events, such as the sixteenth-century Peasant War, instead of those connected to Jewish persecution at German hands, such as Kristallnacht.[35] In their opinion, Nazi acts of genocide were of limited relevance to GDR national history insofar as socialists had been tortured and detained as political prisoners.

This strategy encountered practical challenges in the early 1960s, when the SED began planning the erection of several memorials at those concentration camps that lay within East German borders; the case of Sachsenhausen, situated just north of East Berlin, exposes the level of political myth building and the SED's unwillingness to address the Jewish Question directly. As historian Caroline Wiedmer observes, the GDR pointedly avoided remembrance of Jewish victims, stressing instead the Holocaust's impact on other constituencies:

> If there was any lingering doubt that anyone other than Communists had been held in [Sachsenhausen], it was dispelled by the forty red triangles [atop the GDR's official memorial], which were used to identify political prisoners by the Nazis. . . . Unrepresented were thus, to name just the largest groups of victims, the Jews, the Sinti and Roma, the homosexuals, and the Jehovah's Witnesses (unless some of these were also Communists).[36]

SED foreign policy directives also impacted memorial practices at the camp. In 1960, Sachsenhausen's museum contained the names of nineteen countries from which the detainees hailed but excluded Israel, which the GDR did not officially recognize as a legitimate nation-state. Moreover, in Walter Ulbricht's April 24, 1961, dedication of the memorial, he saluted the "countless martyrs and heroes of the anti-fascist resistance struggle" and proceeded to identify those who had perished at Sachsenhausen: Communists, Social Democrats, Soviet POWs, and citizens of Poland, Luxembourg, Yugoslavia, Holland, Belgium, Denmark, Austria, Hungary, Czechoslovakia, France, and Britain.[37] Conspicuously absent were Jewish victims, in part because the GDR considered them to be a migrant, "stateless people."[38] Such evasion slowly eased as the Sachsenhausen memorial came under scrutiny for blatant discrimination, and in 1961, in an attempt to improve its international reputation, the SED approved the creation of a "Museum of Resistance and Suffering of the Jewish People" at Sachsenhausen, ushering in a new phase of public Holocaust recognition.[39]

The negative reviews of *Jüdische Chronik* that appeared in *Die Welt* and other newspapers offered the GDR an opportunity to redirect accusations of anti-Semitism toward their Western neighbor. In early February, Dessau held a press conference in which he questioned why Western newspapers had overlooked the work's social message, especially given renewed fascist activity in the FRG. He noted that "many of my collected press clippings, which range from August 1964 to December 1965, testify to the evil intentions of the anti-Semitic vandals," emphasizing that it was "pitiable that the West German government has not taken any action against [such present-day violence]."[40] Later that month, the *Norddeutsche Zeitung* (Schwerin) published an interview with Eberhard Kluge, president of the State Radio Committee for Serious Music, who reaffirmed the noble and collaborative nature of *Jüdische Chronik* during a time of heightened anti-Semitism in West Germany.[41] At a later press conference, Herbert Kegel, who would conduct the GDR premiere, dismissed Heinemann's article as "hateful [Western] criticism" and reinforced the sincerity of the East German-born project.[42]

Similarly, the program notes for the GDR premiere stressed that the vandalism that had inspired the *Chronik* had occurred specifically in the FRG and remained topical. The program begins with a pseudo-educational lesson on anti-Semitism, couching it as a West German phenomenon:

> ANTI-SEMITISM: Fascism made use of these means with satanic consequences [and] promised economic recovery through the genocide of the Jews. . . . In 1959, when Jews again began to be cursed and threatened in West Germany and West Berlin, anti-Semitic slogans were [again] characteristically united with fascist [slogans]. What happened once is happening again today [in West Germany].[43]

The bent of these accusations were parroted in the press, for example the *Sächsische Zeitung* (Dresden), which described the cantata as "a chronicle of the darkest Jewish witch-hunt in the Nazi times [that] begins and ends in present-day West Germany."[44] The program also glossed over the work's collaborative nature, commending Dessau for single-handedly "developing [Germany's] political consciousness through the unity of [the *Chronik*'s] humanistic message."[45]

Next-day reviews reiterated the thematic emphases of both the press conferences and the program. The *Liberal-Demokratische Zeitung* (Halle) contextualized the *Chronik* as an extension of the great humanistic legacy of GDR art:

> *Jüdische Chronik* continues . . . the humanitarian German artistic tradition — to take a stand against actual political events through artistic materials. It is a tone set by Hutten and Heine, by Becher and Brecht, by Eisler and Dessau. . . . What bound these five composers . . . and what, at the same time, divorced them from the official *Kulturpolitik* of Bonn, was the collectivity of their humanistic product.[46]

Eastern papers declared the Leipzig performance to be of a higher artistic standard and detailed the audience's rapt attention and sincere response to the work. *Neues Deutschland*, the official paper of the SED, reported that the "solidarity" of the Leipzig orchestra surpassed that of the Cologne ensemble and ultimately imbued the work with "humanism, anti-fascism . . . and great national meaning."[47] The *Freie Erde* (Neustrelitz) seemed most impressed with the audience's reaction to the work: "The predominantly young public followed the shocking and rousing work with emotion and rewarded the excellent interpretation with sustained applause."[48]

Such overwhelmingly positive reviews were intended to contrast with the disparaging comments in *Die Welt*, which the East considered direct evidence of the FRG's continuing anti-Semitism. The *Leipziger Volkszeitung* cited the Eastern performance of the *Chronik* as confirmation of the GDR's dedication to humanistic inquiry and blatantly criticized the Western press for its vitriol: "That *Jüdische Chronik* — as an expression of the humanistic goals of our republic — was performed in Leipzig . . . is just as characteristic of the development of [East] Germany as the disapproval . . . of the successful world premiere in Cologne by the press monopoly in West Germany."[49]

The *Liberal-Demokratische Zeitung* flatly accused Heinemann of "Beckmesserism," due to his desire for unified formalism over communicative potential: "Predictably, [*Die Welt*] reacted to the world premiere with poisonous attacks against its political bent and dismissed the composition as 'sniveling banality.' . . . *Jüdische Chronik* is on the whole an artistic achievement that attests to the high level of national consciousness and responsibility of its creators."[50]

Neues Deutschland even appropriated Adorno's own terminology in an attempt to discredit Western efforts at political atonement: "*Jüdische Chronik* is an avowal and call for a *true* attempt to come to terms with the past, a struggle against the power of the past, which awakens anew in the FRG."

[Emphasis mine][51] Thus, the debate over *Jüdische Chronik*'s cultural and aesthetic value seemed clearly delineated along the West-East axis, a division made clear in a 1966 republication of "representative reviews" in the newsletter of the Eastern Union of German Composers and Musicologists (VDK).[52]

Remembering Red Flags and Broken Glass: 1984–1988

East German use of *Jüdische Chronik* continued in the 1980s as the SED slowly began to introduce events like the Holocaust into their own historical narrative. Realigning the GDR with its German roots required confrontation of both the Nazi and Jewish questions and forced the GDR to recognize the Holocaust "not simply [as] one aspect of Hitler fascism but as part of German history."[53] This belated Eastern version of "coming to terms with the past" reached a pinnacle in 1988, when the SED announced its decision to commemorate the fiftieth anniversary of the Kristallnacht pogrom (November 9–10, 1938) instead of the annual celebration of the 1918 November Worker's Revolution. The idea to commemorate Kristallnacht had originated in 1985 among the members of the Jewish Federation of the GDR, who requested permission to host a modest ceremony in Dresden in memory of the victims of the pogrom.[54] Klaus Gysi, the state undersecretary for religious affairs, recommended postponing the event until 1988 in order to expand its scale and prepare educational broadcasts, noting that the average citizen would have little historical knowledge of Kristallnacht. Ultimately East German media participated in the preparations by presenting television programs and newspaper articles that focused on the "primacy of Kristallnacht in East German collective memory rather [than] on the November Revolution. Numerous articles covered Jewish traditions and history, [which] suggested an unprecedented link between Jewish and German history."[55]

In a memo to the central committee, Hans-Joachim Hoffmann, the GDR's minister of culture, argued that state remembrance of Kristallnacht was "in the anti-fascist spirit and tradition of our land." He cited a 1938 edition of the *Rote Fahne* [Red Flag], then the official newsletter of the German communist party [KPD], which had published an editorial decrying the Jewish pogrom only days after Kristallnacht:

> True to the legacy of the KPD, which condemned these murderous excesses [in the *Red Flag*] and called for solidarity with the victims, the GDR became the homeland for [German] citizens of Jewish faith. In the GDR, they experience attention, social security and protection, equal participation in socialist soci-

ety, and the free and unhindered ability to worship — all of which are a daily reality for them.[56]

Hoffmann averred that the proud tradition of the German *Kulturstaat* might serve the Jewish cause and proposed a series of nationwide events that would utilize the cultural institutions under his jurisdiction, including museum exhibitions, academic colloquia, youth rallies, theatrical offerings, and musical performances.

In May 1988, the Central Committee approved Hoffmann's proposal and set a tentative schedule that included a musical concert in Berlin, a performance of Lessing's *Nathan the Wise*, and the official dedication of the New Synagogue.[57] They also initiated self-serving plans to publicize the events internationally in an effort to improve credibility abroad, foster beneficial trade relations, and counter claims that the GDR espoused an anti-Semitic foreign policy. An official invitation to attend all of the commemorative ceremonies was extended to the State of Israel, an offer complicated by the SED's firm support for the Palestinian cause.[58] Hoffmann also welcomed Jewish diplomats and activists, including Edgar Bronfman, president of the Jewish World Congress, Rabi Phil Hiat, a member of the Union of American Hebrew Congregations, and Itzchak Arad, who sat on the board of directors at Yad Vashem.[59]

As the political speeches and ceremonies fell into place, repertory decisions for the November 8 concert remained mired in negotiations well into October. The original plan for the concert had been modest, consisting of traditional Jewish liturgical music performed by the Leipzig Synagogue choir and the premiere of Thomas Heyn's "Three Yiddish Songs," winner of the Hanns Eisler Prize. As the list of attendees became increasingly high profile, Hoffmann revised the concert to reflect the international diversity of its audience. In August, he announced a new program that showcased prominent composers and musicians from outside the Iron Curtain while communicating the central themes of the Kristallnacht commemoration: protest of antifascist violence, celebration of German-Jewish culture, and commitment to a pan-German atonement for the past. The proposed concert would open with Arnold Schoenberg's Holocaust cantata, *A Survivor from Warsaw*, followed by a performance of Felix Mendelssohn's *Violin Concerto* by Isaac Stern, and concluding with a grand performance of Brahms's *German Requiem*, sung by Jessye Norman, Jewgeni Nestorenko, and the Leipzig Radio Chorus.[60] Here, Hoffmann ran into logistical problems in that the East German Artists Agency protested the program because it featured no native composers or soloists.[61]

A solution presented itself the following month at the second annual Dresden Festival for Contemporary Music, a series of thirty-two concerts that showcased works by an impressive list of avant-garde composers.[62] The opening concert presented musical meditations on the horrors of World War II and included Penderecki's *Threnody for the Victims of Hiroshima*, Udo Zimmermann's *Sieh, meine Augen*, and finally *Jüdische Chronik*, which had unexpectedly become the final piece of the concert when the world premiere of Ernst Hermann Meyer's *Orchesterlieder* was cancelled due to the illness of conductor Herbert Kegel. In heroic fashion, Jörg-Peter Weigle assumed the podium and led the Dresden Philharmonic and the Leipzig Rundfunkchor through the five-movement *Chronik* with only a few days' notice. Reviews in the *Sächliches Tagesblatt* (Dresden) not only lauded his aplomb but also applauded the "long overdue performance" of the *Chronik* in Dresden, which boasted a vital Jewish population and had inspired the state-wide Kristallnacht commemoration: "The [*Chronik*] harkened from an earlier time, but the concert demonstrated how important performances of older works are [and] that [programs] must not be 'new at any price.'"[63] Perhaps these final words resonated with Hoffmann in his desperate situation; shortly thereafter, he hired Weigle and the Dresden Philharmonic to perform *Jüdische Chronik* as the finale to the Kristallnacht concert.

The concert took place on November 9, 1988, in Berlin's Schauspielhaus and presented a chronological program of Jewish music. The concert began with Jewish liturgical music from the eighteenth century followed by one of Mendelssohn's *Orgelwerke* and finally *Jüdische Chronik*. The *Chronik* was well suited for the commemorative concert in that antifascist resistance was at the heart of both its libretto and its political engagement. Moreover, the prologue had previously been interpreted as a specific allusion to the Kristallnacht pogrom, which made the cantata thematically appropriate. The *Chronik*'s diverse composer base also represented the uniting of East and West Germans against what was now a common historical past, although Dessau's pivotal role in its creation was emphasized to assuage East German nationalists. Overall, *Jüdische Chronik*'s collaborative nature underscored the GDR's renewed participation in collective *German* projects rather than the promotion of distinctly East German creations.

Despite its newfound, progressive approach toward the Holocaust, the GDR did not completely abandon its antifascist (anti-West) stance. Such doublespeak appeared in the opening welcome at the Berlin concert of the *Chronik*, in which Dr. Lothar Kolditz, president of the GDR Parliament of the National Front, recognized Jewish suffering during the Holocaust as distinct from other victims but then predictably cited the 1938 edition of the *Rote Fahne* as proof of the GDR's historical severance from the Third Reich:

It was the KPD [who first warned in the *Rote Fahne*]: "True to the proud traditions of the German workers' movement and in the true spirit of the greatest
German poets and thinkers, the KPD raises its voice against Hitler's Jewish
pogrom, which has shrouded the honor of Germany with a deep shame."

Today . . . we in the GDR pledge ourselves to this tradition of engaged anti-
fascism. In that spirit, [we offer] today's concert of undying works by Jewish
composers — a concert of remembrance and a warning to [heed] the historical
[lessons of] fascism, hate, and war.[64]

Press accounts of the concert merely reprinted official proclamations of
the Ministry of Culture and the SED, emphasizing the *Chronik*'s status as a
"united appeal against the re-occurrence of anti-Semitism and neo-fascism
in *West Germany*" and turning a blind eye to discriminatory policies and
actions within the GDR.[65] Thus, despite its recognition of the "Jewish
Chronicle" as a part of its new German historical narrative, the Kristallnacht performance maintained much of the anti-West propaganda from
1966.

Jüdische Chronik: A Cold War Postmemorial

As this essay argues, the cultural prominence of *Jüdische Chronik* was primarily limited to the GDR, where the state often used it as cultural ammuni-
tion in Cold War posturing. Reviewers and politicians alike emphasized the
work's social message over its artistic integrity (often with musical description or critique appearing as an aside) and placed the work in the service
of the state, whether as a didactic educational example or a blatant form of
propaganda. Conversely, the *Chronik* never positioned itself as an icon of
Holocaust memory in the FRG, in part because its premiere had been so
contested along representational lines in 1966.

Genealogical consideration of the *Chronik* helps to identify myriad moti-
vations behind productions of the *Chronik*, illustrating its semiotic versatility in the East German context. The work's collaborative roots provided a
flexible basis of interpretation, which allowed the work to be appropriated
as either an example of Cold War conflict or pan-nationalism. In the early
1960s, as the GDR constructed divisional barriers both ideological and physical, Dessau envisioned the work as an important collective stand against
anti-Semitism, only to be surprised by the withdrawal of the Western composers from the project due to their fear of political repercussions. The 1966
premieres point to greater ideological conflict and also the variegated status
of Holocaust culture in both states, which impacted the reception of *Jüdische Chronik* almost as much as the political situation. From 1970 to 1988,

however, as the GDR reluctantly acknowledged the Holocaust as part of its own historiography, the *Chronik*'s malleability proved beneficial for its cultural longevity. It could now simultaneously reinforce the antifascist foundation of the GDR and articulate a new receptivity to the shared historical acceptance of the Holocaust, allowing the state to appear progressive and yet still culturally distinct.[66] Its hermeneutical openness continues to serve the *Chronik* well; in 2003 it was broadcast on Radio Berlin for the sixty-fifth anniversary of *Kristallnacht* and cited as an example of cultural cooperation that had preceded the reunification of Germany — perhaps part of a new constructed national mythos.

Such interpretive possibilities affected not only official exploitation of the *Chronik* but also aided the revision of individual accounts associated with its turbulent genesis. Of all the composers, Henze had the most tenuous relationship with the work: abandoning its composition before his movement was finished (Dessau would finish "Aufstand" for him), calling for the cancellation of its 1961 performance, and failing to attend the 1966 world premiere. In the 1960s, the political climate proved too stormy for Henze, who distanced himself from the *Chronik* and its engaged message. In 1981, however, he drafted an open "Letter to Young Artists" in which he implored them to creatively protest the injustices of human society. The *Chronik* served as the primary example of his own experience of musical engagement, and he cited its protest not only of fascism but also of individual and governmental silence: "[We] remembered how too often in the past artists had kept their own counsel, and how disastrous their silence had often been in the Third Reich. . . . We all believed that any kind of warning would be preferable to the kind of non-political evasiveness that indicates only indifference and insensitivity."[67] Henze also reaffirmed the shared impetus behind the composition of the *Chronik*, maintaining that each member of the "collective" chose to join the project because of his own negative wartime experiences:

> The five of us had all, each in his own way, been brought face to face with his own life [and had] experienced the gruesome events of the Nazi era. We all had personal experiences to bring to the work: the bitterness of emigration and [marginalization], the horrors of the war, and of the problems that come from belonging to any kind of minority.[68]

Henze's essay thus extends the communal foundation of the *Chronik* beyond the anti-Semitic acts of 1959 to the onset of the Nazi regime in 1933, rooting the work in *German* history rather than *Cold War* rhetoric. This collective spirit clearly inhabits the tone of his essay; rather than speaking from the perspective of an individual, he stresses instead the memories of a collective "we."

Given the diverse reactions to and uses of *Jüdische Chronik* within the GDR, the work seems to operate as a musical postmemorial, a term derived from recent scholarship pertaining to representational postmemory. In *Family Frames: Photography, Narrative, and Postmemory*, Marianne Hirsch defines *postmemory* as a second-generation phenomenon in which "a powerful and very particular form of memory . . . [mediates the Holocaust] not through recollection but through an imaginative investment and creation."[69] Her emphasis lies in the constructed and creative aspect of these artistic works, which not only characterize "the experience of those who grow up dominated by narratives that preceded their birth" but which also serve as a marker of the process of cultural memory itself.[70] The more individualistic nature of postmemory, which Hirsch ascribes singularly to art created by second-generation relatives of survivors, finds translation in the work of cultural historian James E. Young, who deals explicitly with the artistic and political contours of public memorials to the Holocaust; Young argues that these second-generation memorials denote a "vicarious past" and derive from a "received history," noting that the artists' experience of the Holocaust is "a mediated experience, the afterlife of memory represented in history's after-images."[71] For him, a postmemorial transmits specific cultural and political memory when appropriated for (or silenced from) official events and party discourse. These later manifestations often distance the memorial from either its original intent or the historical event it commemorates, creating a sense of "post-ness" or belatedness that define a more trans-generational act of transfer.[72] They transmit not history itself but contemporary ideas about history.

Postmemorials can present several consequences when the discourse generated around the representations exclude certain viewpoints from the realm of official and historical memories. As Hirsch notes, many postmemorials neither recall the past accurately nor facilitate the work of "coming to terms" with the Holocaust; worse, they can actively block memory, functioning more as a revisionist counter-memory used for political gains.[73] The danger lies in their dialogical nature, by which reception of a postmemorial can redirect the work's initial memorial aims and promote instead new, ideological myths. This begs the obvious question — what postmemorial consequences befell *Jüdische Chronik* during its trans-generational reception? When viewed genealogically, the *Chronik* possesses significant cultural depth and danger in that GDR critics and party officials adopted it as a means to advance counter-memories about the Holocaust that promoted political myths and agendas at the expense of true reconciliation. In Dessau's original concept for the work, Kristallnacht, Treblinka, and the Warsaw Ghetto Uprising all become historical reminders of the horrors of Nazi fascism meant to instruct a generation of Germans who had forgotten (or chosen to forget) German complicity in the Holocaust. Its 1966 reception, produced in a variety of journalistic mediums, reoriented the work away from the Holocaust and toward the Cold War; moreover, within the GDR, the piece became a means of transmitting East German cultural and historical supremacy via both journalistic and educational channels. Indeed, even amid the resilient spirit of collectivity and condolence that accompanied the 1988 ceremonies, the SED continued to stress the duplicitous "myth of the antifascist" in their promotional and performance materials. The end result is an aggregate of competing historical interpretations about fascism, the Holocaust, and German postwar legitimacy, which when taken together create an interpretational dynamism and tension via their dialectical interface. In this manner, *Jüdische Chronik* might more aptly be titled "Deutsche Chronik," in that its story commemorates not only the Jewish tragedy of the Holocaust but also East and West Germany's long-term, problematic, and developing relationship with one another and their "shared" past.

Notes

1. Jeffrey Herf, *Divided Memory: The Nazi Past in the Two Germanys* (Cambridge, MA: Harvard University Press, 1997), 1–2.

2. Joy H. Calico, "*Jüdische Chronik*: The Third Space of Commemoration between East and West Germany." *Musical Quarterly* 88 (2005): 97.

3. Calico, "*Jüdische Chronik*," 101.

4. Calico, "*Jüdische Chronik*," 101.

5. Calico's second example, *Die Ermittlung* (1965), does argue strongly for the existence of a "cultural third space" into which both nations directed their understanding of the Holocaust.

6. Hans Werner Heister, "Aktuelle Vergangenheit: Zur Kollektivkomposition *Jüdische Chronik*," in *Paul Dessau: Von Geschichte gezeichnet — Symposium P.D. Hamburg 1994*, ed. Klaus Angermann (Hofheim: Wolke, 1995), 171–72.

7. "Jüdische Chronik: ADN-Gespräch mit Paul Dessau," *Berliner Zeitung*, May 17, 1961.

8. See Ernst H. Flammer, *Politisch Engagierte Musik als Kompositorisches Problem* (Baden-Baden: Verlag Valentin Koerner, 1981).

9. Letter from Hans Werner Henze to Karl Amadeus Hartmann, March 13, 1960, reprinted in Renata Wagner, ed., *Karl Amadeus Hartmann und die Musica Viva* (Münich: R. Piper & Co. Verlag, 1980).

10. Obviously, Dessau's roster could never have been fully inclusive of the wide scope of Germany's social diversity. Indeed, the makeup of the roster exposes also the narrowness of the compositional team, including its lack of gender diversification and the exclusion of composers who espoused Darmstadt's opinion that music should remain abstract and apolitical. Also barred were those composers who did not practice a high modernist approach to composition, including composers of more popular or commercial music intended for mass appeal.

11. Jens Gerlach, Libretto for *Jüdische Chronik* (Berlin: Zeuthen/Mark, 1961).

12. In the end, Henze was unable to complete "Aufstand." Dessau finished the movement for him.

13. See Paul Dessau, *Paul Dessau 1894–1979: Dokumente zu Leben und Werk*, ed. Daniela Reinhold (Berlin: Stiftung Archiv der Akademie der Künste Henschel Verlag, 1995), 111.

14. Paul Dessau, *Let's Hope for the Best: Briefe und Notizbücher aus den Jahren 1948 bis 1978*, ed. Daniela Reinhold (Berlin: Stiftung Archiv der Akademie der Künste, 2000), 111.

15. Telegram from Karl Amadeus Hartmann to Paul Dessau, August 28, 1961, Stiftung Archiv der Akademie der Künste (SAdK), Berlin, Paul Dessau Archiv (PDA), Nr. 1.74.270.2.

16. Letter from Paul Dessau to Boris Blacher, no date (probably late August 1961), SAdK, Berlin, PDA, 1.74.1814.1.

17. Letter from Boris Blacher to Paul Dessau, September 11, 1961, reprinted in Dessau, *Let's Hope for the Best*, 111.

18. Letter from Paul Dessau to Boris Blacher, September 27, 1961, and revised version, September 30, 1961, SAdK, Berlin, PDA, Nrs. 1814.2-3. Also reprinted in Dessau, *Let's Hope for the Best*, 111.

19. Program notes, January 14, 1966, performance in Cologne, SAdK, Berlin, Rudolf-Wagner-Régeny-Archive (RWR), Nr. 497.

20. Program notes, January 14, 1966.

21. Dessau, diary entry, January 14, 1966, reprinted in *Let's Hope for the Best*, 92.

22. Postwar narratives that specifically focused on Jewish suffering were rare in both the FRG and the GDR at the time; instead, narratives tended to focus on the traumatic experiences of Germans during World War II.

23. Theodore Adorno, "What Does Coming to Terms with the Past Mean?" in *Negative Dialectics*, trans. E. B. Ashton (New York: Seabury Press, 1973).

24. This includes the 1961 Eichmann trial in Jerusalem and the 1963–65 Auschwitz trial in Frankfurt.

25. Lynn Rapaport, *Jews in Germany after the Holocaust: Memory, Identity, and Jewish-German Relations* (Cambridge: Cambridge University Press, 1997), 21, 32.

26. Siobhan Kattago, *Ambiguous Memory: The Nazi Past and German National Identity* (Westport, CT: Praeger, 2001), 42.

27. Kattago, *Ambiguous Memory*, 42, 46.

28. Adorno, *Negative Dialectics*, 367.

29. Herbert Eimert, "Ein Bekenntniswerk von fünf Komponisten," *Melos* 2 (1966): 56.

30. Gerhard Koch, "Ost-Westliches Engagement," *Frankfurter Allgemeine Zeitung*, January 17, 1966.

31. "Diese Chronik Missglückte: Zweites Konzert *musik der zeit* im Kölner Funkhaus," *Kölner Stadt Anzeiger*, January 19, 1966.

32. Rudolf Heinemann, "Fasst Musik den Massenmord? Experiment des Westdeutschen Rundfunks: *Jüdische Chronik*," *Die Welt*, January 19, 1966.

33. Kattago, *Ambiguous Memory*, 107.

34. Dan Diner, "On the Ideology of Antifascism," *New German Critique* 67 (Winter 1996): 123–32.

35. Kattago, *Ambiguous Memory*, 87, 99.

36. Caroline Wiedmer, *The Claims of Memory: Representations of the Holocaust in Contemporary Germany and France* (Ithaca, NY: Cornell University Press, 1999), 184.

37. Walter Ulbricht, Dedicatory Speech at Sachsenhausen, April 4, 1961, cited in Herf, *Divided Memory*, 179.

38. Wiedmer, *The Claims of Memory*, 186.

39. Wiedmer, *The Claims of Memory*, 187.

40. "Jüdische Chronik," *Neue Zeit* (East Berlin), February 1, 1966.

41. *Norddeutsche Zeitung*, February 9, 1966.

42. *Norddeutsche Zeitung*, February 9, 1966.

43. Program Notes, February 15, 1966, performance in Leipzig, SAdK, Berlin, RWR, Nr. 497.

44. *Sächsische Zeitung* (Dresden), February 23, 1966.

45. Program Notes, February 15, 1966.

46. "Jüdische Chronik," *Liberal-Demokratische Zeitung*, Halle, February 24, 1966.

47. *Neues Deutschland* (Berlin), March 3, 1966.

48. *Freie Erde* (Neustrelitz), February 17, 1966.

49. *Leipziger Volkszeitung*, February 17, 1966.

50. "Jüdische Chronik," *Liberal-Demokratische Zeitung* (Halle), February 24, 1966.

51. Hans Jürgen Schaefer, "Verantwortung für Heute und Morgen," *Neues Deutschland* (Berlin), January 17, 1966.

52. Verbandes Deutscher Komponisten und Musikwissenschaftler (VDK), "Im Spiegel der Presse," *Informationsblatt* 2 (1966).

53. Kattago, *Ambiguous Memory*, 106.

54. Klaus Gysi, "Gedenkveranstaltung des Verbandes der jüdischen Gemeinden in der DDR aus anlass des 47. Jahrestages des faschistischen Pogroms 1938," July 8, 1985, SAPMO, DY30/9051.

55. Kattago, *Ambiguous Memory*, 107.

56. "Vorlage für das Politbüro des Zentralkomitees. Betreff: Massnahmen zum 50. Jahrestag der faschistischen Pogromnacht vom 9.11.1938," May 26, 1988, SAPMO, DY30/9051. Other articles in the 1938 edition included "Are the Jews Guilty? No. Hitler Is Guilty."

57. Memo, August 25, 1988, SAPMO, DY30/9052.

58. No delegates from Israel attended the performance. See Angelika Timm, *Jewish Claims against East Germany: Moral Obligations and Pragmatic Policy* (Budapest: Central European University Press, 1988).

59. Letter from Loeffler to Jarowinsky, August 18, 1988, SAPMO, DY 30/9052.

60. "Beschlussauszuege von Sitzungen des Politibüro," May 31, 1988, SAPMO, DY30/5178.

61. Memo, August 18, 1988, SAPMO, DY 30/9669.

62. Among the composers featured were Berg, Berio, Busoni, Eisler, Gubaidulina, Schnittke, Schoenberg, Shostakovich, Webern, and Zemlinsky.

63. "Erstmals *Jüdische Chronik*: Zur Eröffnung Sonderkonzerte der Philharmonie," *Sächliches Tagesblatt* (Dresden), October 5, 1988.

64. Dr. Lothar Kolditz, Präsident des Naitonalrates der Nationalen Front der DDR, November 9, 1988, SAdK, Berlin, RWR, Nr. 1439.

65. Gerald Felber, "*Jüdische Chronik*," *Berliner Zeitung*, November 10, 1988.

66. This is not to argue that the *Chronik* was the only musical example; indeed, Dessau had provided music for Peter Weiss's GDR production of *Die Ermittlung* in the late 1960s.

67. Hans Werner Henze, *Music and Politics: Collected Writings, 1953–81*, trans. Peter Labanyi (Ithaca, NY: Cornell University Press, 1982), 274–75.

68. Henze, *Music and Politics*, 275.

69. Marianne Hirsch, *Family Frames: Photography, Narrative, and Postmemory* (Cambridge, MA: Harvard University Press, 1997), 22. See also Andrea Liss, *Trespassing through Shadows: Memory, Photography, and the Holocaust* (Minneapolis: University of Minnesota Press, 1998).

70. Hirsch, *Family Frames*, 22. Aleida Assmann supports Hirsch's notion in her study of how national and political memory join with cultural and archival memory to form a brand of cultural memory which is trans-generational and mediated solely through symbolic systems of representation. See Aleida Assmann, *Der lange Schatten der Vergangenheit, Erinnerungskultur und Geschichtspolitik* (Munich: Beck, 2006).

71. James Young, *At Memory's Edge: After-Images of the Holocaust in Contemporary Art and Architecture* (New Haven, CT: Yale University Press, 2000), 3–4. See

also his *The Texture of Memory: Holocaust Memorials and Meaning* (New Haven, CT: Yale University Press, 1993).

72. Hirsch talks expressly about the "post-"designation of postmemories in her essay, "The Generation of Postmemory," *Poetics Today* 29, no. 1 (Spring 2008), 106.

73. Hirsch, *Family Frames*, 24.

AFTERWORD

From Voice to Violence
and Back Again

J. MARTIN DAUGHTRY

They warn us that there may be inspirations
from below, as well as from above. — *The Duke of Argyll*

1. We begin with breath, the life-sustaining act:

Inhale slowly.
Exhale slowly.
Repeat.

Inhalation introduces fresh energy into the organism; it marks the body's submission to the cyclical microrhythms of life (i.e., it is the upbeat to exhalation's downbeat); and it represents an accumulation and crystallization of potential. Potential what? Potential everything: with inhalation, anticipation builds, anything is possible, action is imminent. *She took a deep breath, and then she* — laughed, sobbed, jumped, took flight, pulled the trigger, burst into song — whatever she did, she *acted*. Inhalation precedes a multitude of acts, one of which is simply more breathing. Even if this is all that follows, more breathing equals life, which makes inhalation the emphatic (if temporary) deferral of the void. *She took a deep breath, and then she —*

Inhale slowly.
Exhale slowly.
Repeat.

2. The metaphysical significance of breath has been the object of formal reflection for at least twenty-five centuries. From the Confucian *qi* ("breath,"

"life-force") to the Sanskrit *prana* ("breath," "vital energy") to the works of Anaximenes of Miletus, the pre-Socratic thinker who regarded air as the fundamental substance from which all things earthly and divine are fashioned, breath and breathing have regularly been placed in a tight relation with the flow of spiritual energy and psychic rejuvenation. In the English language, for nearly five hundred years, the term "inspiration" has connected the drawing in of breath with the drawing in of spiritual enlightenment.

Adriana Cavarero, musing on fellow philosopher Emmanuel Levinas's preoccupation with the breath, contends that, for Levinas,

> breath . . . introduces the theme of the soul that, like *ruah* [Hebrew: "breath," "holy spirit"], belongs to the semantic family of respiration: in Latin, *anima*, in Greek *anemos*; or else, *psyche* from the verb *psycho*, "to breathe"; or even *pneuma* [ancient Greek: "spirit," "wind," "breath"] itself.[1]

In *Otherwise Than Being or Beyond Essence*, Levinas draws upon the concepts of *psyche* and *pneuma* to position breathing as one of the foundations of ethical relations. To breathe in the breath of one's interlocutor, of one's other, is to take that person into oneself, to open oneself into a relation of hospitality. In his words, "breathing is transcendence in the form of opening up."[2] Silvia Benso describes Levinasian breathing as "a deep inspiration — an inspiring, breathing the other in as well as a being inspired, animated by the other."[3] The moment of inspiration, for Levinas, is a signal moment of being-in-the-world, with others, ethically.

Beginning with the ancients from regions throughout the world and stretching, with remarkable continuity, into the modern era, inspiration has been placed within an ethical matrix that privileges unmediated communication (with the other, with the environment, with the divine); positive energy (corporeal and spiritual); and peace and serenity. To breathe in, in this sense, is to be born anew. But we can't sustain inspiration indefinitely: at some point, we must exhale. And exhaling, equally broadly, has been read across the centuries as a metonym for death. (It's not an accident that we call both "expiration" in English.) The respiratory cycle can thus be read as a microcosm of the life cycle, which begins with our first inhalation and ends when we "give up the ghost" with our dying breath.

I want to stake out this spot, the pivotal instant that separates inspiration and expiration, as a rich metaphorical starting place for a few closing thoughts about the relationship of music to violence. Actually, my chosen topic overlaps with music, but also stands apart from it: what I really want to talk about is *voice*, and the ways that voices — both within and outside musical contexts — resonate within the field of the social, which, as it happens, is the field in which violence also takes place. The instant following inspiration and preceding expiration is an ideal moment to consider this topic, for at this moment of held breath, we haven't yet acted, and so can pause and reflect upon everything that we might do or not do with that breath, everything that we've done before and can repeat or not repeat, every utterance, every song, every scream, every silence. I begin with some general comments on voice, vocality, and violence, and then move into the specific terrain that the essays in this volume cover.

Inhale slowly.
Hold.
Exhale slowly.
Repeat.

3. In addition to its life-sustaining function, inspiration is also the prelude to, and necessary condition for, giving voice.

Inhale slowly.
Hum softly for the length of one full breath.
Repeat while reading further.

A curious thing, voice. Many before me have noted how deeply uncanny it is, this thing that is produced deep inside our bodies but resonates outside them, thus blurring the line between interiority and exteriority, between self and world.[4] Many too have remarked upon the unstable relationship between the sonorous voices that surround us and our nonsonorous "inner voices," the envoiced thoughts we hear in moments of isolation and quietude. Losing the ability to control these latter voices, or to distinguish them from sonorous voices, has long been equated with insanity; while learning to listen to one's inner voice(s) and harmonize them with ethical action is seen as the path to self-knowledge.[5] And many have pointed to the radical degree to which meaning seems to adhere to vocal sounds; even the most brief and incoherent sound, the clearing of the throat or a hesitant "uh," appears absolutely pregnant with significance, an apparently prelinguistic significance that creates the sensation of a body communicating without being mediated by language — or even by a controlling consciousness.[6] The cough, the stutter, the warble, the snort all seem to be the voice voicing itself despite your best efforts to tell it what to say.

4. Here's another curious fact: the human vocal apparatus is composed exclusively of elements whose primary biological functions have nothing to do with voice.[7] The lungs, which act as the bellows for our vocal organ, also rid the body of toxins and deliver the fresh oxygen that the body demands. The lips, teeth, tongue, soft palate, and throat, which allow us to perform the complex articulatory tasks that constitute speech, are used to process

food and move it into the digestive tract. Even the vocal folds, which seem custom designed for vocalization, are vital gatekeepers that prevent food and liquids from entering the trachea. When a foreign substance slips by the epiglottis — when something "goes down the wrong tube" — the vocal folds adduct to create the air pressure necessary to blow foreign substances out (aka coughing).

When the body is working at peak efficiency, breathing takes on a steady, constant rhythm. (Think of how you breathe when you're running or otherwise exerting yourself.) Talking and singing involve a necessary repurposing of the lungs, vocal folds, nose, mouth, and a diverse collection of muscles, bones, cartilage, nerves, and synapses over roughly two-thirds of your body. To vocalize is to make a (normally) conscious decision to employ the body in an activity that reduces, if only temporarily, the body's ability to meet its biological imperatives. In this sense, with the exception of the newborn's first cry, which, physicians surmise, performs the vital function of jump-starting the lungs, the act of vocalization is a bodily eruption that is simultaneously an *interruption* of the body's natural life-sustaining rhythms.

Inhale slowly, then read the following aloud in one breath:

"In order to deliver this sentence in one breath I would need to deprive my body of the oxygen it requires for a time span that would no doubt become increasingly uncomfortable (depending on the speed of my delivery of course) but one that would be justified in my mind by the great importance to me of what it is that I have to communicate to my listeners."

Repeat.
While jogging.

5. In focusing on the voice's fundamental strangeness, psychological volatility, and supersaturation as a vehicle for meaning, and in presenting voice as an interruption rather than a physiological given, I am gesturing toward the ever-present element of artifice in vocality. I use the word *artifice* here not in the sense of "deception" or even "artificiality" but rather in the sense of "constructedness" and even "theatricality." To wit: while we can think of voice as a biological attribute or human capacity, something that we innately "have," we can also profitably conceive of voice as an event, and not just any kind of event, but a performance. Our reasons for undertaking vocal performances are seldom purely biological — even our screams of fright and "uncontrollable" laughter are socially conditioned. We may not always be in control of this social performance, but it is a performance nonetheless.

Richard Schechner's famous definition of performance as "twice behaved behavior" is applicable to the performance that is voice.[8] For like the more formalized and stylized performances that Schechner had in mind, we are never really voicing "for the first time"; we are always voicing "for the second to the *n*th time," and we are in a state of constant *audition*, in the sense of listening but also in the sense of "trying out," as we release our voices into the world. As our voices' simultaneous creators and auditors, we are constantly judging our vocal performances as they resonate in space. We are, in this sense, in a lifelong state of vocal rehearsal, simultaneously on the stage and in the audience. And just as there is no God-like vantage point from which to experience a theatrical rehearsal in its all-encompassing entirety — just as you can't be on stage, backstage, in the orchestra, and in the balcony at the same time — so is there no position from which we can hear our vocal performance as it exists in the world. The "voice" that I hear as my own is a duet comprised of vibrations conducted through my skull directly to my ears as well as vibrations emanating from my mouth that travel to my ears through the air. (Wherever there is an echo or room reverberation this duet becomes a trio.) As a result, I am constantly listening to my voice and never hearing precisely that which is heard by others. In this sense, and in a way that Schechner may not have foreseen, I am constantly in a state of "me behaving . . . as if I am 'beside myself' or 'not myself.'"[9] This nonidentity of our experience of our own voice and everyone else's experience of our voice is frequently a source of anxiety, because it means that our voice in the world is never doing precisely what we think it is, what we want it to do. It is never projecting the exact "I" that you intend to project, or experience yourself projecting. As a performance, then, voice is always somewhat wild, *unheimlich,* experimental, never fully under control.

6. Vocal performances — of self, of art, of violence, of all three together — aren't simple reflections of our mind at work: they are also "at work" in their own right.[10] The things we say and sing and shout generate effects in the world. They can inspire and intimidate, tickle and infuriate. Their vibrations set other bodies in motion, provoking an immediate physical reaction from all who are within earshot, and often provoking thought, bemusement, pain, confusion, and other sundry delayed reactions. At its most powerful, vocal performance contains within itself the notional possibility of reconfiguring the world: "*I have a* dream *today!*" "*La historia es nuestra y la hacen los pueblos.*"[11] "*Poekhali!*"[12] In our mediatized age, some voices ring out, resonate, and are fixed in recordings — and, at least potentially, in collective memory — as instances of unique force, in which semantics fuse with timbre and cadence and the moment at hand to produce powerful transhistorical affect. Many musical vocal performances carry the aura of this kind of transformational power as well, as devotees of Bach or Umm Kulthum or

Appalachian folk Christian singing or Tumbuka healing rituals would surely attest.[13]

More often, however, voices-in-performance don't refashion the world, or if they do, they do so in a microscopic, intensely local way. In a posthumously published critique of speech act theory, anthropologist Michelle Rosaldo demonstrated how cultural expectations and proscriptions shape, in ways both subtle and profound, the ways in which selves are conceived, and consequently, the ways in which utterances are received. "The 'force' of acts of speech," she argued, "depends on things participants expect; and . . . such expectations are themselves the products of particular forms of sociocultural being."[14] Without theorizing voice per se, her work calls into question the notion of voice as a universal, uniform phenomenon. Rosaldo's cautionary note — "accounts of verbal action cannot reasonably proceed without attention to the relations between social order, folk ideas about the world, and styles of speaking"[15] — serves as a reminder that vocal performances are both embodied *and* emplaced, products of both the selves that make the sounds *and* the social collectives that make the sense.[16] This profound fact both shapes and delimits the primary effect of voices, without impinging upon a voice's ability to continue to circulate in mediatized form, generating various kinds of unforeseen sense among diverse audiences.

As Leslie Dunn and Nancy Jones assert, our voices generally resonate within "an intersubjective acoustic space" in which meaning is the product of both the vocalizer and the auditor, the performer and the audience.[17] I will foreshadow a bit here by saying that, if we acknowledge that voices can interpellate as well as communicate, and wound as well as console, then this "intersubjective acoustic space" becomes a fraught space, a space in which voices instigate, interact with, militate against, and at times disappear within violent acts.

Inhale slowly.
Call out into the darkness.
Listen for a response.
Proceed with caution.

7. What vocal performances also do, albeit also microscopically, incrementally, is reconfigure the body that engages in the performance. Nina Eidsheim notes:

> Learning to use the vocal apparatus in a particular way not only contributes to the shaping of vocal timbre, but the behaviors learned in this training are also "written into" the texture of the body. Thus singing is a practice manifested in the physical entity, the body, as are other physical practices or activities. The

way the voice is daily used, as any everyday physical activity, is discernable in the body. The patterns of our physical activities as female and male, as racially, nationally, and socioeconomically categorized people, shape our bodies, and thus shape the voice. And it is this *shaped voice* that we hear. There are therefore two bodies: first, there is the body with which we are born, which does not possess any inherent timbral limitations. Second, there is the body that is shaped over time, a body that most likely has been asked to take a form which expresses categories that matter in a given society.[18]

Eidsheim's work detaches the voice from biology proper and places it at the intersection of the embodied subject and culture. With this move, we can come to a provisional understanding of "voice" (or better, "vocality") as a performance that microscopically changes the performer's surroundings *and* the performer herself. As such, voice is, by necessity, a moving target, an embodied and emplaced event that exerts differentially distributed effects upon vocalists and their audiences, an event that relentlessly and fluidly *means*, even if we cannot always fix or articulate its meaning, a performance that is never fully under the performer's control nor fully possessable by the audience, a performance that is the result of a life spent listening to other voices.

> *Inhale slowly.*
> *Holler out joyously,*
> *at the top of your lungs.*
> *How do you feel?*
> *How does your neighbor feel?*

8. Stressing the performativity of the voice puts pressure on the connotative field that has accrued around voice in the modern, industrialized West and elsewhere. (This field of associations was in large part the target of Derrida's famous [1967] critique of "phonocentrism," but it survived his onslaught and persists to the present day.) Its exact shape is variously configured from one person to the next, but the following elements are common enough that they will seem intuitive to many of us:

a. voice = presence. At its most fundamental, voice would appear to point to the corporeal presence of a speaker. "What a voice, any voice, always says," writes Steven Connor, "no matter what the particular local import may be of the words it emits, is this: this, here, this voice, is not merely *a* voice, a particular aggregation of tones and timbres; it is voice, or voicing itself. *Listen, says a voice: some being is giving voice.*"[19] As an index of presence, the voice is associated with the body, with liveness, and with proximity — with being within earshot.

But Connor — a scholar of, among other subjects, ventriloquism — knows that the voice's relationship to presence is more complicated than it may first appear. Voices, to put it bluntly, may be thrown, making the absent present and the present appear to be absent. Moreover, life in a world of digitized media forces us to contend with multiple forms of disembodied, mute, layered, granular, and often spectral "presences" that confound the tight indexical association of voice with a singular, living, present body.[20]

b. voice = essence. In the modern era, voice has emerged as a strong metaphor for the distillation of an individual's (or a collective's) identity, personality, or even soul. Writers and artists experiment and struggle with different techniques until they "find their own voice." In musical, theatrical, and cinematic contexts, audiences often apply this metaphorical idea of essence to the performer's sonorous voice, creating a sounding voice that appears to express not just the protagonist of the song/play/film but the life experience of the person doing the vocalizing.[21] In listening to a voice, we think we can hear a life. In the United States, the equation of voice with personality has acquired juridical status through court cases that recognize a "distinctive voice" as the property of the vocalist.[22]

But while we can all think of moments when we were transfixed by a voice, when that voice seemed to be speaking the deepest, most essential truths about its owner, it is clear that "one's true voice" is not something that you find, but that you construct, and that voice (authorial or sonorous) is constructed in part through our mimetic, dialectic, dialogic, and polyphonic relationships with the voices (authorial and sonorous) that surround us from birth. Voice is, in this sense, not the essence of self, but essentially relational: our voices are responses to a lifetime of calls. Eidsheim's work on the lifelong shaping of vocal timbre powerfully demonstrates this point. More broadly, the notion that there is one essential "self" that is in an isomorphic relationship with a singular "voice" doesn't stand up to scrutiny or scholarship. Voice is not the essence of a unitary self but an instrument through which our different personalities, our many overlapping "selves," are projected out into the world. "The light is *green*, asshole!" "Hey baby, you look *good*." "Yes, mother."

c. voice = agency. In Western democracies, voice is a ubiquitous and transparent metaphor for agency within the sphere of representational politics. On the eve of every election, we are entreated to "make our voices heard" because our "voice counts." Likewise, in the aftermath of elections, we are told that "the people have spoken." These rhetorical moves present voting as akin to speaking in a kind of idealistic Habermasian public sphere. Much feminist scholarship, while critical of the hidden discriminations that underlie the public sphere, takes this essential relationship between voice and agency at face value, seeking to "give a voice" to those who have been disenfranchised (or "silenced") by hegemonic structures.[23] Dunn and Jones agree that the metaphor equating voice and agency "has become so pervasive, so intrinsic to feminist discourse that it makes us too easily forget (or repress) the concrete physical dimensions of the female voice upon which this metaphor was based."[24]

But merely having a voice, or even using it, is not equivalent to the exercising of agency. Voices can be dismissed as insane, they can be coded as noise, they can be, and are frequently, simply ignored. Shouting in the streets is not always an effective strategy if the decision makers are in a palace, or a bunker. This disconnect — between the metaphor (in which having a voice means not just being heard but being heeded) and the various effects that sonorous voices have in the world — is fundamental.

9. Why are these metaphors so persistent if they are so clearly inadequate? One reason is that in intimate situations, in situations of relative peace and quiet in which individuals are talking and listening to each other, our voices often provide us with a visceral sensation of presence, essence, and agency. You and I speak softly to one another, I taste your breath in my mouth, and you taste mine in yours. I hear myself (or close enough — see point 5 above) and I hear you, speaking softly to me. In hearing you I feel (rightly or wrongly) that I know you. And in talking to you and listening to you, I feel (again rightly or wrongly) that I myself am being heard, and heeded. This sensation can be even more intense when I am not talking with you but singing with you.

But these metaphors also gather strength outside of such intimate encounters. I submit that much of this strength comes from the voice's mythical function in Western-oriented modernity. To be specific, I want to argue that the voice metaphor is a myth that refracts vocal exchanges through the prism of ideas that are rooted in Enlightenment liberalism. Within the context of this myth, your voice asserts that: (1) you are a unique, autonomous individual (i.e., it asserts your presence); (2) you are a rational being capable of knowing and communicating your needs and desires (i.e., you are in touch with your essence); and (3) you have the power to act according to your individual wishes (i.e., you have agency). Under the influence of these associations, voice becomes an index, and a stand-in, for an individualist, rational, democratic worldview. This worldview and the voice-presence-essence-agency metaphor support one another. Voice thus deployed presents you to yourself as an autonomous, rational, empowered individual — despite any evidence to the contrary.

Of course, this individualist conception of voice is not the only one to have emerged in world history. It stands in contrast, for example, with the vocal myth that emerged in the immediate postrevolutionary years in the Soviet Union, a period in which lexicons and manners of writing and speaking were bent to the nascent contours of the newly (if only theoretically) enfranchised proletariat. Voice in the revolutionary state did not bespeak autonomy and individual agency but rather the meticulously constructed collective identity of a unified people marching together into the bright future. According to Michael Gorham, this homogenization of the Soviet voice was the conscious product of the political elite. In the years following the revolution, Gorham notes, "the impure voice of the people — and the peasantry in particular — was being cleansed from the palate of public discourse."[25] Further:

> The voices of the cultural peripheries . . . were purged of their regional and dialectical identities and were linguistically "collectivized" into a reinvented and safely controlled image of a *Soviet*-Russian people, a rural proletariat. Those unable or unwilling to adapt to the new standards found their voices quickly and literally muted from the various spheres of public discourse.[26]

The whiff of violence that can be detected in this quote, the "literal" muting of voices for speaking out of turn or out of style, is an indication of the degree to which control of the vox populi can be important for the establishment and maintenance of state power. The Western modern vocal myth is not being consciously manipulated by governments as the Soviet myth was — and that is an important difference — but it too helps to perpetuate larger state and corporate structures, and it too involves the symbolic silencing of marginal populations who are not recognized as enfranchised members of the imagined community. In any polity, there are voices that, whether heard or not, are never heeded.

Inhale slowly.
Wait for your partner to speak.
Whenever he speaks, shout until he stops speaking.
How do you feel?
How does your partner feel?

10. Within the context of its Enlightenment framing, however, voice is presented as violence's opposite. According to the connotative field that surrounds voice, to speak is to communicate with one's others, to sing is to commune with them, and both together are the antithesis of killing. In a world where to speak is to be heard and heeded, agency in the guise of voice would appear to be the common property of humankind, and the

necessary condition for politics, and therefore peace. Hannah Arendt's concept of violence relies upon a notion of speech/voice that conforms to this mythological model:

> Where violence rules absolutely, as for instance in the concentration camps of totalitarian regimes, not only the laws . . . but everything and everybody must fall silent. It is because of this silence that violence is a marginal phenomenon in the political realm; for man, to the extent that he is a political being, is endowed with the power of speech. The two famous definitions of man by Aristotle, that he is a political being and a being endowed with speech, supplement each other and both refer to the same experience in Greek *polis* life. The point here is that *violence itself is incapable of speech*, and not merely that speech is helpless when confronted with violence. Because of this speechlessness political theory has little to say about the phenomenon of violence and must leave its discussion to the technicians.[27]

The idea of violence as speechless strangely dovetails with the Romantic notion of music beginning "when words leave off" that Pegley and Fast mention in their introduction to this volume. If we take these two ideas together, the following schema emerges: (1) violence, whose incapacitating brutality places it in opposition to speech (here presented as a civilizing force), occupies one extreme; and (2) music, whose transcendent expressiveness places it in opposition to speech (here presented as the residue of ordinary life), occupies the other. In this schema, voice is the sound of humanity, music is the sound of the gods, and violence is the negation of both.

In an influential article grappling with language use within the context of the twenty-first-century conflicts in Iraq and Afghanistan, Mary Louise Pratt begins by affirming that the conventional portrayal of language — and by implication voice — places it in a zero-sum relationship with violence: "Common sense locates, and often theorizes, violence as that which lies beyond words, that which erupts when words fail. War breaks out when diplomacy breaks down; war stops when dialogue resumes, or dialogue resumes when war stops."[28] But Pratt goes on to argue that language and violence are less opposed to one another than they are imbricated with one another:

> Aggression, the anthropologists say, is biological; violence is social. The embedding of violence in language and language in violence is what makes it social. Violence might erupt when interlocution stops, but *where there is violence, language is nearly always present*, supplying meanings and alibis and inflicting injuries of its own. Violence usually relies on discursive accompaniment to

give it meaning. This framing marks the social character of violence and manages its dangers. In war, these powers get weaponized.[29]

Pratt discusses an incident in which an American combat unit was sent on a mission to flush out a group of Taliban fighters who were hiding in a village north of Kandahar; the previous day, the fighters had killed an American and an Afghan soldier. The convoy approached the village with "huge speakers mounted atop the vehicles blar[ing] Pink Floyd at top volume." An American psychological operations specialist ordered his Afghan interpreter to hurl abusive language and taunts at the unseen Taliban, calling them "scared," "lady boys," "a disgrace to Islam," and "cowardly dogs," among other epithets. Both the music and the shouting were designed to be as offensive as possible, as the soldiers worked to anger the Taliban fighters so much that they would feel compelled to reveal themselves and fight.[30]

Pratt claims to be discussing language here, but she tacitly acknowledges that it is primarily when language is *envoiced* that it participates in the social phenomenon of violence. Words given voice in Dunn and Jones's "intersubjective acoustic space" can wound, and as Pratt explains, these wounds help accomplish the aggressors' objectives: "trained practitioners of verbal abuse have no doubts about the effectiveness of verbal aggression." Using tactics that include "intimidation, vilification, . . . derision . . . [and] threatening and demeaning interpellations," vocal aggressors, in times of war and peace, seek to infiltrate their victim's consciousness, so that hateful speech inseminates the victim's inner voice.[31] Quoting Denise Riley and Jean-Jacques Lecercle's provocative work on linguistic violence, Pratt argues that "inner speech, the voice in the head, is 'our own constant ongoing performance of who we are,' a constant flow that is social and transpersonal." It is this voice in the head that is "the carrier of linguistic injury." In the words of Riley and Lecercle, "injurious speech echoes relentlessly, years after the occasion of its utterance, in the mind of the one at whom it was aimed. . . . The curse does work."[32] By repeating hateful speech to an addressee, the vocal aggressor ventriloquizes the victim's inner voice, taking it out of the victim's control and thereby inducing the kind of psychic trauma that is one of the more subtle but most pervasive by-products of violence, be it military or domestic. In this way, voices resonating in space don't just encounter a violent world — at times, they help construct it.

Of course, shouting curses at someone is not the same as shooting bullets at them. But shooting people, it must be said, is often preceded, accompanied, and followed by shouting, and screaming, and sobbing, and laughing, and singing, and all manner of vocal expression, both ritualistic and improvised. Our voices are actions that set the stage for further action, and that action can bend toward or away from violence, sometimes in keeping with our intentions, sometimes in contradiction to them.

Inhale slowly.
Think of a hateful word.
Speak it forcefully,
in a public place,
to a child.
Evaluate the effects.

11. For several years now, I have been working on a study of the sonic dimension of the Iraq war [which was, at the time of this writing, ongoing — JMD]. While this work doesn't deal with voice specifically, there are several moments at which voices leap into the foreground. One such moment involves the practice, more common at the beginning of the conflict, much rarer in more recent years, of U.S. service members listening to loud music while on motorized patrols. While some of this listening took place for the reasons that Pratt describes, more often service members claimed to be doing it for reasons similar to the reasons they listened to loud music in civilian life: "pumping [oneself] up," passing the time, providing a "soundtrack" for daily activities. My Iraqi civilian interlocutors were deeply troubled, even disgusted, when they encountered Humvees in their neighborhoods with music blaring. To them, this practice was audible proof that the foreign soldiers were treating war not as duty or a necessary evil but as play and as aesthetic spectacle. According to them, copies of homemade videos of soldiers engaged in violent acts to the accompaniment of a metal or rap soundtrack, which soldiers make to entertain themselves and their friends, have reportedly been sold in VCD form throughout Iraq in an attempt to attract more civilians to the insurgency.

These are not the only videos in circulation. Insurgents regularly post videos of successful IED attacks against U.S. troops; hundreds of them are available on the Arabic-language Internet. In the vast majority of these videos, the lethal explosion is followed by the voices of unseen insurgent men, chanting "Allahu akbar" (Allah is great) in raised voices that perform a type of devotional ecstasy. When my American interlocutors view these videos, they are deeply troubled, even disgusted. Based on the videos and other experiences, some have drawn the erroneous conclusion that Islam is an essentially violent religion.

One does not have to copy any of these interpretive moves, or succumb to the temptation of ascribing false equivalences to violent acts, in order to be struck by the frequency with which stylized, scripted vocal performances (live and recorded, musical and declamatory) are found in disconcertingly close proximity to violent acts in contemporary combat zones.

12. Here is another, even more disturbing, instance of voices — musical and declamatory — found in close proximity to violence. This is taken from an undated account of the Rwandan genocide written by Colette Braeckman:

> The most popular station of all was RTLM [Radio Télévision Libre des Milles Collines], the Thousand Hills Radio Television. It was known for having the best disc jockeys in Rwanda and for its attractive mix of African music, news programming, and political analysis. Founded in 1993 and owned by family members and friends of President Habyarimana, the station preached an extremist message of Hutu supremacy, but *many apolitical Rwandans became listeners because of the music it played*. In fact, their hearts and minds were being prepared for genocide. When the killing was unleashed on April 6, it became clear what the owners and managers of the station had created — an infernal pulpit from which the message to kill could be disseminated throughout Rwanda.[33]

13. Returning to the conflict formerly known as the Global War on Terror, my colleague Suzanne Cusick has meticulously documented the U.S. military and intelligence service's practice of using music within the context of interrogation in Iraq, Afghanistan, and Guantànamo Bay, Cuba. In one of several articles on the topic, she quotes former interrogator Tony Lagouranis, whose first-person account of an interrogation at Mosul Air Force Base in Iraq demonstrates the fluidity with which vocal violence mixes with other forms of sensory manipulation:

> After bagging his head while checking him out of the prison late at night, we threw him roughly in the back of a pick-up truck. . . . We drove him around the base for about twenty minutes, [then] we dragged him out of the truck and forced him to stand in the middle of the container. His breathing was heavy after hearing the metal doors slam and the bolt fall into place. It was completely dark. We'd staged it perfectly. In his mind, we were getting ready to seriously mess him up.
>
> As [the detainee] knelt, we put the flashing light directly in front of his sandbagged face and the boom box, at full volume, just off to the side. The music . . . consisted of industrial-style guitars, beating drums, *and lyrics delivered in a moan/shout style, the singer obviously trying to sound like the Prince of Darkness himself.* It blasted out of the speakers and ricocheted around the container. . . .
>
> And as [the detainee] knelt, *we took turns yelling our questions into his ears.* His head twisted around as he tried to figure out where we were. *After about a half*

hour, he started moaning. I imagined he was crying behind his sandbag. *We pushed forward, getting harsher with our words.* My throat was sore, my ears were ringing, and the lights were disorienting.[34]

How are we to feel about vocal exchanges like this one? Cusick frames the use of sustained loud music as inflicting "psychic rather than physical pain." This type of pain "attacks its target and causes self-betrayal in the intrasubjective space that many religious traditions call the soul. It is when soul and body together collapse in the catastrophe of self-betrayal that resistance is not just futile but impossible."[35] In the incident described above, live and recorded voices fuse into an overwhelming onslaught. The only way to bring an end to the pain is for the detainee to use his voice in the confessional mode demanded by the interrogator.

My primary objective in describing these events in Rwanda, Iraq, and elsewhere is not to judge them. (The task of judging would require more time and contextualizing information than I have at my disposal.) Rather, I mention them here in order to point out ways in which the voice, in both musical and declamatory contexts, can be utilized as a trigger for violence, or as an instrument of violence in its own right. In the light of these and countless other events, it is clear that we need a definition of violence that does not put it in opposition to voice, or to music.

14. Having contemplated voice as:

a physiological process

an interruption of bodily rhythms

a performance

a source of anxiety

an agent of change in the world

a practice that changes the body

a mythological trope

a lack of control

a prelude or postlude to violence

an index of ongoing violence

an invitation to violence

violence itself . . .

now (and only now) I am ready to talk about the beauty of singing.

15. It is only against the background of the work, and the damage, that voices accomplish in the world that a discussion of music and violence can

take place. And it is only against such a troubling background that the profound life-affirming potential of the voice and music can be evaluated. In the essays included in this volume, we find musical actors engaged in a range of activities that articulate in various ways with objective violence, subjective violence, and violent memory. The majority of the musical voices herein described are positioned in opposition to violence. We read of vocal music that: engages in an attempt to memorialize a traumatic past (Ritter, Wlodarski); articulates messages of tolerance amid the persistent fact of violence (Vicente); and models cross-cultural reconciliatory relationships (Miller). Collectively these essays reveal a vocal epistemology that frames voice, and more narrowly vocal music, as a force that can be effectively deployed in opposition to violence. In the end, this is perhaps the most important thing vocal performance can attempt to do. It is precisely because voices are so often used to violent purposes, as I hope to have demonstrated above, that the instances in which they are used to reconciliatory ends are both noteworthy and inspiring. When a potential bomb becomes a balm, this is news.

Other authors in this volume describe vocal performances that relate to violence in different, more oblique and complicated ways. In these essays, the musical voice acts, variously, as: an ambivalent agent, creating unpredictable effects on both sides of a world war (Baade); a force that simultaneously is distorted by and exacerbates ethnic tensions in an atmosphere of civil war (Baker); and a galvanizing instrument for the performance of a number of overlapping but distinct political affiliations within a chronically violent timespace (McDonald). Musical voices are not explicitly aligned against violence here, but are intertwined with violence in more difficult configurations, at times subjugated to it, at times moving against the current of violent events, at times moving in two directions at once. Nuanced work that tracks this movement, such as the work in these essays, is crucial for those who seek to gain a more comprehensive understanding of the ways in which musical voices resonate through, interact with, and support violent acts.

Even the two essays that do not deal primarily with musical voices contribute to our understanding of ways in which voice and violence can intersect. Nicholas Attfield's probing chapter on the evolution of rhetoric within a German music publication over the course of WWI points to the important role that patriotic songs and national anthems played in the drive to establish nationalist unity in Germany. And Jim Deaville's detailed discussion of the use of instrumental music during news broadcasts analyzes the ways in which musical sound has become integrated with the declamatory voice of the newscaster. Currently, the relation between the two is so strong that we might profitably examine the nightly news as an experimental composition for voice and instruments. In fact, the numerous online entities engaged in the musicalization of news broadcasts — the so-called "auto-tuning the news" that has become a ubiquitous meme on the Internet over the past few years — appear to be making an ironic commentary on the mediascape along precisely these lines.[36]

16. This is the unstable ground upon which the current volume lies. In the context of the violent acts that the authors describe, it is clear that we can no longer afford the luxury of a purely celebratory attitude toward music or voice. I doubt that we ever could. We spend our lives listening to the voices that surround us, and listening to ourselves engage with those voices mimetically, dialectically, dialogically, and polyphonically. But one of the precursors of violence, and one of its enabling conditions, is the practice of engaging with voices competitively, in a zero-sum relation in which vocalizing silences other potential voices and falling silent (e.g., in order to listen) is tantamount to defeat. This kind of competition takes place rhetorically, but also musically. Bruce Johnson and Martin Cloonan, in their recent book on popular music and violence, state this point forcefully:

> That music is complicit in relations of power is a truism of popular music studies. Less often recognized is that musical transactions are therefore double-edged. Every time music is used to demarcate the territory of self or community, it is incipiently being used to invade, marginalize or obliterate that of other individuals or groups.[37]

We can see this kind of territorialization in a number of the essays in this volume. But we can also see efforts to deploy musical voices in configurations that are more inclusive than exclusive, voices that interpellate listeners into communities that are more ecumenical than fundamentalist. As scholars of music, it is important for us to document both of these approaches, and to seek to understand their interrelationship.

17. At the end, I return to the beginning, to breath, to the utopian thrill of inspiration. Among its many more direct uses, this volume has compelled me to think critically about the twenty-five-century tradition that equates inhalation with spiritual strength and psychic rejuvenation. And my critical thought is this: for those traditions that equate the drawing in of breath with the drawing in of metaphysical sustenance, the presumption is that we are inspiring clean air under peaceful circumstances. Such an idyllic inspiration, an inspiration that is a rejuvenation, logically leads to a conception of voice that is similarly life affirming, a voice that is the product of the *pneuma*. The difficulty with this proposition is that breathing — living — in proximity to violence does not resemble "transcendence in the form of opening up." Violence threatens the life-affirming prospect of inspiration, both literally

and figuratively. To put it bluntly, war zones are noxious places, and they often bring not the enlightening breath of the other but the stench of death into your lungs. What kind of voice can emerge from the inspiration of the air of violence? What kind of damaged voices can we expect to come out of the toxicity of war? The authors in this volume have begun to answer this question, among many others, and the results are predictably mixed. The bad news is that violence and voice will always coexist, and musical voices will never succeed in putting a permanent end to violence, no matter how much we may want them to. It is important to adopt a sober orientation to the study of voice and of music, an orientation that lays bare the complicated ways in which both are involved in all of the forms of violence that the editors of this volume mention in their introduction, and that the authors also document. At the same time, we can take some solace from the fact that beautiful, life-affirming voices can and do emerge from violence-warped environments. And whether they are performing laments for fallen comrades or odes to post-violent futures, whether they are cataloging atrocities or effecting a temporary escape from war's exigencies, we can be moved by these voices. We can be moved by their sounds; we can be moved by the resilience of the humans that produced them; and we can hope that they move us, if only incrementally, toward a more just life.

Inhale slowly.

Hold.

Prepare to sing an impossibly beautiful tone.

Listen to it in your mind.

Remain silent.

Keep listening to the tone.

Exhale slowly.

Repeat.

Notes

1. Adriana Cavarero, *For More Than One Voice: Toward a Philosophy of Vocal Expression.* (Stanford, CA: Stanford University Press, 2005), 32.

2. Emmanuel Levinas, *Otherwise Than Being or Beyond Essence*, trans. Alphonso Lingis (Dordrecht, The Netherlands: Kluwer Academic Publishers, 1991), 181.

3. Silvia Benso, "The Breathing of the Air: Presocratic Echoes in Levinas," in *Levinas and the Ancients*, ed. Brian Schroeder and Silvia Benso (Bloomington: Indiana University Press, 2008), 23–24.

4. See, for example, Anne Karpf, *The Human Voice: How This Extraordinary Instrument Reveals Essential Clues about Who We Are* (New York: Bloomsbury,

2006); Mladen Dolar, *A Voice and Nothing More* (Cambridge, MA: MIT Press, 2006); Steven Connor, "The Decomposing Voice of Postmodern Music," *New Literary History* 32, no. 3 (2001): 467–83.

5. See Dolar, *A Voice and Nothing More*, 14; Ivan Leudar and Philip Thomas, *Voices of Reason, Voices of Insanity: Studies of Verbal Hallucinations* (London: Routledge, 2000). Media theorist Friedrich Kittler problematizes this reading by presenting the inner voice as a historical phenomenon connected with reading practices in the late eighteenth century, rather than a psychological universal. Friederich Kittler, *Discourse Networks 1800/1900*, trans. Michael Metteer (Stanford, CA: Stanford University Press, 1990 [1985]).

6. See David Appelbaum, *Voice* (Albany: State University of New York Press, 1990).

7. See Alfred Tomatis, *The Ear and the Voice*, trans. Roberta Prada (Lanham, MD: Scarecrow Press, 2005), 59; Karpf, *The Human Voice*, 23.

8. Richard Schechner, *Between Theater and Anthropology* (Philadelphia: University of Pennsylvania Press, 1985 [2002]). Dunn and Jones adopt and develop Paul Zumthor's usage of the term "vocality" in ways consonant with my framing of the voice as event. Leslie C. Dunn and Nancy A. Jones, "Introduction," in *Embodied Voices: Representing Female Vocality in Western Culture*, ed. Leslie C. Dunn and Nancy A. Jones (Cambridge: Cambridge University Press, 1994), 2.

9. Schechner, *Between Theater and Anthropology*, 37.

10. There is a theory already available for making this point. Founded upon the mid-twentieth-century scholarship of J. L. Austin and John Searle, "speech act theory" offers a model for understanding the work that many vocal performances accomplish. Most famously, Austin focused upon "performative utterances," in which the saying of a thing is coterminous with the doing of that thing: *"I pronounce you husband and wife"; "You're fired"; "I quit."* Such utterances are not so much describing action as conducting action themselves.

11. "History is ours, and it is made by the people." Salvador Allende's final speech, September 11, 1973, www.ciudadseva.com/textos/otros/ultimodi.htm.

12. "We're off!" Yuri Gagarin, April 12, 1961 — the first words spoken during the first manned space flight.

13. See George B Stauffer, *Bach, the Mass in B-Minor: The Great Catholic Mass* (New Haven, CT: Yale University Press, 2003); Virginia Danielson, *The Voice of Egypt: Umm Kulthūm: Arabic Song, and Egyptian Society in the Twentieth Century* (Chicago: University of Chicago Press, 1997); Jeff Todd Titon, *Powerhouse for God: Speech, Chant, and Song in an Appalachian Baptist Church* (Austin: University of Texas Press, 1988); and Steven Friedson, *Dancing Prophets Musical Experience in Tumbuka Healing* (Chicago: University of Chicago Press, 1996), for excellent monographs on these traditions.

14. Michelle Rosaldo, "The Things We Do with Words: Ilongot Speech Acts and Speech Act Theory in Philosophy" *Language in Society* 11, no. 2 (1982): 228–29.

15. Rosaldo, "The Things We Do with Words," 213.

16. For examples of socially and historically situated conceptions of the voice, see Emily Wilbourne, "La Florinda: The Performance of Virginia Ramponi Andreini" (PhD diss., New York University, 2008), 335, and Geneviéve Calame-Griaule, "Voice and the Dogon World," in *Notebooks in Cultural Analysis vol. 3*, A Special Issue on "Voice," ed. Norman Cantor (Durham, NC: Duke University Press, 1986), 51. I am using the word "emplaced" here in the sense outlined by David Howes: "While the paradigm of 'embodiment' implies an integration of mind and body, the emergent paradigm of *emplacement* suggests the sensuous interrelationship of body-mind-environment. This environment is both physical and social, as is well illustrated by the bundle of sensory and social values contained in the feeling of 'home.' The counterpart to emplacement is *displacement*, the feeling that one is homeless, disconnected from one's physical and social environment. A sense of displacement is often the plight of the socially marginalized." David Howes, *Empire of the Senses: The Sensual Cultural Reader* (London: Berg, 2005), 7. When applied to the voice, the emplacement/displacement relationship gives us the means to discuss the imbrication of voice and politics in the grounded way that I call for in section 13 of this essay.

17. Dunn and Jones, "Introduction," 2.

18. Nina Eidsheim, "Voice as a Technology of Selfhood: Towards an Analysis of Racialized Timbre and Vocal Performance" (PhD diss., University of California, San Diego, 2008), 35.

19. Steven Connor, *Dumbstruck: A Cultural History of Ventriloquism* (Oxford: Oxford University Press, 2000), 4 (emphasis added).

20. See Jason Stanyek and Benjamin Piekut, "Deadness: Technologies of the Intermundane," *TDR* 54, no. 1 (2010): 14–38 for a treatise that fundamentally rewrites the relationship between voice and presence.

21. See Laurie Stras, "The Organ of the Soul: Voice, Damage, and Affect," in *Sounding Off: Theorizing Disability in Music*, ed. Neil Lerner and Joseph N. Straus (New York: Routledge, 2006), 173–84.

22. *Tom Waits v. Frito-Lay Inc., et al.*, 978F.2d 1093 (9th Cir. 1992); available at www.law.umkc.edu/faculty/projects/ftrials/communications/waits.html (accessed December 31, 2010).

23. See Nancy Fraser, "Rethinking the Public Sphere: A Contribution to the Critique of Actually Existing Democracy," in *Habermas and the Public Sphere*, ed. Craig Calhoun (Cambridge, MA: MIT Press, 1992), 109–42.

24. Dunn and Jones, "Introduction," 1.

25. Michael S Gorham, *Speaking in Soviet Tongues: Language Culture and the Politics of Voice in Revolutionary Russia* (Dekalb: Northern Illinois University Press, 2003), 149.

26. Gorham, *Speaking in Soviet Tongues*, 152.

27. Hannah Arendt, *On Revolution* (London: Penguin, 1963 [1990]), 19 (emphasis added).

28. Mary Louise Pratt, "Harm's Way Language and the Contemporary Arts of War." *PMLA* 124, no. 5 (2009): 1516.

29. Pratt, "Harm's Way," 1516 (emphasis added).

30. Pratt, "Harm's Way," 1517.

31. Pratt, "Harm's Way," 1523.

32. Denise Riley and Jean-Jacques Lecercle, *The Force of Language* (New York: Palgrave MacMillan, 2004), 47, quoted in Pratt, "Harm's Way," 1523.

33. Colette Braeckman, "Incitement to Genocide," *Crimes of War Project*, n.d., www.crimesofwar.org/a-z-guide/incitement-to-genocide-2/ (accessed December 30, 2010) (emphasis added).

34. Tony Lagouranis and Allen Mikaelian, *Fear Up Harsh: An Army Interrogator's Dark Journey through Iraq* (New York: NAL Caliber, 2007); Suzanne Cusick, "'You Are In a Place That Is Out of the World . . .': Music in the Detention Camps of the 'Global War on Terror,'" *Journal of the Society for American Music* 2, no. 1 (2008): 10 (emphasis added).

35. Cusick, "'You Are In a Place That Is Out of the World,'" 17.

36. The musical group the Gregory Brothers are the most prominent practitioners of this technique. See www.youtube.com/show/autotunethenews (accessed December 30, 2010).

37. Bruce Johnson and Martin Cloonan, *The Dark Side of the Tune: Popular Music and Violence* (Surrey, UK: Ashgate, 2009), 4.

Bibliography

Abu Sha'ira, D. *Dalil Lil-Aghaniya Al-Wataniya Al-Filistiniya: Fakr wa Maqawma [Guide to Palestinian Nationalist Songs: Conception and Resistance]*. Damascus: Dar Al-Shajara Lil-Nashr, 2004.

Adorno, Theodor W. *Negative Dialectics*. Translated by E. B. Ashton. New York: Seabury Press, 1973.

Adorno, Theodor W. *Prisms*. Translated by Samuel Weber and Shierry Weber. Cambridge, MA: MIT Press, 1983.

Adorno, Theodor W. "What Does Coming to Terms with the Past Mean?" In *Bitburg in Moral and Political Perspective*, edited by Geoffrey H. Hartman, 114–29. Bloomington: Indiana University Press, 1986.

Agamben, Giorgio. *State of Exception*. Translated by Kevin Attell. Chicago: University of Chicago Press, 2005.

Allan, Stuart, and Barbie Zelizer, eds. *Reporting War: Journalism in Wartime*. London: Routledge, 2004.

Allende, Salvador. "History Is Ours, and It Is Made by the People." September 11, 1973. www.ciudadseva.com/textos/otros/ultimodi.htm (accessed March 10, 2011).

"Allies Gaining Ground." *Times* (London), November 9, 1914.

And, Metin. "The Mevlana Ceremony." *The Drama Review* 21, no. 3 (1977): 83–94.

Andersen, Lale (dir.), and Walter Baumgartner. "Lili Marleen." *Telefunken A 10862*, 1949 (reissued on compact disc 1 of *Lili Marleen*).

Andersen, Lale (dir.), and Michael Jary. "Lili Marlene." *Decca C 16027*, 1948 (reissued on compact disc 3 of *Lili Marleen*).

Andersen, Lale (dir.), and Michael Jary. "Lili Marleen." *Decca F 49076*, 1948 (reissued on compact disc 1 of *Lili Marleen*).

Andersen, Lale (dir.), and Bruno Seidler-Winkler. "Lied eines jungen Wacht-postens (Lili Marleen)," Electrola EG 6993, 1939 (reissued on compact disc 1 of *Lili Marleen*).

Anderson, Benedict. *Imagined Communities: Reflections on the Origin and Spread of Nationalism*. 2nd edition. London: Verso, 1991.

Anderson, Bonnie. *News Flash: Journalism, Infotainment and Bottom-Line Business of Broadcast News.* San Francisco: Jossey-Brass, 2004.

Appelbaum, David. *Voice.* Albany: State University of New York Press, 1990.

Araújo, Samuel, and Members of the Grupo Musicultura. "Conflict and Violence as Theoretical Tools in Present-Day Ethnomusicology: Notes on a Dialogic Ethnography of Sound Practices in Rio de Janeiro." *Ethnomusicology* 50, no. 2 (Spring/Summer 2006), 287–313.

Arendt, Hannah. *On Revolution.* London: Penguin, 1963 [1990].

Arendt, Hannah. *On Violence.* New York: Harcourt, Brace & World, 1970.

Arlen, Michael J. *Living-Room War.* New York: Viking, 1969.

Askew, Kelly M. *Performing the Nation: Swahili Music and Cultural Politics in Tanzania.* Chicago: University of Chicago Press, 2002.

Assmann, Aleida. *Der lange Schatten der Vergangenheit, Erinnerungskultur und Geschichtspolitik.* Munich: Beck, 2006.

Audeh, Ida. "Narratives of Siege: Eye-Witness Testimonies from Jenin, Bethlehem, and Nablus." *Journal of Palestine Studies* 31 (2002): 13–34.

Auslander, H. Ben. "'If Ya Wanna End War and Stuff, You Gotta Sing Loud': A Survey of Vietnam-Related Protest Music." In *American Popular Music: Readings from the Popular Press*, Volume 2: *The Age of Rock*, edited by Timothy Scheurer, 179–84. Madison, WI: Popular Press, 1990.

Austin, J. L. *How to Do Things with Words.* Cambridge, MA: Harvard University Press, 1962.

Baade, Christina. *Victory through Harmony: The BBC and Popular Music in World War II.* New York: Oxford University Press, 2011.

Bach, Steven. *Marlene Dietrich: Life and Legend.* New York: William Morrow, 1992.

Baer, Adam. "The Sounds of War: Rating the Networks' Theme Music." *Slate*, April 17, 2003. www.slate.com/id/2081608 (accessed February 7, 2009).

Bainimarama, Voreqe. Address to the United Nations General Assembly, September 28, 2007. Excerpt of full transcript from *Pacific Islands Report.* http://pidp.eastwestcenter.org (accessed October 16, 2007).

Baker, Catherine. *Sounds of the Borderland: Popular Music, War and Nationalism in Croatia since 1991.* Farnham, UK: Ashgate, 2010.

Baker, Catherine. "When Seve Met Bregović: Folklore, Turbofolk and the Boundaries of Croatian Musical Identity." *Nationalities Papers* 36, no. 4 (2008): 741–64.

Barks, Coleman, et al. *The Essential Rumi*, 2d ed. New York: HarperCollins, 2004.

Baroud, Ramzy. *Searching Jenin: Eyewitness Accounts of the Israeli Invasion, 2002.* Seattle, WA: Cune Press, 2003.

Başat, Başak Güneş. "Whirl to Achieve Oneness." *Hürriyet Daily News and Economic Review*, April 15, 2008. http://www.hurriyetdailynews.com/h.php?news=whirl-to-achieve-spiritual-oneness-2008-04-15 (accessed May 17, 2010).

Baudrillard, Jean. *The Gulf War Did Not Take Place*. Translated by Paul Patton. Bloomington: Indiana University Press, 1995.

Beaumont, Peter. "Ten-Day Ordeal in Crucible of Jenin." *Guardian*, April 14, 2002.

Becker, Judith. *Deep Listeners: Music, Emotion, and Trancing*. Bloomington: Indiana University Press, 2004.

Bellamy, Alex J. *The Formation of Croatian National Identity: A Centuries-Old Dream?* Manchester: Manchester University Press, 2003.

Benjamin, Walter. *Reflections: Essays, Aphorisms, Autobiographical Writing*. Translated by Edmund Jephcott. Edited and with an introduction by Peter Demetz. New York: Schocken Books, 1978.

Benso, Silvia. "The Breathing of the Air: Presocratic Echoes in Levinas." In *Levinas and the Ancients*, edited by Brian Schroeder and Silvia Benso, 9–23. Bloomington: Indiana University Press, 2008.

Berg, Rick. "Losing Vietnam: Covering the War in an Age of Technology." In *The Vietnam War and American Culture*, edited by John Carlos Rowe and Rick Berg, 115–47. New York: Columbia University Press, 1991.

Bergeron, Katherine, and Philip V. Bohlman, eds. *Disciplining Music: Musicology and Its Canons*. Chicago: University of Chicago Press, 1992.

Bergmeier, Horst, and Ranier E. Lotz. *Hitler's Airwaves: The Inside Story of Nazi Radio Broadcasting and Propaganda Swing*. New Haven, CT: Yale University Press, 1997.

Bergmeier, Horst, Ranier Lotz, and Volker Kühn. Liner notes to *Lili Marleen an Allen Fronten: Das Lied, seine Zeit, seine Interpreten, seine Botschaften*. Bear Family Records, BCD 16022 GL, 2005.

Berkey, Jonathan P. *The Formation of Islam: Religion and Society in the Near East, 600–1800*. Cambridge: Cambridge University Press, 2003.

Beverly, John. *Testimonio: On the Politics of Truth*. Minneapolis: University of Minnesota Press, 2004.

Bhim, Mosmi. "The Impact of the Promotion of Reconciliation, Tolerance and Unity Bill on the 2006 Election." In *From Election to Coup in Fiji: The 2006 Campaign and Its Aftermath*, edited by Jon Fraenkel and Stewart Firth, 111–43. Canberra: Australian National University E Press and Asia Pacific Press, 2007.

Biccum, April. "Marketing Development: Live 8 and the Production of the Global Citizen." *Development and Change* 38, no. 6 (2007): 1111–26.

Bierman, John and Colin Smith. *War Without Hate: The Desert Campaign of 1940–1943*. New York: Penguin Books, 2004; published as *The Battle of Alamein*, 2002.

Bilbija, Ksenua, et al., eds. *The Art of Truth-Telling about Authoritarian Rule*. Madison: University of Wisconsin Press, 2005.

Billig, Michael. *Banal Nationalism*. London: Sage, 1995.

"Biography." *The Official Anne Shelton Website*. www.anne-shelton.co.uk (accessed December 2, 2008).

Blacher, Boris, et al. *Jüdische Chronik*. Libretto by Jens Gerlach. Berlin: Zeuthen/Mark, 1961.

Blacking, John. *How Musical Is Man?* Seattle: University of Washington Press, 1973.

Bodroghkozy, Aniko. "*The Smothers Brothers Comedy Hour* and the Youth Rebellion." In *The Revolution Wasn't Televised: Sixties Television and Social Conflict*, edited by Lynn Spigel and Michael Curtin, 201–20. New York: Routledge, 1997.

Bohlman's, Philip V. *Music, Nationalism and the Making of the New Europe*. 2nd edition. New York: Routledge, 2011.

Borer, Tristan Anne. "Truth Telling as a Peace-Building Activity: A Theoretical Overview." In *Telling the Truths: Truth Telling and Peace Building in Post-Conflict Societies*, edited by Tristan Anne Borer, 1–57. Notre Dame, Indiana: University of Notre Dame Press, 2006.

Born, Georgina, and David Hesmondhalgh, eds. *Western Music and Its Others: Difference, Representation, and Appropriation in Music*. Berkeley: University of California Press, 2000.

Bourdieu, Pierre. *The Logic of Practice*. Translated by Richard Nice. Stanford, CA: Stanford University Press, 1990 [1980].

Bourdieu, Pierre, and Loïc J. D. Wacquant. *An Invitation to Reflexive Sociology*. Chicago: University of Chicago Press, 1992.

Braeckman, Colette. "Incitement to Genocide." *Crimes of War Project*, n.d. www.crimesofwar.org/thebook/incitement-genocide.html (accessed December 30, 2010).

Brandes, Friedrich. "An unsere Leser." *Neue Zeitschrift für Musik* 81 (1914): 469.

Brett, Sebastian. *Peru Confronts a Violent Past: The Truth Commission Hearings in Ayacucho*. New York: Human Rights Watch, 2003.

British Broadcasting Corporation Written Archives Centre. Programmes as Broadcast, Forces: October 18, 1942.

British Broadcasting Corporation Written Archives Centre. Radio File R19/1153/1: Entertainment/Anne Shelton Programmes (1942–44).

British Broadcasting Corporation Written Archives Centre. Radio File R27/178: Music General/Lili Marlene (1942–47).

British Broadcasting Corporation Written Archives Centre. Special Collections S24/54/9, 14, 23, 26: Madden/Wartime Radio Diary.

Brock, Gordon. "The Official Lili Marleen Page." In *20,000 Volkslieder, German and Other Folksongs*, edited by Frank Petersohn. http://ingeb.org/Lieder/lilimarl.html (accessed April 30, 2009).

Brown, Wendy. *Regulating Aversion: Tolerance in the Age of Identity and Empire*. Princeton, NJ: Princeton University Press, 2006.

Brubaker, Rogers. *Ethnicity without Groups*. Cambridge, MA: Harvard University Press, 2004.

Burt, Jo-Marie. *Political Violence and the Authoritarian State in Peru*. New York: Palgrave Macmillan, 2007.

Burt, Jo-Marie. "Quien Habla Es Terrorista: The Political Use of Fear in Fujimori's Peru." *Latin American Research Review* 41, no. 3 (2006): 32–62.

Butler, Judith. *Frames of War: When Is Life Grievable?* London: Verso, 2009.

Butler, Judith. *Precarious Life: The Powers of Mourning and Violence*. New York: Verso Press, 2006.

Butler, Judith, and Gayatri Chakravorty Spivak. *Who Sings the Nation-State? Language, Politics, Belonging*. London: Seagull Books, 2007.

Calame-Griaule, Geneviéve. "Voice and the Dogon World." In *Notebooks in Cultural Analysis*, vol. 3. A Special Issue on "Voice," edited by Norman Cantor, 15–60. Durham, NC: Duke University Press, 1986.

Ćaleta, Joško. "Trends and Processes in the Musical Culture of the Dalmatian Hinterland." *Music and Anthropology* 6 (2001). www.fondazionelevi.org/ma/index/number6/ma_ind6.htm (accessed February 4, 2009).

Calico, Joy H. "*Jüdische Chronik:* The Third Space of Commemoration between East and West Germany." *Musical Quarterly* 88 (2005): 95–122.

Cameron, John, and Anna Haanstra. "Development Made Sexy: How It Happened and What It Means." *Third World Quarterly* 29, no. 8 (2008): 1475–89.

Campbell, David. "Representing Contemporary War," *Ethics & International Affairs* 17, no. 2 (Fall 2003): 99–108.

Cánepa Koch, Gisela, ed. *Identidades representadas: Performance, experiencia, y memoria en los Andes*. Lima: Pontificía Universidad Católica del Perú, 2001.

Caruth, Cathy, and Thomas Keenan. "'The Aids Crisis Is Not Over: A Conversation with Gregg Bordowitz, Douglas Crimp, and Laura Pinsky." In *Trauma: Explorations in Memory*, edited by Cathy Caruth, 256–72. Baltimore: Johns Hopkins University Press, 1995.

Cavarero, Adriana. *For More Than One Voice: Toward a Philosophy of Vocal Expression*. Stanford, CA: Stanford University Press, 2005.

Central Intelligence Agency. "A Look Back . . . Marlene Dietrich: Singing for a Cause." *CIA Featured Story Archive*, October 23, 2008. www.cia.gov/news-information/featured-story-archive/marlene-dietrich.html (accessed December 1, 2008).

Chand, Ganeshwar. *Papers on Racial Discrimination, Volume 1: The CERD Papers*. Lautoka: Fiji Institute of Applied Studies, 2005.

Chaudhry, Mahendra. "Taking Stock of 2005 and Looking to the Future." Paid advertisement. *The Fiji Times*, December 31, 2005.

Chickering, Roger. *Imperial Germany and the Great War, 1914–1918*, 2nd ed. Cambridge: Cambridge University Press, 2004.

Chion, Michel. *Audio-Vision: Sound on Screen*. Translated by Claudia Gorbman. New York: Columbia University Press, 1994.

Clarke, Eric F. "Jimi Hendrix's 'Star Spangled Banner.'" In *Ways of Listening: An Ecological Approach to the Perception of Musical Meaning*, 48–61. New York: Oxford University Press, 2005.

Cohen, John. *Dancing with the Incas*. Film. University of California Extension Center for Media and Independent Learning, 1991.

Cole, Catherine. *Performing South Africa's Truth Commission: Stages of Transition*. Bloomington: Indiana University Press, 2010.

Colla, Elliott. "Sentimentality and Redemption: The Rhetoric of Egyptian Pop Culture Intifada Solidarity." In *Palestine, Israel, and the Politics of Popular Culture*, edited by Ted Swedenburg and Rebecca. L. Stein, 338–64. Durham, NC: Duke University Press, 2005.

Comisión de la Verdad y Reconciliación (CVR). *Informe Final de la Comisión de la Verdad y Reconciliación*. Lima, Peru: CVR, 2003.

Cone, Edward T. *The Composer's Voice*. Berkeley: University of California Press, 1974.

Connor, Steven. "The Decomposing Voice of Postmodern Music." *New Literary History* 32, no. 3 (2001): 467–83.

Connor, Steven. *Dumbstruck: A Cultural History of Ventriloquism*. Oxford: Oxford University Press, 2000.

Cook, Nicholas. *Music: A Very Short Introduction*, 2nd ed. Oxford: Oxford University Press, 2000.

Cooper, David. *The Musical Traditions of Northern Ireland and Its Diaspora: Community and Conflict*. Farnham, UK: Ashgate, 2009.

Coxshall, Wendy. "From the Peruvian Reconciliation Commission to Ethnography: Narrative, Relatedness, and Silence." *Political and Legal Anthropology Review* 28, no. 2 (2005): 203–22.

Cross, Charles. *Room Full of Mirrors: A Biography of Jimi Hendrix*. New York: Hyperion, 2005.

Culler, Jonathan. "Deconstruction." In *Deconstruction: Critical Concepts in Literary and Cultural Studies*, edited by Jonathan Culler, 52–71. New York: Routledge, 2003.

Curiel, Jonathan. "Can Rumi Save Us Now? Life and Words of the Popular 13th-Century Persian Poet Have Special Meaning for a 21st-Century World Torn by War, Genocide and Hatred." *San Francisco Chronicle*, April 1, 2007.

Cusick, Suzanne. "Music as Torture/Music as Weapon." *Revista Transcultural de Música/Transcultural Music Review* 10 (2006). www.sibetrans.com/trans/trans10/cusick_eng.htm (accessed July 15, 2010).

Cusick, Suzanne. "'You Are In a Place That Is Out of the World . . .': Music in the Detention Camps of the 'Global War on Terror.'" *Journal of the Society of American Music* 2, no. 1 (February 2008): 1–26.

Czarnowski, Gabriele. "Hereditary and Racial Welfare (*Erb- und Rassenpflege*): The Politics of Sexuality and Reproduction in Nazi Germany." *Social Politics* (Spring 1997): 114–35.

Dack, James. "Sacred Music." In *The Cambridge Companion to Haydn*, edited by Caryl Clark, 138–49. Cambridge: Cambridge University Press, 2005.

Danielson, Virginia. *The Voice of Egypt: Umm Kulthūm, Arabic Song, and Egyptian Society in the Twentieth Century.* Chicago: University of Chicago Press, 1997.

Daverio, John. *Robert Schumann: Herald of a "New Poetic Age."* New York: Oxford University Press, 1997.

Deaville, James. "Selling the War in Iraq: Television News Music and the Shaping of American Public Opinion." *Echo: A Music-Centered Journal* 8, no. 1 (2006). www.echo.ucla.edu/Volume8-Issue1/roundtable/deaville.html (accessed February 7, 2009).

Deaville, James. "The Sounds of American and Canadian Television News after 9/11: Entoning Horror and Grief, Fear and Anger." In *Music in the Post-9/11 World*, edited by Jonathan Ritter and J. Martin Daughtry, 43–70. New York: Routledge, 2007.

Degregori, Carlos Iván, ed. "Heridas abiertas, derechos esquivos: Reflexiones sobre la Comisión de la Verdad y Reconciliación." In *Memorias en conflicto: Aspectos de la violencia politica contemporaneae,* edited by Raynald Belay et al. 75–85. Lima: Embajada de Francia en el Perú, Instituto de Estudios Peruanos, Instituto Francés de Estudios Peruanos, and Red Para el Desarrollo de las Ciencias Sociales en el Perú, 2003.

Degregori, Carlos Iván, ed. *Jamás tan cerca arremetió lo lejos: Memoria y violencia politica en el Perú.* Lima: Instituto de Estudios Peruanos, 2003.

Deleuze, Gilles. *Cinema 2: The Time-Image.* Translated by Hugh Tomlinson and Robert Galeta. London: Continuum, 2005.

Der Derian, James. *Virtuous War: Mapping the Military-Industrial-Media-Entertainment Network.* Boulder, CO: Westview Press, 2001.

Derrida, Jacques. *Of Grammatology.* Translated by Gayatri Chakravorty Spivak. Baltimore: Johns Hopkins University Press, 1998 [1967, orig. trans. 1974].

Derrida, Jacques. *Rogues: Two Essays on Reason.* Translated by Pascale-Anne Brault and Michael Naas. Stanford, CA: Stanford University Press, 2005.

Derrida, Jacques. "The 'World' of the Enlightenment to Come (Exception, Calculation, Sovereignty)." Translated by Pascale-Anne Brault and Michael Naas. *Research in Phenomenology* 33 (2003): 9–52.

Dessau, Paul. *Let's Hope for the Best, Briefe und Notizbücher aus den Jahren 1948 bis 1978.* Edited by Daniela Reinhold. Berlin: Stiftung Archiv der Akademie der Künste, 2000.

Dessau, Paul. *Paul Dessau 1894–1979: Dokumente zu Leben und Werk*. Edited by Daniela Reinhold. Berlin: Stiftung Archiv der Akademie der Künste Henschel Verlag, 1995.

"Die neunte Sinfonie in Kriegszeit." *Neue Zeitschrift für Musik* 82 (1915): 301–2.

"Diese Chronik Missglückte: Zweites Konzert *musik der zeit* im Kölner Funkhaus." *Kölner Stadt Anzeiger*, January 19, 1966.

Dietrich, Marlene. "Lili Marlene." Columbia/Legacy CK 53209, 1993 (1954) (reissued on compact disc 7 of *Lili Marlene*).

Dietrich. Marlene (dir.), and Jimmy Carroll. "Lilli Marleen." *Marlene Dietrich Overseas*, Columbia GL 105, 1951 (reissued on compact disc 1 of *Lili Marleen*).

Dietrich, Marlene (dir.), and Charles Magnante. "Lili Marlene." Decca 23456, 1945 (reissued on compact disc 2 of *Lili Marleen*).

Dietzsch, Paul. "Heine und Chopin." *Neue Zeitschrift für Musik* 84 (1917): 123.

Diner, Dan. "On the Ideology of Antifascism." *New German Critique* 67 (Winter 1996): 123–32.

Dolar, Mladen. *A Voice and Nothing More*. Cambridge, MA: MIT Press, 2006.

Donovan, Robert J., and Ray Scherer. *Unsilent Revolution: Television News and American Public Life, 1948–1991*. Cambridge: Cambridge University Press, 1992.

Draber, H. W. "'Christus' von Felix Draeseke." *Neue Zeitschrift für Musik* 79 (1912): 113–14.

Drakulić, Slavenka. *Café Europa: Life after Communism*. London: Abacus, 1996.

Dugundžija, Mirjana. "Hitmejker koji je Severinu pretvorio u megazvijezdu." *Nacional*, May 28, 2002.

Dunn, Leslie C., and Nancy A. Jones. "Introduction." In *Embodied Voices: Representing Female Vocality in Western Culture*, edited by Leslie C. Dunn and Nancy A. Jones 1–13. Cambridge: Cambridge University Press, 1994.

Đuras, Dora. "Nedu su pet puta vraćali na binu." *Arena*, September 11, 2003.

During, Jean. "What Is Sufi Music?" In *The Legacy of Medieval Persian Sufism (1150–1500)*. Vol. 2 of *The Heritage of Sufism*, edited by Leonard Lewisohn, 277–87. Oxford: Oneworld Publications, 1999.

Dvornik, Boris. "Lipa li si, Mare moja." *Večernji list*, July 6, 1991.

Dymond, Greig. "Benefit Concerts: An Abbreviated History." January 21, 2010. www.cbc.ca/news/arts/things-that-go-pop-blog/2010/01/benefit-concerts-an -abbreviated-history.html (accessed November 14, 2010).

Edensor, Tim. *National Identity, Popular Culture and Everyday Life*. Oxford: Berg, 2002.

Edmondson, Ray. "The Voice of Australia: *Cinesound Review*." *Metro: Media & Education Magazine* 137 (2003): 138–40.

Edwards, Paul. *Historical Dictionary of the Korean War*, 2nd ed. Lanham, MD: Scarecrow Press, 2010.

Eidsheim, Nina. "Voice as a Technology of Selfhood: Towards an Analysis of Racialized Timbre and Vocal Performance." PhD diss., University of California, San Diego, 2008.

Eimert, Herbert. "Ein Bekenntniswerk von fünf Komponisten." *Melos* 2 (1966): 56.

Ellis, John. "Broadcast TV as Sound and Image." In *Film Theory and Criticism: Introductory Readings*, edited by Leo Braudy and Marshall Cohen, 5th ed., 386–87. New York: Oxford University Press, 1999 [1982].

Engstrom, Nicholas. "The Soundtrack for War." *Columbia Journalism Review* 42, no. 1 (2003): 45–47.

Ercan, Mustafa. "Sufi Music Concert at Church." *Hürriyet Daily News and Economic Review*, May 17, 2010. http://www.hurriyetdailynews.com/n.php?n =kilisede-tasavvuf-musikisi-konseri-2010-05-17 (accessed May 17, 2010).

Ergüner, Kudsi. *Journeys of a Sufi Musician*. Translated by Annette Courtney Mayers. London: SAQI, 2005.

"Erstmals *Jüdische Chronik:* Zur Eröffnung Sonderkonzerte der Philharmonie." *Sächliches Tagesblatt* (Dresden). October 5, 1988.

Fabijanović, Anči. "Neki se vraćaju, drugi odlaze." *Večernji list*, January 3, 1990.

Fareanu, Alexander. "Johann Gallus Mederitsch." *Neue Zeitschrift für Musik* 85 (1918): 293.

Fast, Susan, and Kip Pegley. "*America: A Tribute to Heroes:* Music, Mourning, and the Unified American Community." In *Music in the Post 9/11 World*, edited by J. Martin Daughtry and Jonathan Ritter, 27–42. New York: Routledge, 2007.

Fast, Susan, and Kip Pegley. "Music and Canadian Nationhood Post 9/11: An Analysis of *Music without Borders: Live.*" *Journal of Popular Music Studies* 18, no. 1 (2006): 18–39.

Fast, Susan, and Kip Pegley. "Operation Enduring Freedom, the Neo-Liberal Subject and the Concert for New York City." Unpublished manuscript.

Felber, Gerald. "*Jüdische Chronik.*" *Berliner Zeitung*, November 10, 1988.

Felber, Rudolf. "Der Wille zur Kunst," *Neue Zeitschrift für Musik* 84 (1917): 341–44.

Feldman, Walter. "Musical Genres and Zikr of the Sunni Tarikats of Istanbul." In *The Dervish Lodge: Architecture, Art, and Sufism in Ottoman Turkey*, edited by Raymond Lifchez, 187–202. Berkeley: University of California Press, 1992.

Feldman, Walter. *Music of the Ottoman Court: Makam, Composition and Early Ottoman Instrumental Repertoire*. Berlin: Verlag für Wissenschaft und Bildung, 1996.

Fielding, Raymond. *The American Newsreel: A Complete History, 1911–1967*, 2nd ed. Jefferson, NC: McFarland and Company, 2006.

Fiji Island Bureau of Statistics. 2007 Census. www.statsfiji.gov.fj (accessed November 12, 2007).

Fischer, Jens Malte. *Richard Wagners "Das Judentum in der Musik."* Frankfurt-am-Main: Insel, 2000.

Flammer, Ernst H. *Politisch Engagierte Musik als Kompositorisches Problem.* Baden-Baden: Verlag Valentin Koerner, 1981.

"Forces Like the Radio 'Girl Friends.'" *The Evening News* (January 16, 1942). [BBC WAC press clippings].

Franz Fanon, *The Wretched of the Earth.* Translated by Constance Farrington. New York: Grove Press, 1963.

Fraser, Nancy. "Rethinking the Public Sphere: A Contribution to the Critique of Actually Existing Democracy." In *Habermas and the Public Sphere*, edited by Craig Calhoun, 109–42. Cambridge, MA: MIT Press, 1992.

Freie Erde (Neustrelitz). February 17, 1966.

Friedlander, Shems. *The Whirling Dervishes: Being an Account of the Sufi Order, Known as the Mevlevis, and Its Founder, the Poet and Mystic, Mevlana Jalalu'ddin Rumi.* New York: Macmillan, 1975.

Friedson, Steven. *Dancing Prophets: Musical Experience in Tumbuka Healing.* Chicago: University of Chicago Press, 1996.

Gagnon, V. P., Jr. *The Myth of Ethnic War: Serbia and Croatia in the 1990s.* Ithaca, NY: Cornell University Press, 2004.

Garmaz, Željko. "Uvijek sam bila žena borac pa mi Srbi zovi balijka s pendrekom!" *Globus*, April 1, 1994.

Garofalo, Reebee. *Rockin' the Boat: Mass Music and Mass Movements.* Cambridge, MA: South End Press, 1992.

Gay, Peter. *Weimar Culture: The Outsider as Insider.* New York: Harper & Row, 1970.

Geissler, F. A. "Moderne Musik und moderne Kultur," *Neue Zeitschrift für Musik* 79 (1912): 567.

Gerlach, Jens. Libretto for *Jüdische Chronik.* Berlin: Zeuthen/Mark, 1961.

Giddens, Anthony. *Modernity and Self-Identity: Self and Society in the Late Modern Age.* Cambridge: Polity Press, 1991.

Glamuzina, Kaye. "Melanesia: Fiji." In *Grove Music Online*, edited by L. Macy, 2007. www.grovemusic.com (accessed December 11, 2007).

Goldsworthy, David. "Fijian Music." In *The Garland Encyclopedia of World Music, Volume 9: Australia and the Pacific Islands*, edited by Adrienne Kaeppler and J. W. Love, 774–76. New York: Garland Publishing, 1998.

González, Eduardo. "La globalización del derecho a la verdad." In *Memorias en conflicto: Aspectos de la violencia politica contemporanea*, edited by Raynald Belay et al., 181–92. Lima: Embajada de Francia en el Perú, Instituto de Estudios Peruanos, Instituto Francés de Estudios Peruanos, and Red Para el Desarrollo de las Ciencias Sociales en el Perú, 2003.

Goodman, Tanya. *Staging Solidarity: Truth and Reconciliation in a New South Africa.* Yale Cultural Sociology Series. Herndon, VA: Paradigm Publishers, 2007.

Gorham, Michael S. *Speaking in Soviet Tongues: Language Culture and the Politics of Voice in Revolutionary Russia*. Dekalb: Northern Illinois University Press, 2003.

Gorriti, Gustavo. *The Shining Path: A History of the Millenarian War in Peru*. Translated by Robin Kirk. Chapel Hill: University of North Carolina Press, 1999.

"Grabschrift 1914 bei Bixschoote." *Neue Zeitschrift für Musik* 82 (1915): 37.

Grandin, Greg, and Thomas Miller Klublock, eds. *Truth Commissions: State Terror, History, and Memory*. Special issue of *Radical History Review*, volume 97. Durham, NC: Duke University Press, 2007.

Grandmont, Charles. "Massacre of 14 Women Haunts Montréal Ten Years Later." *National Post*, December 5, 1999.

Greenberg, Joel. "Amnesty Accuses Israeli Forces of War Crimes." *New York Times*, November 4, 2002. www.nytimes.com (accessed July 14, 2010).

Greenberg, Robert D. *Language and Identity in the Balkans: Serbo-Croatian and Its Disintegration*. Oxford: Oxford University Press, 2005.

Gubar, Susan. "This Is My Rifle, This Is My Gun: World War II and the Blitz on Women." In *Behind the Lines: Gender and the Two World Wars,* edited by Margaret Randolph Higonnet, 227–59. New Haven, CT: Yale University Press, 1987.

Gugelberger, George, ed. *The Real Thing: Testimonial Discourse and Latin America*. Durham, NC: Duke University Press, 1996.

Gupta, Akhil. "Blurred Boundaries: The Discourse of Corruption, the Culture of Politics, and the Imagined State." *American Ethnologist* 22, no. 2 (1995): 375–402.

Gysi, Klaus. "Gedenkveranstaltung des Verbandes der jüdischen Gemeinden in der DDR aus anlass des 47. Jahrestages des faschistischen Pogroms 1938." July 8, 1985. SAPMO, DY30/9051.

Hallin, Daniel C. *The "Uncensored War": The Media and Vietnam*. New York: Oxford University Press, 1986.

Hammond, William M. *Reporting Vietnam: Media and Military at War*. Lawrence: University Press of Kansas, 1998.

Hayner, Priscilla. *Unspeakable Truths: Confronting State Terror and Atrocities*. New York and London: Routledge, 2002.

Hegarty, Marilyn E. "Patriot or Prostitute? Sexual Discourses, Print Media, and American Women during World War II." *Journal of Women's History* 10, no. 2 (Summer 1998): 112–36.

Heinemann, Rudolf. "Fasst Musik den Massenmord? Experiment des Westdeutschen Rundfunks: Jüdische Chronik." *Die Welt*. January 19, 1966.

Heister, Hans Werner. "Aktuelle Vergangenheit: Zur Kollektivkomposition *Jüdische Chronik*." In *Paul Dessau: Von Geschichte gezeichnet — Symposium P.D. Hamburg 1994*, edited by Klaus Angermann. 171–90. Hofheim: Wolke, 1995.

Henze, Hans Werner. *Music and Politics: Collected Writings, 1953–81.* Translated by Peter Labanyi. Ithaca, NY: Cornell University Press, 1982.

Herf, Jeffrey. *Divided Memory: The Nazi Past in the Two Germanys.* Cambridge: Harvard University Press, 1997.

Hersh, Seymour. "The Gray Zone: How a Secret Pentagon Program Came to Abu Ghraib." *New Yorker*, May 24, 2004, www.newyorker.com (accessed November 13, 2011).

Heuss, Alfred. "Der Foxtrott im Konzertsaal," *Zeitschrift für Musik* 90 (1923): 54–55.

Heuss, Alfred. "Arnold Schönberg — Preussischer Kompositionslehrer." *Zeitschrift für Musik* 92 (1925): 583–85.

Heuss, Alfred. "Über Franz Schrekers Oper 'Der Schatzgräber.'" *Zeitschrift für Musik* 88 (1921): 567–70.

Heuss, Alfred. "Wird es endlich dämmern? Zur Mahagonny-Theaterschlacht am 9. März im Neuen Theater zu Leipzig." *Zeitschrift für Musik* 97 (1930): 395.

Hilmes, Oliver. *Der Streit ums "Deutsche": Alfred Heuss und die Zeitschrift für Musik.* Hamburg: von Bockel, 2003.

Hirsch, Marianne. *Family Frames: Photography, Narrative, and Postmemory.* Cambridge, MA: Harvard University Press, 1997.

Hirsch, Marianne. "The Generation of Postmemory." *Poetics Today* 29, no. 1 (Spring 2008): 103–28.

Hobsbawm, Eric. "Introduction: Inventing Traditions." In *The Invention of Tradition*, edited by Eric Hobsbawm and Terence Ranger, 1–14. Cambridge: Cambridge University Press, 1983.

Holzem, Johann. *Der lange Weg zum Ruhm: Lili Marleen und Belgrade 1941.* Meckenheim: Warlich Verlag, 1997.

Horsley, William. "Turks Cool Towards 'Unfaithful' Europe." *BBC News*, November 6, 2006. http://news.bbc.co.uk/2/hi/europe/6121106.stm (accessed November 6, 2006).

Howes, David, ed. *Empire of the Senses: The Sensual Culture Reader.* Oxford: Berg, 2005.

Hübner, Otto R. "Zukünftige Musik." *Neue Zeitschrift für Musik* 82 (1915): 193.

Hudelist, Darko. "Neda Ukraden otvorila mi je glazbene vidike." *Globus*, March 30, 2001.

"Hullo Troops." *Parade* (April 18, 1942): 1, 3.

Ignatieff, Michael. *Blood and Belonging: Journeys into the New Nationalism.* New York: Farrar, Strauss, and Giroux, 1993.

Iordanova, Dina. *Cinema of Flames: Balkan Film, Culture and the Media.* London: BFI, 2001.

"Islam-West Rift Widens, Poll Says." *BBC News*, January 21, 2008. http://news.bbc.co.uk/2/hi/europe/7200514.stm (accessed January 23, 2008).

Jackson, Carlton. *The Great Lili.* San Francisco: Strawberry Hill Press, 1979.

Jansen, Stef. "The Violence of Memories: Local Narratives of the Past after Ethnic Cleansing in Croatia." *Rethinking History* 6, no. 1 (2002): 77–93.

Jaramillo, Deborah Lynn. "Ugly War, Pretty Package: How the Cable News Network and the Fox News Channel Made the 2003 Invasion of Iraq High Concept." PhD diss., University of Texas, 2006.

Jaramillo, Deborah Lynn. *Ugly War, Pretty Package: How the Cable News Network and the Fox News Channel Made the 2003 Invasion of Iraq High Concept.* Bloomington: Indiana University Press, 2009.

Jelin, Elizabeth. *State Repression and the Labors of Memory.* Translated by Judy Rein and Marcial Godoy-Anativia. Minneapolis: University of Minnesota Press, 2003.

Jennings, Humphrey (dir.). *The True Story of Lili Marlene.* Ministry of Information, 1944.

Jewell, Derek. "Lilli Marlene: A Song for All Armies." In *Alamein and the Desert War*, edited by Derek Jewell. 147–56. London: Sphere Books, Ltd., 1967.

Johnson, Bruce, and Martin Cloonan. *The Dark Side of the Tune: Popular Music and Violence.* Surrey, UK: Ashgate, 2009.

Jorgensen, Darren. "Death Star, or How I Learned to Stop Worrying and Love Globalization." *symplokē* 15, nos. 1–2 (2007): 206–17.

Jović, Dejan. "'Official Memories' in Post-Authoritarianism: An Analytical Framework." *Journal of Southern Europe and the Balkans* 6, no. 2 (2004): 97–108.

"Jüdische Chronik: ADN-Gespräch mit Paul Dessau." *Berliner Zeitung.* May 17, 1961.

"Jüdische Chronik." *Neue Zeit* (East Berlin). February 1, 1966.

"Jüdische Chronik." *Liberal-Demokratische Zeitung*. Halle. February 24, 1966.

Jünger, Ernst. *The Storm of Steel: From the Diary of a German Storm-Troop Officer on the Western Front.* No translator given. New York: Howard Fertig, 1975.

Kaiser, Georg. "Neues von Johann Adolf Hasse." *Neue Zeitschrift für Musik* 79 (1912): 1–3.

Kaneko, Ann. *Against the Grain: An Artist's Survival Guide to Peru.* Film. New Day Films, 2008.

"Karagöz Not Turkish, Greek Minister Says." *Hürriyet Daily News and Economic Review*, July 15, 2010. http://www.hurriyetdailynews.com/n.php?n=turkish-karagoz-confuses-greek-minds-2010-07-15 (accessed July 15, 2010).

Karpf, Anne. *The Human Voice: How This Extraordinary Instrument Reveals Essential Clues About Who We Are.* New York: Bloomsbury, 2006.

Kartomi, Margaret. "Towards a Methodology of War and Peace Studies in Ethnomusicology; The Case of Aceh, 1976–2009." *Ethnomusicology* 54, no. 3 (Fall 2010): 452–83.

Kattago, Siobhan. *Ambiguous Memory: The Nazi Past and German National Identity.* Westport, CT: Praeger, 2001.

Kellner, Douglas. "From Vietnam to the Gulf: Postmodern Wars?" In *The Vietnam War and Postmodernity*, edited by Michael Bibby, 173–98. Amherst: University of Massachusetts Press, 2000.

Kellner, Douglas. *The Persian Gulf TV War.* Boulder, CO: Westview Press, 1992.

Kellner, Douglas. "The Persian Gulf TV War Revisited." In *Reporting War: Journalism in Wartime*, edited by Stuart Allan and Barbie Zelizer, 136–54. New York: Routledge, 2004.

Kellner, Douglas. "The Persian Gulf War Revisited" (long version). www.gseis .ucla.edu/faculty/kellner/papers/gulfwarrevisited.htm (accessed February 7, 2009).

Kelly, John D., and Martha Kaplan. *Represented Communities: Fiji and World Decolonization.* Chicago: University of Chicago Press, 2001.

Kendrick, Michelle. "Kicking the Vietnam Syndrome: CNN's and CBS's Video Narratives of the Persian Gulf War." In *Seeing through the Media: The Persian Gulf War*, edited by Susan Jeffords and Lauren Rabinovitz, 59–76. New Brunswick, NJ: Rutgers University Press, 1994.

Kerman, Joseph. *Concerto Conversations.* Cambridge, MA: Harvard University Press, 1999.

Kerman, Joseph. "Representing a Relationship: Notes on a Beethoven Concerto." *Representations* 39 (1992): 80–101.

Kerman Joseph, et al. "Beethoven, Ludwig van." In *Grove Music Online, Oxford Music Online.* www.oxfordmusiconline.com (accessed November 12, 2010).

Kirkpatrick, Rob. *1969: The Year Everything Changed.* New York: Skyhorse Publishing, 2009.

Kittler, Friedrich. *Discourse Networks 1800/1900.* Translated by Michael Metteer. Stanford, CA: Stanford University Press, 1990 [1985].

Kivy, Peter. "Music as Narration." In *Sound and Semblance: Reflections on Musical Representation*, 159–96. Princeton, NJ, 1984.

Koch, Gerhard. "Ost-Westliches Engagement." *Frankfurter Allgemeine Zeitung.* January 17, 1966.

Kohut, Adolph. "Wagner und seine Mutter." *Neue Zeitschrift für Musik* 80 (1913): 377–80.

Kolar-Panov, Dona. *Video, War and the Diasporic Imagination.* London and New York: Routledge, 1997.

Konta, Ana. "U Zagrebu pjevam slomljena srca." *Arena*, February 24, 2005.

"Konya Targets 10 Mln Tourists in 2013." *Hürriyet Daily News and Economic Review*, November 1, 2008. http://www.hurriyetdailynews.com/h.php?news=konya -targets-10-mln-tourists-in-2013-2008-01-11 (accessed December 3, 2008).

Kracauer, Siegfried. *Theory of Film: The Redemption of Physical Reality.* New York: Oxford University Press, 1960.

Kramer, Lawrence. "Musical Narratology: A Theoretical Outline." *Indiana Theory Review* 12 (1991): 141–62.

Kramer, Stanley (dir.). *Judgment at Nuremberg.* United Artists, 1961.

Kruhak, Mirela. "Intimna sam s Duškom Lokinom samo kad je riječ o pjesmi." *Arena*, August 21, 1993.

Kučinić, Diana. "Granata prekinula sevdalinke." *Večernji list*, November 26, 1992.

Kusić, Dane. "Positivity of Music and Religion in Turkey." *Narodna umjetnost: Hrvatski casopis za etnologiju i folkloristiku* 34, no. 1 (1997): 147–78.

Lagouranis, Tony, and Allen Mikaelian. *Fear Up Harsh: An Army Interrogator's Dark Journey through Iraq.* New York: NAL Caliber, 2007.

Lal, Brij V. *Broken Waves: A History of the Fiji Islands in the Twentieth Century.* Honolulu: University of Hawaii Press, 1992.

"Lale Andersen — Lied eines jungen Wachtpostens (Lili Marlen)." www.youtube .com/watch?v=r9hW7dMWqjs (accessed April 24, 2009).

Lamprecht, Karl. "Geistige Mobilmachung." *Neue Zeitschrift für Musik* 81 (1914): 481–82.

Laušević, Mirjana. "Some Aspects of Music and Politics in Bosnia." In *Neighbors at War: Anthropological Perspectives on Yugoslav Ethnicity, Culture and History*, edited by Joel M. Halpern and David A. Kideckel. 289–302. University Park, PA: Pennsylvania State University Press, 2000.

Lawrence, Amy. "Marlene Dietrich: The Voice as Mask." In *Dietrich Icon*, edited by Gerd Gemünden and Mary R. Desjardins. Durham, NC: Duke University Press, 2007.

Lawrence, Bruce B., and Aisha Karim, eds. *On Violence: A Reader.* Durham, NC: Duke University Press, 2007.

Leebaw, Bronwyn. *Judging State-Sponsored Violence, Imagining Political Change.* New York: Cambridge University Press, 2011.

LeFranc, Sandrine. "¿Cómo acabar con el desacuerdo? Las Comisiones de la Verdad como lugar de construcción disensual de la historia." In *Memorias en conflicto: Aspectos de la violencia politica contemporanea*, edited by Raynald Belay et al., 193–223. Lima: Embajada de Francia en el Perú, Instituto de Estudios Peruanos, Instituto Francés de Estudios Peruanos, and Red Para el Desarrollo de las Ciencias Sociales en el Perú, 2003.

Lehrke, Gisela. *Wie Einst Lili Marleen: Das Leben der Lale Andersen.* Berlin: Henschel Verlag, 2002.

Leipziger Volkszeitung. February 17, 1966.

Lerner, Neil, and Joseph N. Straus, eds. *Sounding Off: Theorizing Disability in Music.* New York: Routledge, 2006.

Leudar, Ivan, and Philip Thomas. *Voices of Reason, Voices of Insanity: Studies of Verbal Hallucinations.* London and Philadelphia: Routledge, 2000.

Levinas, Emmanuel. *Otherwise Than Being or Beyond Essence.* Translated by Alphonso Lingis. Dordrecht, The Netherlands: Kluwer Academic Publishers, 1991.

Levinson, Jerrold. "Music as Narrative and Music as Drama." *Mind and Language* 19, no. 4 (2004): 428–41.

Lewis, Bernard. *The Jews of Islam.* Princeton: Princeton University Press, 1984.

Lewis, Bernard. "The Roots of Muslim Rage." *Atlantic Monthly* 266, no. 3 (1990): 47–60.

Lewis, Franklin D. *Rumi Past and Present, East and West: The Life, Teaching and Poetry of Jalâl al-Din Rumi.* Oxford: Oneworld Publications, 2000.

"Lili Marlene." *International Lyrics Playground.* http://lyricsplayground.com (accessed 30 April 2009).

"Lili Marlene." www.youtube.com/watch?v=MOolUXnAs-U (accessed September 12, 2011).

Lili Marleen an Allen Fronten: Das Lied, seine Zeit, seine Interpreten, seine Botschaften. Bear Family Records, BCD 16022 GL, 2005.

"Lilli Marlene by Anne Shelton." www.youtube.com/watch?v=7gBCWMseKw8 (accessed August 12, 2011).

Linke, Uli. *Blood and Nation: The European Aesthetics of Race.* Philadelphia: University of Pennsylvania Press, 1999.

Liss, Andrea. *Trespassing through Shadows: Memory, Photography, and the Holocaust.* Minneapolis: University of Minnesota Press, 1998.

Lombardi, Francisco. *La Boca del Lobo.* Film. Inca Films, 1988.

Luković, Petar. *Bolja prošlost: prizori iz mužičkog života Jugoslavije 1940–1989.* Belgrade: Mladost, 1989.

MacDonald, David. "The Quest for Purity: Linguistic Politics and the War in Croatia." *Slovo* (London) 15, no. 1 (2003): 5–21.

Maček, Ivana. "'Imitation of Life': Negotiating Normality in Sarajevo under Siege." In *The New Bosnian Mosaic: Identities, Memories and Moral Claims in a Post-War Society*, edited by Xavier Bougarel, Elissa Helms, and Ger Duijzings. 39–57. Aldershot, UK: Ashgate, 2007.

Mackey, Eva. *The House of Difference: Cultural Politics and National Identity in Canada.* London: Routledge, 1999.

Maeckel, Otto Viktor. "Musik und Künstler des feindlichen Auslandes." *Neue Zeitschrift für Musik* 81 (1914): 533–36.

Malak, Amin. *Muslim Narratives and the Discourse of English.* Albany: State University of New York Press, 2005.

Marks, Alexandra. "Persian Poet Top Seller in America." *Christian Science Monitor*, November 25, 1997.

Marx, Karl. *Capital: A Critique of Political Economy: Volume III — Part II, The Process of Capitalist Production as A Whole.* Edited by Friedrich Engels. New York: Cosimo Books, 2007.

Matelita Ragogo, "Dance Could Bring Harmony to Ethnically Divided Pacific Nation." *Agence France Presse* (July 22, 2002).

Maus, Fred. "Music as Drama." *Music Theory Spectrum* 10 (1988): 56–73.

Maus, Fred. "Music as Narrative." *Indiana Theory Review* 12 (1991): 1–34.

Maus, Fred. "Narrative, Drama, and Emotion in Instrumental Music." *Journal of Aesthetics and Art Criticism* 55, no. 3 (1997): 293–303.

Maus, Fred. "Narratology, Narrativity." In *Grove Music Online, Oxford Music Online*. www.oxfordmusiconline.com (accessed November 11, 2010).

McClary, Susan. *Feminine Endings: Music, Gender and Sexuality*. Minneapolis: University of Minnesota Press, 1991.

McClary, Susan. "Getting Down Off the Beanstalk: The Presence of a Woman's Voice in Janika Vandervelde's Genesis II." *Minnesota Composer's Forum Newsletter*, February 1987.

McDonald, David A. "My Voice Is My Weapon: Music, Nationalism, and the Poetics of Palestinian Resistance." PhD diss., University of Illinois, 2006.

McDonald, David A. "Poetics and the Performance of Violence in Israel/Palestine." *Ethnomusicology* 53 (2009): 58–85.

McDowell, John. "Folklore as Commemorative Discourse." *The Journal of American Folklore* 105, no. 418 (1992): 403–23.

McDowell, John. *Poetry and Violence: The Ballad Tradition of Mexico's Costa Chica*. Champaign-Urbana: University of Illinois Press, 2008.

Mendoza, Zoila. *Creating Our Own: Folklore, Performance, and Identity in Cuzco, Peru*. Durham, NC: Duke University Press, 2008.

Menocal, María Rosa. *The Ornament of the World: How Muslims, Jews, and Christians Created a Culture of Tolerance in Medieval Spain*. Boston: Little, Brown and Co., 2002.

Merriam, Alan. *The Anthropology of Music*. Evanston, IL: Northwestern University Press, 1964.

"Mevlana Museum Expects Record Numbers of Tourists." *Hürriyet Daily News and Economic Review*, October 10, 2007. http://www.hurriyetdailynews.com/h.php?news=mevlana-museum-expects-record-number-of-tourists-2007-10-22 (accessed October 12, 2007).

Mihaljević, Mario. "Prestar sam i prekomotan da bih špijunirao izvođače." *Globus*, December 31, 1993.

Mihovilović, Maroje. "Novokomponirani poziv u rat." *Večernji list*, August 22, 1993.

Mikac, Nevenka. "Ja sam kraljica hrvatskog turbo folka!" *Večernji list*, April 28, 1996.

Miller, Kevin C. "A Community of Sentiment: Indo-Fijian Music and Identity Discourse in Fiji and its Diaspora." PhD diss., University of California, Los Angeles, 2008.

Milton, Cynthia. "Public Spaces for the Discussion of Peru's Recent Past." *Antípoda* 5 (2007): 143–68.

Mitton, Yvonne. "Mercan Dede, The Visual DJ." January 15, 2006. *World Music Central.org.* http://worldmusiccentral.org/2006/01/15/mercan-dede-the-visual-dj/ (accessed December 1, 2007).

Montoya, Rodrigo, et al. *Urqukunapa Yawarnin: La Sangre de los Cerros.* Lima, Peru: CEPES, Mosca Azul Editores, and UNMSM, 1987.

Moodley, Kogila "Canadian Multiculturalism as Ideology." *Ethnic and Racial Studies* 6, no. 3 (1983): 320–31.

Mujkić, Asim. "We, the Citizens of Ethnopolis." *Constellations* 14, no. 1 (2007): 112–28.

Muller, Carol. "American Musical Surrogacy: A View from Post-World War II South Africa." *Safundi* 7, no. 3 (July 2006): 1–18.

Murray, DJS. "Tattoo." *Grove Music Online, Oxford Music Online.* www.oxford musiconline.com. (accessed April 30, 2009).

Muśćet, Bojan. "Skladao sam domoljubne pjesme i prije pobjede HDZ-a!" *Slobodni tjednik*, March 19, 1993.

Naini, Majid M. *Mysteries of the Universe and Rumi's Discoveries on the Path of Love.* Delray Beach, FL: Universal Vision Research, 2002.

Nasr, Seyyed Hossein. "Islam and Music: The Legal and the Spiritual Dimensions." In *Enchanting Powers: Music in the World's Religions*, edited by Lawrence E. Sullivan, 219–35. Cambridge: Harvard University Press, 1997.

Nattiez, Jean-Jacques. "Can One Speak of Narrativity in Music?" *Journal of the Royal Music Association*, 15, no. 2 (1990): 240–57.

"Neda Ukraden nepoželjna u Gradiški." *Svet*, July 11, 2003.

Nedeljkov, Milovan. "Putuj Evropo, ne čekaj na nas." *Večernji list*, March 20, 1994.

Neues Deutschland (Berlin). March 3, 1966.

Newcomb, Anthony. "The Polonaise-Fantasy and Issues of Musical Narrative." In *Chopin Studies II*, edited by J. Rink and J. Sampson, 84–101. Cambridge: Cambridge University Press, 1994.

Newcomb, Anthony. "Schumann and Late Eighteenth-Century Narrative Strategies." *19th-Century Music* 11 (1987–8): 164–74.

Newham, Paul. *Therapeutic Voicework: Principles and Practice for the Use of Singing as a Therapy.* London: Jessica Kingsley Publishers, 1997.

Nicholson, Mavis. *What Did You Do in the War, Mummy? Women in World War II.* London: Chatto & Windus, 1995.

Nideffer, Robert. "Bodies, No-bodies, and Anti-bodies at War: Operation Desert Storm and the Politics of the 'Real.'" PhD diss., University of California at Santa Barbara, 1994. http://proxy.arts.uci.edu/~nideffer/BNAatWAR/ (accessed February 7, 2009).

Nietzsche, Friedrich. *Jenseits von Gut und Böse: Vorspiel einer Philosophie der Zukunft.* Stuttgart: Reclam, 1988 [1886].

"9/11 Was Not Only Against USA, But Also Against Islam." *The Rumi Forum.* http://www.rumiforum.org/server/index.php?option=com_content&task =view&id=308&Itemid=57 (accessed October 23, 2007).

"'No Jenin Massacre' says rights group." British Broadcasting Corporation, May 3, 2002. http://news.bbc.co.uk/2/hi/middle_east/1965471.stm (accessed on July 14, 2010).

Nora, Pierre. "Between Memory and History: Les lieux de mémoire." Translated by Marc Roudebush. *Representations* 26 (1989): 7–25.

Norddeutsche Zeitung, February 9, 1966.

Norton, Robert. "Reconciling Ethnicity and Nation: Contending Discourses in Fiji's Constitutional Reform." *The Contemporary Pacific* 12, no. 1 (2000): 83–122.

"Noten am Rande." *Neue Zeitschrift für Musik* 81 (1914): 490.

"Noten am Rande." *Neue Zeitschrift für Musik* 82 (1915): 301–2.

"Noten am Rande." *Neue Zeitschrift für Musik* 84 (1917): 171.

"Novel Discs for Your Shelter." *Melody Maker* (September 28, 1940): 9.

O'Connell, John Morgan. "Introduction: An Ethnomusicological Approach to Music and Conflict." In *Music and Conflict*, edited by John Morgan O'Connell and Salwa El-Shawan Castelo-Branco, 1–14. Urbana: University of Illinois Press, 2010.

O'Connell, John Morgan. "Music in War, Music for Peace: A Review Article." *Ethnomusicology* 55, no. 1 (Winter 2011): 112–27.

O'Connell, John Morgan, and Salwa El-Shawan Castelo-Branco (eds). *Music and Conflict.* Champaign-Urbana, IL: University of Illinois Press, 2010.

Oliver, Anne M., and Paul Steinberg. "Popular Music of the Intifada." In *Garland Encyclopedia of World Music: The Middle East*, vol. 6, edited by Virginia Danielson, Scott L. Marcus, and Dwight. Reynolds, 635–40. New York: Garland. 2002.

Oliver, Anne M., and Paul Steinberg. *The Road to Martyr's Square: A Journey in the World of the Suicide Bomber.* Oxford: Oxford University Press, 2005.

Oremović, Arsen. "Logično je da ja snimam u Zagrebu!" *Večernji list*, November 17, 2000.

"Ostvarena volja građana." *Večernji list*, June 26, 1991.

Paldum, Hanka. "Ponosna sam što sam, za razliku od Nade Topčagić, ostala vjerna svom narodu." *Balkanmedia*, September 2001. http://muzika14.tripod.com/ interwievs/id33.html (accessed October 14, 2008).

Paldum, Hanka. "Razočarali su me Suzana Mančić, Miroslav Ilić, Neda Ukraden . . ." *Balkanmedia*, October 2001. http://muzika14.tripod.com/ interwievs/id34.html (accessed October 14, 2008).

Palmer, Edgar A. *GI Songs: Written, Composed and/or Collected by Men in the Service.* New York: Sheridan House, 1944.

Parsifal. Neue Zeitschrift für Musik 79 (1912): 173ff.

Pavlović, Pavle. "Nedin visoki C." *Arena*, December 8, 1990.

Payne, Leigh. *Unsettling Accounts: Neither Truth nor Reconciliation in Confessions of State Violence.* Durham, NC: Duke University Press, 2008.

Pektaş, Ali. "Mercan Dede: We Need Tolerance More than Ever." *Today's Zaman*, November 9, 2007. http://www.todayszaman.com/tz-web/detaylar.do?load =detay&link=126632 (accessed December 1, 2007).

Peter, Laurence J. *Peter's Quotations: Ideas for Our Time.* New York: Morrow, 1977.

Peters, Robert. *For You, Lili Marlene: A Memoir of World War II.* Madison: University of Wisconsin Press, 1995.

Pettan, Svandibor. "Music in War, Music for Peace: Experiences in Applied Ethnomusicology." In *Music in Conflict*, edited by John Morgan O'Connell and Salwa El-Shawan Castelo-Branco, 177–192. Urbana: University of Illinois Press, 2010.

Pettan, Svandibor. *Music, Politics and War: Views from Croatia.* Zagreb: Institute of Ethnology and Folklore Research, 1998.

Phillips, Nicola. "Book Review: Michel Chion, *Audio-Vision: Sound on Screen*." *FilmSound.org.* http://filmsound.org/philips.htm (accessed February 7, 2009).

"Pick-Up." *Melody Maker* (September 28, 1940): 9.

Pieslak, Jonathan. *Sound Targets: American Soldiers and Music in the Iraq War.* Bloomington: Indiana University Press, 2009.

Pillai, Raymond C. "Culture and the Fiji Indian." Transcript of Radio Fiji Program, *In My View*, 1978.

"A Plea for Restorative Justice." *Fijilive*, June 17, 2005, www.fijilive.com (accessed October 12, 2007).

Poche, Christian. "Zikr and Musicology." *The World of Music* 20, no. 1 (1978): 59–71.

Pochhammer. "Soll die Kunst in den Streit der Völker hineingezogen werden?" *Neue Zeitschrift für Musik* 81 (1914): 549–50.

"Postala sam zvezda preko noči." *Blic*, May 5, 2004.

Potter, Pamela M. *Most German of the Arts: Musicology and Society from the Weimar Republic to the End of Hitler's Reich.* New Haven, CT: Yale University Press, 1998.

Pratt, Mary Louise. "Harm's Way: Language and the Contemporary Arts of War." *PMLA* 124, no. 5 (2009): 1515–31.

Pribić, Sanja. "Narodnjaci protjerani zbog stida: Televizija tvrdi da brine o dobrom ukusu." *TV Best*, May 30, 1991.

Prica, Ines. "Na tlu trivijalnog: Pismo iz trancizije." *Narodna umjetnost* 41, no. 2 (2004): 141–56.

Prümers, Adolf. "Das deutsche Musikleben und seine 'Entlausung.'" *Neue Zeitschrift für Musik* 82 (1915): 276.

Prümers, Adolf. "Die Überlebenden." *Neue Zeitschrift für Musik* 83 (1916): 89.

Pukanić, Ivo. "Likvidirala sam Nedu Ukraden!" *Globus*, February 26, 1993.

Radano, Ronald Michael. *Music and the Racial Imagination.* Chicago: University of Chicago Press, 2000.

Ragogo, Matelita. "Dance Could Bring Harmony to Ethnically Divided Pacific Nation." *Agence France Presse* [English]. July 22, 2002.

Rapaport, Lynn. *Jews in Germany after the Holocaust: Memory, Identity, and Jewish-German Relations.* Cambridge: Cambridge University Press, 1997.

Rasmussen, Ljerka V. *Newly Composed Folk Music of Yugoslavia.* London: Routledge, 2002.

Ratuva, Steven. "Towards Multiculturalism and Affirmative Action: A Case for Fiji." In *Educating for Multiculturalism*, edited by Jill Cottrell, 65–73. Suva: Citizens' Constitutional Forum, 1998.

Readings, Bill. *The University in Ruins.* Cambridge, MA: Harvard University Press, 1996.

Remarque, Erich Maria. *All Quiet on the Western Front.* Translated by A. W. Wheen. London: Putnam, 1929.

Richmond, Portia. "Never the Twain Shall Meet? Causal Factors in Fijian-Indian Intermarriage." MA thesis, University of Hawaii, 2003.

Riemann Musik-Lexikon, 12th ed. Mainz, 1967.

Rihtman-Auguštin, Dunja. "The Monument in the Main City Square: Constructing and Erasing Memory in Contemporary Croatia." In *Balkan Identities: Nation and Memory*, edited by Maria Todorova, 180–96. London: Hurst, 2004.

Rihtman-Auguštin, Dunja. *Ulice moga grada: Antropologija domaćeg terena.* Belgrade: Biblioteka XX vek, 2000.

Riley, Denise, and Jean-Jacques Lecercle. *The Force of Language.* New York: Palgrave Macmillan, 2004.

Ritter, Jonathan. "Siren Songs: Ritual and Revolution in the Peruvian Andes." *British Journal of Ethnomusicology* 11, no. 1 (2002): 9–42.

Ritter, Jonathan, and Martin Daughtry, eds. *Music in the Post-9/11 World.* New York: Routledge, 2007.

Roach, Joseph. *Cities of the Dead: Circum-Atlantic Performance.* New York: Columbia University Press, 1996.

Rolland, Romain. *La vie de Beethoven*, 28th ed. Paris: Hachette, 1953.

Romero, Raúl, ed. *Música, danzas, y mascaras en los Andes.* Lima: Pontificía Universidad Católica del Perú, 2003.

Rosaldo, Michelle. "The Things We Do with Words: Ilongot Speech Acts and Speech Act Theory in Philosophy." *Language in Society* 11, no. 2 (1982): 203–37.

Rose, Sonya O. *Which People's War? National Identity and Citizenship in Britain 1939–1945.* Oxford: Oxford University Press, 2003.

Rosenberg, Sharon. "Neither Forgotten nor Fully Remembered: Tracing an Ambivalent Public Memory on the Tenth Anniversary of the Montreal Massacre." *Feminist Theory* 4, no. 1 (April 2003): 5–27. doi: 10.1177/1464700103004001001.

Rosenberg, Sharon. "Standing in a Circle of Stone." In *Between Hope and Despair: Pedagogy and the Remembrance of Historical Trauma*, edited by Roger I. Simon, Sharon Rosenberg, and Claudia Eppert, 75–90. Lanham, MD: Rowman & Littlefield, 2000.

Sachs, Albie. "What Is Truth? South Africa's Truth and Reconciliation Commission." Public lecture given at the Chautauqua Institution on June 26, 2002.

Sächsische Zeitung (Dresden). February 23, 1966.

SAPMO. "Beschlussauszuege von Sitzungen des Politibüro." May 31, 1988. DY30/5178.

SAPMO. Letter from Loeffler to Jarowinsky, August 18, 1988. DY 30/9052.

SAPMO. Memo, August 18, 1988 DY 30/9669.

SAPMO. Memo, August 25, 1988, DY 30/9052.

SAPMO. "Vorlage für das Politibüro des Zentralkomitees. Betreff: Massnahmen zum 50. Jahrestag der faschistischen Pogromnacht vom 9.11.1938." May 26, 1988. DY 30/9051.

"Sarajevo, gde je moja raja?" *Kurir*, May 6, 2004.

Schaefer, Hans Jürgen. "Verantwortung für Heute und Morgen." *Neues Deutschland* (Berlin). January 17, 1966.

Schechner, Richard. *Between Theater and Anthropology.* Philadelphia: University of Pennsylvania Press, 1985 [2002].

Schechter, Danny. *Embedded: Weapons of Mass Deception: How the Media Failed to Cover the War in Iraq.* Amherst, NY: Prometheus Books, 2003.

Schechter, Danny. *Media Wars: News at a Time of Terror.* Lanham, MD: Rowman & Littlefield, 2003.

Schechter, Danny. *When News Lies: Media Complicity and the Iraq War.* New York: Select Books, 2006.

Schoenberg, Arnold. *Style and Idea.* Edited by Leonard Stein. Translated by Leo Black. London: Faber and Faber, 1975.

Schorn, Hans. "Klaviere und Klavierwerke für Einarmige," *Neue Zeitschrift für Musik* 84 (1917): 229.

Schrader, Bruno. "Berliner Brief." *Neue Zeitschrift für Musik* 81 (1914): 511–12

Scott, Amy. "La Guerre du Golfe a-t-elle vraiment lieu?" *Libération* (February 6, 1991): 10.

Scott, Amy. *La Guerre du Golfe n'a pas eu lieu.* Paris: Galilée, 1991.

Scott, Amy. "La Guerre du Golfe n'a pas eu lieu." *Libération* (March 29, 1991): 6.

Scott, Amy. "La Guerre du Golfe n'aura pas eu lieu." *Libération* (January 4, 1991): 5.

Scott, Janny. "The President under Fire: The Media; a Media Race Enters Waters Still Uncharted," *New York Times*, February 1, 1998, Late Edition — Final, Section 1:1, www.nytimes.com (accessed February 7, 2009).

Scott, Marion M. *Beethoven*. London: JM Dent, 1974.

Searle, John. *Speech Acts*. Cambridge: Cambridge University Press, 1969.

Seeger, Anthony. *Why Suyá Sing*. Cambridge: Cambridge University Press, 1987.

Shannon, Jonathan H. "Sultans of Spin: Syrian Sacred Music on the World Stage." *American Anthropologist* 105, no. 2 (2003): 266–77.

Shelton, Anne (dir.) and Stanley Black. "Lilli Marlene," Decca F 8434, 1944 (reissued on compact disc 2 of *Lili Marleen*).

Shelton, Anne (dir.) Paul Fenoulhet, "The Wedding of Lilli Marlene," Decca F 9148, 1949 (reissued on compact disc 5 of *Lili Marleen*).

Shiloah, Amnon. "The Meeting of Christian, Jewish, and Muslim Musical Cultures on the Iberian Peninsula (before 1492)." *Acta Musicologica* 64, no.1 (1991): 14–20.

Shiloah, Amnon. *Music in the Islamic World: A Socio-Cultural Study*. Detroit: Wayne State University Press, 1995.

Shishido, Rika. *Die Neue Musik-Zeitung (1880–1928): Geschichte, Inhalt, Bedeutung*. Göttingen: Hainholz, 2004.

"Sing a Song from London." *Parade* 7, no. 81, Cairo (February 28, 1942): 16.

Singh, Anendra. "Making It Big on the Local Music Scene." *Fiji Times*, September 10, 1986.

Singing the Living Tradition. Boston: Unitarian Universalist Association, 1993.

Skender, Melisa. "D Dvornik i ET pjevaju za Pale Records u piratskom izdanju." *Večernji list*, June 29, 1997.

Small, Melvin. *Covering Dissent: The Media and the Anti-Vietnam War Movement*. New Brunswick, NJ: Rutgers University Press, 1994.

Solie, Ruth. *Musicology and Difference: Gender and Sexuality in Music Scholarship*. Berkeley: University of California Press, 1995.

Somerville, Ian Keith. "The Ramayan Mandli Movement: Popular Hindu Theism in Fiji, 1879–1979." MA thesis, University of Sydney, 1986.

Sonneborn, Daniel A. "Music and Meaning in American Sufism: The Ritual of Dhikr at Sami Mahal, A Chishtiyya-Derived Sufi Center." PhD diss., University of California, Los Angeles, 1995.

Sontag, Susan. *On Photography*. London: Allen Lane, 1978.

Sontag, Susan. *Regarding the Pain of Others*. New York: Farrar, Straus and Giroux, 2003.

Soundtrack to War. Directed by George Gittoes. Documentary film. Sydney, Australia: Gittoes and Dalton Production, 2005.

Spector, Bert. "A Clash of Cultures: The Smothers Brothers vs. CBS Television." In *American History, American Television*, edited by John E. O'Connor, 159–83. New York: Frederick Ungar, 1983.

Sponheuer, Bernd. "Reconstructing Ideal Types of the 'German' in Music." In *Music and German National Identity*, edited by Celia Applegate and Pamela Potter. Chicago: University of Chicago Press, 2002.

Stan, Adele M. "War Porn with a Beat." *Tapped: The Group Blog of the American Prospect*, July 19, 2006. www.prospect.org (accessed February 7, 2009).

Stanyek, Jason, and Benjamin Piekut. "Deadness: Technologies of the Intermundane." *TDR* 54, no. 1 (2010): 14–38.

Stauffer, George B. *Bach, the Mass in B-Minor: The Great Catholic Mass*. New Haven, CT: Yale University Press, 2003.

Steinberg, Michael. "The Late Quartets." In *The Beethoven Quartet Companion*, edited by Robert Winter and Robert Martin, 215–45. Los Angeles: University of California Press, 1994.

Sterling, Terry Greene. *Illegal: Life and Death in Arizona's Immigration War Zone*. Guilford, CT: Lyons Press, 2010.

Stiftung Archiv der Akademie der Künste. Dr. Lothar Kolditz, Präsident des Naitonalrates der Nationalen Front der DDR. November 9, 1988. Berlin: Rudolf-Wagner-Régeny-Archive. Nr. 1439.

Stiftung Archiv der Akademie der Künste. Letter from Paul Dessau to Boris Blacher, no date (probably late August 1961). Berlin, Paul Dessau Archiv. 1.74.1814.1.

Stiftung Archiv der Akademie der Künste. Program notes, January 14, 1966 performance in Cologne. Berlin, Rudolf-Wagner-Régeny-Archive. Nr. 497.

Stiftung Archiv der Akademie der Künste. Program notes, January 14, 1966 performance in Cologne. Berlin, Rudolf-Wagner-Régeny-Archive. Nr. 497.

Stiftung Archiv der Akademie der Künste. Program Notes, February 15, 1966 performance in Leipzig. Berlin, Rudolf-Wagner-Régeny-Archive. Nr. 497.

Stiftung Archiv der Akademie der Künste. Telegram from Karl Amadeus Hartmann to Paul Dessau, August 28, 1961. Berlin, Paul Dessau Archiv. Nr. 1.74.270.2.

Stokes, Martin. "Introduction: Ethnicity, Identity, and Music." In *Ethnicity, Identity, and Music: The Musical Construction of Place*, edited by M. Stokes, 1–33. Oxford: Berg, 1994.

Stradal, August. "Anton Bruckners erste Sinfonie in c-moll." *Neue Zeitschrift für Musik* 79 (1912): 69–71, 81–83.

Stras, Laurie. "The Organ of the Soul: Voice, Damage, and Affect." In *Sounding Off: Theorizing Disability in Music*, edited by Neil Lerner and Joseph N. Straus. 173–84. New York: Routledge, 2006.

Sweeney, Regina. *Singing Our Way to Victory: French Cultural Politics and Music during the Great War*. Middletown, CT: Wesleyan University Press, 2001.

Tagg, Philip. "An Anthropology of Stereotypes in TV Music?" *Svensk Tidskrift för Musikforskning* 71 (1989): 19–42.

Tagg, Philip. "Music, Moving Images, Semiotics, and the Democratic Right to Know." In *Music and Manipulation: On the Social Uses and Social Control of*

Music, edited by Steven Brown and Ulrik Volgsten, 163–86. New York: Berghahn Books, 2006.

Tappert, Wilhelm. "Feinde ringsum! Krieg gegen die deutsche Musikwissenschaft." *Neue Zeitschrift für Musik* 81 (1914): 518.

Tappert, Wilhelm. "Unsere Musikprogramme und Deutschlands Feinde. Eine Anregung." *Neue Zeitschrift für Musik* 81 (1914): 487.

Taruskin, Richard. "Nationalism." In *Grove Music Online, Oxford Music Online*. www.oxfordmusiconline.com (accessed November 11, 2010).

Taylor, Diana. *The Archive and the Repertoire: Performing Cultural Memory in the Americas*. Durham, NC: Duke University Press, 2003.

Taylor, Paul. *Žižek and the Media*. Cambridge: Polity Press, 2010.

Theidon, Kimberly. *Entre prójimos: El conflicto armado interno y la política de la reconciliación en el Perú*. Lima: Instituto de Estudios Peruanos, 2004.

Thompson, Mark. *Forging War: The Media in Serbia, Croatia and Bosnia-Herzegovina*. London: Article 19, 1994.

Thussu, Daya Kishan. *News as Entertainment: The Rise of Global Infotainment*. London: Sage, 2007.

Timm, Angelika. *Jewish Claims against East Germany: Moral Obligations and Pragmatic Policy*. Budapest: Central European University Press, 1988.

Titon, Jeff Todd. *Powerhouse for God: Speech, Chant and Song in an Appalachian Baptist Church*. Austin: University of Texas Press, 1988.

Tom Waits v. Frito-Lay Inc., et al., 978F.2d 1093 (9th Cir. 1992). Available at www .law.umkc.edu/faculty/projects/ftrials/communications/waits.html (accessed December 31, 2010).

Tomatis, Alfred. *The Ear and the Voice*. Translated by Roberta Prada. Lanham, MD: Scarecrow Press, 2005.

Tomić, Vladimir. "Sin mi je rođen kao princ, umro kao pas, a pokopan kao kralj!" *Globus*, October 16, 1992.

Tucker, Joshua. "Mediating Sentiment and Shaping Publics: Recording Practice and the Articulation of Social Change in Andean Lima." *Popular Music and Society* 33, no. 2 (2010): 141–62.

Tucker, Joshua. "Sounding Out a New Peru: Music, Media, and the Emergent Andean Public." PhD dissertation (ethnomusicology), University of Michigan, 2005.

Tucker, Ken. "Talk, Then Action: Summing Up the Persian Gulf War Coverage." *Entertainment Weekly* 57 (March 15, 1991). www.ew.com/ew/article/0,,313645,00. html (accessed February 7, 2009).

Turino, Thomas. *Moving Away from Silence: Music of the Peruvian Altiplano and the Experience of Urban Migration*. Chicago: University of Chicago Press, 1993.

Turino, Thomas. *Music as Social Life: The Politics of Participation*. Chicago: University of Chicago Press, 2008.

Turino, Thomas. "The Music of Andean Migrants in Lima, Peru: Demographics, Social Power, and Style." *Latin American Music Review* 9, no. 2 (1988): 127–50.

Turino, Thomas. *Nationalists, Cosmopolitans, and Popular Music in Zimbabwe.* Chicago: University of Chicago Press, 2000.

Turino, Thomas. "The State and Andean Musical Production in Peru." In *The Nation-State and Indian in Latin America*, edited by Joel Sherzer and Greg Urban, 259–85. Austin: University of Texas Press, 1991.

"Turkey to Celebrate Rumi's Birthday with a Giant Sema Performance." *Hürriyet Daily News and Economic Review*, September 28, 2007. http://www.hurriyetdaily news.com/h.php?news=turkey-to-celebrate-rumis-birthday-with-a-giant-sema -performance-2007-09-28 (accessed September 30, 2007).

Ugrešič, Dubravka. *The Culture of Lies: Anti-Political Essays.* Translated by Celia Hawkesworth. London: Phoenix, 1998.

Ukraden, Neda. "Beograd je za sve bolji osim za svoju decu i Srbe." *Balkanmedia.* www.balkanmedia.com/magazin/dzungla/7/index.html (accessed 23 October 2006).

Ukraden, Neda. "Publika u Hrvatskoj i Sloveniji se zaželela Nede Ukraden." *Balkanmedia*, September 2001. http://muzika14.tripod.com/interwievs/id22 .html (accessed 14 October 2008).

Unger, Max. "Beethoven 'der Belgier.'" *Neue Zeitschrift für Musik* 81 (1914): 557–59.

Unger, Max. "Das Vierteltonsystem und die moderne Musik." *Neue Zeitschrift für Musik* 79 (1912): 161–63.

Unger, Max. "Friedrich Brandes. Zu seinem 50. Geburtstag am 18. November." *Neue Zeitschrift für Musik* 81 (1914): 548.

Urbain, Oliver, ed. *Music and Conflict Transformation: Harmonies and Dissonances in Geopolitics.* London: I.B. Tauris & Co., 2008.

"Urednici pamte samo prošlost." *Glas javnosti*, November 26, 2000.

Uzelac, Gordana. "Franjo Tudjman's Nationalist Ideology." *East European Quarterly* 31, no. 4 (1998): 449–72.

Velikonja, Mitja. "Ex-Home: 'Balkan Culture' in Slovenia after 1991." In *The Balkans in Focus: Cultural Boundaries in Europe*, edited by Barbara Törnquist-Plewa and Sanimir ResiÐ, 189–207. Lund: Nordic Academic Press, 2002.

Verbandes Deutscher Komponisten und Musikwissenschaftler. "Im Spiegel der Presse." *Informationsblatt* 2 (1966).

Vergara, Albilio. *La Tierra Que Duele de Carlos Falconí.* Ayacucho, Peru: Universidad Nacional de San Cristóbal de Huamanga, 2010.

Verhey, Jeffery. *The Spirit of 1914: Militarism, Myth and Mobilization in Germany.* Cambridge: Cambridge University Press, 2000.

Vicente, Victor A. "The Aesthetics of Motion in Musics for the Mevlana Celal Ed-Din Rumi." PhD diss., University of Maryland, 2007.

Vicente, Victor A. "Sounds Like Sufi Spirit: Sufism in Popular Music and Culture." *İzmir Ulusal Müzik Sempozyumu Bildiriler Kitabı*, edited by Paolo Susanni and Uzay Bora. Yaşar University, 2010. http://izmirulusalmuziksem pozyumu.yasar.edu.tr/ulmusebk.pdf (accessed December 1, 2007).

"Viet Sweep: Troops Take Cong Stronghold, 1967/02/28 (1967)." *Internet Archive Collection of Universal Newsreels*. http://archive.org/details/1967-02-28_Viet _Sweep (accessed February 7, 2009).

Virilio, Paul. *Desert Screen: War at the Speed of Light*. Translated by Michael Degener. London: Continuum, 2002.

Virilio, Paul. *War and Cinema: The Logistics of Perception*. Translated by Patrick Camiller. London: Verso, 1989.

von Treitschke, Heinrich. *Historische und Politische Aufsätze*. 4th ed. Leipzig: S. Hirzel, 1871.

Voreqe Bainimarama, address to the United Nations General Assembly, September 28, 2007. Excerpt of full transcript from *Pacific Islands Report*. http://pidp .eastwestcenter.org (accessed October 16, 2007).

"Voreqe Bainimarama's Press Statement," December 5, 2006. www.fijitimes.com/ extras/TakeOverAddress.pdf (accessed December 5, 2006).

Vukšić, Branko. "Doživio sam uzvraćenu ljubav." *Večernji list*, August 12, 1994.

Vuletić, Dean. "Generation Number One: Politics and Popular Music in Yugoslavia in the 1950s." *Nationalities Papers* 36, no. 5 (2008): 861–79.

Wade, Bonnie C. *Imagining Sound: An Ethnomusicological Study of Music, Art, and Culture in Mughal, India*. Chicago: University of Chicago Press, 1998.

Wagner, Renata, ed. *Karl Amadeus Hartmann und die Musica Viva*. Münich: R. Piper & Co. Verlag, 1980.

Wagner, Richard. "Der deutsche Geist. Aus Wagners Schrift 'Was ist deutsch?'" *Neue Zeitschrift für Musik* 81 (1914): 485.

Waley, Muhammad Isa. "Contemplative Disciplines in Early Persian Sufism." In *Classical Persian Sufism: From Its Origins to Rumi*. Vol. 1 of *The Heritage of Sufism*, edited by Leonard Lewisohn, 497–508. Oxford: Oneworld Publications, 1999.

"The Wedding of Lili Marlene." *International Lyrics Playground*. http://lyricsplay ground.com (accessed April 30, 2009).

Whitaker, Brian. "'Its Best Use Is as a Doorstop.'" *Guardian*, May 24, 2004. www.guardian.co.uk (accessed November 20, 2011).

Wiedmer, Caroline. *The Claims of Memory: Representations of the Holocaust in Contemporary Germany and France*. Ithaca, NY: Cornell University Press, 1999.

Wiest, Andrew. *Rolling Thunder in a Gentle Land: The Vietnam War Revisited.* New York: Osprey Publishing, 2006.

Wilbourne, Emily. "La Florinda: The Performance of Virginia Ramponi Andreini." PhD diss., New York University, 2008.

Wilson, Richard. *The Politics of Truth and Reconciliation in South Africa: Legitimizing the Post-Apartheid State.* Cambridge: Cambridge University Press, 2001.

Winegar, Jessica. "The Humanity Game: Art, Islam, and the War on Terror." *Anthropological Quarterly* 81, no. 3 (2008): 651–81.

Winter, Jay, and Emmanuel Sivan, eds. *War and Remembrance in the Twentieth Century.* Cambridge: Cambridge University Press, 1999.

Witt, Bertha. "Charles François Gounod. Zum 100. Geburtstag, 17. Juni 1918." *Neue Zeitschrift für Musik* 85 (1918): 129–30.

Wolfe, Charles K., and James E. Akenson, eds. *Country Music Goes to War.* Lexington: University Press of Kentucky, 2005.

Wood, Elizabeth. "Sapphonics." In *Queering the Pitch: The New Gay and Lesbian Musicology,* edited by Philip Brett, Elizabeth Wood, and Gary C. Thomas, 27–66. New York: Routledge, 1994.

Wood, Paul. "'No Jenin Massacre' Says Rights Group." *British Broadcasting Corporation,* May 3, 2002. http://news.bbc.co.uk/2/hi/middle_east/1965471.stm (accessed July 14, 2010).

Wood, William A. *Electronic Journalism.* New York: Columbia University Press, 1967.

Yekta Bey, Raouf. *Mevlevi Ayînleri.* Istanbul: Istanbul Belediye Konservatuarı, 1923–1939.

Yezer, Caroline. "Who Wants to Know? Rumors, Suspicions, and Opposition to Truth-Telling in Ayacucho." *Latin American and Caribbean Ethnic Studies* 3, no. 3 (2008): 271–89.

Yorck, Ruth. *Lili Marlene: An Intimate Diary.* New York: Reader's Press, 1945.

Young, James E. *At Memory's Edge: After-Images of the Holocaust in Contemporary Art and Architecture.* New Haven, CT: Yale University Press, 2000.

Young, James E. *The Texture of Memory: Holocaust Memorials and Meaning.* New Haven, CT: Yale University Press, 1993.

Zakošek, Nenad. "The Legitimation of War: Political Construction of a New Reality." In *Media and War.* Edited by Nena Skopljanac Brunner et al., 109–16. Zagreb: Centre for Transition and Civil Society Research/Belgrade: Agency Argument, 2000.

Žanić, Ivo. *Flag on the Mountain: A Political Anthropology of War in Croatia and Bosnia.* London: Saqi, 2007.

Žarkov, Dubravka. *The Body of War: Media, Ethnicity and Gender in the Break-Up of Yugoslavia.* Durham, NC: Duke University Press, 2007.

Zelizer, Barbie. "Reading against the Grain: The Shape of Memory Studies."
    Critical Studies in Mass Communication 12, no. 2 (1995): 215–39.

Žižek, Slavoj. *Violence: Six Sideways Reflections.* New York: Picador, 2008.

Zlatar, Pero. "Neda Ukraden tuži Republiku Hrvatsku za 200.000 DEM!"
    Slobodni tjednik, April 16, 1993.

Zlatar, Pero. "Tko su poznati Hrvati u Beogradu? Što rade i kako žive?" *Slobodni
    tjednik*, January 8, 1993.

Contributors

NICHOLAS ATTFIELD is a British Academy postdoctoral fellow in the Faculty of Music, University of Oxford. His research addresses German and Austrian music in the late nineteenth and twentieth centuries, with a particular focus on the symphony, opera, and intersections with political and cultural movements. In preparation is a monograph on musical conservatism during the Weimar Republic.

CHRISTINA BAADE is associate professor in communication studies at McMaster University in Hamilton, Ontario. She has published work on popular music broadcasting at the wartime BBC, music and cultural memory, and American klezmer, including chapters in *Big Ears: Listening for Gender in Jazz* (Duke) and *Floodgates: Technologies, Cultural Ex/change and the Persistence of Place* (Peter Lang); articles in *Popular Music, Journal of Popular Music Studies, Atlantis: a Women's Studies Journal,* and *Feminist Media Studies*; and a monograph *"Victory Through Harmony": The BBC and Popular Music in World War II* (2011).

CATHERINE BAKER is a teaching fellow in Nationalism and Ethnic Conflict at University College London and a research assistant at the University of Southampton. She is the author of *Sounds of the Borderland: Popular Music, War and Nationalism in Croatia since 1991* (Ashgate, 2010) and a coauthor of two forthcoming books on languages and coalition military operations. Her work on popular music and politics in former Yugoslavia has appeared in *Popular Communication, Nationalities Papers, Journal of Contemporary European Studies, Ethnopolitics, Europe-Asia Studies,* and *Narodna umjetnost.* Her articles on aspects of international intervention in Bosnia-Herzegovina have been published in *Journal of War and Culture Studies, War and Society,* and *Journeys: The International Journal of Travel and Travel Writing.*

J. MARTIN DAUGHTRY is assistant professor of ethnomusicology at New York University. His work on musical nationalism, voice, and underground media in Soviet and post-Soviet Russia has been published in the journals *Ethnomusicology*, *Poetics Today*, and *Russian Literature*. Currently he is completing a monograph on sound, listening, and violence within the context of Operation Iraqi Freedom. He is also a sound designer for "Virtual Iraq," a virtual-reality PTSD treatment program created by the Institute for Creative Technologies (USC) for use in VA hospitals throughout the United States.

JAMES DEAVILLE is professor in the School for Studies in Art and Culture at Carleton University, Ottawa. He has published in the *Journal of the American Musicological Society*, *Journal of the Society for American Music*, and *Music, Sound and the Moving Image* (among others), has contributed to several books, and is editor of *Music in Television: Channels of Listening* (Routledge, 2011). He has published about music, television, and conflict in *Music in the Post-9/11 World* and *Echo*.

SUSAN FAST is professor in the Department of English and Cultural Studies at McMaster University. Her areas of expertise include representations of gender and sexuality, race and ethnicity, constructions of self and other, and performance and performativity in popular music. She is author of the book *In the Houses of the Holy: Led Zeppelin and the Power of Rock Music* (Oxford, 2001). Her current research project, funded by the Social Sciences and Humanities Research Council of Canada, investigates issues related to gender, race, and normative genre boundaries in rock music, and includes case studies on tribute bands, backup singing, and Michael Jackson.

DAVID A. MCDONALD is assistant professor of Folklore and Ethnomusicology at Indiana University. Since 2002 he has worked closely with Palestinian communities in Israel, Jordan, and the West Bank, researching the role of music and dance in the amelioration of severe sociocultural trauma. His interests include violence, popular culture, gender performativity, and the role of music and dance in the Palestinian resistance movement.

KEVIN C. MILLER holds a PhD in ethnomusicology and a master's degree in library and information studies, both from the University of California, Los Angeles. His research interests include the music cultures of the Pacific and the South Asian diaspora, and the ways in which these music cultures are represented in libraries, archives, and museums. His dissertation, "A Community of Sentiment: Indo-Fijian Music and Identity Discourse in Fiji and Its Diaspora," was completed in 2008. He is currently digital collections coordinator at Pepperdine University in Malibu, California.

KIP PEGLEY is associate professor in the School of Music at Queen's University, Canada, with cross-appointments to the Department of Film and Media, the Department of Gender Studies, and the Graduate Programme in Cultural Studies. Her book, *Coming to You Wherever You Are: MuchMusic, MTV, and Youth Identities*, was published by Wesleyan University Press in 2008. She is a recent recipient of a research grant from the Social Sciences and Humanities Research Council of Canada for her work on music, war, and Canadian identity.

JONATHAN RITTER is associate professor of ethnomusicology at the University of California, Riverside. A specialist in the indigenous and Afro-Hispanic musical cultures of Andean South America, he received his MA and PhD in ethnomusicology from UCLA, and his BA (summa cum laude) in American Indian Studies from the University of Minnesota. He is coeditor, with Martin Daughtry, of *Music in the Post-9/11 World* (Routledge, 2007).

VICTOR A. VICENTE received his BA degree from Franklin and Marshall College before completing graduate studies at the University of Maryland where he earned an MM in historical musicology and MA and PhD degrees in ethnomusicology. He specializes in the musical and movement cultures of Turkey, India, and Portugal and has published on such topics as aesthetics, ritual, politics, tourism, and cultural representation. He is an assistant professor in the Music Department at the Chinese University of Hong Kong, and has previously taught at the University of Maryland, George Washington University, the College at Brockport (SUNY), and at Ege University in Izmir, Turkey.

AMY LYNN WLODARSKI is assistant professor of music at Dickinson College. She received her PhD from the Eastman School of Music and publishes regularly on the relationship between music, memory, and Holocaust representation. Her work has appeared in the *Journal of the American Musicological Society* and the *Journal of Musicology*.

Index

Braeckman, Colette, 256
Brandes, Friedrich, 41, 55n7
breath, metaphysics and metaphor of, 243–45
Bregović, Goran, 75, 76
Brena, Lepa, 65, 77n20
Brendel, Franz, 40
British adoption of "Lili Marlene," 83, 87, 88, 91
Brkić, Dragica, 69
Brown, Wendy, 25
Brubaker, Rogers, 62
"Bula Maleya," 178, 181, 191n19
Bulutsuzluk Özlemi (The Longing for Uncloudiness), 152
Burke, Edmund, 119
Bush, George H. W., 117–18
Butler, Judith, 1, 13–16, 19, 20–21

Calico, Joy, 223
Cambodia, American invasion of, 111, 113
Cameron, John, 6
Campbell, David, 18
canción social ayacuchana, 195–96, 198–99, 200, 204–15, 217n4, 220n28, 221n38, 222n43
Caruth, Cathy, 20
Castelo-Branco, Salwa El-Shawan, 2
Cavarero, Adriana, 244
CBS News, 106
celebrity culture and benefit concerts as symbolic violence, 5–6
Chanel, Shobna, 177–78
charity, positive and negative social attributes, 5–7
Chaudry, Mahendra, 181–82
Christian Indo-Fijians, 192–93n32
Cinema 2: The Time-Image (Deleuze), 105
cinéma vérité style for broadcast network news, 110
Clarke, Eric, 15
Cloonan, Martin, 1, 259
CNN and Persian Gulf War, 105, 114–19
Cold War, effect on collective memory in divided Germany, 223, 235
Čolić, Zdravko, 75
collaborative dance in Fiji, 172, 176–83, 189, 191nn16, 191nn18–19
collective memory of violence, 18–26, 195–96, 199, 218n9. See also Jüdische Chronik; Peruvian memorialization and reconciliation
colonialism and Fijian ethnic divide, 173, 175

commemorative vs. informative discourse, 216
commercializing of Sufi practices, 156–57
compassion fatigue, 18–19
"Concerts for Memory," Peru, 199
concurso, 206
Connor, Steven, 249–50
Connor, Tommie, 92, 96
counter-memories and Jüdische Chronik, 196
coup culture in Fiji, 171, 177, 183–84, 189
creative indexing by Palestinian performers, 140
crisis of sovereignty, 12–13
Croatian national identity, 62, 63–73, 74–75
Cross, Charles, 15–16
cross-cultural performance. See Fiji Islands
cultural mosaic model, 175–76
culture: expectations and reception of vocal performance, 248; identity and political resistance in Peru, 210; Mevlevi Sufi music and intercultural understanding, 165–66. See also Fiji Islands; Ukraden, Neda
Cusick, Suzanne, 256–57
CVR (Peruvian Truth and Reconciliation Commission), 199–204, 215–16, 218n10

dabke, 138, 139
Dalmatian Hinterland music, 75, 79–80n56
DAM (Da Arab MCs), 145–46
Dass, Satvik, 185
David, Mack, 92
Dede, Mercan, 162–63, 165
deferred time vs. real-time news, 107, 109
Degregori, Carlos Iván, 201
Deleuze, Gilles, 105
democracy: new versions of violence against, 12–13; sensate, 14–15, 27. See also Fiji Islands; Peruvian memorialization and reconciliation
Derrida, Jacques, 12
Desert Storm: The Victory, 118–19
Desert War (WWII) and impact of "Lili Marlene" on combat forces, 85–90, 91
Dessau, Paul, 224–27, 230, 235, 238
diegetic and non-diegetic sound in news broadcasts, 105, 109, 111–13, 119–20
Dietrich, Marlene, 93–95, 97
"Die Überlebenden" ("The Survivors") (Prümers), 50–52
Die Welt (review), 228, 231
Diskoton, 68
Dohnanyi, Christoph von, 226

German versions of "Lili Marlene," 83–90, 94–96, 100n32

Germany: anti-Semitism in post-WWII, 40, 56n13, 224, 229–30; impact of "Lili Marlene" for German soldiers, 86, 87–88; national identity, 17–18, 42–48, 57n29, 224, 225. See also *Jüdische Chronik*; *Neue Zeitschrift für Musik*

Ghetto movement of *Jüdische Chronik*, 225

Gilbert, Morris, 91

Goebbels, Josef, 87, 92

Gonzalez, Eduardo, 215

Gorham, Michael, 252

The Gospel Legend Singers at Sufi event, 161–62

The Gulf War Did Not Take Place (Baudrillard), 115

gusle, 79–80n56

Guzman, Abimael, 199, 201, 219n12

Gysi, Klaus, 232

Haanstra, Anna, 6

Hallin, Daniel, 109

Hamas-directed suicide bombing at Netanya's Park Hotel, 129

Hartmann, Karl Amadeus, 225, 226

Hayes, Alick, 90

healing and reconciliation, 18–26, 127–28, 224, 227. See also Fiji Islands; Mevlevi Sufi music; Palestinian identity and protest songs; Peruvian memorialization and reconciliation

Hegarty, Marilyn, 85

hegemony, music's support for, 16, 18, 25–26. See also *Neue Zeitschrift für Musik*; Ukraden, Neda

Heil dir, mein Vaterland (Hüber), *44*, 46

Heinemann, Rudolf, 228

Hendrix, Jimi, 14–16, 20

Henze, Hans Werner, 225, 226, 236–37

Herder, Johann Gottfried von, 16–17

Herf, Jeffrey, 223

Herlihy, Ed, 108

Heuss, Alfred, 54

"Hierba Silvestre" ("Wild Weed") (Lagos), 210–11

high-concept values in news reporting, 114–18, 124n40

Hindu indigenous Fijians, 186–88, 192–93n32

hip-hop (Palestinian), 132–33, 145–46

Hirsch, Marianne, 237

Hoffman, Hans-Joachim, 232–33

Holocaust memory in divided Germany, 223. See also *Jüdische Chronik*

Homovec, Boris, 72

hori, 186

Hoskins, Andrew, 107, 111

Hübner, Otto R., 43, *44*, 47

Huljić, Tonči, 80n60

Humala, Julio and Walter, 211

humanitarian suffering focus of al-Aqsa protest songs, 132, 142

humanizing the enemy and "Lili Marlene," 90, 97

Human Rights Watch, 147n4, 203

Hunter, Mira, 164

IEMPSA record label, Peru, 207

imagined communities, 174–75

Imagined Communities (Anderson), 6262

Im Westen nichts Neues (All Quiet on the Western Front) (Remarque), 49–50

Indian dance, 177, 178–80

indigenous Fijians, 128, 171, 172–74, 190n2, 192n29. See also Fiji Islands

indigenous Peruvians as primary victims of violence, 203

Indo-Fijians, 128, 171, 172–74, 190n2, 192n29. See also Fiji Islands

informative vs. commemorative discourse, 216

infotainment practices in news reporting, 115

inspiration and voice, 243–46, 259–60

In Stahlgewittern (Jünger), 50

interactive poetic spaces in protest songs, 131–32, 146–47

interrogation, violent use of music in, 256–57

intersubjective acoustic space for vocal performance, 248, 254

intertextual songs in Peru, 196, 214

intifada. See Palestinian identity and protest songs

Iraq War (2003–2011), 118, 119, 255–56

Islam and the West, historical tensions, 151–55, 160–62, 166–67n6. See also Mevlevi Sufi music

Islamists vs. secularists, Palestinian, 138–39

Islamist voice in Mais Shalash's work, 141, 142–45

Israel, Bob, 117

Israeli identity accusations against DAM, 145–46

Israeli military operation (ODS) against Palestinians (2002), 129–32, 147n2

Istūra al-Jenīn (Shalash), 142

Jackson, Carleton, 87, 92

Jansen, Stef, 64

Jaramillo, Deborah Lynn, 109, 112

Jelin, Elizabeth, 215

Jenin, Operation Defensive Shield attack on, 129–32, 147n2

Jennings, Humphrey, 83, 91

Jewish Federation of the GDR, 232

Jews and anti-Semitism in Germany, 40, 56n13, 224, 229–30. See also *Jüdische Chronik*

Johnson, Bruce, 1, 259

Jones, Nancy, 248, 254

Jović, Dejan, 75

Judgment at Nuremberg, 97

Jüdische Chronik (Holocaust cantata): composition as social protest/commentary, 224–26; FRG's critical reception, 223, 224–28, 230–32, 235; GDR's reception to and use of, 223, 224–26, 228–37, 238; and German avoidance of Holocaust narrative, 239n22; introduction, 223–24; overview, 196; postmemorial perspective, 235–38

Jugotan, 65, 66

Jünger, Ernst, 50

Kamen na kamen, 65

"Kampfbund für deutsche Kultur" (Rosenberg), 54

Kaplan, Martha, 174–75

Karnatak music, 179, 181

Kellner, Douglas, 104, 115, 116, 117

Kelly, John D., 174–75

Kendrick, Michelle, 118

Khada, Samer, 139

Khalil, Kamal, 136, 137

kirtan, 186

"Klaviere und Klavierwerke für Einarmige" (Schorn), 52, 58n57

Kloditz, Lothar, 234–35

Kluge, Eberhard, 230

Koch, Gerhard, 228

Kölner Stadtanzeiger (review), 228

Konya, Turkey, 153

Kracauer, Siegfried, 105

Kristallnacht commemorative concert in GDR, 232–35

kuchipudi dance, 179

Lagos, Edith, 210–11

Lagouranis, Tony, 256–57

language differences and ethnic divide in Fiji, 173

Lawrence, Amy, 95

Lecercle, Jean-Jacques, 254

Lehrke, Gisele, 96

Leip, Hans, 86, 87, 92

Lepine, Marc, 22

Levinas, Emmanuel, 244

Levinson, Jerrold, 19–20

Lewis, Bernard, 151

liberal communists, 4–5

Liberal-Demokratische Zeitung (review), 231

liberal tolerance, 1, 5–6

life cycle, respiration as microcosm of, 244

"Lili Marlene": Anglo-American popularity of, 84, 89, 91, 92–95; composition and style of, 86–87, 93; Desert War impact on combatants, 85–90, 91; historical background, 83–85; overview, 36; post-war impact of, 95–97; sexuality and sentiment in, 85, 87, 90, 92–96

linguistic markers for ethnicity, and Ukraden's lyrics, 65–66

live performance and recording symbiosis in Peru, 207–8

love of home, "Lili Marlene"'s evocation of, 91

Mackey, Eva, 175–76

Madden, Cecil, 84, 88–89, 91

Maeckel, Otto Viktor, 47

"Mamacha de las Mercedes" ("Virgin of Mercy") (Portocarrero), 209

Mancini, Henry, 107

mandali, 188

Mannheim, Lucie, 94

Mara, Ratu Sir Kamisese, 175, 176

Marković, Ante, 63

martial music/march: in CNN coverage of Persian Gulf War, 117; "Lili Marlene" structure and popularity, 86–87; for Vietnam War-era newsreels, 108

masculinity, Lili Marlene's contribution to soldiers', 84, 85

Maus, Fred, 20

McClary, Susan, 11

McDowell, John, 216

media, news. *See* television news music

media frames, 66, 107, 109, 111–12, 115–16, 119

meke dance, Fiji, 177, 178–80, 191n16

melody of anthem, integrity of, 14–16

re-signification of Peruvian testimonial songs, 212, 215, 222n43

resistance to official discourse in Peru, 199, 204–5, 210, 211–12, 215

restorative justice attempt in Fiji, 182

RFMF Meke Group, 178–81

Riley, Denise, 254

Rojas, Kramer, 213, *213*

romanticism and music as detached from social context, 8–9

Rommel, Gen. Erwin, 83, 88

Rosaldo, Michelle, 248

Rosenberg, Alfred, 54

Rosenberg, Sharon, 22–23

Rote Fahne (Red Flag), 232–33, 234–35

RTU Bill (Promotion of Reconciliation, Tolerance, and Unity Bill), 182–83

Rumi, Mevlana Celal ed-Din, 150, 152–55, 166n5

rupturing silence rhetoric of Peruvian Truth Commission, 203, 204

Rwandan genocide and violence of voice, 256

Sächliches Tagesblatt (review), 234

Sachs, Albie, 203

Sachsenhausen, 229–30

sacred space, Mevlana Museum as, 158

Salant, Richard S., 106

Sarajevo and Ukraden, 65, 68, 69, 71–72, 73–74

savior memory in Peru, 201

Schechner, Richard, 246–47

Schechter, Danny, 114

Scherer, Ray, 110

Schoenberg, Arnold, 9–10

Schultze, Norbert, 86, 87

Schumann, Robert, 40

SDL (Soqosoqo Duavata ni Lewenivanua) party in Fiji, 172, 177, 182–83

SED (Socialist Unity Party) of GDR, 229, 232

sema ceremony, 153, 155, 157, 159

sentimental and sexuality in "Lili Marlene"'s impact, 85, 87, 90, 92–96

September 11, 2011 terrorist attacks, 23–26, 165

Serbian national identity, 62–65, 68–72, 81–82nn72–73

sere ni cumu, 181, 191n16

sexuality and sentiment in "Lili Marlene"'s impact, 85, 87, 90, 92–96

"sexy" world development, 6

sha'bī, 138, 143, 144, 146

Shalash, Mais, 132, 141–45

Shalash, Saud, 141–42

Shaqir, Samih, 137

Sharon, Ariel, 129

Shelton, Anne, 84, 89–90, 93, 96

Shining Path guerillas, 197, 199, 201, 210, 219n12, 221–22n39

Shobna Chanel Dance Group, 178–81

silencing, and voice as opposition to violence, 252–54, 257–58

site of memory, 199, 218n9

Slobodni tjednik, 69

Slovenia, 63, 72

Smith, Colin, 84

social construct, music as, 8

Socialist Federal Republic of Yugoslavia, 62–65, 66, 72, 80n60. *See also* Ukraden, Neda

Socialist Unity Party (SED) of GDR, 229, 232

social performance, voice as, 246–47

social segregation in Fiji, 171–72

Sontag, Susan, 18–19

Soqosoqo Duavata ni Lewenivanua (SDL) party in Fiji, 172, 177, 182–83

Sound Targets (Pieslak), 119

South African Truth Commission, 203

Soviet communal conception of voice, 251–52

speaking the unspeakable and Peruvian Truth Commission, 199–200

Speight, George, 176, 181–82

Spivak, Gayatri, 13–16

Stan, Adele M., 112

stingers for television news, 117

String Quartet No. 14 in C♯ Minor, Opus 131 (Beethoven), 10–12

subjective and objective violence, 4–8, 28–29n11, 151–52, 203. *See also* symbolic violence; war context

Sufi mysticism. *See* Mevlevi Sufi music

symbolic violence: celebrity culture and benefit concerts as, 5–6; defined, 4, 28–29n11; in Fijian coup culture, 177, 183–84; in Germany's use of music for national racism, 17–18; and music's role in promoting violence, 35–37; as Slovenian tool for nation-state establishment, 61; use of *Jüdische Chronik* in, 196; Žižek's in Beethoven analysis, 10–11. *See also* war context

systemic violence, 4, 28–29n11, 37

Tagg, Philip, 117, 120
Tappert, Wilhelm, 45, 47
Taruskin, Richard, 16
tasavvuf, 156, 164–65
Taylor, Diana, 202
Taylor, Paul, 5, 37
television news music: audio-viewer, 115, 121n5; diegetic and non-diegetic sound, 105, 109, 111–13, 119–20; historical background, 106–7, 117, 122n17, 124n42, 126n63; importance of role in affecting audience attitudes, 118–20; introduction, 104–6; news-to-entertainment shift (1970s to 1990s), 113–14, 121n4; overview, 36–37; Persian Gulf War and high-concept values, 106, 107, 114–19, 124n40; Vietnam War, 107–13
testimonial songs (canciones testimoniales), Peruvian, 195–96, 198–99, 200, 204–15, 217n4, 220n28, 221n38, 222n43
testimonias, Peru, 202
thawrī, 138
theatrical newsreel as predecessor to television news, 106, 122n17
themes, musical, for television news, 106–7, 114, 116
The Theory of Film (Kracauer), 105
Thiessen, Karl, 43, 44
Tito, Josip Broz, 62
Toledo, Alejandro, 201
tolerance and coexistence, 1, 5–6, 151–52, 162–65
transformational power of voice/music, 247–48, 253, 260
transnational Arab pop intifadiana, 132, 133–37
trauma, origins of response, 20
Treitschke, Heinrich von, 39
The True Story of Lili Marlene (Jennings), 83, 91
truth commission structure, 200, 218n10. See also Peruvian memorialization and reconciliation
Tucaković, Marina, 65
Tuđman, Franjo, 63–64
Turkey, Mevlevi Order (Sufi). See Mevlevi Sufi music
Turner, Ted, 115

Ugrešić, Dubravka, 60
Ukraden, Neda: Bosnian identity, 65, 68, 69, 71–72, 73–74, 73–75; Croatian identity, 65–66, 68, 69, 72–73; and Dragović,

80–81n61; ethnic biography's importance for acceptance, 67–68; historical background, 62–65; introduction, 60–62; NCFM in Yugoslavia, 65, 66, 72, 80n60; overview, 36; and Sarajevo, 65, 68, 69, 71–72, 73–74; Serb identity, 68–72, 81–82nn72–73; summary of ethnicity choice consequences, 74–76
Ulbricht, Walter, 229
Unger, Max, 45
United States: American adoption of "Lili Marlene," 84, 89, 91, 92–95; national anthem, 13–16, 20. See also television news music
Universal Newsreels, 107–8
Urpicha de Oro "Golden Dove," 207

Valentić, Franjo, 72–73
Večernji list, 66, 67, 68–69, 70
Veled, Sultan, 154
Vera Lynn, 90
Vicente, Victor, 128
Vietnam War, 105, 106, 107–13, 118
violence and music: atonality issue for Žižek, 9–10; benefit concerts, 5–7; collective memory of, 18–26, 195–96, 199, 218n9; defining violence, 4–5, 28–29n11, 183; dual role of music in promoting and mitigating violence, 2–3; evocation, music's role as, 7–9, 10–12; nation state's disarticulation and nature of violence, 12–18; overview of project purpose, 1–3. See also objective and subjective violence; voice, vocality, and violence
virgin/whore archetype, Lili Marlene as, 84, 92–93, 95
Virilio, Paul, 104, 107, 109, 115, 118
"¡Viva la Patria!" (Falconí), 209–10, 214
voice, vocality, and violence: agency, voice as, 250–51; embodiment of voice, 248–49; emplacement of vocal performance, 248–49, 262n16; essence vs. relationality, voice as, 250; inspiration and breath metaphor, 243–46, 259–60; presence, voice as, 249–50; private vs. public sphere and voice, 251; as social performance, 246–47; as transformational power, 247–48, 253, 260; voice as opposition to violence (silencing), 252–54, 257–58; voice's role in politics and violence, 254–60; Western individualist vs. Soviet communal conception of voice, 251–52

Vuatelevu, Saimone, 186–87
Vučković, Severina, 76, 80n60

Wagner, Richard, 40, 46
Wagner-Régeny, Rudolf, 225, 226
war context, 12–13, 35–37. *See also* "Lili Marlene"; *Neue Zeitschrift für Musik*; television news music; Ukraden, Neda
wayno musical form in Peru, 198, 205, 206, 208–9, 210–11, 217n4
"The Wedding of Lili Marlene" (Connor), 96
Weigle, Jörg-Peter, 234
Weill, Kurt, 54
West Bank Palestinian neighborhoods, Israel's ODS attack on, 129–32
Western and Islamic relationship, 151–55, 160–62, 166–67n6. *See also* Mevlevi Sufi music
Western individualist conception of voice, 251–52
whirling shows, Sufi, 157–58
Whitaker, Brian, 127
Who Sings the Nation State? (Butler and Spivak), 13–16
Wiedmer, Caroline, 229
Williams, John, 114
Winegar, Jessica, 155
women as primary performers of "Lili Marlene," 85, 89

Wong, Walter, 197
world music, Sufi and Western blendings, 163
World War I. See *Neue Zeitschrift für Musik*
World War II. *See* "Lili Marlene"; National Socialists

xenophobic desire to remove the musical other from German life, 45–46, 47, 57n29

Yabaki, Konisi, 183
Year of Rumi, 154
yeşil, 162
Yorck, Ruth, 84
Young, James E., 23, 237
Yugoslavia, 62–65, 66, 72, 80n60. *See also* Ukraden, Neda
Yurtsever, Hasan Ali, 165

zabavna, 65, 72–73, 77n19
Zapfenstreich (Tattoo), 87, 99n26
zeffa, 138, 139
Zeitschrift für Musik. See *Neue Zeitschrift für Musik*
Zelizer, Barbie, 196
zikr ceremony, 158–62, 163, 164
Zink, Rudolf, 86
Žižek, Slavoj, 4–12, 19, 28–29n11